ENGLISH EPIC AND HEROIC
POETRY

The Channels of English Literature

Edited by OLIPHANT SMEATON, M.A.

ENGLISH EPIC AND HEROIC POETRY.
By Professor W. MACNEILE DIXON, M.A., University of Glasgow.

ENGLISH LYRIC POETRY.
By ERNEST RHYS.

ENGLISH ELEGIAC, DIDACTIC, AND RELIGIOUS POETRY.
By the Very Rev. H. C. BEECHING, D.D., D.Litt., Dean of Norwich, and the Rev. RONALD BAYNE, M.A.

ENGLISH DRAMATIC POETRY.
By Professor F. E. SCHELLING, Litt.D., University of Pennsylvania.

ENGLISH SATIRIC AND HUMOROUS LITERATURE.
By OLIPHANT SMEATON, M.A., F.S.A.

ENGLISH PHILOSOPHERS AND SCHOOLS OF PHILOSOPHY.
By Professor JAMES SETH, M.A., University of Edinburgh.

THE ENGLISH ESSAY AND ESSAYISTS.
By Professor HUGH WALKER, LL.D., St. David's College, Lampeter.

THE ENGLISH NOVEL.
By Professor GEORGE SAINTSBURY, LL.D., University of Edinburgh.

ENGLISH HISTORIANS AND SCHOOLS OF HISTORY.
By Professor RICHARD LODGE, University of Edinburgh.

ENGLISH CRITICISM.
By Professor J. W. H. ATKINS, University College of Wales.

J. M. DENT & SONS, LTD.

ENGLISH
EPIC AND HEROIC
POETRY

BY

W. MACNEILE DIXON, M.A.

PROFESSOR OF ENGLISH LITERATURE IN THE
UNIVERSITY OF GLASGOW

LONDON: J. M. DENT & SONS LTD.
BEDFORD STREET, STRAND · 1912
NEW YORK: E. P. DUTTON & CO.

To

E. M. D.

WHOSE EMBROIDERIES WILL OUTLAST

MOST MODERN SENTENCES.

BEOWULF

NEVER again the galley under sail
Shall by the shining cliffs and forelands steer;
No more the Warden of the Coast shall hail
The bold seafarers in their battle gear;
The treasure-blade, the cup of price, the spear
Rust in the burial mound with helm and mail;
No more of Dragon's den and misty mere,
Of Grendel and his Dam shall be the tale.
Hrothgar is gone, and Wiglaf long ago
At the last rampart met the stroke of fate;
No journeys now the byrnie by his side
Makes with the Earl, or Atheling lying low;
Nor thee a second time can Time create,
Viking and kinsman, in thy mournful pride.

PREFACE

FOR friendly assistance while these sheets were passing
through the press I am indebted to my colleagues,
Mr. Ritchie Girvan and Mr. Robert Dewar (now
Professor of English Literature at University College,
Reading). I have to thank Mr. Girvan also for the
translations which appear in the appendix and for
many valuable suggestions in the early chapters.

W. MACNEILE DIXON.

THE UNIVERSITY, GLASGOW.
September, 1912.

CONTENTS

xi

ENGLISH EPIC AND HEROIC POETRY

CHAPTER I

THE IDEA OF EPIC

IF we ask *what is an epic ?* a hundred critics hasten across the centuries to our assistance. Not alone Aristotle, a fixed star in any region of philosophical inquiry, who, as Roger Bacon said, had " *the same authority in philosophy that the Apostle Paul had in divinity,*" but *longo intervallo* writers like Longinus, Horace, and Petronius may be consulted, all curious in the matter, and later, learned and very numerous, a great army of eager law-givers, the Humanists of Italy and their successors in France and England. One might well anticipate illumination from so noble a company in the obscurest field. Yet since it was from the consideration of one poet alone, although so royal a poet as Homer, that Aristotle derived his light, and since the whole subsequent procession, down to the last of Renaissance critics, leads back, an unbroken chain, to the unerring master, the discussion of epic poetry became in effect the discussion of Homer, " *the mighty sea mark* " by which not only the critics, but the poets also of former ages, were content to steer, and epic might well have been defined as " a poem written in imitation of the *Iliad*." To Homer's indeed was added the sacred name of Virgil, the most faithful disciple, " *the moon of Homer,*" but " *Nature and Homer were, he found, the same,*" we are told: no type but that of the Greek epic appeared possible.

Thus Renaissance criticism kept its eye steadily fixed upon the *Iliad* and the *Æneid*, shining exemplars, and it is the more

A

surprising that, when questions of interpretation or of imitation arose, we none the less find ourselves embarked upon " *a troubled sea of noises and harsh disputes.*" True and full appreciation of the matters at issue would be tedious—strange to our manner of thinking—but from selected judgments of the leading commentators the student may gather something to his purpose.

Le Bossu, a great name, convinced himself and not a few others that in the *Iliad* Homer purposed to illustrate a general truth—" *a misunderstanding between princes is the ruin of their states.*" Homer, he would have us believe, was a political philosopher, who perceived that petty principalities, like those of Greece, frequently quarrel to their disadvantage. To point his moral the poet, it would seem, invented a story. The names, the exploits, the characters of the heroes, Achilles, Agamemnon, Hector, were then selected, as was the siege of Troy, to serve the purpose of the general plan, to illustrate the chosen and weighty thesis. Le Bossu defined epic, therefore, as " *a composition in verse intended to form the manners by instructions disguised under the allegories of an important action.*" It is easy to agree with Lord Kames, however, that the ethical fervour of Le Bossu betrayed him when he demanded that before the story or even the name of the hero the precept must be selected, and that his definition " *excludes every epic poem founded upon real facts, and perhaps includes some of Æsop's fables.*" Let us consult less exigent moralists. Pressing more directly towards the centre, Davenant, in the preface to *Gondibert*, supporting his practice by his theory, would have the subject of the epic chosen from ancient times. Thus, he argues, the poet will escape bondage to well-known history, have freedom to expand his wings, and examples of lofty virtue will be more credible, withdrawn into the vaguer realm of the past, than among contemporaries, whom we are slow to believe better than ourselves. Some votes for this contention are given him. Kames is in agreement, " *familiarity,*" he tells us, " *ought more especially to be avoided in an epic poem, the peculiar character of which is dignity and elevation : modern manners make no figure in such a poem.*"

Yet Lucan, to whom Corneille confessed greater indebtedness than to Virgil, preferred themes of recent date, and historical characters whose names were fresh in men's minds, trusting perhaps a safer instinct. Tasso, again, steering a middle course, advised a subject neither too old nor too new—readers, he thought, do not bear well with changes introduced by the poet into histories familiar, and are interested but languidly in things far off or foreign manners. Some respect for history, if history is at all to be drawn upon, might, we may allow, be legitimately required, but what respect? Is Virgil to be censured because, in choosing Dido for his heroine, he presumed "*to make a lady die for love two hundred years before her birth?*"

Turning from this problem—choice of subject—where no firm principle seems to have been at any time accepted or even outlined, to another—the proper duration of epic action—there is Aristotelian authority for great elasticity. The best examples of tragedy limited the action "*to a single revolution of the sun.*" But the scale of epic he saw admitted, nay even demanded, enlarged dimensions, and it was required to submit to the more easily satisfied principle that the beginning and the end must be within the scope of a single view, a phrase perhaps to be interpreted simply—"*of such a length as can be read in a day.*" Minturno, however, would restrict the canvas of the epic poet, permitting him only the events of a single year, and Ronsard allows no more. Horace, not venturing himself upon so wide a sea as epic, was prepared nevertheless to legislate for his friends: an episode or episodes in the life of the hero he thought, with his accustomed moderation, should provide sufficient material, but Giraldi held, both in theory and practice, that the whole biography of the hero was indispensable.

The discussion of the hero's character exhibits similar disagreement. Unlike the hero of tragedy, who should not, according to Aristotle, be either faultless or a ruffian, the epic hero should be perfectly virtuous, says Tasso, but, argues Dryden, it is not necessary that the manners of the hero should be immaculate; they are practically good if they are of a piece, and though Achilles is the protagonist of the *Iliad* we must

abhor his cruelty to a dead enemy, and the sale of that enemy's
body, Hector's, to his father Priam.   That the hero of epic should
be pre-eminent in war was, however, generally conceded, and
some critics charge Virgil, the supreme master, with a grievous
fault, that he made Æneas "*fitter to be the founder of an order of
monks than of an empire,*" and chiefly pre-eminent in tears. "*The
praise of an epic poem is to feign a person exceeding Nature,*"
argues Alexander in his pleasant *Anacrisis,* "*with all the per-
fections whereof a man can be capable, every deficiency in that
imaginary man being really the author's own.*"   Alexander is all
for "*soaring above the course of Nature*" in epic, though it be
"*agreeable with the gravity of tragedy that it be grounded upon a
true history,*" and of Virgil he complains that by attenuating
the courage of Turnus, who dies like a dastard, Æneas is robbed
of the higher glory that springs from triumph over valour.

We pass to other, but hardly less contentious matters.   No
commentator ventured to challenge the Aristotelian canon that
the epic poem must possess unity.   There is no greater horror
than the sprawling poetic monster, of which one can view the
parts but never the whole; yet wherein, one may ask, consists
the idea of unity, if, as Castelvetro allows, not alone the doings
of a single person, but even the multifarious actions of a whole
nation, may in the epic properly be recalled?   Once more, a
chief support and ornament of heroic poetry—the machinery of
Olympus, the interest of Heaven in the affairs of earth—was
not easily to be thought away.   Yet here the critical battle
raged, perhaps, most fiercely.   For Voltaire it was a faded
dream: "*Lucan is to be commended for having laid the gods
aside,*" and thus given proof that "*the intervention of the gods
is not absolutely required in an epic poem.*"   Yet what to substitute?   The allegory of the *Henriade* has not found many
admirers, the new spiritualities were fainter than the old, dim
shadows of dim abstractions.

> " What Homer saw, what Virgil dreamed, was truth,
> And died not being divine; but whence, in sooth,
> Might shades that never lived win deathless youth? "

Lucan, indeed, attained a measure of success without assistance of the gods, and the nature of things, it may be, supplies no overpowering argument to recall them, yet for the majority of the French critics the law of their presence was immutable, nor was it easy to break with so delightful a tradition. Machinery such as Homer's, belonging to the religion of his race and country, Virgil's even, was inevitable and proper; the Christian poet owed elsewhere his allegiance. Doubtless Ossian was rightly praised by Blair; he found the tales of his country full of ghosts and spirits, he stood on the border of debateable land, he had claims upon his country's beliefs. But the plan and limits of the supernatural in epic poetry—that problem, greatly complicated when the turbid tributaries of mediæval romance began to flow into the pure classical stream, had been foreshadowed by the doubts of Longinus, who thought it a sign of age and declining power in Homer that the *Odyssey* harboured romantic fictions. That the Renaissance, more classical than the classics, would tolerate the Gothic strain was unthinkable, and Tasso after an adventure in the forbidden field hastily retreated into the safer region of allegory. His afterthought of a symbolical sense for his romantic inventions saved him from the impending sword of ecclesiastical censure, but only to incur the contempt of the literary critic. " He could not be insensible," is Voltaire's commentary, " that such wild fairy tales, at that time so much in fashion not in Italy only, but in all Europe, were altogether inconsistent with the gravity of epic poetry. In order to cover this defect he printed a preface, in which he pretends all his poem is but a shadow and a type. The army of the Christian princes, says he, represents the body and the soul. Jerusalem the figure of true happiness, which cannot be obtained but by labour and difficulties. . . . The spells and illusions of the enchanted forest shadow out the false reasoning into which our passions are apt to mislead us. . . . However, the ridiculous explanation which Tasso gives, with so much gravity, of his extravagance, cannot impose upon mankind." Hobbes was of the same opinion—" There are some that are not pleased with fiction unless it be bold not only to exceed the *work*, but also the *possibility* of nature: they would have impenetrable armours, enchanted castles, invulnerable bodies, iron men, flying horses, and a thousand other such things which are easily feigned by those that dare. . . . Beyond the actual works of nature a poet may now go; but beyond the conceived possibility of nature, never." What is this but the rejection of the ever-lasting child's mind in man, a solvent of his eternal dream? So also Kames. "A situation can never be intricate, nor the reader ever in pain about the catastrophe, as long as there is an angel, devil, or magician to lend a helping hand." The Renaissance would have us rational at any price, and poetry, the old house of vision, must open her doors to logic and to reason. Poetry was haunted, the metaphysical Cowley held, by unnatural monsters, until the coming of the champion, Davenant, who succoured it.

> " Methinks heroic poesy till now
> Like some fantastic fairyland did show;
> Gods, devils, nymphs, witches, and giants race,
> And all but man in man's best work had place.
> Thou, like some worthy knight, with sacred arms
> Dost drive the monsters thence, and end the charms."

But hear, on the contrary part, Dryden, an unexpected ally— " I am of opinion that neither Homer, Virgil, Statius, Ariosto, Tasso, nor our English Spenser, could have formed their poems half so beautiful without those gods and spirits, and those enthusiastic parts of poetry which compose the most noble part of all their writings. 'Tis enough that, in all eyes and religions, the greatest part of mankind have believed the power of magic and that there are spirits or spectres which have appeared. This, I say, is foundation enough for poetry." Bishop Hurd, too, was for magic and mystery. " I stick to my point and maintain that the fairy tales of Tasso do him more honour than what are called the more natural, that is, the classical parts of his poem. His imitations of the ancients have indeed their merit, for he was a genius in everything. But they are faint and cold, and almost insipid, when compared with his Gothic fictions. We have made shift to run over the passages he has copied from Virgil. We are all on fire amidst the magical feats of Ismen, and the enchantments of Armida. . . . I speak at least for myself; and must fully own, if it were not for these lies of Gothic invention, I should scarcely be disposed to give the *Gierusalem Liberata* a second reading." *Quot homines, tot sententiae.*

The worship of antiquity involved the Renaissance in strange doctrine. Pope's counsel, though fervid in expression, is not foreign to reason—

> " Be Homer's works your study and delight,
>   Read him by day and meditate by night;"

but *imitatio,* defined by Jonson as the power " *to convert the substance or riches of another poet to his own use,*" received, from Vida and others, even larger interpretation. Borrowing, naked and unashamed, was not a virtue, it was a duty.

> " Come then, ye youths, and urge your generous toils,
>   Come strip the ancients, and divide the spoils."

It was the poet's business, his art also, to transfer, from the golden books of Homer and Virgil, spirit and idea, word and phrase, to his own pages, with care indeed, as of a man handling precious things, and skilfully to make them his own, altering it might be the position, the original order, the immediate reference. For this poetic method a great weight of authority might be adduced, but we are not yet on firm, incontestable ground. Voltaire, the sceptic, thought it less easy than the eloquent Vida supposed to steal dexterously. Trissino, he comments, " *was justly fond of Homer, and yet his great fault is to have imitated him, for imitation requires more art than is generally believed.*" Homer may venture upon details, for example, which in him do not offend, but no modern writer will make it " *his particular care to describe with accuracy how such a colonel was wounded through the bladder, and such a captain in the kidneys.*"

For his avoidance of this very imitation so cordially recommended by others Davenant is expressly praised, and by Cowley again, because he " *scorn'd to live by robbing the dead,*" and Young goes further, " *The less we copy the divine ancients we shall resemble them the more.*" Davenant himself speaks with pith and distinctness, illustrating by simile, when he says,

" *Whilst we imitate others we can no more excell than he that sails by others maps can make a new discovery.*" The doctrine of imitation found its limits of application by the close of the seventeenth century, and was finally dissolved in the crucible of humour. " *In his ode upon the taking of Namur,*" says Kames of Boileau, " *he demands with a most serious countenance whether the walls were built by Apollo or Neptune? and in relating the passage of the Rhine,* ANNO 1672, *he describes the god of that river as fighting with all his might to oppose the French monarch.*" Addison, anticipating a torrent of verse on the occasion of a general peace, derives ironical satisfaction from a public warning to the poets—" I do strictly require every person who shall write on this subject to remember that he is a Christian, and not to sacrifice his catechism to his poetry. In order to it, I do expect of him, in the first place, to make his own poem, without depending upon Phœbus for any part of it, or calling out for aid upon any of the Muses by name. I do likewise positively forbid the sending of Mercury with any particular message or dispatch, relating to the peace, and shall by no means suffer Minerva to take upon her the shape of any pleni-potentiary concerned in this great work. I do further declare, that I shall not allow the destinies to have had a hand in the deaths of the several thousands who have been slain in the late war; being of opinion that all such deaths may be well accounted for by the Christian system of powder and ball. I do therefore strictly forbid the poets to cut the thread of any man's life upon any pretence whatever, unless it be for the sake of rhyme." [1]

The discussion, interminable and inconclusive, of literary problems arising out of the consideration of epos during the sixteenth and seventeenth centuries prompted some to the pious wish that " *England were as free from critics as it is from wolves,*" and make it easy to accept Davenant's opinion that " *Learning is not knowledge, but a continual sailing by fantastic and uncertain winds towards it.*" Ask what question we will, the simplest, we are plunged in difficulty. Is it the nobility of the subject that makes the great epic? Then Tasso outdoes Homer, for his

[1] *Spectator,* 523.

theme is pre-eminently magnificent, while the author of the *Iliad* makes, admittedly, a first-rate poem but out of a second-rate subject. Is the success of the hero essential? Then what of Milton, whose hero is discomfited, whose "*giant foils the knight, and drives him out of his stronghold to wander through the world with his lady errant*"?

Spenser

Thus it would appear possible one by one to take the rules prescribed by critical authority and to show them disputed, or it may be violated, by the epic poets, and not alone the unsuccessful poets. Into the obscurer region of minutest detail the debate has been, and might again be carried. But what profit to inquire gravely, with Gibbon, whether "*exact catalogues of the armies sent into the field are an essential part of epic poems*," whether the supernatural machinery should be taken from the religion of one's country, as Dennis required, or derived from nature as less likely to offend the prejudices of readers, as Howard would have it: or again, whether the Christian poet labours under any serious disadvantage because "*the hell of the Gospel is not so poetical as that of antiquity*." Amid sentences like these, which excite interest only in so far as they demonstrate how the centre of critical inquiry may shift in one or two generations, there may be met flashes of sudden insight, even such sane and enduring deliverances as that of Voltaire, "The same fancy which invented poetry, changes every day all its productions, because it is liable itself to eternal vicissitudes. . . . Use alone has prefixed the name of epic particularly to those poems which relate some great action. Let the action be simple or complex, let it lie in one single place, as in the *Iliad*, or let the hero wander all the world over, as in the *Odyssey;* let there be one single hero, or a great many; happy or unfortunate; furious as Achilles, or pious as Æneas; let them be kings or generals, or neither of them; let the scene lie upon the Indian Ocean, as in the *Lusiada* of Camoens; in the West Indies, as in the *Araucana* of Alonzo of Ercilla; in Hell, in Heaven, out of the limits of our nature, as in Milton; the poem will equally deserve the name of epic, unless you have a mind to honour it with another title proportionable to its merit."

To have fulfilled all the requirements of Renaissance criticism would have taxed the resources of genius however lofty, and before the attempt the most ambitious might well have sat down to consider the chances of success in an enterprise charged first and last with momentous difficulties. On two points, however—probably on no others—the debate fell silent. Epic, it was agreed, was narrative poetry, and the heroic poem, truly such, and despite the contrary judgment of Aristotle, was in Dryden's words, "*undoubtedly the greatest work which the soul of man is capable to perform.*" To fail in a task of this magnitude, it may have been felt, involved no disgrace, certainly few among the poets turned away from it with firmness. Ambition lurked in the recesses of many minds. Yet in England, with the exception of Milton, and in some measure Spenser, those who essayed the glorious enterprise failed, and many went no further than to choose the site and measure the ground for the high design. Jonson planned a "*Hero-ologia of the worthies of this country roused by fame.*" Dryden dreamt of the epic laurel with a poem on "*King Arthur conquering the Saxons, or Edward the Black Prince subduing Spain for Pedro the Cruel.*" Pope confessed to like aspirations. "*I wrote things, I'm ashamed to say how soon. Part of an epic poem when about twelve. Deucalion was the hero of it.*" Another appears to have been on hand soon after—"*The epic poem which I began a little after I was twelve was Alexander, Prince of Rhodes. I wrote four books toward it of about a thousand verses each, and had the copy by me, till I burnt it by the advice of the Bishop of Rochester.*" This was "*the child of self-love begot upon innocence.*" Yet another was contemplated later on Brutus, with the scene in England. These were splendid visions, and doubtless the imagination of every poet since was haunted in youth by the battlements and towers of such cloudy palaces.

> "Ten thousand glorious systems would he build,
> Ten thousand great ideas fill'd his mind;
> But with the clouds they fled, and left no trace behind."

The great refrained, but some of the smaller men exhibited a finer, if less discriminating valour. Davenant wrote three

books of his *Gondibert*, and earned at least the admiration of his
contemporaries; Aaron Hill two on *Gideon*, Cowley four of his
Davideis, Wilkie nine of his *Epigoniad*, Glover twelve of his
Leonidas, thirty of his *Athenaid*, while Sir Richard Blackmore
eclipsed even Homer by the production of four complete epics,
Prince Arthur, ten books, *King Arthur*, twelve, *Eliza*, ten, *King
Alfred*, twelve.   The seventeenth and eighteenth centuries, to
carry the matter no further, are littered with complete theories,
and with the fragments or inanimate remains of unread epics.
Nor were the critics slow to urge the venture upon the poets.
Hayley, in an elaborate didactic poem, endeavoured " *to remove
prejudices which obstruct the cultivation of epic writing*," and
argued that a national epic was the " great *desideratum* " in
our literature.   He addressed his persuasions to his friend
Mason, whom he generously styled—

> " Judge and master of the lyre,
> Harmonious chief of Britain's living choir."

The rural deities, he assured Mason, called him, Flora was
already occupied in weaving a wreath for his brow to match
that woven by Ceres for Virgil:—

> " O be it thine the higher palm to gain,
> And pass him in the wide heroic plain! "

This was surely encouragement enough, yet Mason hesitated!
Not to the critics can the failures of the poets fairly be charged.
They set forth the principles, they interpreted the successes of
the ancients, with admirable patience they revealed the mystery.
But unhappily criticism faces the past while it urges its disciples
to face the future; unhappily, too, wise only after the event,
and thus perpetually halting after doing, it is compelled to alter
its principles with each successful achievement in creation.
Each victory of art requires a new theory to succeed and explain
it.   Hence " *we have in every art more rules than examples*,"
hence, too, " *that critical war which never ceases among the learned* "
seems the inevitable and accompanying shadow which may
advertise the presence of genius but never assists at its
production.

Two things reveal themselves as we contemplate the parade of Renaissance theorising—that it was thought possible

> " To write receipts how poems may be made; "

and that no distinction appears to have been drawn by any writer between the authentic and the literary epic, between the heroic poem, which, like Homer, grows up out of the soil and belongs to no single generation, and the epic of culture, the work of a single individual, projecting his imagination into a distant age. Till the final triumph of the Romantic school at the end of the eighteenth century it lingered—the misapprehension of the true nature of poetical power and inspiration that delighted in the excogitation of rules for the control and influence of artistic invention. Imagination, said Dryden, must " *have clogs tied to it lest it outrun the judgment.*" It survived even the jibes of Sterne[1] and the cold irony of Swift's *Recipe to make an Epic Poem*, with its calm announcement—"*I shall here endeavour, for the benefit of my countrymen, to make it manifest that epic poems may be made without genius, nay without learning or much reading. . . . It is easily brought about by him that has a genius, but the skill lies in doing it without one.*" The other misapprehension, which made it possible to confuse the epic of growth and the epic of culture, which made it possible to think of Homer as the work of an earlier Virgil, was dispelled only when the labours of scholars and ethnologists showed that heroic poetry proper—distinguished from imitations of it by poets in learned times—was the product of an unlettered age, an historical document, the only surviving record of times unchronicled, fashioned by generations of bards from the myths and traditions of their race. It became easy, the distinction once made, to discover that the " *accretion epic* " had borne its own flower and fruit, that the freedom and natural vigour, as of youth, were there, while the invented epic, sacrificing of necessity the qualities it could not produce, might display the maturity

---

[1] Sterne, *Tristram Shandy*, iii. 12.—" And for the epick poem, your lordship bid me look at—upon taking the length, breadth, height, and depth of it, and trying them at home on an exact scale of Bossu's—'tis out, my lord, in every one of its dimensions.—Admirable connoisseur! "

of mind, the intellectual balance and symmetry of adult age. That compensation which experience can supply may be required of it—clearness of intention, intelligent scheme, artistic finish; the graces of youth are beyond recall. How should we think of this first kind of epic, the authentic type? We should certainly not think of it as a fixed, final, inalterable form. The true epic poems we possess, the poems which imposed the type, which set the pattern, to which we immediately turn our thoughts at the mention of the word, are for us of a certain form, but only because for some reason, such as reduction to writing, that form has been preserved. The *epic process* was stayed at a particular point, at the moment when that form had been reached. We become acquainted with heroic poetry then at a moment in its development, the moment simply at which the movement was arrested. Epic, let us say, is a type of poetry caught and fixed at a given stage, poetry which would not have been exactly as it is had the movement been stayed a generation or two earlier or a generation or two later. The Homeric canon, for example, *Homer* as we know him, is a portion only of a much larger volume of Trojan and Theban epics. Many of its features are due to the fact that it was a selection made in the interests of Athens. *Homer* did not mean the same thing to Æschylus, a Greek of the fifth century B.C., as to Plato, a Greek of the fourth century. In the fifth century *Homer* meant far more than the *Iliad* and the *Odyssey*. Quotations before the fourth century were made by Pindar, for example, which are not to be found in our text, and there are inconsistencies in that text to be explained only by reference to other versions of the story elsewhere told. *Beowulf* similarly is a part only of a far larger body of similar poetry, a part which chanced to survive and nothing more. That accidental survival shows us the epic process at a certain stage, as it happens in this case a stage when further development ceased. But neither *Homer* nor *Beowulf* possesses any authority as forms fixed by nature or as law-giving. They may be admired and imitated, but we are misled if we think of them as the exclusively *right* form to which all others must approximate or be ruled out as heretical.

We are misled, too, if we think of *Homer* or *Beowulf* as primitive poetry. Their selection of language, their breadth of interest, their poetic art, their very length and elaboration prove that these poems, which may seem to us simple and unsophisticated, are in truth late arrivals on the world's stage and have behind them generations of experienced singers. Yet the true epic belongs to a period in which the immediate pressure of nature is felt. The heroes of *Homer* and *Beowulf*, as Hegel observed, provide themselves with the necessities of life, with horses and weapons and food. They arm themselves for the fight. They may be smiths and carpenters without loss of dignity. They are not served, like the knights of chivalric times, by their squires and attendants. And since we judge of poetry, not by the intellect only, not as art alone, but by its wealth of human interest, the elementary and unchanging things take hold of us, the freshness of the early world, and make of authentic epic poetry a possession for all time. Romance may go astray in dull days in search of fantasies, but the taste of every age is met when men build their own walls and ships, yoke their own horses to the chariot, or contend, as did the Homeric heroes, in the boxing-match or the foot-race.

When the poet is himself a part of that which he describes, as one fancies it was with " Homer " or the *Homeridæ*, or at least in closest sympathy with its essential elements, not separated from it by any critical superiority, how clear and bright the picture! Whereas in such a work as Virgil, consummate art as it is, one perceives that the field of the author's personal experience is altogether remote from the shadowy land to which he guides us, and that he is trusting to his imagination to revive far-off forgotten things, merely to project a credible and pleasant fiction. The distinction is obvious and imperative, yet it may be pressed beyond truth and the clear facts.[1] Homer, to whom Virgil was confessedly a debtor, owed, who can say how much, to previous bards, nor was the process by which the poet of culture moulded his work wholly and absolutely dissimilar from that which

---

[1] Professor Jebb in his *Homer* (pp. 17-19) seems to me to make the distinction too formal and precise.

Homer, the last of his line, himself employed. We distinguish not so much by the process, the method of invention, as by the tone and temper. The mood of Homer, the mood of Virgil, how unlike they are! The poem too, which has been slowly woven from the myths and memories of a race, reaching perfection by the aid of time, which has passed from the keeping of one generation to that of another—not without loss and gain in oral transmission—which served its race as Bible, law, and story book, we cannot describe as a species distinct and separate, rather as the whole world of poetry, not yet split and parcelled into provinces, into variety of form. We describe it better as the complete library of an age which possessed no other drama, no other history, no other music in the largest, the Greek sense. Primitive epic comprised, out of it proceeded all subsequent narrative, but not narrative only; all the later types and fashions of artistic invention, the drama itself, were latent in it. There, as in the reef of metal, lay all forms of art, all the poetic fashionings of the future. Thus developed, narrative of subsequent ages, in its wide range of style and manner, is a limb of the parent tree, or it may be, as in the epic of Virgil or Milton, a cutting planted and fostered to courtly elegance in cultured soil.

The English people alone — it is a unique fact — possess examples both of natural and imitative epic. If any stranger asks who is their epic poet, they can answer: " *We have two, neither to be pronounced inferior to the other, the author of ' Beowulf,' a great heroic poem, indisputably of the authentic type, and Milton, whose ' Paradise Lost,' with the possible exception of the ' Æneid,' is the most admirable of poetic achievements in the heroic manner.*" For if the natural epic that reaches or approaches full development is rare in the history of the world, hardly more numerous are the artificial epics that have attained high celebrity. So hard a thing it is to build the perfect structure of heroic dimensions, which, like the mediæval cathedral, encloses a hundred vistas of delight within its pillared aisles and chapels, and dominates without, in tower and spire and buttressed battlements, the whole countryside, a monument for age-long wonder and satisfied contemplation.

To conclude that heroic poetry is one, seems best, that however later poets have diversified their material, however brilliantly introduced new ornaments or decorations, they are
essentially followers, even if unconscious, of a great tradition,
copyists of a pattern long ago laid down in antiquity. The
essential matters of heroic poetry, the thing itself, as one might
say, are fixed, and finally fixed, by the life and character of
primitive times. Remote in a sense its interests lie, a great
way off from those of our protected and systematised lives.
Its outlook upon men and things reflects far other surroundings,
a long-vanished world. Nevertheless the interests of this very
world, though vanished as a world, must in some sort be retained
by the modern poet if he plan an heroic poem. It is still
possible, the heroic poem, only so far as the refinements and
restrictions of civilisation have not expelled, wholly and finally,
from the circle of human interests, those earlier interests of the
heroic age. Between us and our pre-Christian ancestors, and
beneath the differences, there remain resemblances, human and
indomitable; heroic qualities remain heroic qualities, great
doings are great doings still, adventures await the adventurous.
Poetry, however, no longer mistress of the whole intellectual
field, no longer history and philosophy, art and music, religion
and morals and law, has resigned something of her epic power.
Prose has encroached upon that once virgin territory, and after
successive and successful invasions, set up new sovereignties.
The ancient, wide, and undivided realm is split and rent into
many kingdoms. Perhaps it is no longer possible for the epic
poet to secure scope and verge enough for his undertaking, or
universal attention for his selected theme.[1] The horizons of
human life have widened, but so vastly widened that the epic
poet can no longer include them however far-seeing his vision,
no longer, as did Homer, weave " *so many histories together as
contain the whole learning of his time.*" His province is not, and
can never again be, co-extensive with the entire world of men's
thoughts and actions. Yet no petty province will suffice. The

---

[1] Coleridge appears to have thought *The Destruction of Jerusalem* the
only subject now left.

great epic owes much of its dignity to the mere spaciousness of
its action, its majestic proportions. The grandeur of the
Colossus, the grandeur of Sphinx or pyramid belongs to a poem
sustained through twelve or twenty books. Before the world
itself, a living wonder, was open to the traveller, in the more
leisurely periods of human history, before the newspaper gave
to every reader his daily budget of news from the ends of the
earth, before the mighty extension of human interests due to
science, the poem of epic dimensions made no impossible
demand upon its audience. Impatience of mere length it is
not, rather the enforced poverty of its interests, competing with
many others, that overshadows modern epic. But if it may no
longer be expected on the scale of antique magnificence, heroic
poetry may still be ranged among permanent types, and of this
type the essential features were presented once and for all in
such poetry as *Homer* and *Beowulf*. Where are we to look for
successful departure from the tradition? Ariosto followed it
when he announced his intention—

> " Of loves and ladies, knights and arms I sing,
> Of courtesies, and many a daring feat; "

he recalled, though in an age remote from the heroic and concerned with an order of ideas—the feudal and chivalric—very
foreign to it, something of the feeling with which one reads the
true epic or saga. He proposes to us the same kind of pleasure
as the older poets proposed, engages our interest in the same or
similar situations, in lofty and hazardous actions, and in persons
suited to their performance, in " *such things as both in war and
peace were fit to be practised by princes.*"

To draw between authentic and literary epic then a final distinction, if possible, is not desirable, nor is it desirable or possible
to distinguish by rigid definition the heroic and the romantic
poem. Had romance, that subtle element, that Arabic perfume,
been altogether absent from Homer, its exclusion from the epic
of latter days might, with show of reason, have been required
by the severer legislators. By some the demand indeed was
made, but presently recoiled upon its makers. For it became
necessary to show that Homer was wholly innocent, and to

B

explain the presence of the quite open and obvious romance in the *Odyssey*, a poem dim with its beauty, steeped in its " *incomparable haze*." To ask of the disciples that they should be purer than their divine master was to ask too much. The streams could not be expected to rise higher than their sacred fount. Romance then, agreeably present from the first, firmly entrenched, as one might say, although often denounced as illegitimate, enlarged its province and seemed likely at times to usurp the whole domain. It may please us to distinguish, to untwist and unlay the composing strands, but no one can indicate the moment at which poetry ceases to be heroic because it is too romantic. Nevertheless, if one lays down the heroic poem and takes up a romance, one perceives usually that the story overpowers the characters, that it is told for its own wonderful sake rather than for the sake of the persons whose temper or " humour " it illustrates. It is thus less of a drama. Or it may be one perceives another thing, that romance has more of the author in it, more of his peculiar notions and feelings. It is by contrast too inward, too much coloured by trains of reflection to permit the action independent life, a clear, commanding superiority of interest. A cultivated curiosity may well indulge itself in such discoveries, but definitions are tyrannous.

" Literary compositions," as Lord Kames said, " run into each other precisely like colours: in their strong tints they are easily distinguished; but are susceptible to so much variety and of so many different forms that we can never say where one species ends and another begins. As to the general taste there is little reason to doubt, that a work where heroic actions are related in an elevated style will, without further requisite, be deemed an epic poem."

And we may remind ourselves, and before all things, that the term epic, definite enough in meaning, can bear no narrow interpretation. Had the numerous embodiments of the mythical history of Greece, that have been lost, come down to us, the governing idea of epic poetry might well have been profoundly modified. In this, as in so many other ways, we are under the

dominion of Hellas. Yet—we are accustomed to overlook it—
after Homer, as well as before him, there flourished epic poets
without number. The names and fame of some survive, like
Peisander of Rhodes, and Anyte, "*the feminine Homer.*"
Before Virgil there were epic poets not a few, like Nævius and
Ennius, and after him imitators and successors till the rôle of
classical poets closes with Claudian. Remember this—leaving
out of account, for instance, that Hesiod's epic, unlike Homer's,
is didactic, written rather to instruct than to please—leaving
out of account also the heroic poetry of Western Europe, and it
will not be by any single canon, nor by any exclusive prejudice
that we shall be justified in judging of a new type. The classical
kinds alone were not one but many. Nor is there justice in the
demand that in a world where all changes, the forms of poetry
should be forbidden to change, that the poet, a slave to the past,
should be requested to conform the picture of his own age to
a pattern outgrown, that battles should for ever remain Homeric.
"*All our understandings,*" as Daniel said, "*are not to be built
by the square of Greece and Rome. We are the children of nature
as well as they.*" [1]

The rules, like that for the exclusion of the marvellous
or fantastic element, laid down by the critics, would have
excluded from the rôle of epic poets, if rigidly applied, names
the most brilliant, had they not indeed made of it a total blank.
Yet impatience, however justified, of the absurd demands and
manifest contradictions of the law-givers has its danger if it
hurry one into a contempt for all rules of art. Like Nature,
art too has its laws; the difficulty is to ascertain them. They
are not written large upon its surface, nor are Nature's, yet we
may perhaps believe them in part discoverable, even if subtle
and withdrawn. A complete exposure of the laws either of art
or Nature, laws knit and folded into the very texture of existence,
would tax an archangelic intelligence. By such a method, on
the other hand, as that of comparison, health and excellence
may be found in alliance with certain principles, disease and
absurdity with their neglect or rejection. Restrictions may be

[1] *Defence of Rhyme.*

wholesome. The Indian epics, to take an obvious example, the *Mahabharata* and the *Ramayana,* take thought neither for the unity nor credibility of their narratives. In one the hero uproots mountains and destroys armies at a blow, in the other the foremost warriors slay their foes not singly, but in earthquake fashion by hundreds and by thousands. The bow, which in the *Ramayana,* Rama, like Ulysses, has to draw, is so vast a weapon that it has to be brought into his presence on a cart dragged by five thousand men. In these poems the poet lets loose his fancy to revel in a wilderness of the wildest and most meaningless fiction. The men in the Eastern epics easily outdo the gods of Homer. It is the same with Cuchullin, the hero of the Irish saga. He has seven pupils in each eye, his' war shout summons to him goblins and demons, he possesses a mantle of invisibility, in his paroxysms of rage flames stream from his mouth, his countenance is distorted beyond all recognition, and a jet of blood taller than the mast of a ship shoots up from the centre of his head. When he meets Ferdia the fury of the combat drives the river by which they fought out of its accustomed bed; when he slays the men of Erin, six score and ten kings are his victims and the number of the common folk beyond enumeration.

With all allowance for the scale of epic action, the great scale —and with Milton's example before us, we may hesitate to discuss the true limits of credibility—with due extension also of the field of belief in ages less informed than our own, it will still be wise to contend for limitation and moderation in art as among the guides to excellence. *" No work from which probability is altogether banished can make a lasting and deep impression."*

> " Tell not your reader in a thundering verse,
> I sing the conqueror of the universe! "

Even in the most elevated heroic passages, even in the delineation of greatness we must see ourselves. As Æsop so contrived it that we discern human characters even in the animal world, so in the epic the deeds of the divine ones may eclipse, but barely eclipse, those of men.

To read in the *Ramayana* or *Mahabharata* or the Cuchullin

saga will go far to assuage the disorder of resentment which too close a study of critics and legislators so frequently evokes.

Restriction rather than inspiration belongs to the nature of criticism, to warn rather than prescribe. It belongs to its nature also to reject rather than welcome, to make narrow the way and difficult the entrance. In the place of rules, principles which lead to exclusion, one may seek principles of inclusion, one may group and compare those narrative poems which by the world's consent have attained some measure of success, one may enumerate such characteristics and qualities as they appear to possess in common, and thus reach, by easier paths, the idea or controlling conception of epic poetry.

Epic, for instance, one notices, usually depicts a victorious hero. It cannot well do otherwise. For in such a poem the interest is rather national than individual. The hero represents a country or a cause which triumphs with his triumph, whose honour would suffer from his defeat. In *Paradise Lost* the event is unfortunate. But Milton chose a subject—the Fall of Man—without national attachments. In tragedy the interest is personal, not tribal or racial, the sympathy of the spectators is a human sympathy, such a concern as might be felt by any man of any birth or country. There is the distinction of tragedy — the world poem. Its hero may suffer defeat unattended with dishonour, without loss even of esteem or affection. But the failure of the epic hero—unless indeed it be a failure like that of Roland or of Beowulf, if one may speak of it as a failure when death follows victory—would it not have the character of a national disaster?—a subject manifestly unfitted for a national poem.

It was claimed by Dryden for the epic poem that it preceded drama and gave laws to it. Clearly it was so, and clearly too its interest, like that of drama, is dependent upon action and character, upon the story and the persons. These two, upon either of which it might be imprudent to lay the major stress, are the pillars of epic. The poet cannot lean upon one of these, its main supports, and neglect the other. Further, the action, as perceived by Aristotle, must be great or important action, and the characters great or important characters. Of themselves great actions and great characters impart that dignity, the uplifting strain, without which the poem lays no claim to epic honours, a certain elevation of tone, proper to the theme and the conduct of the theme. Nor is it sufficient that this dignity or elevation be occasionally felt, it must pervade the whole, it must be sustained throughout. Here, perhaps, the features of epic are first seen to diverge from those of dramatic poetry. "*The heroic poem narrative is called an epic poem*," said Hobbes, "*the heroic poem dramatic is tragedy*." Yes, but in drama for purposes of representation the march of events must be swift, and the poet aims at a concentration of effects, whereas in epic the action moves slowly, with a kind of unhurried stateliness, and can only achieve elevation, grandeur, by the mass or volume of its interests. It may seek to enlarge the volume of these interests by the introduction of numerous sudsidiary characters, or by the diversity of its minor incidents, or by the variety of its episodes, or by the romantic charm of its scenery—by any or all of these. Inclusive and complex, where drama is intense, epic narrative can achieve no more than a diffuse unity. By close-knit texture, by swift progress drama essays to enchain the attention, so that without loss neither eye nor ear can wander: the epic poet holds his reader in easier captivity, "*making it as pleasant as a summer passage on a crooked river, where going about and turning back is as delightful as the delays of parting lovers*." The larger its area, the area of human interest and human experience covered by it, provided the main action be not submerged in the flood of detail, the higher, one may confidently assert, will be the measure of its success. For while conciseness, rapidity, intensity belong to the soul of drama, the epic, diffuse, leisurely, spacious, of necessity unfolds its action with circumlocution; what it yields to drama—and it must yield in depth and heat of emotion —it attempts to recover from it in extent of picturesque and engaging surface. Tragedy is a rapid mountain torrent plunging through dark valley and gloomy ravine; epic a broad and equable steam moving with unhurrying and level sweep through the broad and shining plain. *"Its eloquence,"* as Longinus said of Plato, though *"like the noiseless lapse of a mighty river is nevertheless sublime."* The art of the epic poet is the art of deliberate amplification. To retain and heighten our interest without satisfying it he will check his step, he will pause to describe the hero's sword or shield, or weave a simile or turn aside into some Elysian meadow. He is skilled in delays, in the creation and management of suspense. He will take no count of time while he enriches and decorates his theme, sweeping, as into a treasure house, all that lies within the wide horizons of human experience. Like Homer's, the epic may contain matter for many dramas, but matter held in solution, nor can we, with Aristotle, unreservedly prefer tragedy as a higher form on the ground of its superior concentration. *"Is the moon,"* asks Dryden, *"a more noble planet than Saturn because she makes her revolution in less than thirty days, and he in little less than thirty years ?"* To each belongs its proper excellence. Thus though tragedy, vivid and realistic, presents actual scenes and persons to the spectator's eye, these are not themselves the poet's work, they are incident to the dramatic representation, and the advantages are purchased at a price. For all dramatic art is circumscribed by the conditions of its presentation to an audience. Things seen will ever fall short of things imagined; the recorded strength of Ajax, the beauty of Helen partake of a certain divinity, whereas *"when the picture of Achilles is drawn in tragedy he is taken with those warts and moles and hard features by those who represent him on the stage."* True it is that when in drama the past is brought forward into the present, and realised as a part of immediate and actual existence, placed as it were in the very foreground of our life, the story it tells must move heart and nerve the more it seems to partake of reality. Epic narrative, which carries the imagination into the past, leaning upon that only, and invests its hero in the flowing robes of fable, is eminently of a dream-like texture, which may charm and gratify, but can hardly agitate the soul. Yet how sovereign is the power which can transmute passions and wounds and death, the dreadful things of tempest and battle, into objects of tranquil and delighted contemplation, exquisitely touched to beauty by the poet's art and the divine friendliness of distance. The happiness it confers need not be happiness less complete because it is the happiness of romantic vision, of the child's fairy tale. Since the infirmity of our natures makes more credible a greatness and a goodness far off than near, epic is the natural home of ideals—there lies open to it a region forbidden to tragedy, the shining region to which imagination guides, the underworld of Virgil, the Hell, or Heaven, or Paradise of Dante or of Milton.

In the centuries during which the ideal of heroic poetry was in debate Homer was without serious rival. He is without rival still, though learning has discovered flaws and cracks in the crystal, and made familiar many a song and saga, the names of whose heroes the Renaissance critics had never heard. Exclusive study of the classical type of epic may easily blind the judgment to the distinctive beauties of such poetry as *Beowulf, Roland*, or the *Cuchullin* saga—they emanated from races which never felt the compelling pressure of Greek ideals, and represent far other conditions of national life. Yet heroic poetry is one; whether of the East or West, the North or South, its blood and temper are the same, and the true epic, wherever created, will be a narrative poem, organic in structure, dealing with great actions and great characters, in a style commensurate with the lordliness of its theme, which tends to idealise these characters and actions, and to sustain and embellish its subject by means of episode and amplification.

How far, when one attempts such a definition, attempts an essay or a volume upon " epic poetry," is one guilty of an intellectual error, the error " known as *the theory of artistic and literary classes* "?   " Even the most refined of these distinctions," argues Croce, " those that have the most philosophical appearance, do not resist criticism; as, for instance, when works of art are divided into the subjective and the objective styles, into lyric and epic, into works of feeling and works of design. It is impossible to separate in æsthetic analysis the subjective from

the objective side, the lyric from the epic, the image of feeling
from that of things. From the theory of the artistic and
literary classes derive those erroneous modes of judgment and
of criticism, thanks to which, instead of asking before a work
of art if it be expressive, and what it expresses, whether it
speak or stammer, or be silent altogether, it is asked if it be
obedient to the *laws* of the epic poem or to those of tragedy,
to those of historical portraiture or to those of landscape
painting. Artists, however, while making a verbal pretence of
agreeing, or yielding a feigned obedience to them, have really
always disregarded these *laws of styles*. Every true work of art
has violated some established class and upset the ideas of the
critics, who have thus been obliged to enlarge the number of
classes, until finally even this enlargement has proved too
narrow, owing to the appearance of new works of art, which
are naturally followed by new scandals, new upsettings, and—
new enlargements." [1]

Croce is, in the main, no doubt right, though it would be
difficult to prove, for instance, that " *every true work of art has
violated some established class* "; easy, indeed, to prove the
contrary. But the world has long been aware that art has a
history, that there is such a thing as development, that the
literary and artistic classes, terms like *tragedy* or *epic*, whatever
natural propriety they possess, continually require enlargement.
It has, too, long been aware that art is expression, and that
what we value in the artist is his power of expression. If he
fails here he fails altogether. What other success, we may
naturally ask, can he have?

> " Your music's power your music must disclose,
>   For what light is, 'tis only light that shows."

In the scientific treatise, or the political discourse, or the
philosophical system our eyes are fixed, so to say, in another
direction, we are on the look-out for knowledge, or enlighten-
ment, and for the sake of intellectual gains are prepared to
overlook formal defects. Scientific or philosophical writers

---

[1] *Æsthetic, as Science of Expression and General Linguistic*, translated
from the Italian of Benedetto Croce by Douglas Ainslie, pp. 60 and 61.

make us certain offers and we accept them, but the offer made by the artist is simply the offer of expression; he professes form, and by form he must be judged, we can accept from him nothing less. Yet the difficulty is that in the study of art or literature one moves constantly from one field to another, from the field of scientific to that of æsthetic values. Criticism itself may be, often is, both science and art. Classification, for example, of authors and of works, is frequently found convenient, even necessary. It is convenient to place together for purposes of comparison the *Iliad* and *Beowulf*, Virgil and Milton, to discuss under the same title poems which resemble each other, have points in common, follow the same models, aim at giving the same kind of pleasure. Such a method has its uses and cannot be abandoned. In this field we exercise the logical judgment. But in a moment we may leave it to appraise the work of Homer or of Tasso as poetry, as art, and in this field the æsthetic judgment guides and controls us. For this reason literary criticism, which partakes of a double character, scientific and æsthetic, passes continually in the same volume and on the same page from one form of mental activity to another. Recognise that they are different forms, that the classifications or descriptions given have nothing philosophical about them, that nothing in the constitution of nature dictates or justifies their use, and we escape all dangers; we may continue to employ the customary definitions, the current and convenient classifications, to speak of epic or lyrical or elegiac poetry, of odes and ballads, of tragedies and sonnets. Such phrases are perfectly well understood and one needs no apology for their use. Only if when we employ definitions, often helpful, we imagine ourselves in search of an eternal law, imagine the distinction, for example, between epic and romance as something rigid and final, is the warning necessary. Meanwhile they serve their turn. Not until the last stone is laid is it time to knock away the scaffolding.

CHAPTER II

THE matter of the authentic epic is usually traced to the earlier lays and ballads of the race from which it springs. In it the student discovers not the mind of one skilful artist only, but the minds of many previous makers. And not alone these minds, but the more general mind of a people, the diffused evidence of their creeds and customs, their traditions and experiences. The authentic epic, even in its finished and final form, is, in one sense, primitive poetry, the poetry of an age unlettered, and by contrast with our own uncivilised. But it suggests peoples still more primitive than those to whom it first gave pleasure, and periods more remote than that in which it was composed. It contains hints and references which open up vistas into epochs far withdrawn even from its own gaze, and we know it for a building whose walls were raised by men generations apart from those who laid its foundations. Stones cut from ancient and forgotten quarries, and smoothed with ruder instruments, half-effaced tracings that speak of earlier and superseded plans, fragments of primæval masonry—relate its history. Strictly true it is that—

> " Learned commentators view
> In Homer more than Homer knew."

The poets before Homer were in a measure the architects of his fame; artists, of whom the maker of *Beowulf* had never heard, laboured in his cause. But these again had their predecessors, and before the lays and sagas which the epic poet knew must have flourished a still earlier world of song. The epic — a highly developed form of art—could not have come to birth save for the cruder poems it took up and transformed, and these were in their turn more finely wrought than the earliest narratives and lyrics of men in the infancy of society. The history of poetry is thus, like that of law and custom, a continuous and unbroken history, nor can it be supposed that when its curve dips out of sight, or we miss a connecting link, that the chain of development was severed. It is we who are at fault. The arts advance with the advance of civilisation, and they accompany it steadily back to the drawings by the cave-dwellers of elk or mammoth, and the choral dance of the savage tribe.

Yet one must acknowledge it too hard a task for criticism to trace, fully or exactly, the stages of the journey from choral dance to epic or drama in the story of any people. Criticism can but indicate at most the probable line of advance, piece imperfectly together records and observations of races often far separated in time and space—records and observations perhaps so widely sundered as excavations in Crete and the burial customs of the Hottentot. The scholar is involved, when he ponders the epic problem, in questions the most difficult and disputable of ethnology and philology. An equipment of learning, not rapidly nor easily acquired, is demanded even for their consideration, and they carry one far from the paths of pure literature. Take such a matter as the origins of our own English and Scottish ballad literature, by comparison simple, yet in sharp debate. Enter upon the far remoter field of the origins of *Beowulf*, one is instantly entangled in a forest of conjectures. No one will deny that ballad or epic—any selected ballad or epic—is part of a continuous whole, part of a national literature, yet to ascribe to it not merely its rank and dignity as a poem, but its true date and place in literary and social history, to determine its relations with the poetry that preceded and the poetry that followed, that is a task of real magnitude, more easily outlined than completed.

The earliest poetry of all races—it is not altogether a conjecture—appears to have been the ballad-dance. For in the earliest social gatherings the rude music and song were never dissevered, never practised apart. In rhythmical gesture, for a sense of rhythm appears to be as old as humanity, the village assembly gave expression to its pleasure or sorrow, and when words or cries were added to or accompanied the physical movements, they fell, of nature and necessity, into the swing or beat of the dance. The earliest song, indisputably then, was simply a chorus, often indeed meaningless, but invariably rhythmical, for it followed a pattern already provided. The refrain or chorus of the modern song—linking civilisation with barbarism—leads back to the most primitive of social arts. Poetry for long in the history of mankind was produced and never otherwise produced than under social conditions, at a gathering of the community. The dancing, the singing, the music —these were one, and of the composing strands of the single art the language or words were originally of least import; emotion found expression before thought, and authorship is a phrase without meaning at this stage of human history. Speculation hardens to the inevitable conclusion—collect the evidence from the history of ancient Greece or of the Hebrews, from the observations of travellers among uncivilised races in the past or in the present—that the choral dance and its attendant music are the invariable and preceding conditions of song, the sources of poetry are in these communal efforts of the clan. *"Sometimes they are magic incantations, sometimes they are war-songs, sometimes they are songs of marriage, sometimes they are dirges of death. In some the gestures predominate, and in others the rude music, in others the refrain of a few simple words. But the main points to be borne in mind are that these elements are confused together, and that the mere presentation of the words alone cannot enable us to imagine the true nature of primitive song."* [1] Poetry for long—who knows how long?—can have been little more than a repetition of words, names, phrases of some suggestive value to the group of dancers. Add to these reiterated cries the simplest improvised dialogue, or add to them the simplest improvised narrative, a mere reference to familiar facts—and one has this primitive ballad.[2] Narrative indeed

[1] Posnett's *Comparative Literature*, p. 127.
[2] As Barbour says of Sir John Soulis' feat of arms—
    " Young women quhen thai will play
      Syng it emang thame ilka day."—*Brus*, xvi. 521, 522.
Compare the way in which ballads are sung down to modern times in the Faröe Islands—
    " Their greatest amusement is dancing. Old and young take part in it. . . .

by means of dialogue—the most ancient form of narrative—
possesses advantages great and obvious. Of its age "*we have
proof,*" as Blair remarks, "*in the books of the Old Testament,
which, instead of narration, abound with speeches, with answers
and replies. Thus in the Book of Genesis : ' Joseph said unto
his brethren, Whence come ye ? and they answered, From the land
of Canaan we come to buy food. And Joseph said, Ye are spies ;
to see the nakedness of the land are ye come. And they said unto
him, Nay, my lord, but to buy food are thy servants come : we are
all one man's sons ; we are true men, thy servants are no spies.
And he said unto them, Nay, but to see the nakedness of the land
you are come.*' " [1] So in our own ballads, many of them, by way
of question and of answer, by the way of conversation the story
is told, a method old as the art of story-telling itself. In many
of them are imbedded too, as in a glacier are imbedded the stones
and debris of a distant region, the refrain or chorus which has
travelled far, and links our own with the earliest forms of poetry.
It would seem then that the history of the poetic art—by a
gradual subordination of the chorus either to dialogue or narrative—relates the encroachment of the individual upon the public
domain. He distinguishes, he asserts himself, and slowly the
community withdraws into shadow; further and further it retires
into obscurity till at last it becomes passive altogether, no longer
itself the maker, merely now the audience to whom the poem
is recited or sung. For long indeed it will hold its ground, a
sharer in the mood, by participation in the refrain, but finally
driven from its own, submits, as in the political sphere, to the
superior person, to the ministry of the skilled, professional
artist. "*They lightened their labours by songs,*" says Mungo

They use no instrumental music but dance to songs. It is now the one
and now the other who leads the song, and all who can sing join in it,
at least in the refrain. . . . The object of the song is not only like dance-
music, to regulate the steps, but at the same time to awaken certain
feelings by its meanings. One can see by the dancers' behaviour that
they are not indifferent to the matter of the song, but with their counten-
ances and gestures take pains to express the various meaning of it. . . .
These songs in the Faröe district are so numerous that the same is seldom
sung a second time the same winter. Most of them are pretty long, yet
are never written down, but retained in the memory."—Prior's *Ancient
Danish Ballads*.

[1] Blair's *Lectures on Rhetoric*, vol. 3, pp. 173-174.

Park, in an often-quoted passage, of one of the tribes visited by him, " *one of which was composed extempore, for I was myself the subject of it. It was sung by one of the young women, the rest joining in a sort of chorus. The air was sweet and plaintive, and its words, literally translated, were these—' The winds roared and the rains fell—The poor white man faint and weary came and sat under our tree.—He has no mother to bring him milk ; no wife to grind his corn.' Chorus. ' Let us pity the white man ; no mother has he,' etc., etc.*" [1]

There are modern parallels to such poetry, nearer to ourselves. Let us take, for instance, the *chanties* of the deep-sea sailor, poems of a primitive type, designed to time and to assist the labour of a body of men engaged in a special task, the weighing of an anchor or hoisting of a topsail. It exists, there is a large body of it, but in no fixed or final shape; it changes continually, forms and dissolves and forms anew; new verses sung to old tunes, old choruses fitted to new words, old words to new choruses. Here is a specimen, curiously similar in method and manner to the most ancient tribal song—

The Chantyman sings.	There was a ship—she sailed to Spain,
Chorus.	O Roll and Go;
Chantyman.	There was a ship—she sailed to Spain,
Chorus.	O Tommy's on the topsail yard.

There was a ship came home again,
O Roll and Go;
There was a ship came home again,
O Tommy's on the topsail yard.

What do you think was in her hold?
O Roll and Go;
What do you think was in her hold?
O Tommy's on the topsail yard.

There was diamonds, there was gold,
O Roll and Go;
There was diamonds, there was gold,
O Tommy's on the topsail yard, etc.[2]

Clearly the leader may introduce into his line anything he wishes, clearly the poem may vary and proceed indefinitely. Adjusting itself to the work in hand, it need never be exactly

[1] Mungo Park's *Travels in the Interior Districts of Africa*, 1810, p. 296.
[2] For this and other specimens see Mr. John Masefield's *A Sailor's Garland*.

repeated, inspiration and fancy are free to alter its phrases. The leader may draw upon his memory or invent as the humour takes him, nor is he under obligations to previous singers. Improvisation is here easy, and author's rights are unknown.

In poetry so elementary there is nothing to represent even the germ of epic narrative. The pure choral lyric or the dirge usually tells no story. And the poem, even when it deals with a situation, is merely static, the situation, presented and left, without preface or continuation, seems suspended in air. One notices how characteristic this abrupt opening is, how it clings to all primitive poetry, and is found there long after some progress towards the conduct of narrative has been made. One notices too in early narrative a blending of the dramatic or dialogue method with repetition, not the mere choral repetition, but that form of it which makes for clearness and assists the hearer to grasp the story.

> " ' O aro you come for sport, young man?
> Or are you come for play?
> Or are you come for a sight of our bride,
> Just on her wedding day? '
>
> ' I'm neither come for sport,' he says,
> ' Nor am I come for play;
> But if I had one sight of your bride,
> I'll mount and ride away.' "[1]

Herder looked upon communal poetry, and rightly, as the product of a stage in human history, that stage in which one fancies there existed perfect homogeneity, or if homogeneity can never be perfect, complete sympathy among the units who made the clan or tribe.[2] With the community the individual identified himself, he harboured no separate interests, no private thoughts, no lonely emotions. Singing, dancing, music were not then individual pursuits, pastimes, occupations, they were tribal doings, doings in common. And if so, poetry was then also the product of a group, before the persons of the group had found themselves in some mood of intellectual independence. To retrace the steps from modern poetry to that of less advanced

---

[1] *Katharine Jaffray.*
[2] I have made use in this chapter of some sentences of my own, taken from an article in the *Quarterly Review*, on *English and Scottish Ballads.*

peoples is to pass from complex to simpler types both in form and substance, and approaching the true primitive period, one enters the field of refrain and chorus. Press back still further and the refrain becomes more and more dominant, until the individual note is altogether quenched, silenced amid the voices of the throng. At length the chorus itself dwindles to mere iteration, a series of cries without intellectual filling, accompanying ever the beat of the dance, and poetry—that is articulate and musical speech—sinks below the surface of the emotional sea. Less and less a personal utterance, decreasing in self-consciousness and mentality it passes into mere tribal feeling.

" In the ballad-making age," as Ten Brink puts it, " there was no production, there was only reproduction," by which he means that there was " a common stock of traditions, memories, experiences, held in common by large populations, in constant use on the lips of numberless persons, told and re-told in many forms, with countless changes, variations, and modifications; without conscious artistic purpose, with no sense of personal control or possession, with no constructive aim either in plot or treatment, no composition in the modern sense of the word. Such a mass of poetic material in the possession of a large community was in a sense *fluid*, and ran into a thousand forms almost without direction or premeditation." [1] Or as Professor Gummere describes it—" all was in flux; out of a common stock of tradition, by a spontaneous and universal movement, song rose and fell according to the needs of the community." [2] " Let us imagine," says Ten Brink, " an epoch when the same culture, the same sentiments, the same expressions are the property of a whole community. . . . Imagine a poetry oscillating perpetually between reminiscence and improvisation."

Some demands upon the imagination are made, it may be, by such suggestions, but imagination must be called to the service of any theory, for these epochs, the ballad-making epochs, precede by many centuries the coming of the student

---

[1] H. W. Mabie's Introduction to *A Book of Old English Ballads*.
[2] F. B. Gummere's Introduction to *Old English Ballads*. See also **his** *Beginnings of Poetry*.

and scholar. One can adduce no specimen of the authentic ballad—to parallel the paleolithic remains of the man of science—as it fell hot from the lips of the community. It existed no longer than it was sung or recited, it left no trace in rock or river-bed. In the words of Steinthal, quoted by Professor Gummere, " Dip from the brook a pailful of water, and you have captured no brook; write down a version of some folk-song, and it is no folk-song more. There is no stability about it: among Russians or Servians a song of eight or ten lines has endless variations. An Italian girl sang a song several times, but each time sang it with a difference: when asked the reason, she said she could not help it, as the thing came to her so—*mi viene così.*"

We have our own ballad literature. It is not ancient, no stanza of it in its present shape earlier than the fourteenth century, yet there is clear evidence of an earlier art, not merely in the repetitions, the refrain, the variety of the versions—all difficult to understand, if one thinks of these poems as purely the invention of the minstrel. It is the artistic method as a whole and the primitive outlook upon the world that surprises one. Here are qualities hardly explicable as the result of oral transmission; the mental qualities of a society not yet broken into groups, not yet separated by differences of rank, occupation, opinion, of a society which improvised its own entertainment. To the peasant group at the festival improvisation comes easily, its simpler thoughts and feelings run, as do the sailor *chanties*, into rhythmical speech far more readily—with curious ease indeed—than those of civilised societies. For the meaning of civilisation is each man to his own task; it creates distinctions, artificial barriers, self-consciousness. The gates of natural utterance are closed by it, for no man knows the mind of his neighbour. And men are shy of self-expression when they are not sure of answering sympathies. Had the improviser in the primitive group composed at the dictate of his own imagination, wandering in strange seas of thought, had he felt and thought alone, there had been no primitive poetry. His limits were the limits of a common tradition, his metre was fixed by the beat which his hearers provided, he recalled to his audience events and phrases as familiar to it as to himself, any hearer might in his turn take up the strain.

Are they necessarily remote, the conditions, under which the community or group produced its own poetry, without the aid of professional assistance? Remote in a sense they are, but rather perhaps in respect of mental conceptions than of the lapse of time. For among the peasantry of many races poetry of the communal type, or poetry that approaches it, survived, even now survives, side by side with the more elaborated artistic forms which succeeded and seemed to extinguish it. But it is shy of scientific inquiry, it avoids rather than seeks the light. As Mr. Greig has shown in his *Folk-Song of Buchan* there exists to this day in rural Scottish districts an immense body of song, of which one might remain perfectly unaware even if one spent a lifetime in its neighbourhood. Persisting, untouched and uninfluenced by the official literature of the country, it is independent of print. Neither the songs themselves nor the music to which they are sung come from books, they never find their way into collections. To the country folk, who create them for their own pleasure, they owe existence; children of their parents' festal hour they hasten to hide themselves at the stranger's approach. Without national significance are these waifs of song, without interest for the world of rank and fashion. They are not the work of professional entertainers, they never seek the publicity of the market or the journal. Yet it persists, this body of song, generation after generation, continually and without ado adapting itself to alterations in custom, drifting with the tides of change, perpetually adjusting itself to the subtle unobserved variations in speech; while it bears then no sign of age it is never really young, for it renews itself as does the foliage of the plant or the grass of the fields.

One must conceive for the background of poetry a society of this kind,[1] in which the separation of class from class, to us primal, in which the specialised activities of modern life were wholly unknown. All society was at one time as one class is

[1] See F. B. Gummere's *Beginnings of Poetry*.

now.   With the coming of the minstrel all is changed, the mystic brotherhood is dissolved.   He comes with the new social order, with the elements of disruption into classes; his coming coincides with the beginnings of aristocratic government, of high and low, of rich and poor, of power and impotence.   For the true minstrel, whether in his lordly or lowly days, is a society entertainer, seeking the company of rank and wealth or, after the invention of printing, a livelihood in the countryside.   The true folk-song, the unadorned poetry of the common people would have been his scorn, the scorn of the artist for the vulgar.   The singer known in the hall or castle would have been as unwilling to give his talents to the service of the village as they to hear or appreciate his refined and courtly performance.   The true minstrel does not pass from the village to the court, nor in bad times from the court to the village; he is the scion of the ruling class to whose taste he ministers, or he is in later days an itinerant musician of the pedlar type.

And when it is said that the progress of the poetic art is marked by the growing silence of the group, and the gradual transference to the individual of the leading part in composition as well as execution, it is not meant that the group really becomes silent, that the countryside or village community ceases to sing and begins to listen, but that as always it continues to sing to itself, following the leadership of one of its own members; it is meant that the *centre of historical interest* passes clean away from village community to clan or tribe, organised politically, and *with it shifts the centre of literary interest*.   The village life continues indeed, its art remains, but they have become stationary, they have passed from the light into the shadow, for history follows the star of power and the arc of political change, and passing the village by seeks the castles of the chiefs and the palaces of the kings.   " *Humanum paucis vivit genus*."   *'Tis for a few the human race exists*.   The music of the people has no currency with the ruling aristocracy. Pursuing its own ideals, far different ideals, that literature of the aristocracy becomes the official, the national literature, and its poets, growing up with it, are important officers of state, the chroniclers and historians of the doings of heroes and of princes. Everywhere the subjects of the most ancient song are domestic as the interests of its makers are domestic, and what historian has the village community ever found to chronicle its story, or what story has it to chronicle? Everywhere in primitive folk-song, for example, the place of women is a large one, but with epic or the beginnings of epic we pass into a man's world, the field of politics and war. With the aristocratic minstrel one enters then the field of events which have more than merely human or personal or family significance, which touch the fortunes of a tribe or nation.

In a sense, therefore, there is a flaw or breach in poetic development here: the poetry of the people is not progressive, nor can it reach out towards elaborate forms. Opposed to it are the inexorable limits of the average intelligence. To be distinguished would be fatal to it, to rise above general requirements, the tastes of its audience, it dare not. For the development, in any real sense, of the drama or of narrative the village or rural community can do nothing; it can only continue to minister to its own local and emotional necessities. Higher than that of the lowest intelligence in the interested group its standard can hardly be, at any time or anywhere. Thus its beauty will be an unconscious beauty as of children at play. In appreciative circles under the stimulus of many large and growing interests distinction in art, complexity in material, are welcome; they are distasteful and impossible in the communal group. Briefly advanced art is acceptable only to the alert and advanced intelligence. But the heroic age, the age of epic beginnings, is not primitive, it is really an advanced epoch in the history of civilisation, whose art, like its constitution, is already mature and distinguished. When an audience capable of appreciating his skill is present, the gifted artist puts forth all his powers, since he knows it willing and able to reward him. And with the ruling class, where he is occupied with issues beyond the ken of the countryside, with tribal or national rather than village or domestic, more personal concerns, he is to be found. The affairs of leading men, the doings of princes and chiefs, the heroic episodes, the splendid achievements claim him and give scope to his talents. Thus in an unlettered age he becomes the official repository of the traditions, the heroic lore of his tribe, he becomes the chronicler of the great and memorable things. In the memory of the bard, the only library of the age, are stored the fact and fable which make the history and religion of his people.

In early art poetic form is closely linked with political constitution. To each change in that constitution it would be easy to show a corresponding change in the history of art. Even the beginnings of epic then are impossible while society is perfectly homogeneous, for epic requires eminent persons, distinguished while they are representative; it requires a sense of nationality and pride in that nationality, it requires a theme of more than domestic interest. But here, it must not be overlooked, in the heroic age, though there are distinctions of class, there is a far closer bond between the chief and his people, a bond of common interests and not dissimilar occupations, than is to be found in later stages of society. The king in heroic times is not, like the knight in the age of feudalism, separated from his followers by a different code, different manners, and different weapons. Hence the lay that is sung in the chief's presence is not unsuited for the recreation of his people. They understand it as well as the nobles, its sentiments are theirs, and it has currency throughout all the classes of which the fighting society is composed.

National poetry—and true epic is national poetry—arises and arises only when there is a national spirit to call for it, and this spirit, which made the nation, which achieved a political unity, which created a constitution and laws, will create poetry also, informed by a similar unity and expressive in like measure of nationality. The achievements, the aspirations of a people are not written in their outward history alone. But the unity which makes epic is at once broad and closely-knit. No mere clan or tribe can compass it, it must rest on foundations so wide that the world has laid few capable of supporting it. Nor is this all. One may speak of the pre-existence of the epic hero.

The epic-making people must find a hero worthy of it—or create him—it must find some deed of national significance wrought by him, or ascribed to his prowess, around which may be placed with easy propriety the details of daily life, the beliefs and customs and traditions of the race, so that as a whole the narrative shall be more than a narrative, a meeting place of all emotions held in common and a source of inspiration, since it ministers not only to national pride, but has constant reference to names, and things, and places familiar.

Epic literature implies, too, as Professor Ker tells us, " not merely certain favourite themes—combats, battles, killing of monsters, escapes, or defences—but a diffused sympathy for the heroic mood among the people for whom the epic is made. We may suppose that when the epic poem flourishes there is, among the contemporary people who are not poetical, something like the epic frame of mind, a rudimentary heroic imagination which already gives to mere historical events and situations a glimmering of their epic magnificence. The ' multitude ' in an heroic age interprets life heroically; and it is this common vague sentiment of heroism, not any bare unaccommodated thing in itself, with which the epic poets make their beginning. Their real life is heroic, because it seems so, both to them and to their unpoetic fellows and hearers." [1]

Of the Anglo-Saxon poetry which preceded *Beowulf* no specimens survive. How is it then possible to study the epic process in the ancient literature of our race? Frankly, it is not possible. Yet a process not wholly dissimilar is before us in the development of the modern ballad, if we are willing to allow a certain permanence in human habit, a certain recurrence in the methods of the mind. Our English and Scottish ballads—it matters not when they were composed — probably represent, just as the fo lk-song of Buchan represents, a type older than *Beowulf*, though *Beowulf* was no doubt composed seven or nine hundred years earlier. The democratic, the unofficial, the unprogressive type of poetry—which preserves, though it has outgrown, communal features, indicates earlier social conditions, less complex

[1] *The Dark Ages*, p. 84.

interests, and far simpler artistic form—is there in unmistakable guise. These ballads of ours, modern as they are, may in some cases be the lineal descendants of Germanic ballads, composed before the coming of the Saxon. Though not a word remain the same, though every cadence be altered, the relationship is not of necessity affected. For the folk-song has no fixed text, and accommodates itself with easy fluency, in every generation, to local, temporary, or linguistic requirements. It differs at every rendering, for it is no man's property; it can never fall out of date, for if it does not renew itself on the lips of each singer, it passes into complete oblivion. It lives and dies and lives again with each new recital.

Thus, though we cannot trace back any of our existing ballads to the moment when they parted company from their original choral associations, though they may be and usually are indeed in their present shape the work of individual makers, we are deceived if we think of them as the simple and original compositions of the fifteenth-century balladist. Their stuff is the stuff of which primitive or communal poetry is everywhere composed, their form and structure, their sentiments and situations betray an unsophisticated art. Few things are more certain than that popular poetry continued to flourish in most communities while the more advanced individualistic and progressive art in the hands of the gleeman or scôp, to use the names given in our early literature to the professional singer, was elsewhere collecting epic material.

To the aristocratic and warring society then we must look for our epic beginnings, to the ruling group, whose acts and sayings are of political importance and become history, whose literature is song and chronicle, concerned with their ancestors and themselves, a literature representative and official.[1] Like the early village community in one thing the aristocratic society in its

---

[1] Since writing the above I have seen Mr. Chadwick's recently published and valuable *Heroic Age*. We may, I think, accept his *four stages* in the history of heroic poetry—" To Stage I. belong the court poems of the *Heroic Age* itself "—a stage from which nothing has survived; " to Stage II. the epic and narrative poems based on these "—like *Beowulf* and the other Anglo-Saxon poems we possess; " to Stage III. the popular poetry of the eighth and following centuries; to Stage IV. the German poems of the twelfth and following centuries, composed at a time when heroic subjects had again come into favour with the higher classes."

earliest stages makes its own poetry. All its members are singers. The themes are no longer domestic, the method no longer choral, but skill in song is not yet purely professional skill. The recitative or narrative to which all are interested listeners is within the power of all. The harp goes round at the feast—Achilles himself was not above the art—and from the common stock of tales or myths, known to all, each chief or warrior can shape a song. They were not of necessity inventors, but as they told and re-told, heard and re-heard the stories, memory and imagination were at work together, and the singer passed insensibly into the maker. From rendering familiar things to the creation of new phrases, new figures, was an easy and inevitable step, nor did he himself recognise the moments at which he became an independent poet. Then as families federated into tribes, as petty monarchies superseded patriarchal rule, the themes enlarged and altered, and the rank and standing of the bard underwent corresponding change. The skilful singer rose to independent position. As Alcinous or Agamemnon had each his minstrel, so among the Teutonic tribes the bard appears to have had his own place of honour. A member of the *comitatus*, a member of the chief's council, a man of mark and consequence, or when a wanderer as well as minstrel everywhere welcomed in the ruling circles with rich gifts, the poet in the heroic age sat of right among the nobles. "*Thus as they wander*," says the Old English *Scôp's Tale*, "*they give utterance to the needs of men, and their expression to their thanks. Everywhere south and north they meet some one learned in song, a liberal giver, who wishes before his courtiers to display his lordship and magnify his state, till all things end, both light and life. Fame comes to him who under heaven distributes praise.*" The minstrel of this age when he spoke of battles spoke of what he knew. It is related of Olaf the Saint that in his last fight, where he was slain, he kept about him his Icelandic Scalds, placing them within the shield-burg, that they might see and hereafter speak from their own knowledge, and that two of them fell by his side.

We are debarred, as I have said, from a study of the narrative art as it developed in the early history of the Teutonic tribes, as we are debarred from a study of the lays which preceded the *Iliad* or the *Niebelungenlied*. Into the obscure and misty regions of epic origin we can nowhere force our way. But conjecture based upon the materials supplied in the great authentic epics themselves may seek and obtain assistance from examination of the progress of narrative art in ballad poetry of comparatively late date. From the primitive song in which the refrain predominates to the simple story in the form of dialogue our own ballads conduct the inquirer to the elaborated narrative, and from that to the complex poem, which unifies a mass of earlier matter, introduces the interests of character and of diversification, adds episode and enriches description with details, and thus points clearly enough to the heightened epic manner.

In the earliest stage of our ballad poetry—doubtless in the earliest stage of all ballad poetry—the story is altogether above interest in character, the situation is presented for its own sake, and witnessed as a street scene might be witnessed, there happening before our eyes. Torn from the book of life, a moment's picture, without preface or conclusion, to be watched, as children watch, it is no more than an incident which arrests a passing attention. The central figure, a hero without a home or habitation, resembles all others, a man is a man, a woman a woman. Or if they are more than this the man is brave or bold, the woman fair. To distinguish individuals or localities no touch is given, no clue offered. Suffused with human feeling the simplest ballad is, but feeling unexpressed, secretly hidden in the heart of the situation, such elemental emotion as the child may understand. At this stage, because village interests are chiefly domestic, and because only the simplest human feelings are admissible, woman, as already noted, plays a large part in art as in life. She is not yet pushed into the background to leave room for the mightier issues of nationality and statecraft. Then later, in the more developed art, slight details, added touches of colour, creep in—it is May morning or New Year's day—or we learn something of what has preceded and what followed, how the situation arose and what came of it. With increasing skill repetitions dwindle, the refrain falls away, character begins to play a part in the story. In some groups, like the Border ballads, the hero is already a conspicuous person, eminent in a society that knows and appreciates his qualities; the landscape too reflects the district to which he belongs. The Robin Hood ballads again show us a hero of defined type surrounded by members of his band, the central and distinguishable figure, the natural leader of a body of faithful followers. In these ballads the surroundings are those of recognisable country, the simpler human emotions — such domestic relationships as mother and son, sister and brother— have been superseded by those of a group larger than the family. We enter the region of class or class feeling. Robin Hood and his band are a community within a community, separate and sufficient for themselves. Like the king's court they have their own habitations, their own ways of thought, their own pursuits.

The *Gest of Robyn Hood* instructs us further. It is a little popular epic and clearly an artist has been at work. The composing strands are earlier and simpler songs, but how far the poet is an inventor, that is not possible to determine. He has aimed, one sees, at a unification of pre-existing materials: in the fact that incidents separated from each other are always brought into touch and harmonised, that he is never or rarely discovered to have lost sight of facts previously mentioned, to have confused times or places; the constructive sense is apparent, too, in the prevision, which holds the future in view, keeping an eye on the plot and the consistency of character.

One may thus travel in our ballad literature, noting differences, from the earliest type hardly severed from the choral song—a simple scene or situation involving one or two figures only, not yet differentiated characters — to narrative further and still further complicated, harbouring at each stage new sources of interest, presenting a more and more crowded stage, till one meets character fully developed, if not for its own sake, at least for the sake of the enrichment of plot which it brings. At what stage did the conscious minstrel appear? It is not altogether easy to answer. These ballads of ours are clearly not of the type that compose themselves, yet their authors, whoever they were, have missed the path to fame; not one name is preserved. Some may have been, no doubt indeed were, deliberately composed, but of others it would be misleading to speak of an original version, and vain to make search for the original words. Some are the work of the lower order of minstrels, " adapted," as Professor Courthope says, " by the professors of the declining art of minstrelsy from the romances once in favour with the educated classes." Others however, though we cannot trace them back more than three or four hundred years, have their roots in popular tradition, and fell late in their history into the hands of the professional singer. Once sophisticated it is no easy task to distinguish a traditional ballad from the inventions of the minstrel, but we cannot forget that far behind him lies that mighty field of choral song. Who will tell us—bearing in mind the refrain, the repetitions, the varieties of version, bearing in mind " *the sameness of tone, of incident, of legend, of primitive poetical formulæ in the ballads of Scotland, France, Provence, Portugal, Italy, Greece* "—that we are not here dealing with poetic matter of vast antiquity?

How little knowledge can be gleaned of origins is revealed if one considers the Robin Hood ballad cycle, which might be classed under the title " *historical*." The popularity of these songs has been, from the first recorded mention of them, extreme, their hero has a niche secure in the heart and imagination of the nation. Who then was Robin Hood, and at what date were the ballads composed? " A tale of Robyn Hood " is a very old proverb for an idle and untruthful story, but no mention of Robin in official literature is made before the reign of Edward III. The author of *Piers Plowman* (about 1362) refers to " *Rhymes of Robin Hood* " as " *better known to idle fellows than pious songs.*" The next reference is in Wyntoun's *Scottish Chronicle*, written about 1420, when Robin Hood and Little John are mentioned. But the first reference to Robin as an *historical* person occurs in a passage of the *Scotichronicon*, a work partly written by Fordun, Canon of Aberdeen, between 1377 and 1384, and partly by his pupil, Abbot Bower, about 1450. Bower's part of the chronicle is very untrustworthy; he largely interpolated the work of his master, and sometimes with the absurdest fictions. Among these interpolations appears the name of Robin Hood for the first time in history.

" *At this time* (sc. 1266) *from the number of those who had been deprived of their estates arose the celebrated bandit, Robin Hood (with Little John and their accomplices), whose achievements the foolish delight to celebrate in comedies and tragedies, while the ballads upon his adventures sung by the jesters and minstrels are preferred to all others.*"

The hero then of the most popular cycle of English ballad poetry is never mentioned by any contemporary historian or chronicler, but is conjectured into existence by an untrustworthy writer at a date two hundred years before his own. " Robin Hood," in the words of Professor Child, " is absolutely the creation of the ballad muse.   The earliest mention we have of him is as the subject of ballads.   The only two historians who speak of him, as a ballad hero, pretend to have no information about him except what they derive from ballads, and show that they have none other by the description they give of him: this description being in entire conformity with ballads in our possession, one of which is found in a MS. as old as the older of these two writers."   Ritson connected the main personages in this popular cycle with characters in the old morris-dances.   Wright suggested that Robin Hood was " one among the personages of the early mythology of the Teutonic people," and a German scholar, Kuhn, has endeavoured to prove that Robin is no other in name and substance than the god Woden.   The serious study of origins is not greatly advanced by such hypotheses, but if the origin of so popular a cycle baffle the scholar, what success may one expect in the search for the original of some unattached ballad?   " The first thing that strikes one in reading the *Mabinogion*," said Matthew Arnold, " is how evidently the mediæval story teller is pillaging an antiquity of which he does not fully possess the secret: he is like a peasant building his hut on the site of Halicarnassus or Ephesus; he builds, but what he builds is full of materials of which he knows not the history, or knows by a glimmering tradition merely; stones, 'not of this building,' but of an older architecture, greater, cunninger, more majestical." The ballad minstrel in our own land was often too a pillager of antiquity, not always employing indeed material of a great or majestic architecture, but the traditions and memories of the simple folk who for many a hundred years in " the dark backward and abysm of time " had lightened their labour and heartened their courage and soothed their grief by the divine enchantments of song.

The type of poetry varies with the stage of a people's social and political progress; it varies too with its prevailing interests. Tacitus describes our Teutonic ancestors as a singing folk and as a race of warriors. Such a race would render into song the deeds and praise of heroes, the joy of battle, the glory of victory, the burial of a chief fallen in conflict. And from such material, the lays and hymns that reflected an heroic age, is everywhere drawn the material of authentic epic. But the epic is always a late product, which awaits a fortunate moment. Not one or two races, but many appear to have had their heroic age; how comes it that the epic poetry of the world is so limited? It is true that epic poetry is limited if one thinks of the epic as a complete and rounded whole, an heroic narrative with a beginning, a middle, and an end, its episodes fitly placed, its characters appropriately grouped, its form artistically ordered. But if one's requirements be less stringent, it is barely true. Far from scanty is the epic poetry of Europe, if that title be accorded to narrative in the lofty style, to great stories greatly told.[1] For the appearance of that splendid star, the finished epic, man must wait upon the heavens. A rare friendliness of circumstances, a lucky fortune must attend its birth, if the representative child of the race is to be well-favoured and perfect in every limb. At the great festival of Panathenæa,

[1] See Mr. Chadwick's *Heroic Age*, already mentioned, for a most interesting note on " *a living heroic poetry* " among the Mohammedan population of Bosnia. Among points worthy of notice are (1) the variety of forms in which a story is told, " never repeated," even by the same poet, " in exactly the same words; " (2) the reproduction melting into creation; (3) the absence of written texts; (4) the ease with which the longest poems are memorised.

held every few years, or at similar earlier festivals, through centuries the Ionian bards recited their heroic lays, and Homer became the Homer we know. At such national gatherings a common worship, a common stock of traditions made vivid the sense of kinship; the spirit of unity was visibly abroad. In their pride and happiness the poets produced their finest wares, and the critical sense of a vastly interested audience—exercised through generations—gradually imposed an order and a purpose upon the whole mass of this heroic poetry. A process of acceptance and rejection, the unconscious criticism of assemblies, silently moulded the *Iliad* as we possess it. No such good fortune has attended any other body of heroic poetry in any quarter of the world. In France the continuity of national life was broken when the northern tribes met Christianity and the influences of Roman civilisation. In Scandinavia the progress of culture was too slow, the conditions of the life-struggle too severe, to permit the artistic development without which the epic cannot realise itself, or reach maturity. There the epic form competed unsuccessfully with the lyric. Among Teutonic peoples the Old English poem of *Beowulf* approached most nearly to complete and finished epic. In many ways comparable to the *Iliad*—a great and moving work of art—it is yet manifestly far less complex, less elaborate. "*We have in Beowulf a half-finished epos, as if frozen in the midst of its development.*" It is so frozen because at no stage in their history were the people from whom it sprang welded into political unity. Many such poems were doubtless laid under contribution for the *Iliad*, or, let it be said, that *Beowulf*, dealing with somewhat the same type of material as Homer, carried it to a different conclusion along a path of its own. There is the same background of war, of clan feuds, of heroic enterprises. But the *Iliad* was wrought into a national book for the Greek world, it was the literature of those gatherings where the various branches of the Greek race met to celebrate their common ancestry and traditions. *Beowulf*, never a national Bible, a national treasury, hardly more than a tribal possession, attains as much of unity as was possible to it, not final or complete, yet higher than that attained in the poetry of the Scandinavians or the Franks. Noble indeed it is, but of a nobility below that of the Greek epic, the absolute culmination, the apex of the epic process.

> " The writer of the famous Trojan war
> And of Ulysses' life, O Jove, make known,
> Who, whence he was; for thine the verses are,
> And he would have us think they are his own."

Of the lays which preceded *Beowulf* we learn a little from that poem itself. " *At times one of the king's thanes, with memory stored with old tales, invented new words for them, skilfully woven. He began to relate Beowulf's adventure with deft cunning, and happily to tell the story, fitting word to word.*" [1] Of such songs as this, one may safely conjecture, was the cycle composed to which the author of *Beowulf* was indebted. Some of them are even imbedded in the text as episodes, as is Finnsburh.[2] The poem itself is of higher range and rises above such fragments by its greater elaboration and far greater dignity, its later heightened and lordly style, its emphasis on character, its wider sweep of interest which includes and transcends the single episode.

Strange it is that in that well-defined type, whose counterparts in early Germanic days preceded *Beowulf*, the heroic lay, our literature is lacking. It is lacking too in the literature of Germany. To find it one must go to Denmark, to that very district in which probably the lays from which *Beowulf* emerged had their origin. The Danish heroic ballads are numerous, and like *Beowulf* they are concerned with the sea and sea-faring. Castles and armour and weapons with which the English epic makes us familiar are there; there too gifts are interchanged between heroes; there one hears of martial doings and military expeditions; there, as in *Beowulf*, names are given to favourite weapons—these and many another feature, foreign to our own ballads, the fierce feuds, the combats with dragons and supernatural enemies, recall *Beowulf*. No traces of this heroic world, curiously enough, remain in our popular literature. We have the heroic epic itself, but the tradition, the stories from which it sprang, were left behind in the land of their ancestors when our forefathers became Englishmen.

---

[1] *Beowulf*, vv. 867 ff.   [2] Vv. 1068 ff.

CHAPTER III

THE branch of the Teutonic peoples to whom *Beowulf*, a poem of the migrations, belongs, came to England in the fifth century. The early Angles and Saxons knew nothing of any civilisation existing in Britain; they discovered it for themselves in the fourth century, and the sea-rovers pronounced it a good land, rich in booty. By the fifth Rome had withdrawn her protecting legions, and the invaders, at first mere freebooters, who raided and sailed away, began to make winter settlements on the coasts they had pillaged, and to press inland when driven by necessity. Soon little kingdoms grew up, first Kent, then Essex and East Anglia and Northumbria. The pirates, changing their modes of life, turned settlers and farmers, and for six hundred years our literature is Anglo-Saxon. What did they carry with them into England, these newcomers? What poetry or history in which no mention is made of England, but which preserved the earlier traditions of the race? Many an old lay and ballad, many a hymn, many a battle-song no doubt, but little remains. The only indisputable specimens of that literature are *Widsith, The Lament of Deor, Brunanburh, Waldhere, Finnsburh*, and the incomparable *Beowulf*. From these the rest must be conjectured, yet from these it is not impossible to frame a conception of the races from which they emanated.

When our ancestors came to these shores they were polytheists, whose gods, not omnipotent, though powerful deities, dwelt in Asgard, where Odin, chief of the twelve mighty ones, had his Valhalla, whither he summoned all warriors who fell in battle.[1] The constitution of the Saxons was a species of free

---

[1] These are Scandinavian forms. We know little or nothing about *English* pre-historic religion.

monarchy, in which kingship is of the patriarchal type, and the monarch the friend and shepherd of his people. The chief or earl had his followers, the *comitatus* described by Tacitus, but his own distinguished descent or prowess gave him pre-eminence. Outside the *comitatus* stood the nation of freemen, less wealthy than the earl's retainers, but more independent, men free to speak and not unwilling to defend their words with blows. An emotional though fierce folk, warriors all, they were little given to agriculture or the peaceful arts; of many tribes probably, but tribes not inhabiting for long any fixed geographical area. These tribes met and mingled or fought, coalesced or separated into new groups, for ever in unrest. They were plunderers, when plundering was possible; they battled as they lived in smaller or larger groups, perpetually swaying back and forward as the tides of war or conquest or defeat determined. One who has read De Quincey's *Revolt of the Tartars* can figure to himself the movements of these untamed northern multitudes, who crossed the Rhine and Danube as the fever of battle, the scourge of famine, or who knows what strange impulse drove them. To rule among such wild and turbulent tribes was to be a wielder of weapons, a master of rude eloquence, a tempest-lover and cloud-compeller. These men knew no towns—no city or town is mentioned in *Beowulf*—regarding them even in the conquered lands as tombs; they felt imprisoned within walls, *praelio gaudentes*, they were most at home in the battle-camp or in their galleys threshing over angry seas.

Curious it is that of these indubitable ancestors of ours we know almost nothing. There are the accounts given by Tacitus in his *Germania*, and of Jordanes, himself a Goth, in his *De Rebus Geticis*, written in the sixth century. But of that long history of the German peoples before they drove their terrible wedges into the vast structure of Roman civilisation, we are almost wholly ignorant. And of documents which teach us anything of their beliefs and ways of life, their methods of warfare, their social and political constitutions, there are, besides *Beowulf*, but few and fragmentary remains. None of the arts save that of poetry were sufficiently advanced to leave any monuments. Of their architecture and metal work, their music or drawing, we can only judge from fibulæ or pieces of armour recovered from burial mound or earthwork, or from the scanty remains of some ancient burgh. And though for many a century in their own northern lands the German races must have climbed from primitive savagery to a civilisation that contained noble elements, the long and painful progress is a matter of inference rather than of recorded facts. It is for this reason that *Beowulf*, even were it not an epic of high dignity and poetic worth, must rank as priceless—an historic picture, the only picture extant, of a world long departed and irrecoverable. It illuminates the vast dim tract of an unknown human story, ages of lives; it recreates for the modern man the world of Northern Europe in the pre-Christian era; it gives meaning and content to such bare outlines as are provided by historians and chroniclers; to arms and armour, jewels and ornaments recovered from ditch and barrow, to the broken timbers of old galleys, to the moats and mounds of old townships, it adds a real and living interest. From this poem alone, taken with the remains of ancient German civilisation which the museums preserve for us, is possible at least the partial reconstruction of a society which endured many a hundred years, and yet is otherwise almost wholly beyond our ken, a society whose features, however unconscious of it we may be, are still represented in the political and social order of these our islands. Here is our race in the vigour of its early prime, in this mirror we catch reflections of our own national features, for a moment the curtain is raised upon scenes of a forgotten life shared by millions through centuries of time.

It was a life in many respects like that described by *Homer*, though a gulf of ages separates the two poems—not less than fifteen hundred years. Homer's heroes belong to the age of bronze, *Beowulf* to the age of iron. Homer has the courtlier air, though the Christian poet has also somewhat softened and humanised the spirit of the times. Homer speaks of Fate much as does *Beowulf*, he has the same delight in weapons and armour, the arrow sings, the mail rattles with him as in the Anglo-Saxon epic, his heroes boast in the same strain; the dead Homeric hero, like Beowulf, is placed upon a funeral pyre and the ashes when the body is consumed placed in a like burial mound or barrow. For both a dirge is sung, and like ceremonies take place around the tomb. The warriors in *Homer* would have understood and fraternised with Beowulf and his men, have exchanged gifts with them in the same fashion as with their own countrymen, fought against or side by side with them not as strangers but men of the same world.[1] Yet in *Homer* there is evidence of refinement and even luxury, of the sumptuous arts which adorn life, unknown to *Beowulf*. Hrothgar's hall is of wood, Troy itself was a walled city, and the palace of Priam was built of stone. Andromache in the *Iliad* orders her handmaidens to set a great tripod on the fire that Hector " *might have warm washing when he came home out of the battle.*" In the palace of Menelaus in the *Odyssey* there is " *flashing of bronze through the echoing halls, and the flashing of gold and of amber and of silver and of ivory.*" In the high-roofed hall of Alcinous " *brazen were the walls which ran this way and that from the threshold to the inmost chamber, and round them was a frieze of blue, and golden were the doors that closed in the good house. Silver were the door-posts that were set on the brazen threshold, and silver the lintel thereupon, and the hook of the door was of gold. And on either side stood golden hounds and silver, which Hephaestus wrought by his cunning. . . . And without the courtyard hard by the door is a great garden, of four plough-gates, and a hedge runs round on either side. And there grow tall trees blossoming, pear-trees and pomegranates, and apple-trees with bright fruit, and sweet figs, and olives in their bloom.*" [2]

The student approaches the closer study of this noble poem as the mariner some difficult coast. The land looms up through a forbidding haze of formidable and inconclusive exegesis. For a thousand years after its completion it lay undiscovered, and when brought to light became the centre of a second and equally

---

[1] See for a more detailed comparison Mr. Chadwick's *Heroic Age*, which I saw too late to make use of in this volume.
[2] Butcher and Lang, *Odyssey*, Bks. iv and vii.

heated " Homeric " problem.   First catalogued and described by
Humfrey Wanley in 1705 as " a fine example of Anglo-Saxon
poetry " when found by him among the manuscripts of Sir
Robert Cotton—by whom it had been no doubt bought at the
dispersion of some monastic library—it was damaged by the fire
which destroyed many of the Cottonian manuscripts in 1731.
In 1753 it passed to the keeping of the British Museum, was
copied there by Thorkelin, a Danish scholar, in 1786, and the
first edition of it, printed by him, with a Latin translation,
appeared in 1815.   Five years later it was first translated into
a modern language, Danish, by Grundtvig, from the publication
of whose version dates the stormy debate, darkened by personal
passions, which has since raged round it, a debate whose
thunders still mutter round the academic horizon.

The MS. is the work of two scribes, men of the tenth or
eleventh century, who were possibly unacquainted with the
language they transcribed.   They wrote clearly however, and
though capitals and punctuation are irregular, separate words
sometimes run together, and the lines do not correspond to the
verses, *Beowulf* may be regarded as a fine MS.   There is little
doubt that it was copied from a much earlier original or reproduction of an original probably of the seventh century.[1]

It has been argued that Beowulf was an historical person,
who fell in Jutish battle in the year 340, and that the poet was
his contemporary; it has been much more generally believed
that he is the creation of the epic muse.   Beowulf's name does
not appear in history, his deeds are obviously mythical.   It has
been held again that he was a relative of Hygelac (identical with
the Chochilaicus mentioned by Gregory of Tours), king of the
Geats, who fell in battle against the Franks in the sixth century,
that he gained great renown among Danes and Angles for his
martial exploits in the campaign in which Hygelac perished,
and that to this hero was added the fame of the mythical Beow
or Beowa, of the lineage of the gods, the slayer of dragons.
A mortal, by his valour grown to greatness, thus entered the

---

[1] There are at least two intermediate stages between our MS. and the
seventh century.

Norse pantheon, and put on the glory of a fabled and divine hero. The name Beowulf has been very variously interpreted—by one scholar as the mist-cleanser, he who purified the marsh land from fever; by another as the builder; by another as the harvest-god (from *bewod*, a knife); by another as Bee-wolf, the honey hunter. Grendel, the monster he overcame, is, says one, the god of the high tides, the ravagers of the low coastlands; he is, says Skeat, the polar bear; he is, insists another, merely a personification of the malarial marsh-fog. But the ingenuity of the scholar often taxes the patience without illuminating the mind of the student, and in this region at least philology has won no triumph. Nor has it yet been demonstrated that the Geats of the poem were Jutes, or Swedish Goths as Ettmüller maintained.

We have been asked to believe that the poem was composed in Denmark and brought to England by the later Teutonic invaders; that it was composed in Sweden; that it had its birth in Northumbria and describes with peculiar exactness the Yorkshire coast near Whitby. By some critics it has been confidently ascribed in its present form to a single poet, by others to as many as six heads and hands. It has been argued that it was wholly the work of a Christian monk of the eighth century, laying under contribution a large body of heathen saga, and again that it was developed in Mercia, having passed in an early pagan form from Northumbria, and received the final Christian touches, perhaps in Kent, as late as the ninth century. By one authority it has been ascribed to Bishop Hygeberht of Lichfield, a councillor of Offa, by another to the poet Cynewulf. It is purely pagan, say others, who would excise, as manifest interpolations, some three hundred lines which contain the Christian references. That can be no Christian poem in which Christ is never mentioned, nor his mother, nor the central doctrine of the Trinity.

The problems remain; *Beowulf* keeps its secret well. Hardly perhaps to be finally and fully solved, time will be on the side of research and many chapters will be added to the book of investigation. Meanwhile the mystery of its origin enhances perhaps rather than diminishes its commanding interest. For at least we are sure that it is a genuine document, the work of our forefathers, the men of our own blood who gave us the language we speak. We are sure, too, that it is a poem of which the materials at least were transmitted orally. That it was subjected to alterations we know, to those gains and losses which are inseparable from the poetry of growth, which distinguish the authentic epic from the inalterable work of an individual in an age of advanced culture, wrought on a plan devised and foreseen from the inception. *Beowulf* thus opens, and opens magnificently, with characteristics proper to its age and type, the history of our English literature, the unbroken history of a thousand years, with a chapter prophetic of its later splendour.

The language of *Beowulf* is West Saxon [1]—though there are traces of both Northumbrian and Mercian dialects—and the metre — that of all ancient Germanic poetry — alliterative. Each line falls into two parts, the sections divided by a pause at the end of a word. In each four syllables are stressed, not less than two in each part, and of these stressed syllables, which correspond to naturally-accented syllables in the word, two at least begin with the same letter. Other unstressed syllables may be added and a great diversity in the actual length of the line is thus possible, sometimes as few as eight, sometimes as many as twenty syllables compose the line. The third stressed syllable in the line gives the rime, one or both of the preceding stressed syllables must begin with the same letter (all vowels being regarded as the same), the fourth or last avoids the letter though it may correspond with that beginning another stressed syllable. The place of end rime is thus taken by initial rime which is only found in accented syllables. " *Middle pause so strong as to be more than pause only, alliteration, accent, and substitution of equivalenced groups instead of rigid syllabic uniformity—these are the four pillars of the structure of Anglo-Saxon prosody.*" [2] It is probable that in recitation the stresses were

---

[1] Or late West Saxon, with some traces of old West Saxon forms.

[2] Saintsbury's *History of English Prosody*, vol. i, p. 24.

marked not only by the voice but by an accompanying beat on
some musical instrument.   To a certain ruggedness this verse
adds a splendid if somewhat barbaric vigour, the crash of
swords upon helmets.   The martial ring and weight of it are,
if not caught, at least suggested by Tennyson's translation of
The Battle of Brunanburh :

> " Slender reason had
> *He* to be glad of
> The clash of the war-glaive—
> Traitor and trickster
> And spurner of treaties—
> He nor had Anlaf
> With armies so broken
> A reason for bragging
> That they had the better
> In perils of battle
> On places of slaughter,
> The struggle of standards,
> The rush of the javelins,
> The crash of the charges,
> The wielding of weapons—
> The play that they play'd with
> The children of Edward.

> Never had huger
> Slaughter of heroes
> Slain by the sword-edge—
> Such as old writers
> Have writ of in histories—
> Hapt in this isle, since
> Up from the East hither
> Saxon and Angle from
> Over the broad billow
> Broke into Britain with
> Haughty war-workers who
> Harried the Welshmen, when
> Earls that were lured by the
> Hunger of glory
> Gat hold of the land." [1]

Though much is disputed, it is not disputed that in *Beowulf*
we possess an authentic heroic lay, in which, though it was
worked over by a Christian poet, is clearly mirrored the life and
mind of pagan Germany, " the very body of the time, its form
and pressure."   The story falls into three sharply defined parts,
each of which is concerned with an heroic exploit.   In the first
Beowulf slays a monster, which has terribly harassed a Danish
king, Hrothgar; in the second he slays a second monster, the

---

[1] The date of the battle was 937.

mother of the first come to avenge her son. After these triumphs the hero returns to his own land, becomes the king of it, rules for fifty years, and in his old age, battling for his people, slays, but is slain by, a dragon who has ravaged his realm. Thus the third exploit, related in the third part of the poem, is widely separated in time from the first and second. The first and second are the feats of his youth, the third of his old age. The unity of the poem, it is at once apparent, is not a close-knit unity. It is a unity of the primitive type, achieved simply by relating all occurrences, otherwise unconnected with each other, to a single person. The unity attained in the *Odyssey* of Homer is of the same type, but there a much more complete story or series of stories is knit together with matchless art, an art beyond the skill of the English poet. The successive great incidents then in the career of Beowulf make the plot. To these others might with ease have been added without adding to the organic or artistic complexity of the narrative, but merely to its length. Yet while this is so, the selected incidents are similar in type and they are appropriate to discover the character of the hero, a character consistent and strongly presented. And a certain sense of unity is also derived from an impression, not vaguely received, that the persons we see, the events we follow, make but the foreground of a crowded scene. Behind them move continually across the stage kings, queens, and warriors; a mighty spectacle of vigorous and passionate life— wars, combats, domestic feuds, loves, treacheries, villainies—is revealed to the alert imagination in stray allusions, and in the subsidiary episodes and songs. To the makers of *Beowulf*, and to its original audiences, its recital was something far different from a mere tale of superhuman prowess; it was an incantation which made memory leap from its couch of slumber, and revived for its hearers in all its names and phrases a well-known world in which they and their fathers had borne a part.

The poem opens well with the legend of an ancient king, the ancestor of the reigning Danish monarch, sprung from the race of the gods, who as a child had come by ship, mysteriously from the sea, to Denmark. This divine one, a good king, ruled mightily, and when the time was come, departed at the command of fate, leaving a successor, a son worthy of him. His funeral is described, the funeral of a viking, the finest glimpse anywhere given us of that splendid rite. The dead man is laid upon the deck of his ship, surrounded by his war-gear, and many a precious ornament, and with a golden standard high above his head sent out into the keeping of the ocean from which as a child he came. From the great deep to the great deep, like the Arthur of romance, from mystery to mystery he goes. Such is the prologue from which the poet turns to recount the woes which befell Hrothgar, a descendant of the divinely sprung monarch — how his folk - hall, the splendid dwelling Heorot,[1] where he and his nobles met in council and at feast, lay deserted, since a grim demon, a traveller of the marches, had slain there many thanes, and by night would seize and devour any who dared dwell there. For twelve winters the dreadful peril had assailed King Hrothgar, bringing him sorrow and shame. Far and wide the evil news was bruited among the adjoining peoples till it came to the ears of Beowulf, a thane of the realm of Hygelac, the Geat, lying to the north of Daneland. With fourteen chosen companions, he, stoutest of heroes, sets forth to bring succour to the harassed monarch. His war galley is launched, and with a fair wind a day's voyage brings them within sight of the shining cliffs and broad headlands of Hrothgar's realm. The landing is a vivid scene. The warriors run their vessel ashore, and the warden of the coast sees the bright shields lifted over the bulwarks. Down to the water's edge, spear in hand, he rides to demand their mission. *" Who are ye in battle-gear who thus speed a tall ship hither over the waters ? "* And Beowulf answers, *" I am Beowulf and friendly is my mission, no other than to bring succour to a king beset by troubles."* The warden of the shore, seated on his horse, receives the hero's assurances of amity. He will himself guide them to Hrothgar's hall, and his men will keep the ship in charge. She is left riding at her anchor, and the party sets out along the stone-laid causeway

---

[1] Heorot means *Hart*, and the hall was presumably so called from its horn-crowned gables.

to the hall. Arrived they set up their shields against the benches and rest their ashen spears against the walls. Beowulf announces himself standing there in helmet and coat of linked mail and is admitted to audience of the king. To Hrothgar hail! he cries. The old man is seated among his earls, and listens to the young adventurer's account of himself and his proposal, his desire to do battle alone with Grendel, the fiend that harasses Heorot. Hrothgar remembers Beowulf and his father Ecgtheow, a bench is set for him and his companions, the mead is poured for them by a thane from an embossed ale-stoup, from time to time the gleeman sings, and there is joy of heroes. A certain Unferth, a thane of Hrothgar's, jealous that a stranger should undertake more than he himself or a man of his own people, taunts Beowulf as one mightier in words than deeds. The young warrior defends himself, boasts his valour, and questions that of his assailant. The rough jests evoke a great din of laughter, the feast proceeds, and the queen herself, gold-adorned, mindful of courtesies, bears round the costly ale-cup, and gives friendly greeting to the young chief. The old king, the shepherd of his people, is in cheerful mood, and nourishes good hopes of Beowulf's hardihood. But as the dusk advances the company rises, and Beowulf is left to watch and face the onslaught of the savage Grendel. Proudly he discards his helmet and his mail shirt, nor will he retain even his rich-hilted and long-tried sword. He is resolved to meet the monster on equal terms.

Thus far the poem is neither more nor less than history. Not possibly history in the sense of actual events of any given day or year, true to the details of persons and localities, but history in the far wider and truer sense of a faithful rendering of a world that once had real existence. Poetry, as Aristotle said, deals with the universal, history with the particular. It is not *what Alcibiades did or suffered*—with such things the historian proper must concern himself—but with that wider area of possible and likely things that the poet is occupied. And so far in *Beowulf* we have vivid pictures of matters familiar in the heroic age of our forefathers, their daily concerns, the things that happened in every hour of their lives. Their ships and sea-faring, their offensive and defensive armour, their political methods and international civilities, their social doings, their streets and houses, their domestic habits, their arts of decoration in hall or on sword or flagon—these are all spoken of with the utmost simplicity, truth, and distinctness. *Beowulf* recreates for us a society which endured for centuries side by side with the Roman empire, a northern society of the aristocratic military type, a society whose chief business was war and plunder, yet which in the very atmosphere of storm and battle made its way towards civility and the arts, and knew the worth, despite its heathen ferocity, of magnanimity and self-sacrifice.

The battle with Grendel strikes a new note, the note of pure imaginative work. "*Then from the moor, from under the misty heights came Grendel, striding.*" The fire-forged hinges of the door give way before him; he seizes a sleeping warrior, tears and devours his flesh, and advancing grasps at Beowulf, the hero himself. But a hand-grip, fiercer than any he had ever known, meets his own, and he would fain have fled to his den of darkness. Then upright sprang Beowulf and straightway grappled with his foe. The struggle grim and great overthrows the ale-benches and the hall resounds with the uproar. Panic seizes the Danes as they hear the din and the terrible cries of the monster. But the unrelaxing grip of the hero at length bursts sinew and bone, tearing Grendel's arm from the shoulder, and the demon, sick to death, flies to his den beneath the fells. With dawn the victory is bruited abroad, and the young warriors ride to Grendel's lair, the demons' mere. There wondering they gaze upon the gloomy waters, seething with blood, proof of the beast's joyless end. Then was there great rejoicing and praise of Beowulf. The youths, light hearted, race their horses on the smooth ground; a thane, skilled in song, chants the story. He chants, too, the lays of Sigemund and of Heremod, songs of far journeys and feuds and many battles. Hrothgar, standing at the entrance of the hall, receives the hero, giving him the thanks that are his due; costly treasures also—a golden standard, a helmet and coat of mail, a mighty treasure sword, and with these eight war-steeds, with bridles and cunningly wrought saddles. To the companions of Beowulf, too, Hrothgar presented gifts. Then song and the sound of feasting resound through Heorot, and Hrothgar's queen herself, bearing the mead-cup to her lord and Beowulf, adds her words of praise, and gives to him gifts of price, a mantle and ring and collar of twisted gold.

Thus ends Beowulf's first adventure, a great story greatly told from the moment in which the young chief launches his ship, the wave-crosser, and sails the swan-path on his splendid errand. His figure as he stands " *bold under helm* " in Hrothgar's hall, surrounded by his followers, the boar crest proudly shining above the cheek guards of their helmets, their grey mail rattling as they move, is conceived in the very spirit of heroic adventure. The society of the Danish king's court is epic society. It is full of types—the diplomatic queen with her graceful and gracious attention to her lord's friends, the wife and daughter, " *peace-weavers*," whose presence refines the banquet and moderates strife, the experienced courtier and counsellor to whom the king turns for advice, the thanes young and old, the braggart, the coward, the bard or harper, cunning with the glee-wood, the crafty smith, all are there, and in the background the fierce faces of the warrior band.

Grendel is no longer to be feared, but not for long is Heorot left at peace. Quickly there came an avenger, the hag, Grendel's mother, a female monster. By night, raging at the death of her son, she enters the hall of the Ring-Danes, seizes and bears away to the fen Æschere, a trusted friend and counsellor of the king. Hastily is Beowulf summoned and the dread news made known to him. " *Sorrow is renewed,*" said Hrothgar, " *Æschere is dead, my war-friend, I know not whither he is borne. I have heard of these monsters who hold as their own unvisited lands, wolf-haunted slopes and windy nesses, perilous places among the fens, where the mountain stream descends beneath the earth under the misty forelands. Not far measured in miles is it from here, where lies the mere. Over it hang rimy thickets, a fast-rooted wood over-shadows the water. No pleasant place is that.*" Proudly answers

Beowulf—" *Better is it that a man should avenge his friend than that he should greatly mourn.   Each one of us comes to his end, let him who may, achieve renown, leaving a famous name.*" [1] Proudly he undertakes the second labour.   A horse is saddled for Hrothgar, and with him fares a band of shield-bearing warriors.   The tracks of the demon are plain to see.   They reach, tracing them, at length the joyless wood overhanging the grey crags.   The water below it stood blood-stained and troubled. Sea-beasts lay on the jutting rocks, dragon-like serpents swam the deep.   Beowulf lets fly an arrow, slays one, and he is dragged ashore.   Then, clad in full armour, with a sword Hrunting in his hand, an ancient treasure-blade, hardened with blood, damasked with poison-twigs, he addresses Hrothgar a second time.   " *Befriend my thanes if battle take me, and send to Hygelac, the Geat, the treasures thou hast given me.   With Hrunting I win fame or death shall take me.*"   So he said and plunged into the depths of the tarn.   A long space was it ere he saw the bottom, the tusks of the crowding monsters burst the links of his mail-shirt.[2]   The demon snatches at him and they rise into a wondrous sea-hall, a cavern above the surface of the water.   By the blaze of a great fire he perceives the she-wolf of the deep, the mighty water-wife, and strikes fiercely at her with his sword.   But for the first time Hrunting fails to bite, and angrily Beowulf casts aside the great blade.   Grasping his foe by the shoulder he hurls her to the ground, but falling she seizes him in her turn, and over-reaching himself Beowulf too

---

[1] Cf. Sarpedon's words in *Homer*—

> " Could all our care elude the gloomy grave
> Which claims no less the fearful than the brave,
> For lust of fame I should not greatly dare
> In fighting fields, nor urge thy soul to war;
> But since, alas! ignoble age must come
> Disease and death's inexorable doom;
> That life which others pay, let us bestow.
> And give to fame what we to nature owe."
> Pope's Translation, *Iliad*, xii. 324.

[2] The monster's dwelling appears to be conceived as a sea-cave whose entrance is below the level of the sea.   See Mr. Chadwick's *Heroic Age* for a comparison of this exploit of Beowulf with that of Grettir in one of the Icelandic sagas, where the monster's cave is beneath a waterfall.

comes to the ground. The fiend stabs at him with a broad knife, brown-edged, but his interlaced breast net, his ring mail, saves him. Staring round in his extremity he spies an old Eotenish sword, huger than any forged by mortals, the work of giants. With the battle-fury in his veins he grasps it, strikes and strikes so furiously that the great blade passes clean through the beast's body. Then turning to where lay his old foe Grendel, with the same weapon he strikes off the head.

All this while the watchers, sick at heart, stared at the mere, all stained with blood, expecting never to see again the Atheling, their friend. And at even the Scyldings departed, his own men waiting and watching against hope. Then at last Beowulf rose through the water, in his one hand Grendel's head, in the other the giant's sword. But, a wonder, the blade was consumed up to the very hilt by the poison of the monster's blood. With great rejoicing is the chieftain greeted and relieved of his armour, and back to the hall the company takes its way, four bearing upon a pole the head of Grendel. Arrived they enter, Beowulf in the midst, and lay their trophy before the old king—a sight to waken fear in all that assembled company. When the tale is told and the golden hilt of the magic sword examined, with its runic legend, Hrothgar, amid profound silence, addresses his trusty friend, praising him in no stinted fashion. He repeats his promises of rich reward and gives orders for the morrow's banquet. With the day, when the weary champion has had his fill of well-won rest, he makes preparations for departure, greatly desiring, he and all his men, to see his own land again. Before his going Hrothgar once more praises Beowulf as an emissary of peace and goodwill between Geats and Danes, presents him with twelve princely gifts, prophesies his future kingship in his own country, and takes leave of his benefactor with tears, knowing they might never meet again. And thus Beowulf departs, marching with his thanes to the shore, where lay their ship, the sea-rover, at anchor. The warden of the coast greets them, and they pile upon the vessel's deck the costly treasures from Hrothgar's hoard. To the coast-warden Beowulf gives a parting gift, an heirloom, a sword with golden scabbard; the sail is hoisted, the timbers hum, the ship shoots out into deep water, the foam white around her prow and track, the wind free for home. Soon are seen the Geatish cliffs, the windy walls, the well-known headlands. The watchman of the haven, who for so long had gazed over the sea for the return of his beloved countrymen, hurries down to bid them welcome and to make the vessel fast. Then laden with their treasures, in the bright sunshine of the afternoon, the heroes came again to Hygelac's lofty dwelling, hard by the sea-wall. Eager for news the king welcomes his kinsman, and while the lady, Haereth's daughter, bears round the mead-bowl, Beowulf relates his adventures. When these are told he delivers to his lord Hrothgar's messages of friendship, and bidding his men bear in the lofty helmet with its boar's crest, the grey mail-coat, the mighty war-sword, he presents them and all the gifts he had received from Hrothgar, adding words of courtesy—" *All my favours are from thee ; I have few near kinsmen, save thee, O Hygelac.*" And Hygelac, not to be outdone in grace, commands that there be brought and given to the young warrior Hrethel's heirloom, a gold-decked sword— no greater treasure in the shape of a sword was there among the Geats, and with it he gave him seven thousand pieces of gold,[1] a house, and chieftain's rank. And so with Beowulf's triumphant return to his native country the second part of the epic comes to an end.

There is a long gap in time between the second and third parts of the poem. In a few lines we are told how Hygelac died, slain in battle, and how he was succeeded, first by Heard-red, his son, and when he too had fallen in war, by Beowulf, who reigned well for fifty years. But in his old age a trouble came upon the venerable king and his folk, the Geats. A monster, a fire-breathing dragon, which had its den in a high stone-barrow by the sea—a place full of mighty treasure hidden there by the last survivor of some perished clan—had been disturbed by an outlaw seeking refuge in the cave. Seizing a cup of price to buy back the forfeited favour of his lord, the

---

[1] Or seven thousand hides, or its equivalent in land and treasure.

man fled back to his home. The dragon waked and sniffed the stranger's track along the rocks, and when night came, wrapped in fire and breathing vengeance, issues from his den. The homesteads far and wide are set in flame, the mansion of Beowulf himself destroyed, and the aged king, fearlessly as of old, resolves to meet and slay his people's foe. Many times, since the days in which he succoured Hrothgar, had he fought for his kinsmen; when Hygelac was slain escaping only by his prowess of swimming, turning ever and again upon his pursuers like a wolf of battle, so that few of them escaped, and again, when king himself, with an army, after long and bitter marches he wrought retribution, and supported the son of Ohthere in warfare over the seas. Thus safe from many encounters he came to his last, sad at heart and filled with foreboding, for he knew that Fate was near at hand. And knowing it he makes a speech of farewell to his friends, recalling his glorious youth—the crash of the charges, the sword-play, the passions, and the feuds. " *Many battles I ventured in my youth, once more will I, the aged shepherd of my folk, go forth to the combat. It shall be at the rampart as Fate, the giver of lots, may decide.*" Then clad in mail and with a fire-proof shield upon his arm he goes down the rocky path to meet the coiled dragon, the warder of the barrow. With a shout Beowulf, standing before the stone arch, roused the monster, and out he came upon him, flaming, curved like a bow. In the first onset Beowulf's great sword, the heirloom of Ing, failed him, and so fiercely terrible was the beast's approach that the hearts of the king's own comrades, Athelings' sons, weakened with terror, and they fled for shelter to the wood hard by. Wiglaf alone came to his aid, Wiglaf, a loved and trusted friend, who never before, for he was young, had stood by his lord's shoulder in the fight. Angry with grief he reproached the cowards, his companions, and sprang into the fight, armed with a famous blade, the ancient blade of Eanmund. In the second encounter Wiglaf's shield is burned down to the boss and Beowulf's sword snaps short, for too strong was his stroke and he overtaxed it, the sword Naegling, though old and grey in battle. In the third he is sorely wounded. But Wiglaf

E

stands to him, and wounds the dragon, and Beowulf, drawing his dagger, stabs and slays it, before his own strength ebbs away. Then, still clear in mind but knowing that death is very near, he suffers Wiglaf to wash his wounds, and lamenting that no son of his can succeed him, speaks of his own reign now at an end, and takes comfort in the memory of past deeds. He would view, before death, the treasure hoard so long guarded by the dragon, the treasure he now leaves to his people. Wiglaf brings it out from the cave, a wondrous spectacle—gold and jewels, beakers and vessels, the possessions of some ancient race, helmets old and rusty, bracelets curiously twisted, and high over all a golden ensign, of handiwork marvellous to behold, wrought with spells, from which there shone so bright a gleam that by its light he saw and examined the riches heaped upon the floor. Upon these, when brought forth, the dying king gazes for a time and then with his last breath gives his parting commands. *" Bid the warriors raise a barrow, after the funeral fire, on the headland at the sea's edge, which shall tower high on Hronesness* [1] *as a memorial for my folk, so that the sea-farers driving their tall ships over the ocean may in after time call it by the name of Beowulf's mound."* Then taking from his neck the golden collar he gave it to the young warrior thane, and with it his ring and helm and coat of mail, and bade him use them well. *" Thou art the last of our stock, the Waegmundings. Fate has swept to their doom all my kinsmen, valiant earls. I must follow them."* So he dies, Beowulf, the king, the representative of his race, beside the dragon he has slain, and with the sea at his feet. He dies lonely, childless, unsupported by any religious consolation, without hope of the future save in the affectionate memory of his folk, but with his duty done. And the poet puts into the mouth of Wiglaf, when his craven comrades creep back from their shelter, the principle upon which this heroic society was founded—*" Better is death for every one of noble birth than unhonoured life."*

A messenger is sent over the headland to the camp, and there are forebodings of wars now that the people's champion is dead.

---

[1] That is *Whale's head land.*

Franks and Frisians and Swedes also, when they have word of
it, will turn, alas, upon the defenceless; many a maid will be
torn from her home, and the grey raven with the wolf be busy
among the slain.   The folk with tears crowd to the shore where
lies the dragon and their hero slain, beside the heaped and
ancient treasure.   Wiglaf addresses them, giving Beowulf's last
message and his due meed of praise ere he makes preparations
for the funeral rites.   The body of the monster is pushed over
the cliff, wood is sent for to build the pyre, and the body of the
king is placed upon a bier and borne away.   Then at Hronesness
a great pyre is built, hung with helmets and shields and coats of
mail, and upon it his sad followers lay the body of their chief.
The fire is kindled, the smoke rises thick above the burning
pile, and mingled with the sound of weeping the roaring flame
fanned by the wind arises till all is consumed.   Then, the
sorrowful rites ended, for ten days the folk of the Wederas were
busy—building a mound high and broad, a beacon in the midst,
surrounded by a wall.   In it they placed rings and jewels, earl's
treasures, and around the mound rode twelve sons of Athelings,
singing a dirge and the deeds of the hero, saying that he was
a king of kings, of men the mildest and gentlest and of honour
very desirous.

Such briefly and omitting the episodes, which amplify but
interrupt it, is the story of the English epic, a poem without
parallel in the literature of the Germanic peoples, and eclipsed
by few in the narrative literature of the world.   Apply the
severest tests and *Beowulf* falls short of true epic greatness in a
dozen essentials.   It is too short—hardly more than three thousand lines, or about the length of three or four books of Homer,
Virgil, or Milton; it is defective in plan; it is insufficiently
varied in interest; it is unequal in texture—the early part
superior to the later; it harbours inconsistencies, such as the
Christian interpolations in a pagan setting; at times the action
waits on speeches, as when Wiglaf goes to the assistance of
Beowulf only after a long discourse; its style is harsh and often
uncertain.   Evidences of primitive art, of primitive ideals and
ways of thought abound in *Beowulf*, the thoughts of childhood

in the language of men.   Yet however and wherever preserved
it has far outgrown the limitations of the ballad art and method.
There is here style, not indeed the matchless style of *Homer*,
perfected by a school of bards, a high speech invented for their
own purposes, yet style—selected words in effective order—
the clear note of distinction.   This is not the language of every
day but of *makers*.   The formality and dignity of the speeches,
the deliberate choice and variation of phrase, the massing of
detail and elaboration of descriptions, reveal the presence of the
careful artist.   That *Beowulf* is far nearer the original martial
songs, its predecessors, than *Homer* is clear, if any evidence be
required, from the absence of the long elaborated Homeric
simile, or aggregation of similes, *comparaisons à longue queue*,
which display the experienced poet decorating his subject with
skilful ease.[1]   In *Beowulf* similes are few—the ship beginning her
voyage is described as " *most like a bird*," or the blade of a
sword flashes " *as when the sun, candle of the firmament, shines
brightly in the heavens*."   Metaphors—the " kenning " or poetic
synonym—are on the other hand common—the sea is " *the
whale's road* " or " *the swan's path*," the ship " *the sea-wood*,"
the sword " *the battle-friend* "—but so rudimentary a power of
comparison indisputably assigns the English poem to an earlier,
less developed stage of narrative art.   Still we have journeyed
far from the beginnings.   Beyond all this, the external elements

---

[1] " Even as ravaging fire kindleth a boundless forest on a mountain's
peaks, and the blaze is seen from afar, even so as they marched went the
dazzling gleam from the innumerable bronze through the sky even unto
the heavens.   And as the many tribes of feathered birds, wild geese or
cranes or long-necked swans, on the Asian mead by Kaystrios' stream,
fly hither and thither joying in their plumage, and with loud cries settle
ever onwards, and the mead resounds; even so poured forth the many
tribes of warriors from ships and huts into the Skamandrian plain.   And
the earth echoed terribly beneath the tread of men and horses.   So stood
they in the flowery Skamandrian plain, unnumbered as are leaves and
flowers in their season.   Even as the many tribes of thick flies that hover
about a herdsman's steading in the spring season, when milk drencheth
the pails, even in like number stood the flowing-haired Achaians upon
the plain in face of the Trojans, eager to rend them asunder.   And even as
the goatherds easily divide the ranging flocks of goats when they mingle
in the pasture, so did their captains marshal them on this side and on that
to enter into the fray."—*Iliad*, ii. 455 ff.   *Translation by Messrs. Lang,
Leaf, and Myers.*   These similes, says Professor Murray, " *are not meant to
be taken all_together; they are alternatives for the reciter to choose from.*"

of form, there is in *Beowulf* an intellectual wealth and a depth of reflection no ballad knows. The world upon which this poet looks out is thronged and bustling as the street of a city. Where the ballad horizon is limited by immediate and village interests, a single scene and one or two lonely figures, before this "*Son of Memory*" a past unrolls in which nations have been born and died, kingdoms won and lost; he recalls tribes and tribal heroes, kings and their kindred, a hundred names of races and of men. He foresees too the future, and looks to it with hope or with foreboding—"*such is the deadly grudge of men, doubtless the Swedish folk will come against us when they have learned that our king is dead.*" The scene shifts easily from the hall to the galley under sail, from the shore to the moors, from day to night, from winter to spring. There is observation of nature and pleasure in good handicraft, and a Stoic creed of life and honour. To carry all this within a single brain, to space and arrange the material, to order and decorate the verse, to present the characters and the sentiments, the appropriate word, the apposite comment, to leaven the whole mass by the infusion of poetic enthusiasm was no mean personal achievement. In *Beowulf* the conscious poet emerges. But there is more than this, the high poetic dawn of insight and imagination. Hard the poem is with the hardness of armour and weapons, of a society that gives and expects no quarter, and of this hardness the interpolated Christian passages afford no real mitigation. "*God, doubtless, can stay the fell ravager from his deeds,*" we read in one passage, and again "*Him*" (Beowulf) "*hath holy God sent to us, as I trust, to us the West Danes, against the terror of Grendel*"; these asides hardly even colour the stark pagan tale.[1] But there are utterances, pathetic and penetrating, moving reflections on human life and destiny that vibrate with truth learnt in the harsh grip of experience. The themes are ancient, no more than the brief glory of man's strength, the relentlessness of fate, the sorrows of the weak or the conquered—foreseeing slaughter and shame and the captive's lot. "*Now is the*

---

[1] The gods have disappeared from Beowulf, the old gods, expelled by the Christian scribe or redactor.

flower of thy strength lasting a while—soon shall it be that sickness or the sword, or the clutch of fire, or wave of the flood, or spear-thrust, or flight of arrow, or blinding age shall take away thy might." [1]   Or again: *" Now that the leader in war has laid aside laughter, revel, and song, therefore shall many a spear, cold in the dawn, be grasped by the fingers, raised in the hand.   No sound of harp shall rouse the warriors, but the dark raven, busy over the fallen, shall send his frequent cry, telling the eagle how he sped at the feast when, with the wolf, he spoiled the slain."* [2]   Or take this, the lament of the last survivor of his clan as he gazes upon the useless treasures of the dead—*" None have I to wield sword or burnish the golden beaker, the treasure-cup of price, the warrior host is gone.   The hard helmet bright with gold must be stripped of its adornment, they sleep who burnished it, whose part it was to furbish the battle-masks.   The corselet that withstood in war, amid the crash of shields, the bite of the sword-edge, moulders with the warrior.   No more will the ringed mail, close to his side, make far journeys with the chieftain.   There is no gladness of the harp, no joy of the glee-wood, no good hawk swings through the hall, no swift steed paws the yard of the stronghold.   Death the despoiler has banished many a one of living kind."* [3]   Trite reflections no doubt, but not more trite than those of Homer, and far beyond the range both in content and expression of the mere balladist. For the epic form, as here, envisages a society; it perceives, beyond the immediate actors from whose affairs the ballad never wanders, wide spaces filled with human interests and human figures.   The ballad fails to supply any background, any depth of stage.   One or two actors or sufferers occupy the immediate scene, and behind them is vacancy.   Again, and it is an indisputable sign of maturer art, political relations in the epic supersede the personal.   It is aristocratic when the ballad is democratic.   There is no talk in *Beowulf* of lovers, of son and mother, of sisters or domestic doings.   The community bond has overpowered that of the family; men and the doings of men, nations and the affairs of nations, are the interests of this

[1] V. lines 1761 ff.   [2] V. 3022 ff.
[3] V. 2252 ff.

literature, rank and the duties of rank are the pillars of this society.

The epic hero is always a fighter, a soldier in some good cause. In the mediæval French epic he is the champion of the true faith against the Saracen; in *Beowulf* he is engaged in a no less holy war with the powers of darkness, the enemies of the whole human race. This is not a war of heroes with other heroes, it is a conflict of man with powers hostile to man. Nothing can be clearer than that *Beowulf* belongs to an age in which nature was felt as unsubdued, in which the elements were unfriendly. His race inhabited the narrow lands, the ridge of unceasing war —the unexplored ocean before him, at his back the equally unexplored and threatening woods. The forest had not yet been cleared nor the protecting walls of the city built. Northern Germany in the pre-Christian centuries can hardly have been a more kindly region than the Central Africa of to-day. The hero in *Beowulf* stands at bay with Nature, exposed to the attacks of strange, uncouth, silent foes. Neither Grendel nor his dam nor the dragon by whom he is slain make use of any speech. Suddenly and mysteriously they issue from the unknown, suddenly and mysteriously as a plague upon the wind. Everywhere in this poem we have the sense of a savage and menacing world—in the scenery, the stormy seas, the sombre forest, the wild unpenetrated country of the interior. Heroic poetry of this order has small concern with ideas; unlike the chivalric epic, it is desperately occupied with doings. Life is wholly strain and pressure, governed by the simplest emotions, the desire of food and drink, of treasure and good weapons. There is no room for love-episode or protracted courtship, no place for gentleness, for subtleties of thought and feeling, no heart for easy humour, small space for the gay sciences. It reads throughout like a stern record of a painful but necessary undertaking. In this society each group is supporting itself with difficulty against famine, the untamed forces of nature, the raids of rival clans, each individual preserving his existence at the spear's point. These men—

" Fierce in their native hardiness of soul,"

are laying the foundations of civilisation and social order, they keep their foothold only by the exercise of eternal vigilance and native valour. The unfriendliness of the physical environment is far more emphasised than the play of motives or the varieties of emotion and character. We are far nearer the elemental conditions of life, the opening days of human history, than with Homer. The nerve of the narrative, the heart of its interest lies therefore in the vivid presentation of a real struggle against deadly odds. Ringed round with enemies the hero proudly takes pleasure in his strength while his strength lasts, he sells his life dearly. When he dies, he would die like Colonsay's fierce lord in Scott, pierced by the lance of De Argentine—

> " Nail'd to the earth, the mountaineer
>   Yet writhed him up against the spear
>   And swung his broadsword round!
>   Stirrup, steel-boot, and cuish gave way,
>   Beneath that blow's tremendous sway,
>   The blood gushed from the wound;
>   And the grim lord of Colonsay
>   Hath turn'd him on the ground,
>   And laugh'd in death-pang, that his blade
>   The mortal thrust so well repaid."

The hero in this epic knows that the day will come when fate will be stronger than he, as it has been stronger than his fathers and kinsmen, when all will seem " *too wide for him, the fields and the homestead*." And a natural melancholy tinges the poet's mood when he reflects that if not to-day then to-morrow in the battle the chief goes the fated way, that the bravest must, in the end, sleep " *den eisernen Schlaf des Todes*," *the iron sleep of death.* The best that can befall, the heart of his desire, is to die the great death, as Beowulf dies, beside the dragon he has slain, or—

> " With heroes' hot corpses
>   High heaped for his pillow."

A dark, capricious fate, whose decrees none can foretell, is the ruler of human destiny—" *It is not an easy matter to escape it,*" says the poet, or " *Fate did not thus ordain for him.*" Yet courage may shield him from the impending blow, " *Often does Wyrd save an earl undoomed when his valour avails.*" The

Beowulf temper is that of the born fighter, the man born never to yield, "*the temper of the fighter who feels that the very Norns themselves must cringe at last before the simple courage of men standing naked and bare of hope, whether of heaven or hell or doom.*"

> " The harder shall thought be, the bolder the heart,
> The mood the more, as lessens our might." [1]

It was the temper of that long roll of Englishmen, soldiers, sailors, adventurers, explorers, to whom retreat was more bitter than death, who, rather than turn back from the task undertaken, challenged the fates themselves—to pluck, how often, glorious success from the very heart of failure. *Beowulf* itself does not end, as it is sometimes demanded the epic should end, upon a note of success and triumph. Or if it end upon a note of triumph, it is triumph touched, as are all human triumphs, with a sense of the invincible hardness of the world. It is at best a losing battle in which mankind is engaged, and Beowulf is throughout his life the leader of a forlorn hope. Again and again he is successful in spite of odds, foot by foot he grapples with destiny unafraid, but he knows that there is but one way, and that he must tread at last the pathway to the shades. The clear-sighted philosophy of the old English epic, undimmed by any dream of hope, disturbed by no metaphysical consolations, has in it the more than Roman fortitude that looks unflinchingly into the burning eyes of Truth.

Of the arts of peace *Beowulf* says little. The skilful craftsman twists collars of gold or bracelets or other personal adornments, but the warrior's weapons are the subject of his peculiar and affectionate regard. The sword, to which perpetual reference is made, is jewelled, carved with runes, often personified and given an individual name, handed down as a precious heirloom, its record preserved in history. The helmet and coat of mail too, the spear and shield, are wrought with a care and skill lavished upon no other possessions. So much are they a part of himself that a warrior is known by his arms. This is true epic feeling. In the true epic manner, too, Beowulf does not

[1] *Maldon*, 312-313.

await the tide of war, he goes out to meet it, and against an enemy of unknown strength, unknown haunts, and unknown resources.   In his labours—the fight with Grendel and his dam and the Fire Dragon—human valour and power as idealised by the poet are matched with supernatural adversaries, vaguely imagined, dwellers in a mysterious country.   The landscape assists to create an atmosphere of the dim and marvellous. A hidden and perilous place is it, the haunt of the mighty stalkers of the mere, and there is none of the sons of men so wise as to know its depths.   " *Thou knowest not yet the spot, the savage place*," says Hrothgar, " *seek it if thou darest.*"   The Athelings follow to the misty mere, " *over steep slopes of stone, a narrow and single path, by many an abrupt cliff, the homes of sea monsters, an unknown road.*"   The dragon of the last combat watches its hoard in a high burial mound, " *beneath it a path unknown to men.*"

In the foreground of the *Beowulf* landscape are the shore, the bold headlands, the wind-swept sea rising clearly before the eyes as in a picture; beyond is a vague region of enchantment— not mountain country, it is significant that mountains are never mentioned in this east coast epic—gloomy fells and shaggy woods, a land of high and dead romance, but romance in which there is neither sunshine nor warmth, in which terror overpowers beauty.   In Celtic story one meets with delightful experiences, exquisite sylvan retreats, meadows rich in flower and fruit, islands of repose and fair winning figures that invite the sea-worn mariner.   There are no such pleasaunces in *Beowulf*.   In *Homer* the divine shapes of gods and goddesses, the holy splendours of Nature and of a world fairer than man's, are discerned through the dust and smoke of mortal battle, or beyond the weary leagues of sundering sea; no veil lifts in *Beowulf* to disclose immortal beauty.   What a life, behind all its courtliness, the grace and chivalry the poet imparts, what a life in the ages before his own this epic pictures—days and nights tossing upon the sea, the bitter North Sea, in open vessels, days and nights of unintermitting battle with foes human and inhuman; the fierce quarrels, the ferocity of war, the bodily strain, the sleepless mental vigilance, rage and storm and slaughter, uncouth terrors, and nowhere a harbour of refuge, nowhere lasting peace or beauty—surely a school for heroes. Nor, as in *Homer*, is the spectacle of life enriched and graced by scenes of domestic happiness, like that of Andromache and Astyanax; *Beowulf* is the story of men and men's work, the pioneer work of the world.

> " *Nunquam has hiemes, haec saxa relinquam,*
> *Martis agros* .   .   .   .   .   .
> .   .   .   .   .   . *ubi copia leti*
> *Tanta viris.*"
>
> *Never shall I leave this wintry land, these stony ways, the fields of war,*
> *where men meet many a form of death.*[1]

Wonder and admiration are the emotions proper to heroic poetry, to wonder and admiration this epic calls us. The hero, unlike the hero of tragedy, Œdipus or Hamlet or Othello, asks for the tribute of our worship rather than of our pity and of our tears. Yet as he goes down the lonely way to death for his people something of affectionate and human compassion mingles with worship and astonishment—here before the dawn of history is written that marvellous tale of the travailing soul, driven by who knows what divine gale, that would not if she could purchase her deliverance from the strange, unprofitable ideals of allegiance to truth and duty.

Two strains are blended in the *Beowulf* narrative, the strain of fact and the strain of fable, the strain of history and the strain of imagination. We know when we read of the hero's voyage, of the handling of the ship, of the arms and armour, of the hall of Heorot, that in describing these things the poet had his eye upon the object, so firm and clear is the drawing. We know when he relates the struggle with Grendel or the Fire Drake that he is telling a story he has heard or has invented. And this is as it should be. It is the mark of the true epic that it weaves together legend and history, things familiar with things told or dreamt or believed. In the poem, as we possess it, the stories of marriages and reconciliations, even some of the genealogies and characters, are no doubt historical; the

---

[1] *Argonautica* (Valerius Flaccus), vi. 335.

representation of manners and customs, of social usages and methods of warfare, making allowance for the refinements of courtesy and chivalry gathered from a later time, are indisputably exact. But to these are added from the mythology and folk-lore of Northern Europe the hero's adventures with the demon and the dragon in the sea cavern or on the lonely moor. All the elements proper to the epic are present, yet all dominated by the central interest, the appeal made in an age which knew the value of heroic and masculine qualities by the figure of Beowulf himself, a good comrade, a leader such as men gladly followed, a chief they proudly served. He is an ideal rather than an individual, and this too is right, the highest conceivable in an heroic age, a man of vast bodily strength, wise in council yet adventurous, hungry of fame, not content to guard but to gain, friendly to his own people and their protector to the point of death, terrible to his enemies, " *a king like to none other in the world.*" He had need of all his valour and resolution for helper he had none. The spiritual atmosphere of the Anglo-Saxon epic is the bleakest of any poem in literature. The Christian sentiments of the scribe or poet serve but to accentuate, to throw into high relief the unparalleled situation that Beowulf faces all the powers of evil without hint or hope of divine or supernatural assistance. There are no gods or goddesses interested in his fate, angels or archangels there are none to call on. In a terrible blank world, empty of all spiritual aid or consolation, he goes down to the battle with dragon or monster. There is no divine cloud to hide his weariness, to shield him from the exultant foe, no good fairy by his side, no heavenly voices to cheer, no miraculous wells for the healing of his wounds. Like Capaneus he might have boasted—

" Virtus mihi numen, et ensis
Quem teneo."
My gods are valour and the sword I bear.[1]

If he conquers, it is well: if he fails, he dies. *Vae Victis !* Nor in death is his heart comforted by hope of recovering lost friends in the other world; with life he leaves all that was dear to him,

[1] Statius, *Thebaid*, iii. 615.

kindred and folk, hall joys, the pleasant glee-wood, and the praises of valour. Sorely unwilling he departs he knows not whither. Yet there are no tears in *Beowulf* as in *Homer*, the man of the North does not shed even such tears as angels weep.[1] And to his folk of the European races, however widely separated in time and circumstance, the spirit of adventure, the unflinching temper in *Beowulf*, still call with resistless power; the motives by which he is governed, desire of fame, of honour, the gratitude and esteem of his kinsfolk and friends, still stir their nerves and keep at bay the monster of the creeping mist, the spiritual despair, that paralyses the energies of Asia.

Rude as is the society depicted in *Beowulf*, savage as are the features of its daily life,[2] bleak and dismal as are its climate and many of its surroundings, crude as are its superstitions, it expresses a certain magnificence of manhood. The unshaken hardihood and fortitude which made the future England utter themselves in every line; in every line there is the ring of iron. We hear it again at Naseby and at Worcester. And not less does it foreshadow in its sombre vein of reflection the Elizabethan drama and the philosophy of English moralists. It is the forerunner of *Hamlet* and of *Rasselas*.

[1] Hrothgar, however, weeps at the parting.
[2] These are significant hints of an earlier savagery. The son of Ecgtheow is praised that he lived justly, " *never, when drunk, slew his hearth companions.*"

CHAPTER IV

FRAGMENTS OF EARLY ENGLISH HEROIC POETRY

Beowulf is not the oldest document in the history of English literature. Assign to it what date you please, it is far older than *Roland* or the *Niebelungenlied*, and in scope and excellence it is incomparable in the age to which it belongs;[1] but older yet is at least part of *Widsith*, "*the far-wanderer*," contained in the wonderful Exeter Book, given by Leofric, first Bishop of Exeter, to his cathedral in the eleventh century. This book, published in 1842 as *Codex Exoniensis*, contains, besides much of the poetry of Cynewulf, that most famous of early English lyrics, *The Seafarer*, and the *Lament of Deor*, a later composition than *Widsith* but to be read with it, since both are occupied with the experiences and fortunes of the professional poet in the heroic age. Neither can be properly described as in itself an epic fragment, but both assist us in the reconstruction of the epic period in Northern Europe. The opening lines of *Widsith* introduce the scôp or gleeman, "*the stitcher of lays*," who tells his story, a story of his wanderings, much of it apocryphal, amid many kindreds and nations.

> " Widsith spoke—
> Unlocking his word-hoard:
> He, who of all men
> Farthest had fared among
> Earth-folk and tribesmen:
> Oft in the hall given
> Gifts that were costly."

He has known many men, rulers and earls, Huns and Goths, Swedes and Geats and Southern Danes, Angles and Sueves

---

[1] There is only one piece of extant Germanic verse which can claim to be as old as *Beowulf* or any of the early English fragments we possess. It is a poem of about seventy lines, the lay of *Hadubrand and Hildebrand*, and tells part of the same story as that told by Arnold in *Sohrab and Rustum*, a story in which the father slays his son in personal conflict. (See for a translation Gummere's *The Oldest English Epic*.)

and Saxons; he has sung at many a court in Italy and Germany, high-born heroes have been his patrons and friends, Guthere of the Burgundians gave to him a ring, Eormanric, King of the Goths too, and Ealdhild the queen, daughter of Eadwine. Of these and many names historical the poem is a catalogue, and behind these far back in the misty irrecoverable past we discern the endless confused feuds and wars among forgotten tribes and once famous leaders, to us no more than names.

> " Fierce was the fray then,
> When by the Wistla wood
> The host of the Hreads fought,
> With swords that were hardy,
> For land and for home with
> Attila's warriors."

Priceless as an antiquarian document the poem is, though shadowy as a primæval forest and as trackless. For we meet the Hrothgar of *Beowulf* and mention is made of Heorot; we hear of Offa and the King of the Franks, and many another hero of our own folk ere their descendants made England, but with these are mingled references to Greeks and Finns, Israelites and Assyrians, Hebrews and Indians, Medes and Persians, where the poet is content to repeat simply a traditional catalogue. As literature *Widsith* is valuable chiefly for its strange suggestiveness, and as a picture in little of the life of a travelling minstrel in the heroic age of the Teutonic peoples. For the rest it is a glorification of the great art of song. The wanderer claims, after the ancient fashion of poets, the power to confer honour even upon monarchs, to write their names and deeds in his immortal story. It is clear that the minstrel is in possession of a great store of heroic legend, that, like the bards before Homer, he was the sole repository of history and tradition, welcomed on his roving commission not only for his knowledge of old family histories, of battles and heroic enterprises far back in the past among the Germanic folk, but for his skill to render into verse, and so perpetuate, the glories of kings and leaders among the living of his own day. He is the typical minstrel of his age.[1]

[1] For a detailed study see *Widsith, A Study in Old English Heroic Legend*, by R. W. Chambers.

The other minstrel's lay, preserved in the Exeter Book, strikes a different note. It is the song of a court poet, a song of encouragement and consolation to himself. The poet is no longer young, he has been superseded by another in the favour of his lord, but with fine cheerfulness recalls others, Wayland, the famous smith, the maker of Beowulf's breastplate, the maker too of Mimming, the great sword mentioned in *Waldhere*, Wayland, who for all his marvellous skill had for comrades care and weary longing; Beadohild, in sore plight, mourning her brother's death; he recalls too Hild and Theodric, and many a sorrowful subject of Eormanric, a wolvish king. If these bore up under their burdens of grief, his own spirit must not fail. And to each stanza of his poem he adds the refrain—

> " That was endured, so this may be."

The *Lament of Deor* is a lyric, important not merely as a document, but as a poem excellent in itself and of singular interest as strophic in form, or at least thrown into the semblance of stanzaic structure by the recurring line just quoted. It is possible that *Deor* is a translation of which the original is Norse, or it may be an English poem imitated from some Gothic lay. Behind *Widsith* and this lyric of regret by a court poet, who has been supplanted in his patron's favour by another bard, there is the same immense background stretching to the horizon of time that meets us in *Beowulf*, the background of history and legend, of tossing spears and shields, of battles and the confused movements of marching tribes, out of which welter spring the names of great leaders, of kings, and queens, and warriors remembered for their valour. Here is a version of *Deor*.

I.

> " Wayland knew the sorrows of exile,
> Masterful earl, he knew its smart,
> Care and longing, companions constant
> Knew, and the winter cold and the aching
> Laming wound that Nithhad wrought—
> Bitter pain to a better man.
> That was endured, so this may be.

II.

Beadohild too, for her brother's death
Stricken at heart, yet more bewildered
Knew too well of her sorrows certain—
Birth of a babe, yet knew no further
What in the end her fate should be.
That was endured, so this may be.

III.

The shame of Hild from many we gathered,
The passion of Geat that had no bounds
Till sorrow of love his sleep consuméd.
That was endured, so this may be.

IV.

For thirty winters Theodric wasted
In Burg of the Merings, full many knew it,
That was endured, so this may be.

V.

Of Eormanric, the wolvish-minded,
In songs we've heard, of his wide domain
Mid Gothic peoples, a tyrant king.
Many a warrior, clothed in misery
Sat despairing, wistful, praying
For the closing day of his evil rule.
That was endured, so this may be.[1]

VI.

Now of myself the tale I tell you—
Once of the Heodenings scôp was I,
' Dear to my master, Deor my name,'
Many a winter, happy my service
Under a good lord, till Heorrenda,
Crafty in song, for himself the guerdon
Gained that the earl-guard granted to me.
That was endured, so this may be."

Of true epic quality are the two fragments, about sixty lines, preserved in a manuscript in the National Library at Copenhagen, entitled *Waldhere* (or *Walter*), which appear to have formed part of an heroic narrative, perhaps the equal of *Beowulf*, in its original and complete form.   The story, of which a part is here told, exists in a mediæval Latin version, *Waltharius*, and it was probably one of the most popular tales of the early Germanic cycle.   Unhappily the portions extant in Old English give only two incidents, the first in which the hero, Walter, pursued by

[1] A probable interpolation of seven lines is here omitted.

F

Guthere and Hagen and their *comitatus*, as he flies from the court of Attila with his betrothed bride, Hildegyth, and a great treasure, during a pause in the fight is, for a moment, weary and disheartened, and is urged to fresh activity by Hildegyth, who reminds him of his former valour; the second that in which Guthere advances, boasting his mighty sword and its history, and is met by the defiance of Walter, and a haughty summons to advance and take possession, if he can, of his armour. These challenges and counter-challenges of chiefs belong to epic poetry from Homer to Milton.

The story as we know it from the Latin version tells how Walter, set upon by Guthere's companions, slays one after another, till Guthere and Hagen only are left. A terrific combat ensues in which all three receive dreadful wounds, and weary of an indecisive fight agree to peace. Their wounds are dressed by Hildegyth, and in high good humour after the wine-cup has gone round Guthere and Hagen return, leaving Walter to pursue his journey to his own country where, on his father's death, he succeeds to the throne and lives and reigns for thirty years. I give a version of the most striking passage.

> " Then did Hildegyth
> To valiance heat him:
> Truly of Wayland
> Weakeneth never
> Work of his hands
> With men, who Mimming,
> Hoary of edges,
> Wield in their war.
> Heroes in plenty
> Blood-boltered, sword-stricken,
> Have tasted its terror.
> Attila's foremost one,
> Let not thy valour
> Droop, nor thy lordship
> Fail thee to-day.
> Now hath the day dawned
> That leadeth thee one way
> Or else another, to
> Ending of life, or to
> Glory that ends not—
> Thee, son of Ælfhere,
> A man amongst men.
> Never at sword-play,
> O chief, have I heard it
> That thou in fear sharing
> Fled from the foe,

> Nor yet at the wall sought
> Safety from warriors,
> Shielding thy body,
> Though on thy breast-byrnie
> The blows of the foemen
> In plenty were ringing.
> But ever in fighting
> Wert thou with the foremost,
> Far in the front of it
> Waging thy war.
> So that I feared for thee
> Too fiercely seeking,
> In clash of the conflict,
> The combat with heroes.
> Now, therefore, on honour
> Bethink thee, and glory
> With fortune thy friend."

Of a portion of the second fragment the following is a free rendering:—

> " Then thus spake Walter,
> High-renowned hero,
> In his hand holding
> Weapon for battle, his
> Trusty war-helper.
> Great was thy hope, O thou
> Friend of Burgundians,
> That Hagen's hand-craft
> Would break me in battle,
> Disable for war.
> Do thou, if thou darest,
> From me, who am weary
> With toil of the conflict,
> My byrnie tear from me,
> That here on my shoulders
> Shines now in its glory
> Bright studded with gold.
> Good armour for Atheling,
> If he with his hands may
> His heart and his life now
> Guard from his foes, for
> It faileth me never
> When close the unfriendly,
> As ye now beset me,
> Beset with their blades."

Of battle pieces there is none finer or more worthy, like *Waldhere*, of a " *son of Homer*," than *The Fight at Finnsburh*, a poem which carries us straight to the mead hall and the feast of heroes, to the songs and stories recited by the bard at tribal gatherings, to the chants that pleased our warlike forefathers. It is, like *Waldhere*, a fragment, and was discovered in the library of Lambeth Palace. Almost certainly it belongs to the same period as the lays from which *Beowulf* was drawn, and for rapidity, vigour, and dramatic fire eclipses perhaps any single passage in that great poem. The interest of *Finnsburh* is enhanced by the fact that it tells part of a story, the conclusion of which is incidentally given in *Beowulf*. Finn, the Frisian monarch, at feud with Hnaef, treacherously invites him as his guest to Finnsburh, but in the night surrounds and attacks the hall in which his guest and *comitatus* are lodged. The portion of the poem that is preserved opens with the moment at which Hnaef, aroused from sleep, calls his men to arms. Singularly Homeric it is in spirit, and may well remind the reader of the twelfth book of the *Iliad*, where Hector and the Trojan allies broke through the Achaian wall. From the minstrel who sings in Heorot we learn that in the end Hnaef is slain, but that Hengist his successor in the leadership works full vengeance for his lord in Finnsburh.

From the following version the contents of the poem may be gathered.

> " Then to his warriors called he, the young king—
> ' *Not from the East this glare, nor from the flight*
> *Of any dragon, nor the hall fire's blaze.*
> *Yet here it burns ; without, the birds of war*
> *And the grey-coated wolf await the slain,*
> *While harsh the war-wood rings, spear answering spear.*
> *There shines the moon mid clouds, to men below*
> *Hateful destruction threatens—Wake you now,*
> *My warriors, wake, and mindful of your lands*
> *With one heart fight, and foot to foot engaged.*'
> Then they rose up, the gold-decked thanes, and girt
> Their swords about them, and those mighty ones
> Sigeferth and Eawa, sprang to the door, and drew
> Steel, and at the other doors Hengist himself
> Ordlaf and Guthlaf stood, and now without
> With Guthere Garulf spake—' *Not yet for thee* [1]
> *The battle at the doors, where some bold chief*
> *May snatch thy weapon* '—fiercely stood he there]
> Armed, and above the voices cried across
> The entrance, hero-like, ' *Who holds the door ?* '
> ' *Sigeferth am I, of valiant sword-men lord,*
> *Warrior well known to fame and used to wars,*
> *Old in the fields of pain ; here waits thee now*
> *Of life or death, whichever thou mayest choose.*'
> Then high in hall arose, mid clashing shields,
> The din of slaughter, and the bone-guards burst
> And the floors groaned, and of the Frisian chiefs
> First in the battle Garulf fell, the son

[1] As too young.

Of Guthlaf, and around him many a man,
A ring of slain—swarthy and sallow brown
The raven circled, while the flashing blades
Gave light as if Finn's burg were all ablaze.
Never of warriors worthier have I heard,
Sixty more noble, who with song and mead
Requited by their lord, gave Hnaef his due.
Five days they fought, and in their fighting none
Of them that held the door fell in that fray.
Then forth there fared a wounded man, his helm
Pierced, as he told, his breastplate hacked, his gear
All shattered, and the shepherd of his folk
Swift questioned all the warriors of their wounds."

Beside *Finnsburh*, though far separated from it in time, must be placed *The Battle of Maldon, or the Death of Byrhtnoth*,[1] a tenth or eleventh century poem, charged with the same spirit of warrior pride and delight in grim, unyielding resistance. The hero and the fight against the Northmen it describes are historical, an authentic document of the times, when—

" Men's cheeks faded
On shores invaded
When shorewards waded
    The lords of fight;
When churl and craven
Saw hard on haven
The wide-winged raven
    At main-mast height;
When monks affrighted
To windward sighted
The birds full-flighted
    Of swift sea-kings."

" The battle took place near the town of Maldon, on the banks of the tidal river Panta, now called the Blackwater. The town lies on a hill; immediately at its base flows one branch of the river, while another, still crossed by a mediæval bridge, flows at a little distance to the north. The Danish ships seem to have lain in the branch nearest to the town, and their crews must have occupied the space between the two streams, while Brihtnoth came to the rescue from the north. He seems to have halted on the spot now occupied by the church of Heybridge, having both streams between him and the town."[2] Anlaf, the Danish leader, with a great fleet, had harried Sand-

Edited in the *Belles-Lettres Series* by Dr. W. J. Sedgefield.
Freeman's *Norman Conquest.*

wich and Ipswich, and in this later descent upon the English coast in 991 was opposed by the old East-Saxon Ealdorman and his followers, who disputed the passage of the river. The poem tells how the Viking Herald, calling across the river in loud and threatening tones, demands tribute from the English as price of the Danes' departure, how it is indignantly refused by Byrhtnoth, how the wily pirates request an unopposed passage of the stream and a fair fight, how the Saxon leader in his pride and confidence waives his advantage of position, and permits his foes to cross, and how the battle is joined. A fierce hand-to-hand struggle takes place, in which Byrhtnoth is slain, but dying still exhorts his men, and around his body his loyal followers fall, fighting to the last.

In *Maldon* for the last time in our literature the old epic strain of *Beowulf* is revived. Once again flames out in a Christian epoch the spirit of the old pagan lays. It was doubtless the work of a Christian, but of a Christian in whom the defence of home and kindred against the Danish sea-robbers, "*the wolves of blood*," had roused the smouldering pagan fires. The author may himself have seen, he must surely have had speech with men who had seen the battle. So vivid a picture, so detailed, so exact in its references to names and places, could hardly have been the work of the unaided imagination. The last stand of Byrhtnoth and his companions around the body of their chief in this the latest of our authentic heroic poems seems to typify the resistance of the epic spirit to the new literature, and its final overthrow. The splendour of *Maldon* rises even above the splendour of a good fight well told, of poetry which is worthy of the indomitable courage it describes. It rises above the splendour of a death-grapple in which men are minded to die rather than give ground, of a Homeric strain in which are exchanged the ringing challenges and defiances of the old heroic world. The splendour of *Maldon* springs from the mingled daring and chivalry to the foe which, casting aside advantage of position, offers a fight on equal terms, from the temper which, in this, as it were, its final utterance, seems to express for us in the words of Byrhtwold, "*the old comrade*," the whole creed of heroism, "*Harder should be the spirit, the heart all the bolder, courage the greater as the strength grows less.*"

Plain as is the style of *Maldon*, plain to bareness, there is perhaps no more spirited or stirring battle piece in the language. From it radiate the best qualities of the English race, its hardihood, its magnanimity, its loyalty, its contempt for cowardice. Such a pillar as that of which Pausanias speaks, "*on which were inscribed the paternal names of those who at Thermopylae sustained the attack of the Medes,*" [1] should mark the spot where this English Leonidas and his people fought and died.   But, if there be no pillar, the poem is their more enduring monument. Some conception of the contents may be gathered from the following versions of portions of the poem.

> " Hard by the shore stood
> The Herald of Vikings;
> Full boastful the sea-farers'
> Errand loud spoke he—
> His word to the earl.
> ' *From sea-rovers bold, I,*
> *To bid thee for safety*
> *Bracelets—a ransom—*
> *To send them and quickly,*
> *Since far for thee better*
> *Is payment of tribute*
> *Than strife of the spears*
> *In battle's fierce fray.*
> *Then purchase thee peace now*
> *With treasure ; and freedom,*
> *Their chief, may'st thou give them*
> *Thy people, from pain.*
> *Take from us seamen*
> *Peace at the price of it,*
> *Gold at our pleasure,*
> *And to our galleys we*
> *Go, on the flood faring*
> *Far on our way.*'
> Answered him Byrhtnoth,
> His buckler uplifted,
> Shook he his spear and
> In anger he answered.
> ' *Hear'st thou, sea-farer,*
> *What say they, my folk here ?*
> *For tribute the spear-shaft*
> *They send you, fell-pointed,*
> *Their swords, and the weapons*
> *That worthless to you are,*
> *The trappings of war.*

[1] Quoted by Pater, *Plato and Platonism*, p. 213.

Sea-rover's Herald !
Bear this for thy saying
Back now to thy people—
Unwelcome the word.
Here an earl standeth—
Not without fame he—
His folk with him stand.
He for his fatherland,
For Ethelred's earth fights,
Fights for his folk and his
Fields and his liege-lord.
Ye heathen are fated
In battle to fall.
For base were the yielding
If ye with our booty
Unfought for, fared ship-ward,
And lightly departing
Bore back with you gold—
Since far have ye journeyed
Within this our land.
But us beseems better
That grimly the game now
Of battle, ere tribute
We tend you, we play.'

Then waded the war-wolves,
The host of the Vikings,
West over Panta,
For water they recked not.
Across the bright river
High bore they their bucklers,
The shipmen their linden shields
Lifted to land.
There 'gainst them Byrhtnoth
Fiercely in readiness
Stood, with his men ranked,
Facing the foemen.
With bucklers close-linked he
Bade them together stand
Fast 'gainst the foe.
Nigh then was the fray and
The fame of the fighting,
Nigh was the doom of men
Fated to fall.
Loud sounded the clamour
The clash of the conflict,
Greedy for carrion
Raven and eagle rose,
Tumult was there.
Forth flew the spears
Sharp-filed, and the javelins
Whetted to slay.
Bows there were busy,
The dart and the buckler,
The battle was bitter.
Warriors on either hand
Fell, and the flower of the
War-folk lay dead."

Maldon is not an epic poem; it is, like *Finnsburh*, an epic episode. It is such an episode as might have filled a book in an epic conceived like that of Homer. It is of course also a belated episode, the event itself occurred too late in history to be taken up into any epic process. From just such lays, however, dealing with matter of the same kind in the same spirit, a great national epic might possibly have sprung.[1] But architectural faculty which enabled the poet or poets of the *Iliad* to invent a scheme, such as the wrath of Achilles, was wanting. By means of that scheme—the absence of Achilles from the war—episode after episode was introduced without destroying the unity of the poem. Room was left for the achievements of other heroes, while the nominal hero sulked in his tent, and a mass of heterogeneous material thus swept within the framework of a single poem. In the *Odyssey* the device employed is a different one. The action waits while Odysseus at the court of Alcinous relates in four books his earlier adventures, into which narrative is set all the matter through which the poet found it inconvenient or impossible to conduct his hero himself. Three more books are occupied with the adventures of Telemachus on his search for his father. The Teutonic epic process reached the episode; it went further, in *Beowulf* it made a practically successful effort to unify several episodes. But to impose unity upon such a complex of episodes and characters as meet us in *Homer* was beyond its strength. At a critical moment in its development it met unfriendly forces. It combated those forces indeed vigorously, imposed its ideals and methods in a field very foreign to that of its own interests, but, sapped of its strength, gradually lost ground, declined, and finally sank below the mind's horizon.

[1] It is held by some critics, perhaps with truth, that the Teutonic lays, such as we possess or can from the fragments imagine, characterised as they are by a certain independence and native sufficiency, had reached the highest development possible to the type, and would not readily have yielded themselves to a process of " stitching " into epos of the eminent or Homeric pattern. See Professor Ker's *Epic and Romance*.

CHAPTER V

THE epic matter, the hero-sagas our ancestors brought with them to England, attained in *Beowulf* its noblest and most comprehensive form. Of this heroic material—there must have been store of it—none was written, and *Beowulf* itself was stitched together from lays for long carried in the memory and orally recited. But its ideals, the ideals of a branch of the Germanic peoples, are there refined and ennobled by contact with Christianity and the Celtic civilisation of Britain. There is clear evidence of an alien influence at work. The heroic sagas—ruder compositions, the image of a ruder society—submitted to the spiritual and softening forces of their altered life when the invaders crossed the North Sea and from pirates became settlers. Of Anglo-Saxon poetry untouched by such influences nothing of importance survives. " *The immigrants in Britain did not,*" as Ten Brink says, " *live with a native population permeated by Roman culture, as in Gaul, and ready to communicate this culture. Only dumb witnesses, monuments of Roman art and industry, spoke to them of the greatness of the people whose place they had taken.*" The settlers preserved their language, they preserved their political constitution, they preserved many of the ancient virtues of the race, yielding only, after a campaign in which for long the issue seemed doubtful, to the Christian creed. That submission was of itself, however, sufficient to prove fatal to the epic impulse. In the campaign against Teutonic paganism Christianity was powerfully assisted by certain features in the political organisation and in the character of the English settlers. Even Christian sentiment discerned in these fierce sea-farers, and in their literature — the old heathen sagas themselves — friendly elements, a high sense of duty, a moral depth and power of feeling, a reverence for the mysterious, a respect for chastity

and the keeping of faith. The new religion found potent allies
in the camp of its foes, something, indeed, approaching the
spiritual temper it desired to inculcate. There was need to
soften the manners, to subdue the ferocity of the old English and
their poetry; there was hardly need in order to transform it for
Christian use, to heighten its seriousness, or altogether to alter
its spirit and character. The ethical ideals, the sense of loyalty,
the generous instincts abroad in it passed easily into religious
literature. Some virtues peculiarly Christian our ancestors must
in the beginning have found it difficult to accept—forbearance,
humility, meekness—yet the converts, once made, displayed a
sincerity of faith and a religious zeal which distinguished the
English branch of the Church among all others. But if
Christianity thus tamed the fiercer characteristics of the race,
it was forced in turn to submit to ideals, political and literary,
grown in a pagan soil.

The early Christian poetry of England is hardly to be
distinguished in temper and spirit, it is not at all to be distinguished in form and method, from that of the earlier heroic
and heathen lays. Nothing at first sight might appear more
alien to Christian feeling and sentiment than the poetry of
battle, to the lamb of peace than the wolf of war. There was
nevertheless an aspect of Christianity, a figure under which
its nature might be partially revealed. It was possible to
represent it as a warfare. Under what better symbol than that
of an age-long conflict between the powers of light and the powers
of darkness could Christianity be presented to a warrior race?
Thus translated into the terms of a life peculiar to them, our
forefathers discovered within the new religion room for the old
ways of thought, the ideals of their military life. Much, particularly in the Old Testament story, found ready acceptance.
The wanderings of the Israelites, the tribal battles, the dis-
affections and revolts—all this they grasped easily. The conceptions, too, of God as " *the Lord of hosts*," a King " *mighty in
battle*," of Satan as a chief in revolt, surrounded by rebel
followers, were in no respect foreign to their mental experience.
In the early literature of the converted English it was inevitable

that Christianity should be transformed into the image of the heroic world. Into its scheme and history entered prince and earl, thane and clansman, all the details of long understood social and political relations. " Wyrd " by natural translation became Providence, Christ a " *man of war* " who invades Hell as a king the territory of his enemy, the saints and patriarchs " *ealdormen* " and " *warriors,*" Abraham " *a bold earl,*" the apostles " *fierce and warlike leaders of the host,*" Peter and Paul " *thanes of Christ.*" The phrases and motives of the old pagan poetry, strangely inappropriate in our ears, passed into the new, and Christianity is forced for a season to accommodate itself to ideals not its own. The revolted " *thanes of Satan* " engage in a hand-to-hand struggle with Christ and his followers, the bow and spear are their weapons, Hell is the prison to which God, the victorious monarch, consigns his captives, loyal service to Him is such allegiance as the warrior owes his chief.

The subjects of this early Christian literature are portions of the Bible story, as in the *Genesis, Exodus,* and *Daniel,*[1] pre-served in a single MS. now in the Bodleian, or narratives of saintly lives like *Juliana,* in the Exeter Book, or tales from the Apocrypha, like *Judith,* contained in the same MS. as *Beowulf,* but in them all are preserved the old seafaring and martial experiences, the old relations between earl and *comitatus,* the old note of exultation in victory, the familiar references to the horny-nibbed raven, the dewy-winged eagle, and the wolf, greedy for slaughter, to the trusty sword and byrnie, the mead-hall, the crowded ale-benches, the gifts, the treasure of rings and jewels. Religious though the subjects are, the treatment remains epic, and only where such treatment is possible is the glow of inspiration felt. The earliest of these poems, *Genesis, Exodus, Daniel,* have been ascribed to a late seventh-century poet, Caedmon, most of the later, *Elene, Andreas, Juliana,* to Cynewulf, a Northumbrian poet of the eighth century. Of Caedmon we know nothing save from the famous passage in Bede's *Ecclesiastical History* (A.D. 731), which describes

[1] *Exodus* and *Daniel* have been edited in the *Belles-Lettres Series* by Professor Blackburn, *Juliana* in the same series by Professor Strunk, *Judith* by Professor Cook.

him as a certain brother of Whitby monastery, "*greatly distinguished and honoured by divine grace*," whose power of song was the gift of God, since he had lived in the world till of advanced years and had learnt nothing of the art, and when the harp went round was accustomed to leave the feast in shame and retire to his home. To him upon one such occasion there came in a dream a man who saluted him, and calling him by his name, requested him to sing. And Caedmon answered, "*I cannot sing.*" Then he who spoke to him replied, "*Yet it is in thy power to sing,*" and Caedmon asked, "*What shall I sing ?*" And the man said, "*Sing the beginning of all things.*" And Caedmon sang, and when he awoke from sleep he remembered all that he had sung, and added to that song others and all to the praise of God. It was formerly usual to ascribe the *Genesis, Exodus,* and *Daniel* all to Caedmon, but it is now customary to regard them as separate poems and the work of different authors. Yet although these works in the form in which we possess them can no longer be claimed for Caedmon, it is probable that he was the author of similar poems, and portions even of these may with probability be assigned to him.

The earlier, or Caedmonian, *Genesis* (which has to be distinguished from an interpolation in the MS. of much later date, about 900, generally known as *Genesis B.*), gives the narrative as in the Scripture story, down to the sacrifice of Isaac; it is followed by the narrative of the passage of the Israelites through the Red Sea as related in *Exodus,* and by a poetical version of the first five chapters of *Daniel,* which leaves unfinished the account of Belshazzar's feast. Of these poems probably the earliest in date of composition is *Exodus,* the next in date *Daniel,* and the latest *Genesis*.[1]

The *Genesis* has a varied interest. Not only does it exhibit that curious blend of Christian and pagan sentiment, and that heightened epic manner so characteristic of early English poetry, it is a poem of rare quality distinguished for the imaginative elevation in the opening description of the creation of the world

---

[1] Part of *Genesis* may be older than either *Exodus* or *Daniel.*

and account of the fall of man.   A worthy precursor, we might
call the author, of the poet of *Paradise Lost*.   Nor is it impossible
that his work was known to Milton in the first printed edition
of 1655 made in Amsterdam, and that he had it in mind
during the composition of his epic.   The passages descriptive
of the Deluge; of the expulsion of the rebellious angels; of the
Hell, "*flaming, yet without light*," "*terrible with fire*"; of Satan
imprisoned behind "*the great bars of rugged iron hammered
hot*"; or such a battle piece as that between Abraham and the
Elamites, prove its author beyond doubt a poet.

> " So they rushed together—Loud were then the lances,
> Savage then the slaughter-hosts.   Sadly sang the war fowl,
> With her feathers dank with dew, midst the darting of the shafts,
> Hoping for the corpses.   Hastened then the heroes
> In their mighty masses, and their mood was full of thought.
> .   .   .   .   Then was hard play there,
> Interchanging of death-darts, mickle cry of war!
> Loud the crash of battle!   With their hands the heroes
> Drew from sheaths their swords ring-hilted,
> Doughty of the edges! " [1]

The *Genesis* is throughout distinguished by a rare activity
of imagination; the descriptions of Satan particularly attain a
surprising reflective depth and solemn splendour.

The *Exodus* is chiefly remarkable for the epic nobility of the
description of the Israelites in their flight from Egypt, the
pursuit by Pharaoh, and the destruction of the Egyptians in
the Red Sea.   Here all the martial ardour of the Teutonic race
flames out.

> " Then they saw
> Forth and forward faring, Pharaoh's war-array,
> Gliding on a grove of spears; glittering the hosts!
> Fluttered then the banners, there the folk the march trod.
> Onwards surged the war, strode the spears along,
> Blickered the broad shields; blew aloud the trumpets.

> " Wheeling round in gyres, yelled the fowls of war,
> Of the battle greedy; hoarsely barked the raven,
> Dew upon his feathers, o'er the fallen corpses;
> Swart that chooser of the slain!   Sang aloud the wolves
> At the eve their horrid song, hoping for the carrion,
> Kindless were the beasts, cruelly they threaten;
> Death did these march-warders, all the midnight through,
> Howl along the hostile trail—hideous slaughter of the host."

[1] For this and the following translations in this chapter I am indebted to
Mr. Stopford Brooke's *History of Early English Literature*.   For alternative
versions see the Appendix.

Daniel contains no such striking passages as meet us in *Genesis* and *Exodus ;* it is more prosaic, more didactic, a poem in which the epic objectivity suffers from the presence of the poet and his personal emotions.

Judith, a fragment which relates the story of Judith and Holofernes, was also formerly attributed to Caedmon. The problem of its authorship remains unsolved, but it is certainly later by centuries than the Caedmonian poems, and though some critics claim for it the highest poetical merit, in the judgment of most readers *Judith* will be found tamer in spirit and more artificial in tone than *Genesis* or *Exodus.* It sprang, however, from the same epic impulse, and endeavours like the rest of this early Christian poetry to substitute, for a purpose, Biblical history for national while it preserved the heroic manner. It was thus possible to attract to the new themes men who still were drawn by racial instinct to the older interests of war and warriors.

Of Cynewulf, who flourished about a hundred years later, we know hardly more than of Caedmon. He appears to have been something of a scholar, to have passed much of his life as a minstrel, to have lived to a great age, and to have been the author of many poems preserved for us in the Exeter and Vercelli books. How many is doubtful, but it is certain that he wrote *Elene* and *Juliana,* since he has himself recorded it by the insertion of runes which spell the name Cynewulf. The influence of Latin Christianity is a marked feature in this poet's work, not merely in the choice and treatment of his subjects, but in the language and construction. The epic impulse, it is apparent, has already suffered from antagonistic influences and the symptoms of a rapid decay are prominent. Lyrical and subjective elements successfully assert themselves, religious zeal overpowers distinctively pagan sentiment. Still, as in the Caedmonian poems, the smouldering fires burst forth even in the work of this scholar and fervid apostle of the Christian creed. *Juliana,* the story of a Christian maid who refuses to wed a pagan, opens like *Beowulf* with the customary *Hwaet !* Hark! by which the Anglo-Saxon scôp called the attention of

his audience to the tale he was about to chant; *Elene*, a story of
the search for the true cross, a poem of Cynewulf's old age and
his masterpiece, strikes the familiar chords; the clash of sword
and shield, the flight of the battle-serpents, the ashen arrows,
the resounding sea, the swan-road over which swing the galleys,
foaming wave-floaters, the treasure gifts in the mead-hall are
not yet forgotten.   For in Cynewulf, even in his old age, and for
all his learning and his saintly tales, there survives the Viking
still.   The *Andreas*, also in the Vercelli book, and by some
scholars attributed to Cynewulf, is filled with the many voices
of the sea and wind.

> " The sword-fish played,
> Through ocean gliding, and the grey gull wheeled
> Greedy of prey; dark grew the Weather-torch;
> The winds waxed great, together crushed the waves,
> The stream of ocean stirred, and drenched with spray
> The cordage groaned; then Water-Terror rose
> With all the might of armies from the deep."

At the period of their conquest of Britain our ancestors were
in the epic stage, and to that stage their extant literature
corresponds.   Their failure to produce a completer or more
perfect form of epic poetry was due in part to their failure to
achieve a higher political unity, which, had they achieved it,
might well have manifested itself in epic of high dignity.   But
political constitution apart, the influence of the new religion
upon the heroic temper and heroic life was in itself paralysing.
Ideas foreign to the experience of these peoples entered and
interrupted the evolution of their poetic genius, the current of
their lives was altered and directed into other channels than
those in which it had been accustomed to flow, heroes unknown
to their national history were presented to them as exemplars,
they were introduced to the art of writing, they came under the
influence of learning and a culture derived from books, their
language itself underwent changes in the loss of inflexion and
gender and its prosody was gradually modified, the importance
of the scôp both as singer and historian was diminished.
To these changes the decline of epic poetry can be directly
traced.   Yet the strength of the impulse towards it appears in

the character of the early Christian literature just spoken of. The epic process is interrupted, it has received fatal injuries, a lyrical and reflective note and a devotional mood foreign to its nature soon appear in it, yet it retains sufficient vitality to impose its form and method upon Christian poetry for several centuries. The first stage in the decline is seen in the subjects of the Caedmonian poems, which are selected in the interests of the new religion. The second appears in the poetry of Cynewulf, who, if not ecclesiastic, was at least educated under ecclesiastical conditions, and draws his material exclusively from Latin sources. To poetry in the age of Alfred succeeded prose, and the epic stream, "*forgetting the bright speed it had*," is lost in the low and level tracts of Church annals and theological homilies.

CHAPTER VI

EPIC AND ROMANCE—CHAUCER

ROMANCE entered as an element into the epic poetry of Homer,
it entered into *Beowulf ;* we may regard it as one of the ultimate
inexpugnable constituents of the narrative art.   No one indeed,
as I have said, can indicate the moment at which poetry ceases
to be heroic because it is too romantic.   A generous contributor
to epic splendour, there comes, nevertheless, a moment at which
we must brace ourselves against the acceptance of romance as
sufficient in itself.   Who will wish to enter on the epic register
the whole stupendous mass of romantic poesy?   These millions
of acres would, if added to our ground of respectable epic
dimensions—

> " Singeing his pate against the burning zone
> Make Ossa like a wart."

Romance is not epic, nor is it necessarily heroic poetry.   Epic,
as in the *Odyssey,* can take up and convert to its own high uses
of episode and amplification an indeterminable amount of
foreign and marvellous matter, but—and here the first distinction emerges—true epic or heroic poetry has its roots in
native soil; it is not an exotic, it is a home growth.   Whatever
meanings, and they are many, that have been attached to
romance, there is involved in it, and invariably, a foreign element,
something brought from a distance, a strange country, or
strange ways of thought.   The wonder and mystery of it, the
secret of the charm hides in its remoteness from the world we
know.   The ideas of epic poetry, the society it pictures, the
hero it praises, the deeds it recalls, to whatever race or country
they are assigned, have in them the genius of that race or
country, as in a mirror is reflected there, if not always historical
fact, at least the shadow of history and national achievements.

Sift from the *Odyssey* the romantic fables brought from far,
omit from Virgil the battles and episodes, the decorative and
picturesque literary additions, and they still exhibit national
attachments; there is still left something to remind us of the
birthplace of this poetry, a solid substratum of life and character,
as it was lived in Greece or exhibited in Rome.

The secondary type of epic, the poems of the bookmen—
and Virgil may be placed in this category also—like *Jerusalem
Delivered* or *Paradise Lost*, have established their own claim to
be included upon the epic roll. Their claim consists in this,
that they follow deliberately the epic tradition, their authors
chose to imitate the manner of the authentic epic. True, they
are not epic in the way that Homer is epic or *Beowulf*, but
in a derived and cultivated manner of their own, yet by virtue
of their discipleship they have made good—it is a matter of
common consent—their right to the great title. The chief
business of heroic poetry is war, the martial deeds of heroes,
and war of a kind with which its authors had commonly
some real knowledge. Virgil had no such knowledge, nor
Milton, but they chose to keep within the tradition. Virgil—

> " Sang of battles and the breath
> Of stormy war and violent death,"

though the rift between his own and the heroic world is visible.
He had, it is clear, no Homeric pleasure in battle, the desire of
it he describes as " *an insane lust.*" The painful incidents of
war he touches with a pathos altogether un-Homeric; he dwells
by preference on its picturesque splendours, its stern array;
he pities the fallen warrior and forgets to exult with the victor.[1]
With Virgil we are already passing away from the heroic strain,
he knows nothing of the passionate Berserker fury, " *the eagle-
bark for blood.*" Virgil was not himself a fighting man, but a
court poet, and he delightfully covers his deficiency in martial
ardour by episodes like that of Dido, exquisite, admired in every
age, by appeals to Roman pride and patriotism, by noble sentiment, and by the exercise of his consummate art. Yet we
cannot exclude Virgil or Milton from the epic company though

[1] *Æneid*, xii. 544-7.

they are themselves remote in experience and feeling from the heroic world—they preserve the epic tradition. With the romantic poets it is otherwise. Mediæval romance neither knew nor cared for the tradition. Pursuing a new avenue to poetic delight, it makes the introduction of surprising unfamiliar things its chief end; it departs wherever possible from the positive ground of human experience. It provides—a second distinction between its aim and the prouder design of heroic poetry—entertainment and provokes vulgar curiosity, not a curiosity about the historical foundation of the tale, nor the characters, but about the mere happenings, the incidents, and occurrences. *Abundat dulcibus vitiis, it abounds in pleasant faults.* Where epic poetry, like *Beowulf*, is based upon a life actually lived, a life familiar to the poet who speaks of what he knows, romantic poetry sets the imagination wholly free and trusts to its novelty, its introduction of magic and marvels, its sentimental subtleties, its extravagances of rhetoric and chivalric idealism. It addresses itself deliberately to the age in which it is produced, presents " *a past that never was present*," a past imagined as the audience for whom it was provided desired to imagine it. Can it be accepted, or any part of it, as falling within the epic field?

With the passing of the heroic age one type of epic becomes impossible, the type which, its literary values apart, possesses interest and worth as an historical document. A new order of literature takes its place, dealing sometimes with new, sometimes with the old themes. Yet though the themes may be preserved the fashion of the handling must alter. The business of the heroic world and of its poetry, for example, is war. In romantic literature the theme remains, war is still one of the major interests. But it is a changed type of war. Battle tends to pass from the foreground into the background as an interest fading, to become unreal, not practically necessary, not every one's and a daily affair, not so much a way of life as a way of amusement or adventure, like hunting or hawking. Men now sometimes doff their armour, cease to be continually on guard, have leisure for other entertainment. The interest of love, hardly visible in the heroic poetry, springs into triumphant prominence. It is treated as a complicated science—there is leisure for that—with intricate problems and logical subtleties which demand constituted courts and parliaments of love for their elucidation. How far can compositions in a world so changed, conceived in so different a spirit, and addressing themselves to so altered an audience be described as epic poetry? To determine the rank of this new romantic poetry we must question its breadth, its elevation, its power of depicting great characters and great situations, in a word its nobility. We must ask how it will bear comparison with the poetry of acknowledged greatness in earlier ages. We must apply to it the test by which all great art must finally be judged, the quality of impressiveness. The critic is not here concerned with the application of a single rule of classification, but with the effort to distinguish greatness from that which is less great, achievement of rare eminence from elevations not infrequently attained. The truth might be conveyed in a sentence: any narrative poetry if it be sufficiently impressive is epic. To say so may appear a cutting rather than a loosing of the Gordian knot. There is, however, but one alternative. With the progress of the world we must invent new terms of description and criticism for all new forms of art. We must decline to apply the old designations to the later works of a later time. Retain them—the simpler expedient—and they ask from us continual expansion, continual readjustment to the growing needs of a civilisation ever increasing in complexity.

Call to mind then the names of Ariosto and Spenser, universally allowed a place beside that of Virgil, and we admit the romantic epic as a legitimate species. And the task of criticism is to discover, after the passing away of the heroic world, after the victory of romance, what narrative poetry in the new mode is of supreme excellence, of a dignity that challenges comparison with the best produced by the ancient races. Criticism may go further. It may seek to determine what epic qualities are to be found in compositions which on the whole fall short of the required dignity or worth, and the causes of their failure. Throughout it will apply the touchstone of absolute merit.

With poetry not in the romantic mode, poetry, that is, which
follows and frankly follows the ancient tradition, the task is
easier. Even when not highly, nor, it may be, at all successful,
such poetry, like Wilkie's or Glover's, for example, puts forward
a special and legitimate claim to attention, because it is an
attempt, though uninspired, to imitate the recognised and
heroic type.

The passing away of the heroic world, the triumph of romance
may in our history be associated with the eleventh century.
" *The difference of the two orders of literature*," as Professor Ker
says,[1] " *is as plain as the difference in the art of war between the
two sides of the Battle of Hastings, which indeed is another form
of the same thing ; for the victory of the Norman knights over the
English axemen has more than a fanciful or superficial analogy
to the victory of the new literature of chivalry over the older forms
of heroic narrative.*" Nor is it without significance that, as the
chronicler tells us, a certain minstrel, Taillefer, rode out before
the Norman host, singing of Roland and of Oliver and the
knights who died at Roncevaux. Romance proper then may be
said to enter European literature in triumphant and conquering
guise late in the eleventh century. As Mr. Wyndham has shown[2]
six centuries prepared for its coming—the centuries which
followed the overthrow of the Western Empire. It had to wait
for a universal language, Northern French, which superseded
the unromantic Latin, it had to wait for the meeting of East
and West, of Celtic and Saracenic influences, it had to wait for
the great feudal and literary court of Henry II. of England and
Eleanor of Poitou and Aquitaine. "Romance is a tissue. In
the twelfth century, when it took hold of the middle ages,
romance displays a deliberate weaving together of many-
coloured strands. Celtic glamour, the uncouth strength of the
North, and marvels from the fabulous East, are interlaced in
one woof which unfolds a continuous story of Europe, from
the Argonauts' quest of the Golden Fleece, by way of the fall
of Troy and the foundation of Rome, to the conquest of Jeru-

[1] *Epic and Romance.*
[2] *The Springs of Romance in the Literature of Europe.*

salem by Crusaders. An examination of these strands reveals that the earliest and most alien are largely mythological. They consist of many attempts made by many races, in different ages and distant countries, to express in symbols their guesses at the origin and destiny, the hopes and fears, of man."

No single poem reduced this vast and tangled growth of ideas to unity, as in the *Odyssey*, "*a tissue of 'old Märchen'*" many strands were woven into a single whole. No poet of supreme genius took possession of this imperial estate. The body of matter was far larger, it was less homogeneous, the ideas abroad in it were more numerous, less in harmony with each other than those which were taken up into the *Odyssey*. Instead of a romantic epic therefore, a modern *Odyssey*, instead of a perfect work of art, comprehending the accumulated imaginative wealth of many tribes and lands, we have cycles of stories, told by innumerable singers—of the *Chansons de Geste* alone a list of more than a hundred has been published—a collection so vast, a treasure-heap of such bewildering extent that no single mind could make itself master of it, or employ all its resources. Barely conceivable is it that any one poem could have caught and presented the spirit of it all, this world within world of human imagining, and the modern epic to match the *Odyssey* remained unwritten, beyond the reach of human wit. France had its *Song of Roland*, Italy its Ariosto and Tasso, England its Spenser, yet these are fragments, and fragments only of the great book of Romance; these are but the "*peaks of a submerged continent*," conspicuous elevations to one who looks back from afar, who misses the minor heights and is hardly aware of the once fertile plains now covered by the waters of forgetfulness. Not that this shipwreck of all but the best is without previous parallel in literary history. "At Rome it seemed," says Professor Tyrrell, "as if the stream of epic poetry would never run dry. On it rolled, carrying on its unrippled surface to the gulf of oblivion Memnonids, Perseids, Heracleids, Theseids, Thebaids, Achilleids, Amazonids, Phæacids, without number. The river of time has happened to throw up a few spars from the wreckage, a few poets, not, perhaps, much better than those it has engulfed—Valerius Flaccus, Silius Italicus, Claudian, all of whom, together with Statius and even Lucan, Scaliger said that he would gladly give for a complete Ennius." [1]

Most authentic and successful epics appear to be the culmination of a process, as was the *Iliad*, as was *Beowulf*, as was *Roland*. The lays that preceded them are in most cases lost to us, but in the romantic period, we can if we will, recover and peruse much that might, without loss, be permitted to die, poems which might have contributed to the supreme epic that never came to the birth. The romantic lays, or poems of the process, pre-epic poems, we might call them, are many, but rarely one hears in them the great accent. The voices of the deep that called Ulysses have fallen silent.

During the whole of the Middle Ages narrative poetry in Latin continued to be written, of quality inferior indeed to that of Valerius or Statius of the Silver Age, but preserving something of the air, something of the old tradition. Albo in the ninth century with his *De Bellis Parisiacae*, and Ekkehard with his *Waltharius*, attained even a touch of distinction and celebrity, and at least presented, till the Revival of Letters brought fuller light, the shadow of a great poetic type. At no period in the history of Western Europe did the classical epic altogether fail. Weak as its representatives became, more bloodless as the centuries passed, a breath of the Virgilian spirit survived in compositions which may have served in a measure to school some of the earlier poets who used Romance languages. But in the seventh and eighth centuries, while the old tradition was barely kept alive by these ghostly survivors of a vanished age, a new epic process, which was to culminate in the *Song of Roland*, took shape in France. Certain heroic songs, to the accompaniment of lyre, or *rote*, a Breton harp, were sung by warriors in the Merovingian epoch, perhaps in connection with a dance, or by *joculares*, the professional minstrels, who were doubtless the authors of the *Chansons de Geste*. Of the earliest of this epic process we possess no examples, as we possess none of that which preceded *Beowulf*, but we know the poems to have been historical,

---

[1] *Latin Poetry.*

to have treated of actual fact. The poets must have been, as in the case of the Anglo-Saxon *makers*, court poets or wandering minstrels, either under the patronage of great lords or dependent upon the contributions of strangers. Doubtless, together with heroic songs they frequently disseminated less edifying matter, nor does it appear probable that in Gaul their rank and dignity was as high as that of the scôp in Northern Europe. Yet equally they were the makers of the tradition, the repositories of history, who supported literature and art in a half barbarous age. It was they, bestowers of fame, who exalted Charlemagne to his supreme place in mediæval history, and though their work has perished, its characteristics, refined and exalted, are visible in Roland and others of the *Chansons de Geste*.

It will be proper here to inquire what epic elements meet us in the romantic literature of Europe from the eleventh century onwards, and it will be convenient to speak of it under the famous divisions of Jean Bodel:—

> " *Ne sont que trois matières à nul home attendant,*
> *De France, et de Bretaigne, et de Rome la grant.*"

matter of France, of Britain, and of Rome.

In the *Roland*, taking this single poem as representative of the French cycle, as in earlier heroic poetry, the historical element, though obscured, is clearly present. The hero is the representative of his race, in whose feats his kinsmen have a part, who confers distinction on those who share his nationality. We are already, however, far from the beginnings. History tells us that a certain " *Hruolandus, Britannici limitis praefectus* " [1] was slain in 778, when the rearguard of Charlemagne's army was defeated by the Basques in the valley of Roncevaux. In *Roland* Charlemagne has become the founder and patron of chivalry, of which he knew nothing, the body of Basques has been replaced by a huge host of Saracens, Roland himself, " *Count of the Marches of Brittany*," is exalted to heroic rank, the combat receives a religious and national character unknown to history, " *dulce France* " has been born a nation, the weapons and place of battle altered, and the marvellous or superhuman element

---

[1] Eginhard's *Vita Karoli.*

transfigures the whole narrative. The spirit of the Song of
Roland is the spirit of the Crusades, the hero is the protagonist
in a war against the enemies of God, and the true story of a
skirmish with mountaineers at Roncevaux has become an epic
and a glory of the world. Not once or twice had the story of
Roland been told before it attained its final and magnificent
form. In that form it captivated all Europe, inspired poets like
Pulci and Ariosto, made the names of its characters household
words in many languages, and remains the pride of France to
the present day. It mirrors the noblest features of feudalism
in the twelfth century as *Beowulf* the noblest features of the
Viking Age.

Roland, then, feudal and Christian though it be, is true epic
poetry, with its roots in history. It is the culmination of a
process not dissimilar to that which produced the *Iliad*. It is
epic also in its preoccupation with the heroic subject, war—
" *Gente est nostre bataille !* " cries Oliver, " a fine fight this of
ours ! "—and the sentence rings true to the type, whether we
take Homer or *Beowulf* as representing it. But the *Roland*,
though finely free and bold in its conduct of the narrative, is
almost a sustained lyric in its fervour and emotional pitch.
Lyrical and popular in origin—for the earliest *Chansons* were
recited to music—it was composed in a metre suitable for song.
The most lyrical of extant epics, it falls short of the highest
reaches of heroic poetry in certain not negligible particulars.
The form is comparatively weak and undistinguished, lacking
in the last refinements of art. In the presentation of character
and life generally—character and life in all their variety, breadth,
and complexity—it is no match for Homer; as an historical
document its value is slight, it gives no help, as does *Beowulf*,
towards a reconstruction of the society it pictures. Yet neither
the " *matter of Britain* " nor that of Rome produced in the
Middle Ages a poem at all comparable with *Roland* in epic
quality, a poem for men, so tense with martial feeling, so noble
in ideals, so full-blooded, simple, and impressive.

Poetry and history, which in the earlier *Chansons de Geste*
were, as in Homer and *Beowulf*, closely interwoven, part com-

pany before we reach the later cycles of romance. Already in *Roland* the connection is slight, in the Arthurian stories true history has sunk altogether below the horizon. In the fourteenth century the separation is complete, and for our history we go to Froissart rather than to the poets, though it is significant of the old alliance that the first book of his *Chronicles*, afterwards recast, was composed in verse. As authentic history becomes less and less in the romances the wonder element gains until it dominates the entire field. From the twelfth century onwards we are in the full flood of the romance of marvel, we associate with writers who no longer sing their compositions, but address themselves to readers, who have become conscious of the requirements of a new audience, and endeavour to gratify it with delightful novelties, with the strange and unexpected, with the subtleties of the new science of courtly love, with modern sentiment. The spirit of curiosity outgoes that of pleasure in the life of the actual world, credibility ceases to be of consequence, and astonishment is to be purchased at whatever price.

With the *Romans d'Aventure* and the Arthurian stories—it is another significant change—women for the first time exert an influence in the world of literature. "*A knight may never be of prowess but if he be a lover*," said Sir Tristram. These were the tales which, in Chaucer's words, "*women hold in full great reverence*." That they formed a conspicuous and important, perhaps the most sympathetic, section of the audience to whom the poet addressed himself there is proof sufficient.

> " In chief these tales the ladies please
> They listen glad their hearts to ease."

The fashionable and elegant society of feudal times, given to the pleasures of tourney, of hawking, and hunting—pleasures which, contrasted with the serious business of war, made the presence of ladies at the pursuits of men possible—demanded a literature which took account of women. And taking account of it not only did the interest of love overshadow that of battle, the ideals that were abroad in romance took higher flight. The courtesies, the tenderness and pathos, the symbolism and spirituality, the tone of thoughtfulness—all reflect, although all are not directly due to, the influence of the feminine mind in this age. We have left behind the heroic and entered the chivalric world. Epic is masculine, romance feminine. A parallel may be drawn from ancient times. "Romance," [1] writes Professor Hardie, " is naturally associated with women and their emotions—if it is concerned with the inner life of feeling it must inevitably deal with the sex which is less actively engaged in the work and business of the world. The Greek states differed very much in their treatment of women. Among the Ionians and Athenians women lived in seclusion, enjoyed little freedom, and had few opportunities of education. The Homeric poems are substantially the work of Ionians. Greek tragedy is Athenian. Neither in Homer nor the Drama is there a romantic tone. The state of things was different among the Dorians and Æolians. It is among them and not among Ionians that romance is to be looked for. Stesichorus was a Dorian poet."

The older epic poetry then was driven from the field by the more popular " *matter of Britain*," its simpler beauty faded before the more brilliant splendours of Celtic imagining. The Arthurian romance, in some respects superior to the "*matter of France*," in others, and these important respects, was inferior to the " *haughty matter* " of epic. Unlike the *Chansons de Geste*, the Celtic stories did not spring from the soil of an actual life once lived, a veritable historical past. Arthur began in myth and never rose into a national hero. Efforts, but unavailing efforts, were made on his behalf. He failed to establish himself firmly and without rival in the national mind. It may have been, indeed, for this among other reasons, that the French epic lost ground before the chivalric legends, in that it was less symbolic, less universal in its appeal, a poem of limited patriotic and national feeling, incapable of that kind of indefinite expansion of meaning and various interpretation which assist the work of art to accommodate itself to the emotional and intellectual needs of progressive civilisation. Arthur—in the account of Nennius, leader in the battles against the Saxons waged by

---

[1] *Lectures on Classical Subjects.*

British kings—is, from the first mention of him, a figure in extremest shadow. This Arthur who, as the story went, came from the unknown, and after his last battle in Lyonesse returned to it, who kept his court in a vague wonderland through whose dark enchanted forests his knights wandered in search of adventure; this Arthur, only to be approached through myth and mystery, supplied by the Celtic imagination, was wholly superhuman, and conceptions of him to suit the needs of many times and minds were easily moulded. Fancy, untrammelled by any order of facts, was free to picture her hero as she would. Thus the absence of strongly defined features of character, though it militated against his acceptance as a national hero, was altogether in his favour as a world figure. The very lack of individuality makes for universality, and Arthur and his knights overthrew on the plains of romance Charlemagne and his peers.

In an inquiry concerning the epic elements present in Arthurian literature the question of origins need not arise, and we may omit, therefore, all reference to the debate which has not yet determined for us the problem whether it sprang from Celtic or French or English—that is Anglo-Norman—sources. Nor need it here concern us how the various legends drifted together, until, with Arthur as centre, matter from far separated quarters was wrought into the wonderful embroidery. Taken as a whole, we have seen, the romances were never brought within the compass of a single poem. It is to the prose narrative of Malory, to his *Morte d'Arthur*, that we must go for the only attempt at unification of the legends in the English tongue, an attempt unrivalled in that it presented by far the most complete version of the romance, renewed at a later day its early popularity, and gave it currency throughout modern literature. Malory's is the only *Arthuriad*, and from Malory, therefore, whatever epic qualities belong to it will best appear. And it will be generally conceded that, despite the splendour of Malory's achievement, this final and most complete rendering of the Arthurian romance is lacking in one great essential of epic, a coherent plot. The stories have little or no connection with one another, and the absence of any important central action, with which they

might have been associated as subsidiary episodes, places the
Arthurian romance, as we possess it, almost at once beyond the
pale of epic. This inherent defect has never been wholly overcome. It appears as conspicuously in Tennyson's *Idylls* as in
the *Morte d'Arthur* itself. Nor is the atmosphere in any satisfying
sense the atmosphere of true epic. The wars of heroic poetry
have become adventures hardly serious beyond the seriousness
of tourney, undertaken for the sake of glory, or for the favour
of ladies—

> " whose bright eyes
> Rain influence and judge the prize
> Of wit or arms, when both contend
> To win her praise, whom all commend."

Love and adventure, knight-errantry, are the topics of this
literature, and to these interests is added that of magic—love
potions, charms, and spells, miraculous arms and armour, giants,
dragons, enchanted castles, the whole sum of marvels gleaned
from the folklore of West and East:—

> " Where wonders wild of Arabesque combine
> With Gothic imagery of darker shade."

" *Always pleasant is it, the wonderful,*" as Aristotle acknowledged, and these interests are indeed sublimated by the spiritual
touch. For the child-like and almost vulgar materials are so
interwoven with Christian ideals, so permeated with symbolic
conceptions, so transfigured by high and mystical vision that
civilisation is profoundly in their debt. Yet how far from
Homer and *Beowulf* we are in this world of moving dreams, of
phantom figures!

From the epic standpoint " *the matter of Britain* " is defective
also in its presentation of character. The vagueness of its
history and geography is matched by the vagueness of its
persons. The knights and ladies of Arthur's court have little
to distinguish them from one another; all the men are bold—as
in the ballads—and all the women fair. But of dramatic inter-
play of character there is almost none. And thus a certain
incurable monotony—reflecting perhaps the monotony of life in
the mediæval castle [1]—hardly assuaged by the introduction of

[1] As the monotony of the *Arabian Nights*, veiled with wonderful skill,
reflects the monotony of life in the harem.

new marvels, accompanies the reader through the endless series
of combats hardly distinguishable from one another, or successful
rescues of distressed damsels, in the clutches of the luckless
giant or dragon that we know is doomed from the first. Yet
that epic might have sprung from this material is undeniable. It
needed the artful handling of a consummate poet, and till " the
sage and serious Spenser " attempted an altogether different
treatment, no such poet presented himself. Nor is impressive
quality more conspicuous if we take instead of the *Arthuriad*
of Malory, the best versions of single legends. These are, it
must not be overlooked, in a different class from the *Roland* or
the *Beowulf* lays, since they are literary compositions at no
stage in their evolution indebted, as far as we know, to the art
of the scôp or the minstrel. Yet in their best examples, like
the fourteenth-century *Sir Gawayne and the Grene Knight*,
though its originality and skilful construction give it a place by
itself, they fall short of that dignity and comprehensiveness
required by epic. They fall short, too, in style, the grand style
that a tradition, supported by generations of skilled and professional singers, may produce, the people never. To examine
the English romances *seriatim*, many of them directly borrowed
from the French, like *Sir Orfes, Sir Launfal*, or *Sir Tristrem*,
would be tedious. Whether so borrowed, or, like *Havelok* and
King Horn, Beves of Hamtoun, and *Guy of Warwick*, romances
with an Anglo-Saxon flavour, which have a tang of the sea
derived from Viking originals, or recall the history of a pre-
Norman England, they exhibit no trace of epic distinction or
breadth. The anonymous romances, view them as we will,
are poems of low artistic value. They belong to the literature
of the people and have a certain kinship to the ballad. One
sees what Hegel meant when he described romance as " the epic
of the *Bourgeoisie*." The *romans d'aventure* now take the place
of the extinct folk-epic. Despite a mediæval love of the
beautiful, interest in combat and martial figures—which is
never wholly absent—their passion for extravagant feats, devotion to the misty abstractions of the schoolmen, and their
remoteness from real life, altogether exclude these poems from

the heroic category. Nor is their historical greater than their literary value, for they are not documents which assist us in envisaging a society that at any time existed or in forming a picture of the period to which they belong. The inferiority of the English romances, of which about a hundred are extant, may be traced to several causes—the degradation of native literature following upon the Norman Conquest, the absence of a tradition in technique and the necessity of meeting the requirements of more popular and less refined audiences—the middle class then rising into prominence—than their French originals. These native lays exerted no influence upon the future literature of the country, though they remained in favour till the fifteenth century or even later, and they are to-day hardly known even by their titles to any save students of literary history. Their true importance is as precursors of the modern novel.

Romance in the Arthurian cycle tends to be reflective, to move away from the pole of action to the pole of thought, to exchange the blue sky, the open field, and men in action for the palace of the mind. It remains akin to epic " *where the interest turns, not upon what a man shall choose to do, but on how he manages to do it ; not on the passionate slips and hesitations of the conscience, but on the problems of the body and of the practical intelligence, in clean open-air adventure, the shock of arms, or the diplomacy of life.*" [1] When it forsakes these and becomes more and more taken up with ideas, more with character in itself than with character displayed through deeds, more with motives than with what has happened, more with what can be seen by the eye of the mind than with what has been or can be seen by the bodily eye, no magic of words can save it, narrative begins to lose the arresting power of heroic poetry. For in all heroic poetry the paramount interest is in the thing itself rather than in thoughts about it. " Crusoe recoiling from the foot-print, Achilles shouting over against the Trojans, Ulysses bending the great bow, Christian running with his fingers in his ears, these are such culminating moments in the legend, and each has been printed on the mind's eye for ever. Other things we may

[1] R. L. Stevenson, *A Gossip on Romance.*

forget; we may forget the words, although they are beautiful; we may forget the author's comment, although perhaps it was ingenious and true; but these epoch-making scenes, which put the last mark of truth upon a story, and fill up at one blow our capacity for sympathetic pleasure, we so adopt into the very bosom of our mind that neither time nor tide can efface or weaken the impression. This then is the plastic part of litera- ture: to embody character, thought, or emotion in some act or attitude that shall be remarkably striking to the mind's eye. This is the highest and hardest thing to do in words: the thing which, once accomplished, equally delights the schoolboy and the sage, and makes in its own right the quality of epics." [1]

Besides the "*matter of France*," the *Chansons*, and the "*matter of Britain*," the Arthurian cycle and the Anglo-Saxon romances, there exists another great division of mediæval narrative, the stories of antiquity, the "*matter of Rome the great*," like the *Tale of Troy* and the *Alexander*, which through various tongues and versions made their way into immense popularity. Curious it is, and indicative of the mediæval reverence for antiquity, that Chaucer's irony at the expense of Arthurian romance, "*those worn-out impressions of the feigned nowhere acts, of Arthur of the Round Table*," should barely appear when he faces towards the ancient legends. The opening lines of *The Wife of Bath's Tale* very clearly betray his attitude towards the chivalric splendours of an outworn day.

> " In tholde dayes of the King Arthour,
> Of which that Britons speken great honour,
> All was this land fulfild of fayerye.
> The elf-queen, with hir joly companye,
> Daunced ful ofte in many a grene mede;
> This was the olde opinion as I rede.
> I speke of manye hundred yeres ago;
> But now can no man see none elves mo."

Both here and in *Sir Thopas*, where in the way of parody he ridicules the knightly romance, the new world has parted company with the old, but the fascination of the still older world of classic fable endured, with power unshaken. The "*matter of Rome*" had, indeed, undergone strange transforma-

---

[1] R. L. Stevenson, *A Gossip on Romance*.

H

tions in its passage through the mediæval mind, but the *Tale of Troy*, even when feudalised, its Greeks and Trojans converted into knights dwelling in castles, fasting and praying like good Catholics, its chiefs into dukes, its women freshly fashioned into ladies and surrounded by kneeling cavaliers, still resisted, as only immortal beauty can resist, the disfigurement of time. A later poet than Chaucer, who himself did not disdain to make a version of part of the Arthurian cycle, seems to have shared his feeling.

> " No part have these wan legends in the sun
>   Whose glory lightens Greece and gleams on Rome.
> Their elders live; but these—their day is done:
>   Their records written of the winds, in foam
>   Fly down the wind, and darkness takes them home.
> What Homer saw, what Virgil dreamed, was truth
> And died not, being divine, but where in sooth
> Might shades that never lived win deathless youth? "

Nothing in its way could well be stranger than the history of the two cycles of legend through which the Middle Ages derived almost exclusively their knowledge of antiquity, the antiquity for which their reverence was as unbounded as it was uncritical. These were the Alexander story and the story of Troy. For generations they equalled, if they did not surpass in popularity, the celebrated tales of Arthur and Charlemagne, and to them the peculiar mediæval interpretation of ancient history and distorted rendering of antique fable are undoubtedly due. Two accounts, both apocryphal, both claiming contemporary knowledge of the events described, made the tale of Troy famous in the Middle Ages—the wholly imaginary narratives of wholly fictitious persons entitled Dares Phrygius and Dictys Cretensis.[1] Of astonishing interest these narratives are, because they so impressed the mediæval mind, drew again with such quaintness and stained with such curious dyes the picture of the classical age as to render it in our eyes rather an original than a copy, but almost more because these forgeries were by far the most influential and successful literary impositions that the world has ever known. It was believed that Dares and Dictys were veracious historians—Dares, who fought on the Trojan side,

[1] See *Dares and Dictys* by N. E. Griffin. Baltimore.

Dictys, a native of Crete and companion of Idomeneus, the suitor of Helen who led a fleet of ships to the siege. By the Middle Ages it was believed that these men lived before Homer —by whom Dares was mentioned as " *a priest of Hephaestus* "— and as authentic prose historians deserved credence far beyond the poet, who—

> " madè lies
> Feigning in his poetries." [1]

Since both claimed to be eye-witnesses of the Trojan war, omitted or rationalised the supernatural machinery of Homer, preserved an air of honesty and accuracy, explained, as did Dictys, that the events before the war were communicated to him by Ulysses, those subsequent to it by Menelaus and Neopto-lemus, or, as did Dares, that he remained in Troy after its capture, and was thus able to state exactly the number of slain and the number of prisoners taken by the Greeks, no hesitation was felt in the acceptance of the whole magnificent fiction. Nor was belief in it easily dissipated. It was accepted by Sidney and Shakespeare in the sixteenth century and by many even among the learned as late as the seventeenth. Of such materials are spun the convictions of centuries, of such the cherished opinions of men! The history of Dares was discovered, the tradition ran, by Cornelius in the fifth century, and by him translated into Latin; that of Dictys, given currency in the same language, was originally written upon bark in Phœnician characters, buried with the author, and by his command, in a metal box, and only brought to light by the accidental inter-vention of an earthquake in the reign of Nero. Nor is this the whole story. The material of these narratives formed the basis of a long poem by Benoît de Sainte-More, in the twelfth century, but it was not destined to make him famous. By some singular fortune the Latin version of a Sicilian, Guido da Colonna, or de Columnis, who says not a word of Benoît de Sainte-More, his original, became the authority for the legend and secured immense celebrity. The prose plagiarist reaped the glory which belonged of right to the poet. So fitly ended the history of a superb deceit.

[1] Chaucer, *Hous of Fame*, 1477.

The Alexander legend, setting forth the life and exploits of Alexander the Great, was no less famous than that of Troy.

> " The storie of Álisaundre is so comune
> That every wight that hath discrecioun
> Hath herd somwhat or al of his fortune." [1]

Of this narrative—the great versions were the French *Roman D'Alexandre* and the English *King Alisaunder*—the chief source appears to have been a book of obscure origins and very early date, declared, probably not without warrant, to have had more readers than any other except the Bible, a Greek book by the unknown Pseudo-Callisthenes, which obtained currency through a fourth-century translation by Julius Valerius, supplemented by later versions and traditions. The Oriental flavours and colours, the Eastern marvels of this fabulous biography profoundly influenced the Middle Age and permeated its romance. So incongruous are its elements—one meets there Darius and Aristotle, Gog and Magog, Amazons and flower-maidens, whose raiment grew on their bodies, red like flowers and white as snow, one hears of Greeks and Babylonians, rivers of Paradise and fountains of immortality—that we accept Alexander as a Christian king without surprise, an earlier Charlemagne surrounded by a feudal court.

Dreams of childhood rather than history indeed it all seems, pieced from a nurse's evening tales. Yet misunderstood and misrepresented as antiquity was in these accounts, and in the mediæval romances which they inspired, they did something by their popularity to prepare the mediæval mind for the acceptance of the same material in the far nobler but still untutored presentation of Chaucer. To know them is to approach him with sympathy, to appreciate his " *infantine familiar clasp* " of the ancient and divine myths, by which, as by some early Italian painter of the Renaissance, things already rare and lovely are made to yield for us new and exquisite sensation.

The exclusion of Chaucer from an account of English heroic poetry might quite well be justified but for his authorship of a

---

[1] Chaucer, *Monk's Tale*, 3821-3823.

single poem, *The Knight's Tale*. Here, because he is the disciple
of Boccaccio in an attempt to follow the epic tradition, and
because this poem illustrates perhaps better than any other in
English the peculiarities of the mediæval treatment of an
antique heroic subject, he may be permitted to fall within our
range.

Boccaccio, like Chaucer, viewed the chivalric romance with
amused disdain, and turned, when he proposed to himself an
epic, to classic models. With these he was familiar, for he had
made Latin versions of both the *Iliad* and the *Odyssey*, and in
his *Teseide*, the first epic in a modern language—a conscious
imitation the most painstaking—omitted none of the traditional
requirements such as Swift in the eighteenth century sarcasti-
cally enumerated in his *Recipe to Make an Epic Poem*. Deities,
battles, episodes, similes—all the ingredients are there and duly
mixed in their proper proportions. But the *Teseide* is a tale
of love rather than war, for Boccaccio, like Virgil, was not at
his best in war, to which "*the hero tears himself away from
king's daughters at the call of country*." His poem fixed for his
more successful followers, Pulci, Boiardo, and Tasso, the metre
—*ottava rima*—suited to their purposes and gave to Chaucer
the suggestion for *The Knight's Tale ;* for the rest it hardly
rose to distinction. Chaucer's poem, a more skilful narrative,
reduces to less than three thousand the ten thousand lines of
Boccaccio's epic, excels it in art and interest, but illustrates
in the same vivid fashion the odd transformation of the classical
into the mediæval, the cross lights of the feudal and chivalric
conceptions playing across the life of the antique world.

Nothing can well be stranger to a reader fresh from the *Iliad*
than the easy familiarity and gaiety of tone, as of one telling a
story to children, with which Chaucer begins his narrative—

> " Whylom, as olde stories tellen us,
> Ther was a duk that highte Theseus . . .
> This duk, of whom I make mencioun "—

or the lightness of touch with which he passes over preliminary
details—

> " I have, God woot, a large feeld to ere . . .
> The remenant of the tale is long y-nough."

With what an unsophisticated air he takes his readers into his confidence, and puts to them the question—

> " Yow loveres axe I now this questioun,
> Who hath the worse, Arcite or Palamoun? "

or inquires blandly, with humorous self-depreciation—

> Who coude ryme in English proprely
> His martirdom? for soothe, it am nat I."

How novel too the heroic type now presented to us. The duke is " *a trewe knight*," " *gentil*," " *of herte piteous*," a philosopher who ponders on the flux of human things—

> " Considereth eek, how that the harde stone
> Under our feet, on which we trede and goon,
> Yit wasteth it, as it lyth by the weye.
> The brode river somtyme waxeth dreye.
> The grete tounes see we wane and wende.
> Than may ye see that al this thing hath ende."

A moral philosopher is he likewise—

> " Thanne is it wisdom, as it thinketh me,
> To maken vertu of necessitee."

Note too the feudal and heraldic accessories. The duke displays his banner, and by it is borne his pennon—

> " Of gold ful riche, in which ther was y-bete
> The Minotaur, which that he slough in Crete."

With what pleasure Chaucer dwells upon " *the riche array of Theseus paleys*," where " *haukes sitten on the perche above* " and " *houndes liggen on the floor adoun*," the marble gates of the tourney ground, the oratories, the ways crowded with spectators, greedy of wonder and eagerly gossiping on the sights and probable issue of the contest in the lists—

> "' Heer three, ther ten, holding hir question."

How he lingers over his description of the bustle and colour, the pageantry so loved by the Middle Age—

> " And on the morwe, whan that day gan springe,
> Of hors and harneys, noise and clateringe
> Ther was in hostelryes al aboute;
> And to the paleys rood ther many a route
> Of lordes up-on stedes and palfreys.
> Ther maistow seen devysing of herneys
> So uncouth and so riche, and wroght so weel
> Of goldsmithrie, of browding and of steel;

> The sheeldes brighte, testeres and trappures;
> Gold-hewen helmes, hauberks, cote-armures;
> Lordes in paraments on hir courseres,
> Knightes of retenue, and eek squyeres
> Nailing the speres, and helmes bokelinge,
> Gigginge of sheeldes, with layneres lacinge;
> Ther as need is, they weren no-thing ydel;
> The fomy steedes on the golden brydel
> Gnawinge, and faste the armurers also
> With fyle and hammer prikinge to and fro;
> Yemen on fote, and communes many oon
> With shorte staves, thikke as they may goon;
> Pypes, trompes, nakers, clariounes,
> That in the bataille blowen bloody sounes."

How remote from the classical spirit and manner are the tapestried picturesqueness, the personified abstractions, the symbolism of the chapels of Venus, of Mars, and of Diana, as of oratories in a Gothic minster.—

> " First in the temple of Venus maystow see
> Wrought on the wal, ful piteous to biholde,
> The broken slepes, and the sykes colde;
> The sacred teres, and the waymenting
> The fyry strokes and the desiring,
> That loves servaunts in this lyf enduren. . . .
>
> Nat was foryeten the porter Ydelnesse . . .
>
> And downward from an hille, under a bente,
> Ther stood the temple of Mars armipotente,
> Wrought al of burned steel . . .
> Ther saugh I first the derke imagining
> Of felonye, and al the compassing . . .
> The smyler with the knyf under the cloke . . .
> . . . . . woodnesse laughing in his rage,
> Armed compleint, out-hees, and fiers outrage . . .
> And all above, depeynted in a tour
> Saw I conquest sitting in greet honour." [1]

How remote too the amorous atmosphere of the tale, the references to May, to the lark, to the dolorous lover—

> " Welcome be thou, faire freshe May—"
>
> " The bisy larke, messager of day
> Salüeth in hir song the morwe grey."
>
> " His eyen holwe, and grisly to biholde;
> His hewe falwe, and pale as asshen colde,
> And solitarie he was, and ever allone,
> And wailling al the night, making his mone."

[1] As Warton points out (*History of English Poetry*, vol. ii. p. 196) the groundwork of this description is taken from the *Thebaid* of Statius, a favourite author in the Middle Ages.

Love, the tyrant, is master of this tale, that Love which in the *Argonautica* refused sleep to Medea when she thought of Jason though it brought happy forgetfulness "*to the mother of sons but lately dead*"—

> " The God of love, A! *benedicite*,
> How mighty and how great a lord is he! "

The lover's first sight of the lady is like a swift sword-thrust—

> " He caste his eye upon Emelya,
> And ther-with-al he bleynte, and cryde ' a! '
> As though he stongen were unto the herte."

The lady herself is "*fresher than the May*," "*fairer than the lilie upon his stalke grene*." There is here matter for a Court of Love—whether the knight who first sees and loves the lady, but thinks her a goddess, or he who loves her second but knows her to be a human creature, is to be the fortunate lover? The delicacy of the final award is in the best manner of the subtle science; Chaucer with infinite art reverses Boccaccio's decision. In the *Teseide* Arcite first sees the lady, but his prize is not her hand—it is victory in the tourney and death. Chaucer gives the first sight of Emely to Palamon, and though to Arcite goes the triumph in the lists, it is by him who loved her first that the lady is finally won.

And behind Love, and behind the decorative classical deities, what dark power of Fate or Fortune in the stars presides over this tale told in Christian times?—

> " Sum wikke aspect or disposicioun
> Of Saturne, by sum constellacioun,
> Hath yeven us this, al-though we hadde it sworn;
> So stood the heven whan that we were born."

What a self-concious touch is that in the description of Arcite's resolution—

> " And with that word he caughte a greet mirour
> And saugh that chaunged was al his colour."

How refined are the chivalric manners when Arcite, about to fight to the death with his rival, offers to bring arms and armour for both—

> "And chees the beste, and leve the worste for me "—

and when the two knights with all gentleness assist each other
to arm—

> " As freendly as he were his owne brother."

And to what height of courtesy does the mortally-wounded
Arcite rise in his last words, as he resigns Emely to his more
fortunate rival—

> " Forget nat Palamon, the gentil man."

How the sentiment of pity dominates the tale, the badge of
knighthood's flower—

> " For pitee renneth sone in gentil herte."

Exquisite the tale is, none more admirably wrought of pathos,
" *of arms and amours*," depicting a conflict between friendship
and love, in which both are victorious, a tale delightful in its
music to the ear, in its picturesqueness to the inner eye, in its
delicacy of sentiment to the heart. It were hard to deny to it
the title " heroic," though times and men and manners have
all been transfigured. But behind it, as never in the older
heroic poetry, there stands the author, gravely smiling at our
pleasure, amused a little at his own success, and hinting now
and again, with an engaging charm, at the humours of a piece
not wholly serious.

CHAPTER VII

EPIC AND HISTORY—LAYAMON—BARBOUR

EPIC, it has been said, " *is a compromise between poetry and history.*" [1] Perhaps, but in what sense a compromise? Is a portion of historical truth sacrificed, or are the graces of poetry limited? Which gives way to the other? Or are there mutual concessions? And when history has become a science is epic no longer possible? " *The poet and the historian differ,*" says Aristotle in the *Poetics*, " *not by writing in verse or in prose. The work of Herodotus might be put into verse, and it would still be a species of history, with metre no less than without it. The true difference is that one relates what has happened, the other what may happen. Poetry, therefore, is a more philosophical and a higher thing than history, for poetry tends to express the universal, history the particular.*" There is nothing to exclude, as Aristotle expressly allows, from the epic category the poem which has an historical theme, for what has actually happened may well " *conform to the law of the probable,*" and in virtue of that quality prove suitable poetic material. [2] The poem which takes its hero from authentic history, and describes again, in the manner proper to poetry, events which are known to have taken place, may be legitimate epic, epic of the secondary type, like that of Tasso. Yet, not by reason of its metre, but as a result of its method, it will still differ from history. For the poet, in one way freer than the historian since he is not bound within the circle of fact, is in another way subject to a stricter law. He must conform to a principle by which the historian is not and cannot be bound, the principle of rigid unity. Historical compositions, as Aristotle is careful to explain, survey a wide region,

[1] F. W. Newman, *Miscellanies*, p. 8.
[2] " What has not happened we do not at once feel sure to be possible; but what has happened is manifestly possible; otherwise it would not have happened."—Butcher, *Aristotle's Poetics*, ix. 6.

" *of necessity present not a single action, but a single period, and all that happened within that period to one person or to many, little connected together as the events may be.*" Thus the poet may be an historian, but he will be a selective historian, whose method involves excision of all matters which cannot be closely knit into relation with his main action, whose contact with his hero and hero's doings cannot somehow be preserved. Clear and close must be the bond between the events narrated, tend they must to one result, march together to one end. No mere loose alliance in time will suffice; a connection far closer must hold together all the parts, as constituents of a single body, in itself complete, intelligible, significant.

Though free of the historical province, therefore, the poet in a cultivated age never in any way or measure encroaches upon the historian. Their paths in advanced society lie far apart, for the one will sacrifice to the truth of fact, as he believes it, the dearest wishes of his readers; the other, as minister to their pleasure, will be tempted "*for the sake of the turn of phrase,*" as was said of Plutarch, "*to make Pompey win the battle of Pharsalia.*" Not until late, however, in national development was this separation possible between the epic and history, between the functions of poet and chronicler. Their aims in the infancy of society are undivided, their parts are one. The poet is the historian of the heroic age. For long the Greeks looked upon Homer as essentially a narrator of historical facts, the *Iliad* was often quoted as an authoritative document, "*a kind of scripture.*" The island of Salamis was on the authority of a single passage assigned to Athens—Thucydides, himself an historian, writing at the zenith of Greek culture, cited the Homeric catalogue of the ships as authentic. While no written records exist, it would not manifestly be easy for a sceptical spirit of discrimination between fact and fiction to assert itself. " Credible " and " incredible " are words of an advanced and sceptical age. The world is full of wonders, and the past may well have been believed more wonderful than the present to men in heroic times. Where scientific doubt was impossible the field of belief was wide, and the singer when he clothed tradition

—that which was in fact universally believed—in new and striking phrases, amplified and decorated it, was himself, doubtless, convinced of the truth of his own tale. Nothing suggested, nothing was to be gained by reluctance in belief. Commonly he sang of his own kin and that of his hearers, and to make their achievements magnificent, magnificent even beyond the mortal prowess of his own day, what hindered? Poetic enthusiasm served its true end when it kindled a passion of pride and desire to emulate the glory of so famous an ancestry. With the progress of civilisation, the growth of cities, the increase of travel, and the interchange of ideas with men of other races a frigid spirit of inquiry arises—like that of Froissart, who made journeys to obtain exact information about men and events— a spirit half-sister to distrust. Hunger for the fact, a huntsman's eagerness after new quarry seizes upon less imaginative men, and the historian, a shrewd brain, presents himself as rival of the poet at the Court of Letters. "*I write what I believe true,*" proudly announced Hecatæus of Miletus, "*for the traditions of the Greeks seem to me many and ridiculous.*" It is the historian's hour when the prosaic present throws its shadow upon the poetic past; when in his attempt to understand the past, he reads the record by the light of his own experience, and reduces that record to the level of his daily life. For long, nevertheless, he remained in some measure a poet still, not wholly scientific, not wholly unwilling to believe in things more wonderful than he himself had seen. Herodotus, says Gibbon—the fully emancipated of the half emancipated historian—"*sometimes writes for children, sometimes for philosophers.*" "*Herodotus is as much a poet in relation to Thucydides,*" wrote Peacock, "*as Homer in relation to Herodotus. The history of Herodotus is half a poem, it was written when the whole field of literature yet belonged to the Muses, and the nine books of which it was composed were therefore of right, as well as of courtesy, superinscribed with their nine names.*" [1] One may imagine that physical improbabilities would first arouse the spirit of scepticism, but it is not easy to fix the limits of the credible. If the intervention of the gods must

[1] *The Four Ages of Poetry.*

be abandoned, men like gods may without so great difficulty be imagined, and feats almost divine substituted for those altogether beyond the limits of belief. The myth gives way to the " *historische Novelle,*" and for a time the historian, though inspired by different emotions, carries on the work of the maker. Herodotus wrote history in prose, but published his work as a minstrel might have done, by reading it aloud to an audience. He adopted, too, the devices of the epic. " *Herodotus knew that every narrative of great length wearies the ears of the hearer, if it dwell without a break on the subject ; but if pauses are introduced at intervals, it affects the mind agreeably. And so he desired to lend variety to his work and imitated Homer.*" [1] Our own early chroniclers employed verse, yet they too chanted their poetic history when chance or occasion offered. Writing and printing deprived the minstrel, or the scôp, of his vocation, but his immediate successors, half poets, half historians, belong to the age of transition, since they had in mind not one, but two, types of audience, the listeners and the readers. How slowly and reluctantly imagination withdraws from the province in which it had been so long supreme! So slowly and reluctantly that the chroniclers of the Middle Ages display it not seldom in a more eminent degree, as they not seldom display a more marked individuality, than the professed poets themselves.

For two centuries after the Norman Conquest it went hard with English literature. Latin, in the work of the ecclesiastics, overshadows the native tongue. The tales and ballads of the people received no favour from the new aristocracy. The literature of the Norman nobles made no immediate appeal to the English. Nor could any revival of English letters take place till the Norman had ceased to be a Frenchman, and made the language of the new home-land his own. Side by side with the monkish scholars and chroniclers lived the men who fashioned the romances, like *Horn* and *Havelok,* translated though they were from the French, in which the national spirit still lived, but Christianity and the foreign conquest had tamed the rude strength

---

[1] *Dionysius* quoted by Professor Bury in *The Ancient Greek Historians,* p. 42.

of our early literature without adding to it a new distinction. The native race, however, in numbers far exceeding the new-comers, gradually took captive their victors, their language, enriched by a fresh current of ideas and an extended vocabulary, imposed itself upon court and legal tribunal, and a new English literature challenges the attention of the historian. One of the earliest, and by far the most noble of English poems after the Conquest is Layamon's *Brut*, the work of a priest of Arley, near the Severn, on the Welsh border. It is a poem of colossal length, more than thirty thousand lines;[1] it is wholly lacking in unity, ranging over far too vast a field and descriptive of events which cover centuries of time; it is without a central theme; it heaps together matters the most incongruous, and bewilders the reader by the multitude of its persons; as a poem it is alive only in parts, as a chronicle it abounds in anachronisms and is wholly untrustworthy; yet Layamon's *Brut* is not merely impressive from its length. Neither garrulous nor puerile, so sincere is the poem, so ample in range, so informed by imaginative vigour that one is surprised into admiration. Of all rhymed chronicles in English the *Brut* has the foremost claim to represent the type. We may indeed reject the type and demand its exclusion from the epic register, but an examination of Layamon's poem must precede the judgment.

The rhymed chronicle, like the early heroic lays, designed to give currency to the facts of national life and history, preserved the memory of memorable things, of great doings and the men who did them. It took up the task which the scôp could no longer accomplish. Layamon's were epic intentions. "*It came to him in mind*," he wrote, in words that a scôp might have uttered, "*that he would tell the noble deeds of England, what the men were named, and whence they came.*" He resembles the scôp in this, too, that he makes no attempt to distinguish myth and authentic record, but is everywhere roused to admiration

[1] Antimachus of Claros or Colophon, it may be mentioned, wrote a *Thebais*, now lost, which though it ran to twenty-four books had not reached the central point of its narrative. Yet he was assigned by Alexandrian critics the second place among epic poets, was preferred by Hadrian to Homer, and enthusiastically admired by Plato, so it is said, who at least remained to listen when all others had left.

by heroic things, the lofty figures in his country's past. This
enthusiasm makes Layamon a poet; it makes the temper of
his work epic and national. The fire and vigour of the old
English battle poetry may be dimmed in the *Brut*, but they
flash out in passages comparable to the descriptions of the
fighting in *Maldon* or *Waldhere ;* the alliterative measure,
though more freely handled, recalls the iron ring of the verse
of *Beowulf*, at times we are " *out of sight of land*," and have
glimpses of the sea " *where nikeres bathe*," or " *a sea wondrously
wild and bitterly enraged*," where are " *labouring ships*," and
" *hail and rain*," and " *waves that ran as if towns there were
burning*." No poet after the Conquest can claim a larger share
of the ancient spirit of Anglo-Saxondom than this " *our English
Ennius*." [1] None of the later days better recalls the heroic age
in language, in style, in poetic animation, in love of great deeds
than the gentle Worcestershire priest, who links the England
of *Beowulf* with that of Chaucer.

This monument of patriotic zeal was probably executed about
the beginning of the thirteenth century, and is usually assigned
to the year 1205. It is extant in two MSS., one perhaps thirty
or forty years earlier than the other. For all its length and
diversity of theme, it contains—so English is it—singularly few
words of French origin, not a hundred in all, a fact the more
surprising since its main source is a French chronicle, the *Brut*
of Wace, which purports to relate the history of Britain from
the destruction of Troy till the seventh century. " Layamon,"
wrote the author of himself, " began to journey wide over this
land, and procured the noble books which he took for pattern.
He took the English book that Saint Bede made, another he
took in Latin, that Saint Albin made, and the fair Austin who
brought baptism in hither; the third book he took and laid
there in the midst, that a French clerk made, who was named
Wace, who well could write, and he gave it to the noble Eleanor,
who was high King Henry's queen. Layamon laid before him
these books, and turned over the leaves; lovingly he beheld

---

[1] A title transferred, by Sir Frederick Madden, from Robert of Gloucester
to a poet with a far stronger claim upon it. Of Sir Frederick Madden's
version of the *Brut* I have made free use in the following pages.

them—may the Lord be merciful to him! Pen he took with fingers, and wrote on book skin, and the true words set together, and the three books compressed together."

It appears doubtful whether Layamon owes anything to the writers he mentions except Wace, who had in turn derived his narrative from Geoffrey of Monmouth. Wace's fifteen thousand lines he expands to more than twice their number, and though from this French original he unquestionably drew the bulk of his matter, so copious were his additions—derived no doubt from sources, including oral traditions, to which as a dweller on the Welsh border he had access—so rich his vocabulary, so spirited his style, so imaginative his temper, that Layamon's is throughout an English book, marked by originality of almost the highest or creative type and possessed of the secret of interest beyond any of his successors in chronicle.

It is not easy to give briefly an idea of this mighty book, the greatest between the Conquest and Chaucer, which tells the whole story, legendary and real, of Briton and Saxon from the fall of Troy to the conversion of England. It relates how Brutus, a descendant of Æneas, after many adventurous wanderings found in the isle of Leogice a temple of marble lofty and spacious, and within an image of the Lady Diana, very noble, "*queen of all the woods on earth.*" Entering alone, bearing in his hand a vessel of red gold full of wine mixed with the milk of a hind he had slain, Brutus called upon the goddess to counsel him whither he should lead his people. Then he took the hide of the hind and spread it on the floor of the shrine and slept there. And as he slept it seemed to him that the Lady Diana beheld him lovingly, and laid her hand upon his head and said: "*Beyond France thou shalt find in the West a winsome land, surrounded by the narrow sea. Thereon thou shalt prosper. There is fowl, there is fish, there dwell fair deer; there is wood, there is water, there is much desert. The land is most winsome; springs there are fair; giants most strong dwell in the land; Albion is the land named, but men there are none. Thereto shalt thou go and a new Troy make there; there of thy kin shall royal progeny arise, and over all lands shall they have fame.*" And when he awoke Brutus promised the Lady Diana a shrine all of red gold in the new land.

And so Brutus and his men departed, going ever north and west. Over the lake of Silvius and over Philisteus and over Malva they sailed, and through the Pillars of Hercules, which were "*tall posts of strong marble stone*," and they saw the mermen whose song no man is ever weary of hearing "*be the day ever so long*," till to land they came in Spain. And from Spain to Armorica they sailed, and to a most fair river the Loire, and there in haven they lay several days and viewed the people. And thereafter fighting arose, and Brutus and his men harried Armorica till the French were beaten, and then blowing his horn he assembled his company, and to the coast they marched, and with a favourable wind on a calm sea, where "*the wild fish played*," they voyaged till they came to Dartmouth in Totnes, and the ships grounded upon the sand. And in this land they found twenty strong giants, Geomagog their chief. And nineteen they slew, and Geomagog they took alive, and Corineus, their strongest man, made a trial of his strength with the giant in wrestling. A grim combat it was, "*breast against breast, bones there cracked*," "*there was full little wanting that Corineus was not overcome*," and "*evilly he was marred*." Nevertheless he took heart and strengthened his arms, and hugged Geomagog that his back brake, and mightily heaved him up and hurled him over the cliff where they fought. And then in the land, the giants being dead, Brutus and the Trojans settled, and built houses and towns, and sowed and reaped and mowed the meadows, and after Brutus, its first ruler, was the land named Britain.

Then of many kings and peoples the chronicle proceeds to tell—of the Huns, and of Silvius, King of Lombardy, who sent over to King Ebrane for his daughters, because his knights found "*the women of Lombardy odious to them*," of the wars that raged incessantly, and of the chiefs who partitioned the land in the days when Romulus built Rome. And many a tale it tells like that of the "*sea-weary men*," "*evilly clad and naked they were, and nothing cared who their limbs saw*," driven from Spain and

I

found by King Gurguint off the end of Orkney, who craved a land for dwelling, for they had had " *many harms, hunger, and much thirst, many conflicts, many strifes on the wild water* " for seven years, upon whom Gurguint had pity and sent them into Ireland, " *where no man ever was since Noah's flood had passed over it;* " or like that of the monster " *out of the sea, from Ireland-ward, a beast most wonderful,* " " *the folk it terrified, towns it ravaged,* " until Morpidus, huge and tall, cruel in fight, who when " *in wrath with any man on the spot would him slay, but so soon as he became calm, did all that men bade him,* " went forth against the monster with sword and quiver full of arrows, a bow most strong, a long spear, at his saddle an axe, and at the other side a knife, and " *rode on his steed as if he would go mad,* " and his arrows all he shot, and smote the beast in the neck with his spear so that the shaft brake, and " *the beast uprose* " and rushed on the steed and bit him through the breast, whereupon the king drew his sword and smote the beast upon the head-bone so that the hilt broke in his hand, and the beast undid his jaws and bit the king in the middle, and so the fight was done, both king and monster dead.

And many hundred winters after Gurguint arose a king, " *Alfred, England's darling,* " and wrote the law in English that was before in British, and hereafter with his Romans Julius Caesar came, " *who conquered all the lands that he looked on with eye,* " " *five and fifty kingdoms,* " who made the calendar that denotes the months of the year, " *a keen knight, over all middle-earth renowned, the wisest man of the world's empire.* " To Britain came Caesar and suffered defeat, though " *like a wild boar he fought,* " and slew an hundred men, so labouring in the battle that " *he was all lathered in sweat,* " and among those with whom he fought was Nennius, whom he smote with his sword so that it bit into the opposing shield, but could not be withdrawn, and Androgeus coming to the help of Nennius Caesar relinquished his brand and turned to flight, and with Nennius, who died of his wound, that sword was buried. " *The steel brand was very broad and very long, thereon were engraven many kinds of letters, on the hilt was engraven that the sword was called in Rome Crocea*

Mors, so the sword hight, because it had much might." And after
his defeat Caesar went to Boulogne, where he built a tower
"*wonderfully fair*," "*never was there any tower that was built
with craft so good as the tower of Otheres. Sixty hundred knights
might sit in the bottom of the tower, and the top of the tower a knight
might cover with his mantle.*" Thirteen months abode he there,
and then into France he went and established his cities, and
after with great armies yet a second time Caesar sailed to Britain
in six hundred ships wonderfully great, and again suffered defeat,
but at length the Britons yielded and paid tribute, and Caesar
returned to Rome. Then Cassibelaune made a great feast for
all his folk, "*merry was the day.*" Two hundred cooks were in
the king's kitchen, and no man may tell all the waiters. Were
slain for this meal twelve thousand good oxen and thirty hundred
harts and as many hinds, of the fowl kind no man may it tell.
And all the wealth and all the gold that was over all this king's
land, it was assembled at the service.

Afterwards king succeeded king, and at the time our Lord was
born came other emperors of Rome, Claudius and Severus, who
built the strong dyke, to keep out the Picts from the north,
from sea to sea, and a wall exceeding crafty, and set knights to
guard it day and night. And there came also excellent men out
of Rome who told of the worship of Christ, and of Peter, and
what he did in Rome and of his martyrdom, and many of the
Britons received baptism, and those who would not the king,
Luces, caused to be slain. And bishops caused the heathen
temples to be cleansed, the heathen vestments cast out of doors,
and the images burnt with fire, and hallowed the temples in
the Saviour's name, and set bishops to direct the folk and
archbishops and clergy to rule.

But when the Romans went to their ships, and left the
Britons to defend themselves, there were in London dreadful cries,
weeping, and sorrow. And the two Earls of Norway, Melga
and Wanis, heard the tidings, and with an innumerable army
broke through the wall and harried the Britons with fire and
sword. And the Britons sent messengers to Rome to bid the
Romans come quickly, but they answered they would never

come, " *on another side we have more than we can uphold.*" So the Britons gathered to a great battle and slew Melga and Wanis and their followers, and " *the women forth marched over woods and fields, over hills and dales, and wheresoever they found any man escaped that was with Melga, the heathen king, the women laughed loud, and tore him all in pieces, and prayed for the soul that never should good be to it.*" And later again were tidings brought to King Vortigern " *that over sea were come men exceeding strange,*" " *the fairest men that ever here came, but they were heathen.*" They were Hengest and Horsa and their followers out of Saxland, and they fought with the Britons at Thanet, and they wrought a treacherous slaughter of Britons at Stonehenge, and possessed the land, " *the noblest in Essex, the baser in Sussex.*" And afterwards the Britons avenged the treachery, and there was fought a great fight, " *steel went against the bones, mischief then was rife ; streams of blood flowed in the ways, the fields were dyed and the grass changed colour.*" And the Britons prevailed and compelled the Saxons to receive Christianity and be baptised.

Such—save the concluding part, about a third, devoted to his chief hero, Arthur—is the matter of which Layamon fashioned his astonishing poem. But even so lengthy a summary hardly more than hints at its wealth of content, fabulous and true. On almost every page starts out an arresting phrase, an attractive tale, a poetic gleam, a dramatic touch, a graphic description or a human sentiment to captivate the reader. Here is told the story of Leir and his daughters, to which Shakespeare was indebted; the story too of Cymbeline and Cloten; of Ferrex and Porrex related again in *Gorboduc*, the first of English tragedies; the story of Pope Gregory and the English captives —" *Truly ye are English, to angels most like ;* " the story of Rowena and the poisoned cup she gave to Vortimer; the story of the voyage and fate of Ariene (Ursula) and her companions. Here too we are told of the Saxon gods and the customs of Saxland; of the comet, " *immense, terribly shining* " that foretold to Uther Pendragon the birth of Arthur; of the building of the tower called Billingsgate, " *now and evermore the name standeth there ;* " of Helen's finding of the cross; of the marvellous flood in Brittany, during which "*it rained blood for three days*," and after of the plague of flies that "*flew in men's eyes and their mouth and their nose, and their lives went all to destruction;*" of Bladud, the father of Leir, "*who boasted that he would fly in likeness of a fowl*," who "*put on wings*," and "*went very high, to the welkin he was nigh,*" but to whom "*the wind came adverse*" so that he fell and was dashed in pieces, and "*the kingdom of its king bereaved;*" and of the founding of Winchester, and Canterbury, and Carlisle, and many another fair burgh; and of the brothers, Belin and Brennes, rival chiefs reconciled by their aged mother, who came to the army of Brennes in "*a tattered kirtle, on her bare feet,*" and with tears which ran over her cheeks implored him to lay down his "*war clothing, and red shield, and long spear, and mighty sword, and believe his mother and love his brother;*" of the marvellous Taliessin who prophesied of the Saviour; and of many kings, Merian, a man most fair "*that women loved him out of their wits;*" and Lud, who loved London above all things, and caused a wall to be made all about it, and "*honoured the burgh, and made it very fair;*" and of the King of Ireland, to whom the Picts sent for wives, and learnt from them the Irish tongue; of popes and monks, captains and ladies, loves and hates, plots and treacheries—a record amazing in its amplitude and containing all things that ever were, so as to awaken in the imaginative reader a sense of infinity making him in some sort "*a spectator of all time and of all existence,*" as of one standing at a point of vantage whence he can survey "*the dark backward and abysm*" of an interminable past, an ocean-like spectacle —wave succeeding wave—of generations, rank on rank, filing past, the incalculable armies of humanity.

All this apart Layamon secures a place in his country's book of remembered names by his account of Arthur, the great "*Christian King of England,*" and his additions to the Arthurian legend. Throughout the chronicle this early, simple patriot takes the British side. The Saxons are for Layamon the invaders of his country, they are pagans against whom the Britons waged a holy war. It is then for Britain rather than

England he stands, and to him belongs not merely the restoration of Arthur to his own kingdom of Britain, but—wherever obtained—much of that peculiar mystical atmosphere which clings around the romance and gives to it a unique place and character in the literature of the world. Layamon first shed upon the cradle of Uther's son the visionary gleam—"*So soon as he came on earth elves received him,*" he relates, "*they enchanted the child with magic most strong; they gave him might to be the best of all knights; they gave him another thing, that he should be a rich king; they gave him the third that he should live long; they gave to him, the prince, virtues most good, so that he was the most generous of all men alive. This the elves gave him, and thus the child thrived.*" To Layamon also we owe the mystic "*passing of Arthur,*" and prophecy of his return—"'*And I will fare to Avalun, to the fairest of all maidens, to Argante the queen, an elf most fair, and she shall make my wounds all sound, and make me all whole with healing draughts. But afterwards I will come again to my kingdom, and dwell with the Britons with mickle joy.*' *Even with the words there approached from the sea a short boat, floating upon the waves; and two women therein, wondrously formed; and they took Arthur anon, and bare him quickly and laid him softly down, and forth they gan depart. . . . The Britons believe yet that he is alive . . . ever yet expect when Arthur shall return.*" For "*whilom was a sage hight Merlin; he said with words—his sayings were sooth—that Arthur should yet come to help the Britons.*"

The magic and mystery wherewith the wondrous tale is clothed are found in no earlier version of the legend than that of Layamon. To him also belong "*the byrnie, fashioned of steel that an elvish smith made with his excellent craft; he was named Wygar, the witty wright,*" "*the helm high of steel named Goswhit,*" the "*spear most fair made in Caermarthen by a smith hight Griffin,*"[1] the particulars—curious and new—of the Round

---

[1] See an interesting paper by Mr. A. C. L. Brown, entitled *Welsh Traditions in Layamon's Brut* (Modern Philology, vol. 1), where good reasons are given for supposing "Griffin" to be a corruption of "Gofan," Irish "Gobban." "In Irish and Welsh, wonderful arms are regularly said to be the work of Gobban." Note also the discussion of the phrase usually translated "Wygar, the witty wright."

Table, " *where the high were even with the low,*" " *a board exceeding fair, whereat sixteen hundred knights and more might sit.*" Here too are found, though not for the first time, "*Excalibur, wrought in Avalun with magic craft,*" Merlin and Guinevere and Gawain, Caerleon and Tintagel. It needed little but the addition of Lancelot and the Grail to make this the complete Arthurian romance, the first clear-cut pattern of the whole.

This Arthur, who " *was to the young for father, to the old for comforter, and with the unwise wonderfully stern, to whom wrong was exceeding loathsome, and the right exceeding dear,*" most Christian of kings, is the true hero of Layamon's poem, for though many stars shine in his heaven, its sun is Arthur. The description of his prowess in battle, " *as the wolf when he cometh from the wood behung with snow,*" and of " *the third greatest battle that ever here was fought,*" when Arthur advanced upon the " *Rome-people,*" with " *high standards, sixty thousand waving with the wind,*" the shields glittering, the byrnies shining, steeds leaping so that " *the earth stirred,*" " *trumpets there blew, horns there resounded with loud voice,*" " *together they charged as if heaven would fall,*" or the description of the last great battle at Camelford, " *where were slain all the brave, Arthur's warriors, high and low, and all the Britons of Arthur's board, and all his dependants, of many kingdoms, and Arthur himself wounded with a broad slaughter-spear, fifteen terrible wounds he had,*" are as spirited as any in English poetry. Had he been content to write an *Arthuriad* Layamon might well have taken rank as an epic poet, for such is his nature that he cannot but make his history an instrument of music.

Layamon's chronicle differs from the true epic not in respect of scope, of general character and intention, nor in respect of the type of matter he handles, nor yet in respect of the spirit of his narrative. These are in essentials as they ought to be. It differs from epic in that the parts are not subordinated to the whole, and again in the absence of clearly-defined types of character. The canvas is crowded with detail, but there is no centre to the picture. No circumference limits his design, the materials are not selected, for nothing is omitted. In such a poem destitute of unity the effect is bewildering. The poet does not come to an end because his plan is completed, but because he has exhausted his knowledge and his imagination. Events in the chronicle impose themselves upon the poet, who subscribes himself slave to mere chronology, for example, as the name implies, nor does it belong to him to determine of what his work shall be composed; whereas in epic the poet emancipating himself from the bondage of "*what has happened,*" selects his theme, arranges his material, groups his figures, rising thus to artistic control not of language and description, not of narrative only, but of the subject itself with which he deals. Escaping from captivity to the fact he projects an entire and self-sufficient world of his own, rounded to a unity of which he is himself the sole author.

In the chroniclers of the thirteenth century who succeeded Layamon poetry wages unequal war with history. The metrical form ceases to have warrant in the pitch of emotion or imaginative presentation of the material. If one asks the crucial question, "Is the value of their work historical or literary?" the answer cannot be, as with *Homer* and *Beowulf*, "It is both." It would indeed be more nearly true to say "It is neither." There is little hope that in these works, impressive only from their length, we shall ever meet beauty face to face, or even for an instant catch the gleam of luminous wings. Nor even as chronicles are they trustworthy. Their value lies elsewhere. It is as historians of times of which they do not profess to write, their own; as documents in which the contemporary mind can be studied that their authors attract and instruct us. Mannyng in his *Handlynge Synne* (early fourteenth century) displays considerable skill as a narrator in his many and often interesting stories, but he is a homilist with didactic aims. Robert of Gloucester (*circa* 1300) provides excellent occasional reading in his *Corpus rerum Anglicarum*, a long account of British history from the Trojan war to the reign of Henry III., of which the last portion only has a record's value. But he affords entertainment for the traveller, and the patriotic note in his eloquent description of

England should secure for Robert grateful, even if only passing attention from his countrymen.

" England is a very good land, I ween of all lands the best, set at the end of the world in the extreme west. The sea goes all about it, as in an island. Of foes they need have no fear, save through treachery of the people of the land itself, as has been seen of yore. From south to north it is eight hundred miles long and two hundred broad, going from east to west in the middle of the country and not at one end. Plenty of all goods may one see in England unless the folk spoil them or years be worse. For England is full enough of fruit and trees, of woods and parks that it is a joy to see, of fowls and beasts, both wild and tame, of salt fish and fresh, and fair rivers as well. Enough of wells sweet and cold, of pastures and meadows, of silver ore and gold, of tin and of lead, of steel, of iron, and of brass, great abundance of good corn, of wheat, and of good wool, there is none better. Waters it hath enough, and before all others three, that are as arms out of the land into the sea, whereby the ships may come and go from the sea and bring to land goods enough, bought at each end: Severn and Thames, the third is Humber."

The *Cursor Mundi* (*circa* 1250), a curious and not unsuccessful attempt to make the prevailing passion for romance minister to spiritual edification, is the work of a northern ecclesiastic whose name is unknown. Men delight in these days, says the author, to hear tales of Alexander and Cæsar, of Brutus and Troy, of Arthur and Charlemagne, of Tristram and Iseult. What is there for him who knows not French? Let English be used by Englishmen, and in their native speech let the unlearned have knowledge of the kind that may amend their lives. And forthwith he enters in a poem of 24,000 lines upon the religious history of the world from the Creation to the Day of Judgment. Wondrous and vast the undertaking, yet it is carried through with unflagging spirit and metrical skill, and so skilfully weaves together its composite material, drawn from many sources, that it achieved a high and deserved popularity.

> " This is the best boke of alle,
> The cours of the werlde men dos hit calle "—

writes one of the copyists of the MS., and its anonymous author may well be allowed for the grandeur of his design honourable mention among the English makers of epic poetry. To these early English chroniclers is due at least the praise of high endeavour in their country's cause, in the fields of national speech, national education, and national history.

If England failed to produce an *Arthuriad*, a national epic, Scotland was more fortunate; she has her *Wallace* and her *Bruce*, the latter at least a poem for which stout champions have claimed epic honours, and with which the history of Scottish literature very nobly opens. The story of the making of an independent Scotland, and of its maker, Robert the Bruce, was indisputably an epic theme of the first order, rich in all the traditional requirements—a national not " a classical diction- ary " hero, distinguished by personal valour and resource; armour and weapons of the heroic period; great personages only subsidiary to the hero, like the good James of Douglas; a magnificent variety of combats, sieges, skirmishes; splendid episodes, as, for example, the last ride of Sir Aymer de Valence, or Bruce's encounter with De Bohun, and a great final battle, which makes him an independent sovereign, glorious and undisputed. So superb a subject might well be expected to yield an epic. It converted the Archdeacon of Aberdeen, John Barbour, scholar and churchman, into a poet. Born in 1320, nine or ten years before the death of Robert Bruce, it is possible, though not perhaps probable, that as a boy he may have seen his hero, the poem itself may have been, at least in part, written in the lifetime of the hero's son, David II., and a pension for " the composition of the book of the deeds of the erstwhile King Robert the Bruce " was, we are told, granted to Barbour within sixty-five years of the Battle of Bannockburn. Thus in closest relation to his theme the poet must have known and spoken with many men who had served and fought under the Bruce himself. Nothing in grandeur of theme was lacking, nothing of patriotism, nothing of the necessary knowledge, nothing of the inspiration which contact with great and stirring events could give. Great was Barbour's opportunity and greatly he took advantage of it. Had he been a poet born, as he was poet made by his love of country and the nobility of his subject, *The Bruce* might well have been more than a notable epic. As it is, though far from comparable with the greatest, Barbour made for himself an imperishable name.

The Bruce is an epic of the secondary type—the work of one man—not of the type we owe to the imagination of a race. Such a poem to reach the highest excellence demands shining poetical powers, educated artistic powers. The famous poems in that category, like Virgil's, are wrought with transcendent skill by men whose whole nature was poetical. Barbour was not primarily a poet at all. Primarily he was an ecclesiastic and a man of affairs. We cannot trace the writing of *The Bruce* to the imperative prompting of the divine spirit, to the mandate of the Muse. Patriotism was " *the mother and nurse of his song*," it was undertaken as a national duty. Compared again with poems like that of Tasso or of Milton, it fails on the side of art, of technique, it belongs to a ruder age, the age of the rhymed chronicle. On the other hand, Barbour inherited no great poetic tradition, no style prepared for him by previous minstrels steeped in the lays and legends of their country. He belonged to no school of " *makers*," he had no share in the bardic spirit. The folk songs, of which he himself speaks, were of a rude and unsophisticated type, and can have afforded him little real assistance. Thus though admirable the theme and dazzling the opportunity, since he belonged neither to a time like Milton's, rich in Renaissance culture, conversant with all forms and models, trained in all refinements of the poetic art, nor to a time like that of the author of *Roland*, who dealt in matter already poetised and ready to his hand, schooled by the numerous singers of the story who preceded him, Barbour, since he stood thus alone and unsupported, achieved only a measure of success. A poem is a work of art and must be judged as art. " Poetical history " is not epic even if the history be true. That cannot in the least help it as a poem, except in so far as the " truth " may inspire or assist the poet while at work. In a sense possibly Barbour stood too near his subject, and it is doubtful whether he gained more than he lost by this proximity.[1]   Advantageous as it may appear, this nearness precluded the poetic and artistic enrichment which prepare the subject for the final and consummate rendering.   Unlike his countryman Burns, who drew largely upon the imagination and the poetic experience of his predecessors, Barbour was a solitary, a lonely figure.   This is not indeed to say that he was a poet altogether original and without models.   He was, for instance, profoundly indebted to the French romance of *Alexander the Great*.   " As regards style and narrative, and even to some extent in plan, the impress of the French romance is vital." [2]   None the less he remains a writer insufficiently supported by native poetic tradition, insufficiently supported by artistic culture, insufficiently supported by a language not completely subdued to his purposes.   Barbour, fortunate in his theme, cannot be reckoned equally fortunate in his times or in his artistic education.   Distinguished he was, but as I have said, rather for patriotic than for poetic passion.   That difficult thing, the fusion of history and poetry, is not perfectly achieved in *The Bruce*.   That Barbour should have failed to write his name as high as that of the great epic poets is not wonderful, what is wonderful is the measure of his success.   He is original, as far as we know, in his use of the octo-syllabic couplet in his own language, a metre admirably adapted for simple narrative, original in his grasp and command of his materials, and in the shaping of his narrative, original in the spirit that animates the whole poem.   The noble simplicity, the chivalric sentiment, the sympathy with heroic deeds, the pleasure in " *the pride, pomp, and circumstance of glorious war* " are all Homeric.

[1] " He was not the first," says Voltaire of Lucan, " who thought a recent history the proper subject of an epick poem, for Varius ventur'd before him (and with success) on such a dangerous undertaking.   The proximity of the times and the notoriety of the events which he took for his theme, were certainly a great clog to his poetical invention (if he had any)." —*An Essay on Epick Poetry*, p. 42.

[2] George Neilson's *John Barbour; Poet and Translator*, to which, as well as to another Glasgow scholar's work, Mr. J. T. T. Brown's *The Wallace and the Bruce Restudied*, all students of Scottish literature are indebted.

" Men mycht se than, that had beyn by,
Mony ane worthy man and wycht,
And mony ane armur gayly dycht,
And mony ane sturdy sterand steid
Arayit in-till so ryche weid;
And mony helmys, and hawbyrschownys,
Scheldis and speris, and pennownys,
And so mony a eumly knycht,
At semyt weill that into ficht
Thai suld vencus the warld all hale." [1]

Homeric too is the lucidity and rapidity of his description of Bannockburn from the first marshalling of the hosts through all the scenes of the conflict till the English turn to flee.

" And Bannokburn, betuix the brais,
Of hors and men so chargit was,
That upon drownit hors and men
Men mycht pass dry atour it then."

Though he called his poem a romance, it is agreed that Barbour proposed to himself the composition of a truthful record

" To put in wryt a suthfast story
That it lest ay furth in memory."

He is without rival on the Scottish side for the history of the time with which he deals, though critics doubt whether we possess the poem in its original form, question too how far the poet overcame the chronicler, and to what degree his knowledge of many particulars was at fault. Much has been made of the singular mistake by which Robert the Bruce is identified with his grandfather—viewed by some commentators not as an error but a deliberate falsification to rescue his hero from the degradation of the oath of fealty to Edward and homage to Balliol—and many demonstrations given that the numbers, according to Barbour's account, engaged at Bannockburn are impossible. Some of the exploits ascribed to Bruce, too, as when he engages two hundred Galloway men single-handed and slays fourteen of them, place some strain upon our faith. Yet if due allowance be made for poetic license, there is little reason to question the authenticity of the facts in general outline. In handling such a theme, even with historical intentions, the poet must be permitted a certain freedom, a certain play of imagination, perhaps

[1] *Sterand*, active; *weid*, clothing; *at semyt*, that it seemed; *vencus*, vanquish; *warld all hale*, the whole world.

in part even unconscious.   Its value as chronicle set aside, the merits of *The Bruce* as a poem will not be denied.   There are everywhere graphic touches as in the description of Douglas, that he had a lisp in his speech which became him wondrous well, or Bruce's comforting of his men, weary and starved, by reading to them romances of Charlemagne, or the grim tale of the " *Douglas larder* " of meal, malt, blood, and wine, or the fierce reply of Edward I. on his death-bed, asked what was to be done with the prisoners taken at Kildrummy, when he said, grinning, " Hang and draw them," or the description of the Bruce at Bannockburn in a hard leather hat with a crown upon it, or the circumstance that in the battle so desperate was the struggle that the combatants fought in silence, raising no cries. All that can delight the boyhood of the mind, all the elements of romance are contained within the covers of this book—the hairbreadth escapes of the hero, his combats against over-whelming odds, his indomitable courage, ready resource, un-ceasing cheerfulness and humour, the plots, the warnings and betrayals, the sieges, skirmishes, and flights through the wild hills, the privations and exposures, the marvellous loyalty and endurance of his friends.   To these Barbour adds the strain of high seriousness.   He is conscious and makes us conscious that all then done and suffered was in the cause of country and for the sake of that freedom he so finely praises.

> " A! Fredome is a noble thing!
> Fredome maiss man to haif liking:
> Fredome all solace to man giffis:
> He levis at ease that freely levis!
> A noble heart may haif none ease,
> Na ellis nocht that may him please,
> Gif fredome failye; for free liking
> Is yearnit owre all other thing.
> Na he, that ay has levit free,
> May nocht knaw weil the propertie,
> The anger, na the wrechit dome,
> That is couplit to foul thyrldome.
> Bot gif he had assayit it,
> Than all perquer he suld it wit;
> And suld think fredome mar to prize
> Than all the gold in world that is.
> Thus contrar thingis ever-mar
> Discoveringis of the tother are." [1]

[1] *Liking*, pleasure, ease; *na ellis nocht*, nor anything else; *yearnit*, yearned for; *dome*, doom; *all perquer*, by heart.

There is perhaps nothing more characteristic of the noble spirit
of Barbour, as there is nothing in itself more engaging, than the
magnanimity which permits him to ascribe the most heroic act
of any described in *The Bruce* to an English knight, Sir Giles
de Argentine.

> " And when Sir Gelis de Argenté
> Saw the king thus and his menie
> Shape them to flee so speedily,
> He com richt to the king in hy,
> And said, ' Sir, sen that it is swa
> That ye thusgat your gate will ga,
> Haifis gude day! for agane will I;
> Yit fled I never siccarly,
> And I cheiss here to bide and die
> Than till lif here and shamefully flee.'
> His bridle than but mair abaid
> He turnit, and agane he rade,
> And on Sir Edward the Bruce's rout
> That was so sturdy and so stout,
> As dreid of nakyn thing had he,
> He prikit, cryand ' Argenté! '
> And they with spearis swa him met,
> And swa feill spearis on him set,
> That he and horse were chargit swa
> That baith down to the erd can ga;
> And in that place than slain was he.
> Of his dede was richt great pitie;
> He was the thrid best knicht, perfay,
> That men wist liffand in his day." [1]

Defective in construction *The Bruce* nevertheless achieves if
not a perfect yet a certain diffuse unity; lacking in the more
subtle qualities of poetry it still commands respect and provides
pleasure. Barbour had the honour of inspiring Sir Walter
Scott, the greatest man of letters his country ever produced, a
service in itself of no mean distinction, and though more than
five hundred years have passed since the appearance of his epic,
no poem has since been written in Scotland which more profoundly influenced Scottish ideals and Scottish character, or
surpassed it in originality and absolute merit.

*The Actes and Deidis of the Illustre and Vallzeant Campioun
Schir William Wallace* [2] (*circa* 1460), though it came a hundred

---

[1] *Menie*, company; *hy*, haste; *swa*, so; *thusgat*, in this manner; *haifis*,
have you; *siccarly*, of a surety; *cheiss*, choose; *but mair abaid*, without
more delay; *naykn thing*, thing of no kind; *prikit*, spurred; *feill*, many;
erd, earth; *dede*, death; *liffand*, living.
[2] The oldest extant copy was made in 1488 by John Ramsay.

years later—claimed by some to surpass *The Bruce* in its mastery of metrical form as it certainly surpassed it in popularity—is far more ambitious but far less noble in spirit, so near indeed to mere rude minstrelsy in sentiment and ideals, so incredible in respect of its matter, that it made its appeal with wholly uncritical audiences. The author of *Wallace* was undoubtedly acquainted with a wide field of romantic literature, for he borrows freely and with composure from many sources, from Chaucer, *Morte Arthur*, and more particularly *The Bruce* itself.[1] What is worse, he repays his borrowings by deliberate falsification of history, and by the sacrifice of Bruce to his own hero. We may, however, admit bright, even if filched, patches in his narrative, passages which will always be quoted, as, for example, the description of his hero, or the lament of Wallace over the Graham—

> " When they him fand, and gude Wallace him saw,
> He lichtit doun, and hynt him fra them a'
> In armis up; behaldand his pale face,
> He kissit him, and cry'd full oft: ' Alas!
> My best brother in warld that ever I had!
> My ae fald friend when I was hardest stad!
> My hope, my heal, thou was in maist honour!
> My faith, my help, strengthiest in stour!
> In thee was wit, fredome and hardinesse;
> In thee was truth, manheid, and nobleness;
> In thee was rule, in thee was governance;
> In thee was virtue withouttin variance;
> In thee the leaute, in thee was great largnas;
> In thee gentrice, in thee was steadfastnas.
> Thou wast great cause of winning of Scotland." [2]

The Wallace succeeded in placing its hero in the front rank of Scottish worthies, but judge it by the best in that kind produced in any land or in any language, and the most ardent of patriots must acknowledge it of lineage not royal. If poesy be "*the clearest light by which they find the soul that seek it,*" the light shed by *The Wallace* is somewhat murky. It is not very beautiful. We are spared indeed no feat of physical prowess, but pondering the hero's character one has disturbing reflections. It were

---

[1] See an able paper by Dr. George Neilson *On Blind Harry's Wallace* in *Essays and Studies* by members of the English Association. Oxford 1910.
[2] *Hynt*, laid hold of; *ae fald*, one fold, single-hearted; *stad*, beset; *heal*, health; *stour*, fight.

best cheerfully to allow that the bent of the author's mind was not, as Barbour's, towards the most excellent things and that *The Bruce* is the true national epic, *The Wallace* never at any time or in any mood to be named among the poems that remain dear to the hearts of men, which, though they have to do with earth, seem to have been composed in a region serener and more fair, some " *garden of the Sun, beyond all seas.*"

CHAPTER VIII

THE ROMANTIC EPIC—SPENSER

MEN of the Renaissance conceived of the poet's country as already surveyed and mapped by the critics of antiquity. They thought it divisible into provinces or " kinds." Of these Aristotle had preferred tragedy to the rest, the Renaissance held that epic was the chief " kind," the most spacious and noble province. Epic was in a special degree national poetry. Greece had her Homer, Rome her Virgil. As a city could not be deemed complete without a cathedral, to lack its epic was a reproach to any people which aspired to great place in the world's history, without it national literature failed of its crowning ornament. It was Spenser's ambition to do for England what Virgil had done for Rome.

Since the word is one and the kinds many, the discussion of English epic has already taken us far from the original or primitive type. Spenser takes us further. Nowhere on this subject—not even in an account of Greek literature—can we speak without qualification. To escape from the business of sub-division and classification is impossible. Give romantic narrative a place—and how exclude it without excluding the *Odyssey ?*—and it must be distinguished from heroic. Further, romantic epic is not of one type but many, and includes poems of very various design, inspired by equally various motives. Italy, richly inventive in forms of narrative, has her Pulci, who adopted the style of the popular stories current among the uneducated; her Ariosto, whose exuberant imagination created an ironical wonderland from the Carolingian and Arthurian legends; her Tassoni, who took his material from real history, but assumed the elevated epic style to ridicule by contrast the trivial events and unheroic personages of his own time; her Forteguerri, whose exaggeration of romantic fiction leads to mere burlesque;

146

her Tasso, whose *Gerusalemme Liberata* drew its plot and some of its characters from the authentic history of the Crusades. Heroic, romantic, serio-comic, satirical, burlesque—narrative poetry in all these kinds has been included among the epics. Italy invented that peculiar type of narrative poetry which, if we except Tasso, was cultivated, each in his own manner, by the poets just mentioned, the type which, exchanging the lofty for the familiar strain, dealt with elevated subjects in a humorous or derisive key. For this mixture of tone—the ironical with the serious, the playful with the heroic, the satirical with the sublime, the ludicrous with the pathetic—parallels may be found in other literatures, but in no other is poetry of this kind at all comparable either in bulk or brilliance with the Italian. To account for it we are asked to remember that the Carolingian romances, when they passed from France into Italy, were rejected by the learned and became the possession of the vulgar. In default of national epic the *improvisatori* converted the *Chansons de Geste* into agreeable entertainment for the market-place. The marvellous became more marvellous, while the finer spirit of the legends vanished at the rude touch of the irresponsible levity and practical philosophy of burgher and artisan. Thus to their loss the chivalric romances had already passed through the distorting medium of the popular fancy, and fallen from their high seriousness before they emerged into the light and air of fashionable favour and were introduced by the sixteenth-century poets to the circles of culture. These poets, while they elevated the style, preserved the tone of the popular narratives, and thus the comic humour of the Italian romantic poems " arises from the contrast between the constant endeavours of the writers to adhere to the forms and subjects of the popular story-tellers, and the efforts made at the same time by the genius of these writers to render such material interesting and sublime." [1] The very choice of the Italian rather than the Latin language sufficed in that age to indicate the absence of serious intention.

---

[1] *The Narrative and Romantic Poems of the Italians*, by Ugo Foscolo, *Quarterly Review*, for April 1819.

The chivalric epic of Italy bears, then, the ineffaceable stamp of its association with the people. But what it lost on the side of sincerity it gained on the side of art. No more artificial form of literature exists or is imaginable. None the less it proved highly agreeable to a cultivated age whose æsthetic sensibilities and educated scepticism were gratified by its skilful artistry and ironical humour. Chaucer at an earlier moment had caught the tone of the chivalric epic by his smiling treatment of a lofty theme in *The Knight's Tale,* and had he been a man of the sixteenth century might have rivalled Ariosto in humorous epic. The poet who fell heir to Italian culture in England was, however, of an altogether different temper. At the cradle of " *the sage and serious Spenser* " the Graces attended, but the more irreverent spirits were absent. In his hands the chivalric poem, though it followed Italian models, preserved at the cost of greater monotony the grand manner of unbending superiority. In *The Faerie Queene,* therefore, we have still another kind of epic, to which no exact parallel can be cited, a kind which substitutes moral allegory for ironical humour. This substitution will be praised or deplored in accordance with the temperament and preferences of the critic. Ruskin need not be expected to share the opinions of Hume.[1] So much is clear: Spenser, the disciple of Plato, philosophising in the vein of his master as interpreted by the Cambridge of that day, secures at a respectful distance admiration and esteem, Spenser the artist the more flattering attention of an audience.

If one shares Ben Jonson's mind—" *Spenser's stanzas pleased him not, nor the matter* "—nothing is easier than to prepare a brief for the *Advocatus diaboli,* to charge his poem with utter lack of unity, to complain that neither man nor woman appears in it, that lifeless phantoms flit there through landscapes as unreal as themselves, that the coming and going of the characters is wholly aimless and irrational, that only by their names can we distinguish one from another, for every lady is " the fairest ever seen," and every knight an exact mirror of chivalry; that so leisurely is the poet's foot-pace, so broken and confused the

---

[1] See Hume's *History* and Ruskin's *Stones of Venice.*

narrative, that no reader, however unsophisticated, will be held from sleep by the story; that as for the " *continued allegory and dark conceit* " imbedded in *The Faerie Queene*, by which the author laid such store, so perplexed and vague is it, so confused, too, the attempted explanation of that and of his general aim—" I labour to pourtray in Arthur before he was king the image of a brave knight, perfected in the twelve private moral virtues as Aristotle hath devised "—that none can follow either one or other, the less so since they are not " *as Aristotle devised*," nor did he devise *twelve* such virtues; that, though we are told these paladins represent each a desirable virtue—Sir Calidore, Courtesy, Sir Guyon, Temperance—none will suffer surprise or hurt if Sir Calidore's name be anywhere substituted for Sir Guyon's, or Sir Scudamour change places with Sir Artegal. If it be answered that against an undertaking like Spenser's these objections have no weight, there remain more damaging accusations. How, it may be asked, can we reconcile the high pretensions of his philosophy and spiritual creed with the sensuous and relaxing atmosphere of the whole poem, as close and languorous as a summer's day, where the music of the flutes of pleasure is heard above the trumpet of duty? There is here surely nothing to alarm the sinner, nothing of the sternness of Dante, the *saeva indignatio* of Swift, the sorrowful impeachment of Langland. The slothful or indifferent may wander light-hearted and at ease in these Epicurean gardens, steeped in luxurious and enervating emotion, peopled by beauties naked and unashamed, provocative " of love's delights," the air perfume-laden from the fields of ancient or amorous legend. Nor is the form of the poem more bracing than the content, in grammar and spelling lawless, in language and rime licentious in every articulation of its limbs. Can this be the highest region of poetry when the human voice is never once heard, nor authentic cry of the heart uttered? If so what praise remains to give when we read poetry which is, in Bacon's phrase, " *drenched with flesh and blood*," Macbeth's " *To-morrow and to-morrow and to-morrow*," or Virgil's " *Sunt lacrimae rerum et mentem mortalia tangunt* "?

There is perhaps no reply but to abate the claim for Spenser, and to place him with the masters of the poetic art rather than with the masters of the soul. In artistry if not unrivalled he is at least without superiors. This supremacy in art gained for him the undivided allegiance of his successors. Jonson is almost singular, for the majority are on his side. No English poet of any age won more immediate and universal acceptance, an acceptance the more striking if we recall the exceptions. Who stood outside his circle? Locke, who preferred Blackmore, and Stubbes, who thought *Gondibert* superior to *The Faerie Queene;* probably all those also who, like Newton, regard poetry as "*a kind of ingenious nonsense.*" [1] Leave aside his immediate imitators, like the Fletchers; Drayton was persuaded that since Homer no one had appeared fitter to undertake a similar task, "*I know not what more excellent or exquisite poem may be written,*" said Meres, Nash styled him the "*heavenly Spenser,*" Browne "*the Muses' highest glory,*" Camden *Anglicorum poetarum nostri saeculi facile princeps,* Milton confessed "*that Spenser was his original,*" "*Faerie Spenser still ranks highest among the poets,*" said Hurd, "*No man was ever born with a greater genius,*" said Dryden, "*I had read him all before I was twelve years old, and was thus made a poet,*" confessed Cowley, "*There is something in Spenser,*" wrote Pope, "*that pleases one as strongly in old age as it did in one's youth.*" For Lamb he was "*the poet's poet,*" Coleridge speaks of his "*indescribable sweetness,*" it was "'*The Faerie Queene*' *that awakened the genius of Keats,*" when he

> "beheld Belphoebe in a brook,
> And lovely Una in a leafy nook,
> And Archimago leaning o'er his book."

To Spenser's credit stands also indubitably the most brilliant metrical invention of our literature, the famous stanza which bears his name; a measure, as its history shows, comparable to blank verse in the range and variety of its harmonies, and superior in liquid and lingering charm, in sheer romantic and musical sweetness.

[1] Byron confessed, however, that he "*could make nothing of him,*" and Landor admits that Spenser "*mostly sent him to bed.*"

No one can sufficiently explain the commanding influence of this poet by saying that he represents the Renaissance, its glory of colour, its richness of fancy, its passionate adoration of beauty, though this is true. All sensuous lovelinesses are gathered in *The Faerie Queene*, as they are gathered in Italian painting, the bewildering delight of "*flowers and founts and nymphs and demi-gods*" massed by the author's "*noble and most artful hands*" within these imperishable stanzas. Spenser magnificently represents Renaissance magnificence, its profusion and princeliness, but it is still more true to say that he seems to represent not a phase of art, not an age of poetry, but to be in some sense the genius of poetry itself, its spirit incarnate. This is his secret. He is entranced, and the Muse has taken possession of the bodily organ. The prosaic elements in life have been distilled away, the crude matter burnt out in the crucible, and what remains is the pure sublimated essence. Doubtless it is not life, for life is three parts prose and reason, but with these the Muse was not concerned. And if we consent to omit the prose, and with the prose the tragedy, what of essential poetry remains outside Spenser? It was his ambition "*to overgo Ariosto*," and he succeeds by gathering into a single poem—such is his proud design—all that had pleased in song and story since the dawn of art among all peoples and at every point of time. So wide he cast it that nothing escaped the meshes of his net. The mood of the Renaissance made possible the tangled texture of old and new.[1] Spenser's chivalry merges into Olympus. He is at ease with the knights and the abstractions, with Sir Tristram, Mammon, and Disdain, as with imagination's elder children, all the unfading hierarchy, the Graces and Goddesses, Cupid and Diana and Apollo. He is an unconditioned poet. There are for him no geographical frontiers, no nations, no space or time. This anthologist, this chooser of the

---

[1] " There is, inside Ara Coeli—itself commemorating the legend of Augustus and the Sibyl—the tomb of Dominus Pandulphus Sabelli, its borrowed vine-garlands and satyrs and Cupids surmounted by mosaic crosses and Gothic inscriptions; and outside the same church, on a ground of green and gold, a Mother of God looking down from among gurgoyles and escutcheons on to the marble river-god of the yard of the Capitol below."—Vernon Lee, *Renaissance Fancies and Studies*, p. 165.

best, swept within his scheme all lovely forms and fancies from
the East and West, rifled, and with deliberation, the poets from
Homer and Apollonius Rhodius, through Virgil and Ovid, to
Ariosto, Tasso, Chaucer, and laid under contribution the whole
book of mediæval legend, matter of France, of Britain, and
of Rome. His river is fed from a multitude of tributaries,
the springs of Parnassus and Helicon, and all the wizard streams
of romance. He borrows not from one or two or a hundred
sources, but impresses the histories, the fables, the mythologies,

> " Exceeding riches, and all precious things
> The spoils of the world."

What a world it is, and what does one not meet there? From
the first lines, a frontispiece, as it were, to all chivalric literature—

> " A gentle knight was pricking on the plaine,
> Ycladd in mightie armes and silver shielde "—

The Faerie Queene is a wilderness of fancy, a tropic maze of
exuberant and inexhaustible creation, the least describable poem
in the world. Each canto—six or seven hundred lines—equals
a book of Homer; each book—twelve cantos—is itself an epic;
the whole—about thirty-five thousand lines—is hardly shorter
than Homer and Virgil combined. Through this enchanted
country, uncircumscribed, horizonless, the reader is borne away
on the smooth-sliding current of the verse as it flows by " *two
and twenty palaces* " and the gardens of old romance. By
" *lowly hermitage* " and " *ancient house*," by woods " *not perceable
with power of any star*," by the Gardens of Proserpina and
Adonis flows the charmed stream, by the " *wandering islands* "
and the Bower of Bliss, by the magic strand of Marinel, with
its gravel of pearls and golden ore. By temples, palaces, and
towers it flows—the Castle of Busirane, with its flaming porch
and tapestries of gold and silk, upon which were wrought " *all
Cupid's wars*," the loves of all the gods; the Castle Joyous,
thronged with guests, a pleasance of flowers and Lydian harmonies; the Temples of Venus and Isis, the House of Pluto, and
Neptune's palace " *walled with waves*." The poet's inclination
is " *to surprise by a fine excess*," the incidents of his romance shall

be amazing and numberless, the personages unmatchable—the girdle of the snowy Florimel, the mirror of Merlin, the Shield of Love, the wondrous horse Brigadore, the sword Mordure, "*wrought in Aetna's flames*" and "*seven times dipped in Styx*," Talus, the iron man, the herbs of magic power—

> " whether it divine tobacco were,
> Or panachoea, or polygony."

And with these a press of knights and "*ladies debonair*" as of some great feudal court, Trevisan and Artegal, Satyrane and Scudamour, Pyrochles and Paridel, Britomart and Belphoebe, upon whom the heavens at her birth "*were favourable and free*"; Pastorella and Hellenore and Amoret, whose names are a summons to beauty; Argante, the Titaness, Braggadochio and Trompart his thrall; a brood of giants, Cormorant and Orgoglio, Corflambo and Ollyphant; shepherds and sorcerers, maids false and fair, hermits and satyrs, Muses and guardian angels, slave-merchants and river gods, sea nymphs and Saracens, brigands and dwarfs and deadly sins—a company innumerable. Add to these a flora and fauna from torrid and from temperate zones, symbolic or legendary or real, centaurs and crocodiles, serpents and lions, bears and tigers, dragons and dolphins and drome-daries, the horrible sea-satyr, "*huge ziffus, whom mariners eschew*," "*sea-shouldering whales*,"

> " Bright scolopendras, arm'd with silver scales,
> Mighty monoceroses, with immeasured tails "—

the Tree of Life, the flower-de-luce, "*Dead creeping poppy and black hellebore*," and

> " every sort of flower
> To which sad lovers were transformed of yore."

Add, too, the Masque of Cupid, the Pageant of the Seasons, the Procession of the rivers of the world—and Spenser's design is apparent, it is an ordered disorder, a calculated confusion, a dream composed of dreams, for admiration and bewilderment and delight.

For the style of Spenser the manifest original was Sackville's *Induction* to the *Mirrour for Magistrates*. If any doubt let him read in verses unsurpassed in the English tongue how in the

winter season the older poet met the lady Sorrow, a figure
piteous as any in Dante's *Inferno*—

> " That, in my doom, was never man did see
> A wight but half so woe-begone as she "—

whose dreary destiny it is to bemoan

> " those
> Whom fortune, in this maze of misery,
> Of wretched chance, most woeful mirrours chose;
> That, when thou seest how lightly they did lose
> Their pomp, their power, and that they thought most sure,
> Thou mayst soon deem no earthly joy may dure "—

and how she guides him to the grisly lake, Avern, "*within the
porch and jaws of hell*," where are Remorse and Dread, Revenge
and Famine, with "*body thin and bare as any bone*," Old Age
and Malady,

> " her sickness past recure
> Detesting physick, and all physick's cure."

As Sackville imagined and described, so Spenser. Take these
stanzas, and there will be no further need of witnesses—

> " By him lay heavy *Sleep*, the cousin of *Death*,
> Flat on the ground, and still as any stone,
> A very corpse, save yielding forth a breath:
> Small keep took he, whom Fortune frowned on,
> Or whom she lifted up into the throne
> Of high renown; but, as a living death,
> So, dead alive, of life he drew the breath.
>
> The body's rest, the quiet of the heart,
> The travail's ease, the still night's fear was he,
> And of our life in earth the better part;
> Reaver of sight, and yet in whom we see
> Things oft that tide, and oft that never be;
> Without respect, esteeming equally
> King *Croesus*' pomp, and *Irus*' poverty. . . .
>
> In midst of which, depainted there, we found
> Deadly *Debate*, all full of snaky hair
> That with a bloody fillet was ybound,
> And breathing nought but discord everywhere;
> And round about were portray'd here and there,
> The hugy hosts, Darius and his power,
> His kings, princes, his peers, and all his flower. . . .
>
> Yet saw I more the fight at Thrasimene
> And Treby field, and eke where Hannibal
> And worthy Scipio, last in arms were seen
> Before Carthago gate, to try for all
> The world's empire, to whom it should befall;
> Then saw I *Pompey* and *Caesar* clad in arms,
> Their hosts allied and all their civil harms. . . .

> *Xerxes*, the Persian king, yet saw I there,
> With his huge host, that drank the rivers dry,
> Dismounted hills, and made the vales uprear,
> His host and all yet saw I slain, pardé:
> *Thebes* I saw, all raz'd how it did lie
>   In heaps of stones, and Tyrus put to spoil,
>   With walls and towers flat even'd with the soil." [1]

In his *Laocoon* Lessing discusses, but without hesitation rejects, the theory of Count Caylus, that the work of a poet may be tested by the number of subjects it offers to the painter.[2] Painting, he argues, uses forms and colours in space, poetry articulate sounds in time, the painter can only express visible and stationary action, the poet progressive action. Because " *the co-existent elements in a scene are inconsistent with the consecutive elements of language,*" the best poets, Homer, for example, paint in such a way that the painter finds nothing or but little with which to occupy himself in their descriptions. " The art of the pen," wrote Meredith, " is to rouse the inward vision, instead of labouring with a drop scene brush, as if it were to the eye; because our flying minds cannot contain a protracted description. That is why the poets, who spring imagination with a word or phrase, paint lasting pictures; the Shaksperian, the Dantesque, are in a line, two at most." [3] If Caylus be right Spenser is supreme, beyond all poets ancient or modern—" *velut inter ignes luna minores,*" *a moon among lesser fires.* But if it be true that *our flying minds cannot contain a protracted description,* how of Spenser's method, prolonged, unflagging, unhurried? He who runs counter to nature can achieve no measure of success. Taking our own stand, let us suspend theory which interferes with artistic pleasure. Here is part of a description, " protracted " over ten stanzas—

> " —Eftsoon there stepped forth
> A goodly lady clad in hunter's weed,
> That seemed to be a woman of great worth,
> And by her stately portance born of heavenly birth. . . .
>
> And in her hand a sharp boar spear she held,
> And at her back a bow and quiver gay,
> Stuffed with steel-headed darts wherewith she quelled
> The savage beasts in her victorious play,

[1] Sackville's *Induction* to *A Mirrour for Magistrates.*
[2] *The Laocoon*, chap. xiv.   [3] *Diana of the Crossways.*

Knit with a golden baldric which forelay
Athwart her snowy breast, and did divide
Her dainty paps; which, like young fruit in May,
Now little gan to swell, and, being tied,
Through her thin weed their places only signified.

Her yellow locks, crisped like golden wire,
About her shoulders weren loosely shed,
And, when the wind among them did inspire,
They waved like a pennon wide dispread
And low behind her back were scattered:
And, whether art it were or heedless hap,
As through the flowering forest rash she fled,
In her rude hairs sweet flowers themselves did lap,
And flourishing fresh leaves and blossoms did enwrap.

Such as Diana by the sandy shore
Of swift Eurotas, or on Cynthus green,
Where all the nymphs have her unwares forlore,
Wandereth alone with bow and arrows keen,
To seek her game; or as that famous queen
Of Amazons whom Pyrrhus did destroy,
The day that first of Priam she was seen,
Did show herself in great triumphant joy,
To succour the weak state of sad afflicted Troy." [1]

Whoever be right, Spenser is not wrong. One may properly
hesitate to test the poet, as Caylus suggested, by the number of
subjects he provides for the artist in colour—other and severer
tests may be applied—but, if any argument prove persuasive,
it will be *The Faerie Queene* itself. It is, as has often been said,
a long gallery of pictures, easily to be transferred to canvas.
Leigh Hunt amused his fancy by a selection from this " *poet of
the painters*," naming the artist for each subject. Raphael for
" *The Marriage Procession of the Thames and Medway* "; Cor-
reggio for " *Cupid usurping the throne of Juppiter* "; Michael
Angelo for " *Sir Guyon binding Furor* "; Titian for " *Venus, in
search of Cupid, meeting Diana* "; Guido for " *Aurora and
Tithonus* "; Salvator Rosa for " *The Cave of Despair* ";
Albano for " *The Nymphs and Graces dancing to a shepherd's
pipe* "; Rembrandt for " *A Knight in armour looking into a
Cave.*"

A good reader will value Spenser for more than one quality,
for his " *visible poetry*," his pageantry of colour, his *copia ver-
borum*, his moonlight atmosphere. But his Circean charm is
perhaps most fully felt in the half unconscious mood of the

[1] *The Faerie Queene*, Bk. II. Canto 3.

listener to music, awake to harmonies of sound but careless of
more than these. Men of active mind, insensitive to verbal
melody, are never numbered among his adherents. They grow
impatient for the progress of the idea while the poet is busy with
its embellishment, they ask for advance in meaning while he
dreamily repeats himself, adding honey-sweet word to word.
One has a suspicion that had Spenser presented himself for
admission to Plato's *Republic* his high and clear intentions
might not have sufficed to secure an entrance, although this
fairyland typifies the country of the spirit and the pursuit of
glory the pursuit of righteousness. A certain discrepancy, a
certain contradiction between the creed and the manner of
stating it might have alarmed the rulers. Yet if, as Plato
argued, " absence of grace and inharmonious movement and
discord are nearly allied to ill words and ill nature, as grace and
harmony are the sisters of goodness and virtue and bear their
likeness, " it is demonstrable that *The Faerie Queene* was
written by a saint, who was also

> " High priest of all the Muses' mysteries."

With Spenser it is not so much the word that tells, as with
Milton—" *The helmèd Cherubim And sworded Seraphim,*" " *the
crystal battlements,*" " *the throne of Chaos,*" " *the marble air,*"
" *Twilight's sober livery,*" " *the angelic guards,*" " *the Attic bird,*"
" *the golden Chersonese* "—nor so much the phrase, as with
Shakespeare, " *I am dying, Egypt, dying,*" " *Behold divineness,
No elder than a boy,*" " *For her own person, It beggar'd all description,*" " *The queen of curds and cream,*" " *He has no children* "—
nor so much the line, as with Chaucer—

> " *His studie was but litel on the Bible.*"
> " *The wrasteling of this world asketh a fall.*"
> " *O paleys empty and disconsolat !* "
> " *His seven wyves walking by his syde.*"

With Spenser it is the stanza or the page; time and space are
necessary to him for the development of his world of beauty—

> " The walls were round about appareled
> With costly cloths of Arras and of Tour;
> In which with cunning hand was pourtrayed
> The love of Venus and her paramour,

The fair Adonis, turned to a flower;
A work of rare device and wondrous wit.
First did it show the bitter baleful stowre,
Which her essayed with many a fervent fit,
When first her tender heart was with his beauty smit.

Then with what sleights and sweet allurements she
Enticed the boy, as well that art she knew,
And wooed him her paramour to be;
Now making girlands of each flower that grew,
To crown his golden locks with honour due;
Now leading him into a secret shade
From his beauperes, and from bright heaven's view,
Where him to sleep she gently would persuade,
Or bathe him in a fountain by some covert glade:

And, whilst he slept, she over him would spread
Her mantle coloured like the starry skies,
And her soft arm lay underneath his head,
And with ambrosial kisses bathe his eyes;
And, whilst he bathed, with her two crafty spies
She secretly would search each dainty limb,
And throw into the well sweet rosemaries,
And fragrant violets, and pansies trim;
And ever with sweet nectar she did sprinkle him." [1]

" *The general end* " of *The Faerie Queene* was, declared the author, " *to fashion a gentleman or noble person in virtuous and gentle discipline.*" Such noble persons distinguished the circle of his intimate friends. Raleigh, " *the shepherd of the ocean,*" the first reader of the poem, like himself for some years an unwilling exile in Ireland, and Sidney, in whom survived all the graces of chivalry, in whom died the last of the knights, were men not unworthy of the age to which Spenser looked back with wistful and idealising gaze. Elizabeth's world in a poet's enhancing eyes could hardly have appeared a less spacious field for heroic endeavour than any in the recorded past, while than Ireland, where, in the dark Kilcolman tower, begirt with gloomy woods and surrounded by savage and despoiled outlaws eager for vengeance on the usurpers, *The Faerie Queene* was written, no more fitting ground for armed and romantic adventure could well have been imagined. " To read," wrote Dean Church, " of Raleigh's adventures with the Irish chieftains, his challenges and single combats, his escapes at fords and woods, is like reading bits of *The Faerie Queene* in prose. As Spenser chose to write of knight-errantry, his picture of it has doubtless gained

[1] *The Faerie Queene*, Bk. III. Canto 1.

in truth and strength by his very practical experience of what such life as he describes must be. *The Faerie Queene* might almost be called the Epic of the English Wars in Ireland under Elizabeth, as much as the Epic of English virtue and valour at the same period."

Spenser's age was heroic, heroes his friends. Around his home in the wild Desmond country many a feat of arms was done. He was a man—we read in a dispatch of the Council in 1598—" *not unskilful or without experience in the wars.*" In that same year he was himself a fugitive, when his castle of Kilcolman was sacked and burnt, and in his own person experienced the disastrous chances, the moving accidents which as a poet he had imagined and described. Yet in *The Faerie Queene* one hardly feels the pressure of events, the overflowing energy of the time. Fever and turmoil are banished from it, the voices of human passion stilled, the noises of the tempestuous world, like that of a receding tide, " *heard, but scarcely heard to flow.*" In *The Castle of Indolence*, by his disciple Thomson, there seems more than a suggestion of *The Faerie Queene* itself—

> " A pleasing land of drowsy head it was
> Of dreams that wave before the half-shut eye;
> And of gay castles in the clouds that pass,
> For ever flushing round a summer sky:
> There eke the soft delights, that witchingly
> Instil a wanton sweetness through the breast;
> And the calm pleasures always hovered nigh;
> But whate'er smacked of noyance or unrest
> Was far, far off expelled from this delicious nest."

No one as he reads *The Faerie Queene* thinks of England at war, of anxious statesmen, like Burleigh and Walsingham, or adventurous seamen on the Spanish main, of the great explorers, of Drake and the Invincible Armada. Nor is it probable that while he wrote Spenser had the stirring events of contemporary history in mind. It is far more probable that as he gazed into his magic glass, and watched the visions rise, they became the reality, and the anxious present receded into the world of shadows gladly forgotten. It is far more probable that in his poetry he sought and found forgetfulness, that it had for him the virtues of an anodyne, than that he attempts to embody there his own experience of life. *The Faerie Queene* is the fruit of solitude and long stretches of solitude. Dreams like these do not visit the city dweller in the intervals of the street cries, the soldier in camp, nor the adventurous voyager on the seas. The architect of these airy palaces, "*pinnacled dim in the intense inane*," had not the dramatist's need "*to work upon stuff*," as Byron phrased it, to feel the throb of existence, to mix with the politicians and soldiers, the lawyers and the burgesses. He needed rather a screen between him and the loud-roaring world—

> " And more to lull him in his slumber soft,
> A trickling stream from high rock tumbling down,
> And ever-drizzling rain upon the loft,
> Mix'd with a murmuring wind, much like the sound
> Of swarming bees, did cast him in a swound.
> No other noise, nor people's troublous cries,
> That still are wont t'annoy the walled town,
> Might there be heard; but careless quiet lies
> Wrapt in eternal silence, far from enemies." [1]

For all that his lot was cast in the fiercer currents of history, Spenser was at heart a reader, a bookman. The invisible is with him the veritable, of which the shows of time are a momentary reflection. And though the defined and stated allegory may without loss, indeed with positive poetic gain, be laid aside, there remains and is diffused throughout his poem a sense that all its scenes, even the combats and pursuits, the sudden encounters of knight with knight, the gardens and palaces, the sculptured groups of graces, nymphs, and fauns—have a significance beyond themselves, beyond their beauty and their art, that in these regions from first to last all is of the spirit. The mirror of Spenser's mind gave back not the image of the exterior world that lay around him but of all that he had read and pondered in romance and poetic history. In *The Faerie Queene*, it may be alleged, we are at a second remove from reality, already transfigured in the books the author knew and followed. Battles have lost their horror and war its ugly side, wounds bring no pain, hate and fear are deprived of their poison, the sting of life is extracted, and the rose itself is without its thorn. Yet not without reason, for it is the idea he pursues.

[1] *The Faerie Queene*, Bk. I. Canto 1.

A day-dream, you may call it, but it is a dream only in significance not in texture. The great masters in the arts are aware
that men never really outgrow their childhood, that from birth
to death they prefer the sensible to the impalpable, and are
happiest and most at home with the things they can touch and
handle. Spenser knew it, and made a picture-book of the
spiritual life. The pictures are sufficient in themselves—such
is his art—nor is any reader required to press beyond them.
There is no other poem in the world which deals with pure ideas
in so concrete a style, which finds so many and such firmly
outlined illustrations for an abstract creed. He speaks of
invisible things as if he saw them. All the accuracy of line
and colour required by the eye are preserved in the philosophic
design addressed to the mind. He is a dealer in mysteries who
works in daylight, who, like Socrates, speaks of lofty and divine
matters in a language cleansed of all pedagogic or metaphysical
intention. The difference between Spenser and other didactic
poets is that he thinks more of his art than his allegory. To
begin with his meaning, his lesson, is wholly to mistake and
wrong him. He is not a reformer turned poet—a man important
in his generation, it may be, but as transient. From the
beginning until the end Spenser is an artist, a passionate lover
of beauty. He would have us, no doubt, believe in virtue and
loyalty. He is an enthusiast for perfection in the moral world.
Nevertheless quite naturally, as one speaking on subjects where
there is no dispute, he writes not to convince his readers, rather
to make them happy in his company. A Puritan, you may
say. Perhaps; but can we call a man a Puritan who never
loses his sense of beauty in his zeal for holiness?

Knighthood is his theme. But while his contemporary,
Cervantes, " *smiled Spain's chivalry away*," and noted with
melancholy Castilian humour how remote and impossible its
ideals had become in a world grown practical and materialistic,
while the Italians, like Ariosto, viewed the old order as a man
might view the games of children and consent to play them for
the amusement of his leisure, Spenser believed the Middle Ages
had seized, by a kind of divine instinct, upon a portion of eternal

L

truth, surely divine and enduring. The ideals of chivalry he separated from the actual age which gave them birth, in which they had never, indeed, been more than counsels of perfection, and set forth the celestial pattern as a thing of unceasing worth. It is his peculiar, his crowning glory that he, beyond all other poets, or for that matter philosophers, perceived the splendour of that immense structure of mediæval idealism, perceived beyond orders of knighthood, courts of love, crusades and quests and mysteries the true import of the visionary scheme. Then, as never before in history, he believed, imagination had been at work transforming life, philosophy had been summoned from heaven, "*where she lost her time*," to reign over terrestrial affairs, in the effort to mould society according to a spiritual design the soul had given convincing proof of its divine origin. Magic had for him no marvel, enchantments no wonder, the mind expanding to its august dimensions was matter for more consuming admiration.

Chivalry, the costly and magnificent plaything of Ariosto, had lost all but a plaything's value. Decorated with poetic art and spiced with humour it served as agreeable entertainment for the elegant society in the Renaissance courts. Ariosto perceived in it no element of truth and professed no serious purpose. In the mind of Spenser, though the outward forms of chivalry, like its weapons and armour, might be outworn, the ideas which inspired and governed it were everlasting. If no longer true it revealed truth. Looking beyond its mundane attachments, its mere historical aspect, he desired to draw the essential pattern, the perfect form, chivalry seen, as it were, through the brain of a disciple of Plato.

Obviously a poem so inward, so enskied, is not epic if we place restrictions upon the word. It forms, as Voltaire complained of the *Lusiad*, " *a sort of epic poetry unheard of before.*" The modern critic will not indeed urge against it Voltaire's objection to the work of Camoens, " *No heroes are wounded a thousand different ways, no woman enticed away and the world overturned for her cause.*" The head and front of Spenser's offence is the plentiful lack of unity displayed by his poem. He himself foresaw that it might well be charged with tediousness and confusion, and since too the Renaissance demanded a theoretical justification for all new forms of art, he had double cause to attempt in prose a defence of his design. He avoided indeed the unfortunate expedient of Tasso, who submitted his poem for criticism to a committee of scholars, each of whom placed a candid finger upon some conspicuous fault, so that nothing from title to conclusion, in plot or diction, escaped censure. Nor did he adopt the bolder and perhaps wiser course of defying criticism, like the Elizabethan dramatist whose prologue announced—

"By God, 'tis good, and if you lik't, you may."

In his letter to Sir Walter Raleigh he urges that though the historiographer "*discourseth of things orderly as they were done,*" the "*poet thrusteth into the middest,*" and that the unity of his design will in the end—an end that never came— become apparent. It does not appear that Spenser found serious objection to the allegory. It was indeed a necessity. Allegory in the Middle Ages sat enthroned over theology, philosophy, poetry. The habit of rejecting the literal for the symbolic sense, supported by antiquity, had become fixed and almost ineradicable. Before Plato allegorical interpretations of Homer were common, Plato and the Neo-Platonists, Plotinus, Porphyry and their followers freely employed it. Philo of Alexandria in the first century, who had made the rivers of Eden typify cardinal virtues, lent to the method the weight of his immense theological authority. Origen, who taught that the expulsion of Adam from Paradise was to be understood as a fall from primitive simplicity, held that the Bible was of little use to those who read it literally. The patristic writings were charged with allegory. St. Augustine and Gregory the Great used it continually for the elucidation of difficulties in a literal reading of the Scripture texts, or to corroborate New Testament history by symbolical interpretation of Old Testament prophecy. Virgil, as well as Homer, it was universally believed, shadowed forth more excellent things under the veil of his mundane history. Dante's *Divine Comedy*, the greatest poem of the Middle Ages, was throughout plainly a palace of symbols. In the *Roman de la Rose*, the most celebrated of the romances, where the mediæval spirit is, if anywhere, fully revealed, an elaborate symbolic scheme is developed of the utmost complexity and ingenuity. For centuries allegory subdued all ways of thought, all forms of mental activity to its peculiar temper. The desire for the wonderful, the mysterious, and miraculous fostered it. In the mist all objects loomed greater. Works not in themselves arresting excited curiosity if they claimed to be occult or cabalistic. The sixteenth century was not prepared to allow high importance to mere historical or poetic narrative. It was imperative for Spenser, if he desired a hearing, to distinguish his work from popular story-telling, the pastime of the vulgar, from trivial ballads and romances without philosophical signi- ficance. His was a serious and therefore a mystical poem, dealing with the great matters, the soul and life and love, " *the excellency of the beauty of supernal and intellectual things.*" [1] He fancied too that the poem would not stand or fall by his conduct of the " *dark conceit* " contained in it, and he was right. Probably no one ever read *The Faerie Queene* for the allegory alone, and few have followed the story with close attention. How many readers have been aware, for example, that at a certain point in each book, the eighth canto, Arthur appears, representing divine assistance, [2] a kind of *Deus ex Machina*, to support his vassal knight? How many have observed that as the poem proceeds the allegorical intention becomes more and more obscured, and in the later books—whether from its difficulty

[1] " I account of Poetrie, as of a more hidden and divine kind of Philo- sophy, enwrapped in blind Fables and dark stories, wherein the principles of more excellent Arts and morall precepts of manners, illustrated with divers examples of other kingdomes and countries are contained; for amongst the *Grecians* there were Poets, before there were any Philosophers, who embraced entirely the studie of wisdome, as *Cicero* testifieth in his *Tusculanes.*" Nash: *The Anatomie of Absurditie*, p. 36 (Huth Library). Reynolds in his *Mythomystes* censures those who never look further into the " golden fictions for any higher sense, or anything diviner in them infoulded and hid from the vulgar, but (are) lulled with the marvellous expression and artful contexture of their fables." *Critical Essays of the Seventeenth Century*, ed. by J. E. Spingarn, vol. 1, p. 149. See also Puttenham's *Arte of English Poesie*.
[2] Except in Bk. III. which being of *Chastity*, the representative of that virtue, Britomart, was in the mediæval view beyond the reach of evil.

or the author's inadvertence—almost wholly disappears? The allegory occasions no reader of this poetry any real discomfort. But many critics have been gravely concerned by the absence of beginning, middle, and end, or of any solid core to the narrative. Again and again have prepossessions in favour of the forms of art already known and esteemed blinded the judgment against high poetic excellence. Faults which detract little from pleasure in the composition are discovered by the comparative method, and the poet is often blamed not because he has failed to delight but because he has dared to be original. There exist nevertheless principles which to violate is to court failure, and of these the principle of unity is probably the most important, a kind of eternal law. It must be allowed that the unity of *The Faerie Queene* is not a conspicuous unity, but it may very well be argued that it possesses unity of a kind, and that kind suitable and sufficient for the author's purposes. Bishop Hurd advanced by far the most reasonable defence of Spenser on this count. Judge of *The Faerie Queene*, he contended, from your acquaintance with classical models, and you are shocked with its disorder, consider it with an eye to its Gothic original and you find it regular. In the days of knight-errantry it was not unusual for the prince at some court festival to assign adventures to his vassals, to charge them with the task of redressing the wrongs of distressed subjects who asked for their monarch's assistance. Upon this idea Spenser laid his foundations. " If you ask then, what is this *Unity* of Spenser's poem? I say, it consists in the relation of its several adventures to one common *original*, the appointment of *The Fairy Queen ;* and to one common *end*, the completion of *The Fairy Queen's* injunctions. . . . This, it is true, is not the classic Unity, which consists in the representation of one entire action; but it is an unity of another sort, an unity resulting from the respect which a number of related actions have to one common purpose. In other words, it is an unity of *design*, and not of action." [1]

The objections are perhaps idle and the defence unnecessary. Pedantry may demand adherence to an approved pattern, but

[1] Hurd's *Works*, vol. ii. p. 300.

discard prepossessions and recognise that the unity resides in the spirit of the composition rather than in the structure, remember that the English poet followed Ariosto, who, if more successful in the management of his story, was equally indifferent to classical laws, and yet had achieved a triumph, bear in mind finally that romantic art aims to interest by multiplicity of detail, by profusion and splendour, and to secure its end must sacrifice that simplicity and precision of form which distinguish and ennoble the great works of antiquity, and it will remain possible to admire and enjoy Spenser without violation of one's literary conscience.   It may be allowed that Phidias was wholly right without admitting that the builders of St. Marks or of Chartres were wholly wrong.   To confess that the art of Sophocles is beyond reproach is not to say that the art of Shakespeare is indefensible.

Epic in all ages and at all stages of culture reflects the life and manners, the tastes and pursuits of the ruling class.   *Beowulf* mirrors the aristocratic society of the pre-Christian English, Virgil is the poet of the imperial court of Augustus, Ariosto of the Renaissance circles of culture which met in ducal palaces. Spenser is equally a court poet.   He wrote for the learned and brilliant coterie that surrounded and worshipped Elizabeth. To the Queen the poem is dedicated, "*to live with the eternitie of her fame*."   She is at once Gloriana, the Queen of Fairyland, and —"*in some places else I do also shadow her*"—she is Belphoebe and Mercilla.   The poem itself was recommended to Elizabethan fashionable society in a series of sonnets, seventeen in number, to Essex, the Queen's favourite, to the Lord Chancellor, to Burleigh, High Treasurer, to Earls and Knights, and finally " *To all the gratious and beautifull ladies in the Court* "—

> " If all the world to seek I overwent,
> A fairer crew yet nowhere could I see
> Than that brave court doth to mine eye present,
> That the world's pride seems gathered there to be."

Sixteenth century England, fully conscious that she had taken her place among the great nations, that she might lack nothing of national splendour and dignity, required her epic.   Mindful that Virgil had turned from pastoral to sing his country's glory,

Spenser was ambitious to answer to the call of patriotism and to exalt his England. He makes his allegory, therefore, personal and historical, as well as general and spiritual—Elizabeth is the Fairy Queen, Mary Stuart, Duessa; Lord Leicester, Arthur; Lord Grey of Wilton, Governor of Ireland, delivers Ireland from the rebels, that is, Sir Artegal succours Irena oppressed by Grantorto; Charles, last of the Nevils, Earls of Westmoreland, famous for his many loves, is Paridel, " *the learned lover*," who " *many weak hearts had subdued*," who wrongs the jealous miser Malbecco by bearing off the faithless Hellenore; Percy, Earl of Northumberland, who was also one of the leaders in the Revolt of the North (1569), is Blandamour, Paridel's friend," " *of fickle mind, full of inconstancies*,"—a false pair of knights; Sir John Perrot, at that time a prisoner in the tower, is Sir Satyrane; Philip of Spain is the Soldan, who plots against Mercilla, a maiden queen, here Elizabeth, and by his " *Swearing and banning most blasphemously* " as he advances against Arthur— intervening as the grace of God—may be recognised as the ally of the excommunicating Pope; the Emperor, Charles V., monarch of Spain, Germany, and the Netherlands, is Geryon, " *of horrible aspect*," a three-bodied monster, who had " *the arms and legs of three to succour him in fight* "; Henry of Navarre is Burbon, " *blushing half for shame*," who throws away his shield of Protestantism, and thus his " *former praise hath blemished sore* "; Sidney, Spenser's friend, the mirror of courtesy, is Sir Calidore, and Pastorella—here the *Arcadia* is glanced at— Frances Walsingham, his wife. By these and a host of other references which comment upon contemporary history from the patriotic point of view, by topographical descriptions, such as those in praise of London, as Cleopolis, " *the fairest city that might be seen*," and of Oxford and Cambridge as " *the double nursery of Arts*," Spenser essays to make his poem English, and acceptable by the aristocratic England of his day. It was accepted the more delightedly that the themes were love and beauty, matter after the Renaissance heart. The taste of the age is seen in a book of the same year, Sidney's *Arcadia*, with its wealth of sentiment, its medley of scenes and persons, all fantastic. *The Faerie Queene* is a pageant such as Elizabeth and her courtiers loved,—philosophy embedded in roses, meanings in masquerades, music joined with painting to produce a delicious intoxication of all the senses. Bold in adventure, fierce in action, determined in policy, these men, when they took their ease, desired to sit at a continual feast, "*a sugred blisse*," where all forms and shapes of beauty promised an eternal spring, and Cupid played among the flowers.

Spenser is inconclusive. Nothing really happens in his poem, nothing is done. *The Faerie Queene* is like a labyrinthine flower, whose unfolding we can watch, or a liquid evening sky upon which, as we gaze, the magic rose appears, to glow and fade. If this be a national epic it celebrates no national undertaking or achievement. No foundation is laid of city or state, no *imperium* established, no Ilion besieged, no Jerusalem captured. It would seem as if we had here a poem typical of the inconclusiveness of all romance, beginning nowhere and leading nowhere; it would seem as if the poetry of romance must logically end in a preference for the dream to the act; must, like the youthful Keats when he cried,

"Hence, pageant history, hence, gilded cheat!"

look upon events as so far and no farther of interest or importance than as matter for the poet's vision. Then romance is parasitic and the antithesis of epic. For epic values the act, as drama values it, knowing that in the act, and not in the emotion which may accompany it, the prompting of the god appears, that act and feeling may not coincide, that the bravest man may, for example, feel fear, and disregarding it triumph the more, that human reluctance to undertake the great deed detracts nothing from its splendour when done. Dr. Johnson hated labour, but how far is the sympathy of the readers who know it estranged from the results of his labour? Romance contrasted with true epic is not only inconclusive then, it is hazardous. It may neglect the substance for the shadow, it may become a mere fitful play of emotions without justification in the pains and pleasures of living. It moves on the edge of emptiness. In respect of form it engages in a hazardous rivalry with classic art, for it tends to overlook "*that simplicity without which no human performance can arrive at any great perfection,*" and "*to derive more from the effect than it has put into the cause.*" Simplicity in design, in composition has no dangers, a hundred wait upon exuberance. The affinity of romance with colour rather than design—and Spenser is surely the greatest colourist among English poets—is hazardous also. "*Colour is the enemy of all noble art,*" said Domenico Neroni, and one sees his meaning. "*It is the enemy of all precise and perfect form, since where colour exists form can be seen only as juxtaposition of colour.*" [1] Spenser on his chosen path plainly skirted many and ever-present dangers. It would be idle to assert that he wholly escaped them. But the lovers of poetry, though they have their moods of estrangement, will return to watch him

> " moving through his clouded heaven
> With the moon's beauty and the moon's soft pace,"

and allow him to be *Castalidum decus sororum—the Muses' pride,* and, may we not add, *patriae,* his country's, also?

---

[1] Vernon Lee: *Renaissance Fancies and Studies,* p. 120.

CHAPTER IX

THE Elizabethan age might well have produced an epic on some great national subject. It was confidently looked for. Poets were numerous, not a few of whom belonged to "*the upper house of the Muses.*" If patriotism could have assisted it was not wanting, for at no period in our history was national pride more conscious or more fervid. "Look on England," exclaimed Massinger,

> " The Empress of the European isles:
> When did she flourish so, as when she was
> The mistress of the ocean, her navies
> Putting a girdle round about the world?
> When the Iberians quaked, her worthies named;
> And the fair flower de luce grew pale, set by
> The red rose and the white?" [1]

Long and spirited poems were written on patriotic subjects by men without any claim to be professional poets. Witness *The Most Honorable Tragedy of Sir Richard Grinvile, Knight,* by Gervase Markham, a voluminous writer on horsemanship and husbandry, which in about fifteen hundred lines celebrates the last fight of the *Revenge.* In art and fervour it proclaims the spirit of the age—

> " For till that fire shall all the world consume,
> Shall never name with Grinvil's name presume."

England—the idea was everywhere accepted—needed only the crowning glory of epic to claim entrance into the select society of the most famous nations, to plant " her roses on the Appenines,"

> " And to teach Rheyne, the Loire and Rhodanus,
> That they might all admire and honour us." [2]

Pride in the present begat pride in the national past. Holinshed's *Chronicles of England, Scotland, and Ireland* were published

[1] *The Maid of Honour.*
[2] Daniel: Dedication of *The Tragedy of Cleopatra.*

in 1577.   Interest in early history became intense and universal, as is proved, for example, by the successive editions of Drayton's *Heroical Epistles*.   Librarians like Cotton and Bodley went to work collecting Old English books.   Apologists for the English tongue arose, requiring that it should supersede Latin for all purposes.   "*Why not everything in English ?*" they demanded.   An army of translators busied themselves transferring to their native speech the riches of the world, that England might lack nothing of knowledge or culture.   Scholars, like Jonson, jealous for the perfection of their language, compiled grammars and prosodies.   Enthusiasm for the older English literature meets us everywhere in the occasional poems and epistles as well as in the more formal works of the time.

> " And I remember you much pleased were
> Of those who lived long ago to hear,
> As well as of those of these latter times
> Who have enriched our language with their rhymes." [1]

Meres in his *Palladis Tamia* rejoices to name English poets equal to those of antiquity: Daniel is England's Lucan, Sidney her Xenophon, Warner her Homer, Spenser her Theocritus, Drayton her Virgil, Shakespeare her Plautus.   So enamoured is he of the idea that he will even find parallels, when possible, with their ways of life or manner of death.   " As Archesilaus Prytanoeus perished by wine at a drunken feast, as Hermippus testifieth in Diogenes, so Robert Greene died by a surfeit taken of pickled herrings and Rhenish wine; as witnesseth Thomas Nash, who was at the fatal banquet."   " As the poet Lycophron was shot to death by a certain rival of his, so Christopher Marlowe was stabbed to death by a baudy serving-man, a rival of his, in his lewd love."

The history, the literature, the language, even the natural beauties of England were claimed to rival or surpass all others, by Drayton, for example, in his *Polyolbion*, and Browne in his *Pastorals*—

> " Hail, thou my native soil! thou blessed spot
> Whose equal all the world affordeth not.
> Show me who can so many crystal rills,
> Such sweet-cloth'd valleys or aspiring hills;

[1] Drayton's *Epistle to Reynolds*.

> Such wood-ground, pastures, quarries, wealthy mines;
> Such rocks in whom the diamond fairly shines;
> And if the earth can show the like again,
> Yet will she fail in her sea-ruling men.
> Time never can produce men to o'ertake
> The fames of Grenville, Davies, Gilbert, Drake,
> Or worthy Hawkins, or of thousands more
> That by their power made the Devonian shore
> Mock the proud Tagus; for whose richest spoil
> The boasting Spaniard left the Indian soil
> Bankrupt of store, knowing it would quit cost
> By winning this, though all the rest were lost." [1]

Nothing—to us who look back upon it—seems wanting in the mood or circumstances of the time. The men of the age themselves believed the stars most friendly. But the Muse had other intentions. Despite " the common wish, *That the Majesty of Handling our History might once equal the Majesty of the Argument*," [2] no national poem worthy of England's greatness appeared. Or rather, let us say, it appeared in a shape hitherto unknown to history. The true national epic is the chronicle play. In 1588, the Armada year, the year in which the young poets, Marlowe and Shakespeare, went up to London, the fever of patriotism burned fiercely. The city was afire. But while the readers of books might be numbered, the drama opened the only book for the million. An unlettered audience, in whom the love of country was eager and passionate, unaccustomed to the printed page, but with "*a tolerance for spoken words*" unknown to our impatient age, required its epic in a form unforeseen by the critics and unauthorised. At that moment to have turned away from so clamorous and ardent a company might well have argued a strange insensibility, a coldness of nature or a critical aloofness to which Marlowe and Shakespeare at least were certainly strangers. For the poet inspired by national enthusiasm, the doors of the theatre stood open, its summons proved irresistible. The drama offered the best medium for the story of England. "*How would it have joyed brave Talbot (the terror of the French)*," exclaims Nash, " *to think that after he had lain two hundred years in his tomb, he should triumph again on the stage, and have his bones new embalmed with the tears of ten thousand spectators at least (at several times), who*

[1] *Britannia's Pastorals*, Bk. II. Song 3.   [2] Bolton's *Hypercritica*.

in the tragedian that represents his person imagine they behold him fresh bleeding." [1]   There is a tradition that Shakespeare in a conversation with Ben Jonson, said that *"finding the nation generally very ignorant of history, he wrote plays in order to instruct the people in that particular."* [2]   But the idea was not Shakespeare's.   A generation earlier John Bale had written his *King Johan,* and its successors were many—such plays as *The True Tragedy of Richard III.,* and *The Contention of the Two Famous Houses of York and Lancaster.*   Marlowe too had attempted—with partial success only—to subdue the epic subject to the dramatic necessities of the day.   The required epic was written by Shakespeare, who, with far greater theatrical skill, relates upon the stage three hundred years of his country's history.[3]   He wrote, or had a share in ten historical plays, in which he treats the more important portions of seven reigns, from the thirteenth to the sixteenth century.   It is a majestic English chronicle from *Richard II.* to *Henry VIII.,*[4] a chronicle whose parts are brought into the indispensable unity in that they breathe throughout the sentiments and traditions of England.   One sees that the method is the reverse of epic. The epic method magnifies and glorifies its subject, withdraws its hero into the distance from the spectator, idealises and makes of him a demi-god, whereas the dramatist brings his kings and statesmen forward out of the past, and realises them as men among other men.   " Shakespeare's kings are not," as Pater wrote, " nor are meant to be great men: rather, little or quite ordinary humanity, thrust upon greatness, with those pathetic results, the natural self-pity of the weak heightened in them into irresistible appeal to others as the net result of their royal prerogative.   One after another they seem to lie composed in Shakespeare's embalming pages, with just that touch of nature

[1] Nash: *Pierce Pennilesse,* p. 89 (Huth Library).
[2] Halliwell: *Introduction to the First Part of the Contention.*
[3] If we include the older Chronicle plays by other authors, we may say that they covered four hundred years of English history, the twelfth to the sixteenth century.
[4] *King John* deals with an earlier epoch, and we may with Schlegel regard it as the Prologue, *Henry VIII.,* as the Epilogue to the others, eight in number.

about them, making the whole world akin, which has infused into their tombs at Westminster a rare poetic grace." [1]

It is unorthodox, in a sense of course not epic at all, yet for that age the best, in spirit national, in temper heroic, so full-blooded and vital that beside it the accepted poems on national themes appear but strengthless academic shades.   There is nothing in Spenser, nothing in Warner, " *Termed*," says Meres, " *of the best wits of both our universities, our English Homer*," nothing in Daniel or Drayton to match

> " This royal throne of kings, this sceptred isle,
> This earth of majesty, this seat of Mars,
> This other Eden, demi-paradise,
> This fortress built by Nature for herself
> Against infection and the hand of war,
> This happy breed of men, this little world,
> This precious stone set in the silver sea,
> Which serves it in the office of a wall
> Or as a moat defensive to a house,
> Against the envy of less happier lands,
> This blessed spot, this earth, this realm, this England,
> This nurse, this teeming womb of royal kings,
> Fear'd by their breed, and famous by their birth,
> Renowned for their deeds as far from home,
> For Christian service and true chivalry,
> As is the sepulchre in stubborn Jewry
> Of the world's ransom, blessed Mary's son."

The English " Histories " achieved all epic aims.   " Plays," said Heywood, " have made the ignorant more apprehensive, taught the unlearned the knowledge of many famous histories, instructed such as cannot read in the discovery of all our English chronicles; and what men have you now of that weak capacity that cannot discourse of any notable thing recorded even from William the Conqueror, nay from the landing of Brute until this day? " [2]

Apart from the dramatists the first Elizabethan to celebrate his country's glory in a long poem was William Warner, a lively lawyer, who, says Meres, " *in his absolute ' Albion's England,' hath most admirably penned the history of his own country from Noah to his time*."   Meres will have it that Warner resembles Euripides and equals Homer, but his ten thousand lines of verse in a seven-foot couplet known as " fourteeners " are now—by those who have read them—less confidently praised.   Too

[1] Pater: *Appreciations*.   [2] *Apology for Actors*, Bk. 3.

ballad-like the trot, too easy the indifference with which he
mingles things vulgar with things stately, too indelicate, shall
we say, the episodes, too undistinguished the language—for all
that Meres claims him as " *a refiner of the English tongue* "—to
sustain the severe contest in which time is usually victorious.
He never achieves the miracle—the fusion of history and poetry
—and his very cheerfulness is perhaps scarcely compatible with
epic dignity.   But duller writers have often been esteemed, and
to spend an evening with him is no hardship.   The rose of
Warner's garden is the famous reference to Fair Rosamond
struck by Queen Eleanor—

" With that she dasht her on the lippes, so dyêd double red,
   Hard was the heart that gave the blow, soft were those lips that bled."

Splendours like this, however, are not numerous in *Albion's
England*.   Here is a specimen of its more ordinary level—an
earlier pastoral invitation than the famous " *Come live with me
and be my love* "—

" Then chuse a shepherd, with the sun he doth his flock unfold,
   And all the day on hill or plaine his merrie chat can hold:
   And with the sun doth folde againe, then jogging home betime
   He turnes a crab or tunes a round, or sings some merrie ryme.
   Nor lackes he gleefull tales to tell, whilst round the bole doth trot;
   And sitteth singing care away, till he to bed hath got,
   There sleepes he soundly all the night, forgetting morrow cares,
   Nor feares he blasting of his corne nor uttering of his wares,
   Or stormes by sea, or stirres on land, or cracke of credite lost,
   Not spending franklier than his flocke shall still defray the cost.
   Wel wot I, sooth they say that say: more quiet nightes and daies
   The shepheard sleepes and wakes than he whose cattel he doth graize." [1]

A great subject—it is often forgotten—does not make, rather
it requires a great poet.   Warner's style, the style of the popular
romancer, excellently suited those portions of his narrative
where nobility was superfluous or elevation inappropriate.   He
is then most happy when at ease in the lighter passages, as, for
instance, when he describes a holiday in Hell—

" Sterne Minos and grimme Radimant descend their duskie roomes;
   The docke was also clear of ghosts, adjourn'd to after-doomes:
   The Furies and the deadly Sinnes, with their invective scroles,
   Depart the barre: the Feends rake up their ever-burning coles:

[1] *Albion's England*, Bk. IV., chap xx.   The story of Curan and Argentile
here told, the best admired and quoted in Warner's poem, became a popular
ballad and is given in Percy's *Reliques*.

The Elves and Fairies taking fists, did hop a merrie round:
And Cerberus had lap enough: and Charon leisure found:
The airy sprights, the walking flames, and goblins great and small,
Had theare good cheere, and company and sport, the Divell and all:
To Tantalus the shrinking flood, nor starting fruit were such:
Nor Titius his bowels did the hungrie vulture touch,
Upon his stone sat Cisaphus: Ixeon on his wheele,
The Belides upon their tubs, no wonted toile they feele
Till in this anticke festivall, these last recited five
Of dignities for dueties there, they earnestly did strive:
And then the quarrel grew so hot, that Hell was Hell againe,
And flocking ghosts did severally their fauctors parts maintaine." [1]

This poetry is without wings, and neither Daniel nor Drayton, who followed Warner, succeeded in imparting powers of flight to their historical verse, though Spenser had faith in Daniel—

" Then rouse thy feathers quickly, Daniel,
    And to what course thou please thyself advance."

" *This poet's well-merited epithet,*" observed Coleridge, " *is that of the ' well-languaged ' Daniel ; but likewise by the consent of his contemporaries no less than of all succeeding critics, the ' prosaic Daniel.' "* [2]

Opinions on a poet reveal more often the reader's requirements than the writer's qualities. " *I hate long poems,*" said Rossetti, which is in substance the judgment of Bagehot also—" *poetry should be memorable and emphatic, intense and soon over.*" Poe was of the same mind—" *I hold that a long poem does not exist. I maintain that the phrase, ' a long poem,' is simply a flat contradiction in terms.*" The wise will not approve these violences. The truth is that impatience of this kind, impatience of the ambitious failures, overlooks, virtually, indeed, would suppress, the higher forms of poetry altogether. If we are to allow only short poems, what of Homer and Virgil, Dante and Milton, *Qui Musas colunt severiores ?* " A long poem," as Keats very truly said, " is a test of invention." The grand style, which, in Arnold's words, " *arises in poetry when a noble nature, poetically gifted, treats with simplicity or severity a serious subject,*" [3] can only be perfectly exhibited in a long poem, a poem of epic intentions. For some, and not the worst class of readers, such a poem takes fuller possession of the mind, more powerfully enlists the imagination, and provides a larger

---

[1] *Albion's England,* chap. xviii.   [2] *Biographia Literaria.* chap. xviii.
[3] *On Translating Homer.*

body of reflective pleasure than any collection of exquisite songs by the best lyrist. The sublime may be attained, as Longinus observes, without passion. Is not the greater poetry, the drama or epic, to be preferred to the little poetry, " the ode and elegy and sonnet "? The lyric, no one will dispute it, sometimes achieves a triumphant perfection, the perfection of the gem—" *one entire and perfect chrysolite,*" and such perfection so excites and fires the mind as to disarm criticism. In the case of the ambitious poem of wider circuit, which deals with varied matter, which moves deliberately, so to say, at different levels, criticism is unavoidable. The poem itself seems to ask for it, one part judges another, *neque semper arcum Tendit Apollo.* Nevertheless the sustained, continuous style which elevates rather than excites, which in appropriate language sets forth some action large and spacious in itself, is not less rare, it is far rarer than the styles successful in brief lyric flights. Because it is rare, it is the more precious. The higher forms of art, deny it who will, tax the reader's powers, as tragedy taxes them, for instance, contrasted with melodrama, and the higher forms are, for this reason, less popular. But who will argue from the popular to the admirable? He only gains all points if the many understand and the few approve him. " A great performance on a small scale "—contradiction seems to lurk in the phrase itself. For rightly to estimate genius one must remember that not quality only betokens power, but quantity also. The names written highest are the names of copious poets, Homer and Shakespeare and Dante; the great ages, the age of Pericles, the age of Elizabeth, were profuse, abundant, affluent. Daniel, then, and Drayton—half-remembered, not wholly successful writers—had at least this in common with their times, they planned nobly; they had this, a touch of greatness, in common with the epic poets, they are not petty or cramped, they are large and generous in design. Daniel's very patriotism is Elizabethan. So rich and full that he calls for a state distinguished in letters as in war, as conspicuous in courtesy as in wealth, a state not less careful of its language than of its policy.

M

To understand Daniel, the dignity of the man, one must read his excellent and profound *Musophilus*, where, under the form of a debate, he espouses the cause nearest his affections against the arguments of Philocosmus. Why, he is asked, should he spend his days, as a poet and scholar, toiling to no end—

> " Now when this busy world cannot attend
> Th' untimely music of neglected lays?
> Other delights than these, other desires,
> This wiser profit-seeking age requires. . . .
>
> How many thousands never heard the name
> Of Sidney or of Spenser; or their books?
> And yet brave fellows, and presume of fame;
> And seem to bear down all the world with looks;
> What then shall they expect of meaner frame,
> On whose endeavours few or none scarce looks?
>
> The world's affairs require in managing
> More arts than those wherein you clerks proceed;
> Whilst tim'rous knowledge stands considering,
> Audacious Ignorance hath done the deed."

Who fights best against Time and Ignorance? replies Daniel. Not these " *great seeming-best of men*," opulent and successful, " *that have poor minds and little else to show*,"

> " And think (like Isis' ass) all honours are
> Giv'n unto them alone; the which are done
> Unto the painted idol, which they bear,
> That only makes them to be gazed on.
> For take away their pack, and show them bare,
> And see what beast this honour rides upon."

" *Who then holds up the glory of the state* " if not the poets, the scholars, the historians? And as for himself and his poetic labours, if one appreciative reader be found, he will be a theatre large enough.

> " But what if none? It cannot yet undo
> The love I bear unto this holy skill.
> This is the thing that I was born to do:
> This is my scene, this part must I fulfil."

And with a burst of prophetic patriotism he foresees world-wide recognition of his country's poetry—

> " who (in time) knows whither we may vent
> The treasure of our tongue?   To what strange shores
> This gain of our best glory shall be sent,
> T'enrich unknowing nations with our stores?
> What worlds in th' yet unformed occident,
> May come refined with th' accents that are ours? "

To say, when one has read *Musophilus*, that Daniel mistook his vocation would be to say too much.   Yet his epic, *The History of the Civil Wars* (1595), a poem of seven thousand lines in eight books, was dead before it was published.   It fails on many counts.   The subject is ill chosen, the affairs of a divided rather than a united people.   Though Lucan made a poem on the rivalry of Caesar and Pompey, civil war is not a happy theme. The story too is told for the sake of its lesson—a cardinal error. Daniel's poem pursues truth with anxious accuracy, with careful impartiality, but the cargo is too heavy for the ship.   " *Truth narrative and past, the idol of the historian,*" is, as Davenant said, " *a dead thing,*" " *truth operative, and by its effects continually alive, is the mistress of poets.*"   " What! all this verse? body o' me," exclaims Justice Clement in *Every Man in his Humour,* " he carries a whole realm, a commonwealth of paper." " A poet!   I will challenge him myself presently at extempore." In his conversation Jonson expressed the same disdain—" *An honest man but no poet* " ; " *He wrote Civil Wars and yet had not one battle in all his book.*"   " *Too much historian in verse,*" " *his manner better suited prose,*" commented Drayton.[1]   These are stiff sayings.   But in spite of them we are not dealing with an inconsiderable author.   A distinguished, a learned, a brilliantly accomplished man his contemporaries, and we too, admit him to have been.   No one who has read Daniel doubts that he can write, and with grace, with force and eloquence.   He can write but he cannot imagine.   With all his poetic zeal, with all his ambition, with all his learning, he fails in the quality for which his age was conspicuous—imagination.   His measured, self-controlled, deliberate style recalls the early eighteenth not the early seventeenth century, it recalls " *the age of prose and reason.*"   For an Elizabethan Daniel distilled little honey.   He has sweet things, witness the exquisite

---

[1] *Epistle to Reynolds.*

> " Care-charmer sleep, son of the sable Night,"

or

> " Let others sing of knights and palladines,"

from the *Sonnets to Delia,* nor can Shakespeare's indebtedness here be overlooked. Daniel was his master in this form. But Sylvester's praise is such as Dryden or Pope rather than Marlowe or Spenser would have coveted—

> " Daniel, sharp-conceited, brief,
> Civil, sententious, for pure accents chief."

An exponent, one of the founders in truth of the classical style in English, a forerunner of the Augustans, a correct poet before Pope, we may justly call him. Of the far-famed eighteenth century " correctness " he gives perhaps the earliest example, desiring, as he tells us in his admirable *Defense of Rhyme,* not " *to mix uncertainly feminine rhymes with masculine,*" to avoid affectation " *in disguising or forging strange or unusual words, . . . displacing our words, or inventing new, openly upon a singularity ; when our own accustomed phrase, set in the due place, would express us more familiarly and to better delight than all this idle affectation of antiquity or novelty can ever do.*" But this very zeal for a disciplined poesy, though it bore its own fruit, making of Daniel, as Coleridge said, a poet whose diction " *bears no mark of time* " and " *more intelligible to us than the transitory fashions of our own particular age,*" worked against rather than for his reputation, since his own age preferred, and his country prefers, as M. Brunetière has told us, the individualistic and eccentric style rich in personal qualities, has even indeed come to regard that poetry as unworthy the name in which it finds

> " No shrine, no grove, no oracle, no heat
> Of pale-mouthed prophet dreaming."

Daniel, in many ways admirably equipped for the contest, failed to secure the epic garland. Others among his contemporaries, in whom the age had even greater faith, failed also. Among them Drayton, born one year after Daniel, and certainly a remarkable, hardly, if anything, short of a great man.

There are few things more arresting in Elizabethan literature than its unceasing occupation with the thought of man's forlorn battle against time and " *the misery of dark forgetfulness*." Some of the finest of Shakespeare's sonnets are wholly governed by it, it recurs with sad persistence in the work of the dramatists, the poets, almost to a man, are tormented by the vision of inevitable decay—

> " Angry with time that nothing should remain
> Our greatest wonder's wonder to express."

The victory of oblivion over the fairest human things, physical beauty, great deeds, the glories of art, the laboured verse of the poets, seems to have haunted the minds of that age with curious and pathetic urgency. And as Caius Cestius planned the pyramid, which stands near the modern Protestant cemetery in Rome, as " *a refuge for his memory*," Drayton, like Daniel, had a mind to secure what he could of remembrance for himself and his country's history, the " *transient immortality* " that alone was possible. He secured it in his *Ballad of Agincourt*—

> " Fair stood the wind for France—"

true ringing metal from the first line to the last, the best memorial in the English tongue of the French wars and the battle—

> " When from a meadow by,
> Like a storm suddenly
> The English archery
> Struck the French horses."

But in the longer flights, for all his power and vigorous patriotism, the verse too often flags, in the *Battle of Agincourt*, for example, a poem of about two thousand lines, whose hero is the same " *Henry the fifth, that man made out of fire*." If anything but absolute and unwearying excellence were tolerable in poetry, none who have read could withhold from Drayton's historical works the epithet " successful." But if we think of them alone we cannot measure him aright, nor understand the praise of his contemporaries. They admired without reservation since they knew the man—" *a pious poet*," says Fuller, " *his conscience having always the command of his fancy, very*

temperate in his life, slow of speech, and inoffensive in company"
—and knew the breadth and variety of his talent, the finished
talent displayed, for instance, in *Idea, the Shepherd's Garland*,
when he followed Spenser, and in his sonnets, also named *Idea*,
of which the famous sixty-first—

> " Since there's no help, come let us kiss and part—"

moved Rossetti to the judgment " *almost the best in the language,
if not quite.*"   Bearing in mind that Drayton had a light as well
as a serious vein, that he could write the *Nymphidia* as well as
the *Polyolbion*, we may understand though we may not agree
with Fitzgeoffrey, who in his *Drake* styled him " *the golden-
mouthed poet, for the purity and preciousness of his phrase,*" or
Tofte, the translator of Ariosto, who in a burst of eloquence
speaks of him as " *not unworthily bearing the name of the chief
archangel* [Michael] *singing after his soul-ravishing manner.*"
Ben Jonson, though his *Conversations with Drummond* display
scant cordiality towards Drayton, wrote verses in his praise
which surprise, however, as much by their unwonted generosity
as their irresponsible exaggeration.   After a reference to the
pastorals, which, said he—

> " made me think thee old Theocritus,
> Or rural Virgil come to pipe to us,"

he continues, in a vein considerably inflated, but perhaps worth
quotation as an example of Elizabethan panegyric—

> " But then, thy Epistolar Heroic songs,
> Their loves, their quarrels, jealousies, and wrongs,
> Did all so strike me, as I cry'd, ' Who can
> With us be called the Naso, but this man!'
> And looking up I saw Minerva's fowl
> Perch'd overhead, the wise Athenian owl:
> I thought thee then our Orpheus, that wouldst try
> Like him, to make the air one volaray:
> And I had styled thee Orpheus, but before
> My lips could form the voice, I heard that roar,
> And rouse, the marching of a mighty force,
> Drums against drums, the neighing of the horse,
> The fights, the cries, and wond'ring at the jars,
> I saw, and read, it was thy Barons Wars! "

Not content with this, Jonson, later speaking of the *Polyolbnio*,
exclaims, " *There, thou art Homer !* " and declares that in

reading the " *Miseries of Margaret the Queen* " his tears " *o'er-flowed and stopt his sight.*" Unhappily we cannot with an easy mind, accept Jonson's laboured estimate. *The Barons' Wars,* a remodelled version of the earlier *Mortimeriados,* may be, as the author called it, " *fit matter for trumpet or tragedy,*" but what of the design? Does it surmount, clear and defined, all the accessories? Are the parts subordinated to the whole? With Drayton the design is not the first, nor perhaps the second thing. As one reads the conviction grows that though his theme be historical, there stands by his side the Muse of romance, not of epic poetry. We know it because the narrative halts while the poet philosophises, or lingers over his love scenes, or adds phrase to phrase, colour to colour, for the enrichment of his pictorial passages. Here, for example, is his account of Richard the Second's life while a prisoner in " *a melancholic room* "—strengthened with " *many an iron bar* "—

> " The ominous raven often he doth hear,
> Whose croaking him of following horrour tells,
> Begetting strange imaginary fear,
> With heavy echoes, like to passing-bells:
> The howling dog a doleful part doth bear,
> As though they chim'd his last sad burying knells
>   Under his cave the buzzing screech-owl sings
>   Beating the windows with her fatal wings.
>
> By night affrighted in his fearful dreams,
> Of raging fiends and goblins that he meets;
> Of falling down from steep rocks into streams;
> Of deaths, of burials, and of winding sheets,
> Of wandering hopeless in far foreign realms;
> Of strong temptations by seducing sprites;
>   Wherewith awak'd, and calling out for aid,
>   His hollow voice doth make himself afraid.'

The Queen's chamber in the *Tower of Mortimer* is adorned, after the fashion of Spenser, with pictures speaking the painter's curious skill, as here—

> " Swift Mercury, like to a shepherd's boy,
> Sporting with Hebe by a fountain brim,
> With many a sweet glance, many an am'rous toy,
> He sprinkling drops at her, and she at him;
> Wherein the painter so explain'd their joy,
> As though his skill the perfect life could limn,
>   Upon whose brows the water hung so clear,
>   As through the drops the fair skin might appear.'

This manner of deliciousness is of course pure Renaissance, the glowing beauty-bloom of Titian, only a few years dead when Drayton wrote. Here again is a meeting between the Queen and her lover—

> " The night wax'd old (not dreaming of these things)
> And to her chamber is the queen withdrawn,
> To whom a choice musician plays and sings,
> Whilst she sat under an estate of lawn,
> In night attire more god-like glittering,
> Than any eye had seen the cheerful dawn,
>   Leaning upon her most-loved Mortimer,
>   Whose voice, more than the music, pleased her ear. . . .
>
> She laid her fingers on his manly cheek,
> The gods' pure sceptres and the darts of Love,
> That with their touch might make a tiger meek,
> Or might great Atlas from his seat remove;
> So white, so soft, so delicate, so sleek,
> As she had worn a lilly for a glove;
>   As might beget life where was never none,
>   And put a spirit into the hardest stone."

The same musical, the same poetic and pathetic charm often appears in the *Heroical Epistles*, of which title he remarks, " tho' heroical be properly understood of demi-gods, as of Hercules and Aeneas, whose parents were said to be, the one celestial, the other mortal; yet it is also transferred to them, who for the greatness of mind come near to gods." These were imaginary letters to and from historical persons, the best known of which are, perhaps, those between Henry II. and Rosamond of the labyrinthine bower. In his own day the most popular of Drayton's compositions, the *Heroical Epistles* are now no better remembered than *The Barons' Wars*. Monotonous and yet never wholly without interest, like the sea, the voyager has frequent sight between port and port of quiet islands from which he parts with lingering gaze, as here in the letter which the Lady Geraldine writes to Henry Howard, Earl of Surrey—

> " O! in a map that I might see thee show
> The place where now in danger thou dost go!
> Whilst we discourse, to travel with our eye
> Romania, Tuscan, and fair Lombardy;
> Or with thy pen exactly to set down
> The model of that temple, or that town;
> And to relate at large where thou hast been,
> As there, and there, and what thou there hast seen;

> Expressing in a figure, by thy hand
> How Naples lies, how Florence fair doth stand;
> Or as the Grecian's finger dipp'd in wine,
> Drawing a river in a little line,
> And with a drop a gulf to figure out,
> To model Venice moated round about;
> Then adding more to counterfeit a sea,
> And draw the front of stately Genoa."

The praise of rusty poems is thankless work. And yet if one enters in an unpossessed and unhasting mood upon Drayton's longer pieces one cannot overlook the sudden elevations, the flashes of the " grand style," by which the greater Elizabethans are known. Meres was not a peculiarly discriminating critic, but he often went astray more wildly than when he spoke of Drayton as one " *by whom the English tongue is mightily enriched.*"

To extend the term " epic " to the " *strange Herculean toil* " of the *Polyolbion* [1] might fairly be declared the final stroke, the *coup de grâce* which deprives it of all meaning. If " *a versified gazetteer*," even though a work of genius, be epic, there is an end to sense in literary criticism. One may, however, call it an heroic poem, not so much in respect of its theme as in respect of its author's valiance. Lowell speaks of Drayton's as " *the period of the saurians in English literature, interminable poems,*" and the author himself, even in that age, seems to have felt some apology necessary for his undismayed undertaking. A touch of defiance well became so doughty an adventurer, and anticipating attack, he strikes the first blow. " *This lunatic age,*" this " *idle humorous world,*" will probably extend no welcome to him, such persons " *as had rather read the fantasies of foreign inventions, than see the rarities and history of their own country delivered by a true native muse.*" But these shall not make him afraid—

> " And ere seven books have end, I'll strike so high a string,
> Thy bards shall stand amaz'd with wonder whilst I sing."

The *Polyolbion*, that is " *The Greatly Blest,*" a punning allusion to Albion, owed much to Camden's *Britannia*, but it is un-

[1] *Polyolbion*, or a chorographicall description of tracts, rivers, mountains, forests, and other parts of this renowned isle of Great Britaine, with intermixture of the most remarquable stories, antiquities, wonders, rarityes, pleasures, and commodities of the same, digested in a poem by Michael Drayton, Esq., London, 1613.

exampled. Probably no such attempt to " poetise " wholly recalcitrant material, if ever made, has met with like success. For the verdict cannot be " *magnificent but unreadable*." The poem can be read and read with pleasure. There is somehow life in it. It is easy to say of such a work that it exhibits presumption in a higher degree than genius, but once afloat on these long rolling lines, no good reader—I do not say will ever nod—will ever lose sympathy with the poet, will ever feel resentment or disgust. Fauna and flora, hill and stream, city and hamlet, forest and fen, sport and labour, trade and war, fact and fiction, a hundred thousand topics occupy him as he marches bravely in thirty " songs " through England and Wales, county by county, from north to south and east to west. If the *Polyolbion* be a failure, and of course in a sense it was doomed from its inception, there is no English poem among failures which so extorts our admiration for its author. It is a failure which excites no ridicule, for had Drayton written nothing else only a surly critic would deny to him the title " illustrious."

Though to such a long and various poem no justice can be done by extracts, one or two may be given from which its general character in the movement of the verse can partially be seen. Drayton is doubtless at his best when he versifies his country's favourite legends, like that of Guy of Warwick, the " *English Hercules*," in Song XIII., which contains also the spirited account of a stag hunt; and some of his descriptions like that of Cotswold (Song XIV.) or London (Song XVI.) are charming in themselves. Here is a passage from " the marriage of the Thames and Isis," which exhibits the personification of which he makes constant and skilful use—

> " Ye daughters of the hills, come down from every side
> And due attendance give upon the lovely bride:
> Go, strew the paths with flowers, by which she is to pass.
> For be ye thus assur'd, in Albion never was
> A beauty (yet) like hers: where have you ever seen
> So absolute a nymph in all things, for a queen?
> Give instantly in charge, the day be wondrous fair,
> That no disordered blast attempt her braided hair.
> Go, see her state prepar'd, and everything befit,
> The bride chamber adorn'd with all beseeming it.
> And for the princely groom, who ever yet could name
> A flood that is so fit for Isis as the Thame?

> Ye both so lovely are, that knowledge scarce can tell,
> For feature whether he, or beauty she excel;
> That ravished with joy each other to behold
> When as your crystal waists you closely do enfold,
> Betwixt your beauteous selves you shall beget a son,
> That when your lives shall end, in him shall be begun.
> The pleasant Surryan shores shall in that flood delight,
> And Kent esteem herself most happy in his sight." [1]

Industrious and patriotic undertakings like those of Daniel and Drayton have a claim upon us even when unsuccessful in the accepted sense. They do more than display the greatness of the age and the men it bred. They assist us in measuring, as minor elevations among mountains enable us to estimate the giants, how far beyond the reach of common minds are the achievements of the world poets, how high rise the peaks beside which the poems of such men, great even in a great age, are inconsiderable, how rare are the gifts equal to the performance of tasks of the first poetic magnitude. So spacious is the work of these writers, so full of fine strokes, that one is in difficulty to explain their lack of a more complete success. Where in poetry of our own day are we to look for the spaciousness which they have almost at command, as here, for example?—

> " A world of mighty kings and princes I could name
> From our god Neptune sprung; let this suffice, his fame
> Incompasseth the world; these stars which never rise,
> Above the lower south, are never from his eyes;
> As those again to him do every day appear,
> Continually that keep the northern hemisphere;
> Who like a mighty king doth cast his watched robe,
> Far wider than the land, quite round about the globe.
> Where is there one to him that may compared be,
> That both the poles at once continually doth see;
> And giant-like with Heaven as often maketh wars;
> The islands in his power as numberless as stars,
> He washeth at his will, and with his mighty hands
> He makes the even shores oft mountainous with sands:
> Whose creatures which observe his wide imperial seat,
> Like his immeasur'd self, are infinite and great." [2]

To explain to ourselves the success of some, the failure of others in poetry, we may call to our assistance the enigmatic word " style." Style is the loadstone, the author's secret of attention. But what style? Daniel at his best has style, Drayton also. Yes, but only at their best. They attract, but

---

[1] *Polyolbion*, Song xv.   [2] *Polyolbion*, Song xx.

as often fail to attract; they are discontinuous. They forget how short must be the intervals which separate the passages where style is in evidence. The absence of vivid words, the intrusion of the insipid or lifeless provoke inattention. The successful style then must be sustained, unwearying, like the heavens divinely upheld. Again, it must be clear, yet not too clear. The style of Pope on the one hand, admirable as it is, yields up all it contains of meaning too readily, that of Donne, on the other, too much of a puzzle, wearies attention in the pursuit. The perfect style at once allures and conceals, allures by its ease and clarity, but leaves room and provides food for further thought. It is neither forbiddingly difficult nor smoothly exhaustive. The poet who would please all readers at all times must do them a mental service, but enlist their own efforts, he must make the path to meaning easy, but withhold its complete and final exposition. " Poetry gives more pleasure when only generally and not perfectly understood," said Coleridge. " An imaginative book," says Emerson, " renders us much more service at first, by stimulating us through its tropes, than afterward, when we arrive at the precise sense of the author." It is for this reason that figures, or images, transport us. They are a sudden light in darkness.

> " I shall keep your honour safe;
> With mine I trust you, as the sculptor trusts
> Yon marble woman with the marble rose
> Loose on her hand, she never will let fall." [1]

For it is their nature to illuminate, and at the same moment to increase the mind's activity, so as to be not only bright in themselves, but, as it were, the parents of further brightness.

[1] Browning, *Colombe's Birthday*.

CHAPTER X

" *I should not think of devoting less than twenty years to an epic poem,*" said Coleridge. " *Ten years to collect materials and warm my mind with universal science . . . the next five in the composition of the poem, and the five last in the correction of it. So would I write—haply not unhearing of that divine and nightly whispering voice which speaks to mighty minds of predestinated garlands, starry and unwithering.*" Such was Coleridge's estimate, the estimate of a poet and critic, of a man, we may allow, qualified to judge, who knew, perhaps none better, the magnitude of this mountain labour. Poetry came easily to him if to any man, one would think, yet the conquest of such a peak was, he knew, no holiday excursion, nor even for genius an easy victory. Turn to Milton, who accomplished what was for Coleridge only a spacious dream. How similar is the estimate. To the " *inward prompting* " must be added, he held, " *industrious and select reading, steady observation, insight into all seemly and generous acts and affairs.*" Having calculated the cost, he paid the price, not sparing himself, in a life-long discipline, devoted, in the words of Keats, " *rather to the ardours than the pleasures of song.*" No such deliberate and prolonged preparation as Milton's for a great poem appears to be anywhere recorded in history, a preparation which amazes as much perhaps by its confidence and determination as by its extent. Educated for literature by the " *ceaseless diligence and care* " of his father, encouraged by his masters—surely not unworthy of praise, these men—who found that the style of his earliest compositions " *by certain vital signs it had was likely to live,*" his thoughts when a lad at Cambridge were already with the subjects to which the " *deep transported mind* " was yet to soar. At Horton, where his

189

studies were protracted far beyond the usual limits, though already a scholar, "*I in the most perfect leisure had my time entirely free for going through the Greek and Latin writers.*" He was "*pluming his wings for a flight.*" When he returned from his travels abroad he was still without any profession save that of poet, still supported by the conviction that "*by labour and intense study (which I take to be my portion in this life), joined with the strong propensity of nature, I might perhaps leave something so written to after times as they should not willingly let it die.*" In this confidence he thought it not "*shame to covenant with any knowing reader that for some years yet I may go on trust with him toward the payment of what I am now indebted.*" The few years passed, almost a generation, indeed, before the debt was paid. Other and less congenial tasks, in which he had, as it were, the use but of his "*left hand,*" prose works upon a multitude of controversial subjects, occupied him, he steered through "*a troubled sea of noises and harsh disputes.*" But the unwavering resolution held, and in 1667, when the poet had almost reached his sixtieth year, *Paradise Lost* was at length finished—"*A yet unwasted pyramid of fame.*" Genius one perceives in this man of course, one perceives also, what is less common in poets, a will of iron.

Nothing in speculative matters appears more certain than that genius may be fortunate or unfortunate in its hour of birth. M. Taine, indeed, in a theory, much talked of a generation ago—the theory of *race, surroundings, epoch*—made genius, talent, almost superfluous in the description of a work of art, so much in the work, it seemed, might be withdrawn from individual endowment and otherwise accounted for. M. Taine's theory, in the opinion of some of us, attractive and brilliant as it was, hardly surprised the last secrets of art or poetry, but its value apart, one must, at least, acknowledge that like other men the child of his time, the poet or artist meets day by day forces friendly or unfriendly to his peculiar gifts and temperament. Lay aside influences from family, home, education, and the traditions, the doings, the manners, the conventions of that larger family his race, that larger home, his country, may well be for him or against him. Still, even with a knowledge of his peculiar talents, were it possible it would be an embarrassing charge to choose the hour of a poet's birth. And the more modest undertaking of criticism like M. Taine's, the attempt to calculate the effect upon genius of circumstances already given and known, must remain in the highest degree puzzling, perhaps in the end impossible. Hard in one's own case to determine the effect of spiritual, moral, or intellectual forces, how much harder in the case of that incalculable activity, genius, to disengage the power of the man from the power of the moment, to distinguish the poet's part in his work from the part which belongs to his race or times. To say with confidence, for example, that here Milton was helped or hindered, there assisted by fortune or defeated, demands some little critical courage. To be born twenty years after the defeat of the Armada, and eight years before the death of Shakespeare—was the hour, one might ask, a favourable one for the coming of a great poet? It meant, surely, that he would have a share in the imaginative freedom, the immense vitality, of the great age, be touched, at least in youth, by its after-glow. Yes, but the heavens were charged with doubtful omens. Dissension more bitter than England had ever known rent the social fabric from top to bottom, and for twenty years the poet breathed the hot and angry air of furious debate. At first sight not much seems favourable here. A country distracted by civil war appears hardly the best ground for the poet, more particularly if his interests be deeply engaged in the struggle. *Inter arma silent Musae.* Yet probably as an epic poet Milton gained even from this experience. Through his middle life, though he wrote little or no poetry, he lived amid historic scenes and historic persons, he was associated with great men and great events. Around him the tides of war ebbed and flowed, armies marched to victory and defeat, soldiers and statesmen came and went in the hours of military and political crisis. On one side the king held his court in the armed camp, on the other the parliament its councils, all England rang with news of battle and sieges. To live through such times was an education for an epic poet.

Milton not only lived through them, he stood at the centre, he was a part of all he saw and heard. For thirty years a student of books, for twenty a student of men and affairs during a supreme national conflict, can we parallel this equipment for heroic poetry before or since his generation? Nor is this all. He was a man of the Renaissance and a man of the Reformation, powerful agents in the spiritual evolution of his age. " *The artist is then most powerful,*" it has been said,[1] " *when he finds himself in accord with the age he lives in. The plenitude of art is only reached when it marches with the sentiments which possess a community.*" One freely assumes, perhaps too freely, that everywhere the Renaissance was friendly to art, everywhere the Reformation its enemy. Yet it is not apparent that placed, as it were, between these contending forces Milton felt any embarrassment. As a man of the Renaissance one easily believes him fortunate, inspired by its love of learning, its worship of beauty, its awakened passion for the past. Remembering that Puritanism regarded life as a dangerous pilgrimage, was hostile to all forms of sensuous pleasure, viewed with suspicion poetry itself, can we think him equally fortunate as a man of the Reformation? For the Puritan thought of the world not as a Paradise in which to enjoy God, but as a place of tribulation and temptation from which God was the only refuge. In his worship, therefore, he desired an inward spiritual communion freed from contact with the things of sense. Where the Catholic temper found support in symbolism, in rich ecclesiastical architecture, vestments, ritual, a dramatic service, and claimed that through these the spirit was uplifted and borne heavenward, the Puritan felt them as barriers, as veils or curtains, to be torn down before spirit could enter into close converse with spirit. Insolence in the finite creature, some would call this temper, a temper essentially irreligious. Yet it has given birth to holiness. Religion may, has indeed lived, but the arts never in this rarefied spiritual atmosphere. They make their appeal directly by way of the senses, they are dependent on rhythms and colour and form. The image perceived, the music felt—these are indispensable,

[1] Mark Pattison's *Milton.*

and the invisible world of spirit can be shadowed forth only in a sensuous garment. Poetry and painting and sculpture, " *three powers in man*," as Blake called them, " *of conversing with Paradise*," became in the mediæval world the handmaidens of religion, they served in the sanctuary. But the Reformation viewed them as hindrances, as idolatrous attempts to substitute for inward holiness and penitent prostration of the soul before God, the pomp and glory of men's hands. Clearly the Puritan suffered from disabilities, but as clearly he gained heights of seriousness. Baxter dates one of his epistles, " *London, at the door of Eternity*." Such a mood, even if it be disinclined to dip its pencil in the hues of the rainbow, often rivals in imaginative passion the inspiration derived by secular poets from love or patriotism or heroic enterprise.

Yet had Milton been a typical Puritan he must have suffered as a poet. That he was not such a Puritan, that his religion was the religion of John Milton,[1] is plain beyond debate.[2] The other churches were heretical, he excommunicated in turn the Anglicans, the Presbyterians, the Independents. If we can think of him as a Puritan at all—he was of " *no church*," says Johnson—it would appear that he escaped the cramping influences of the current theology while he drew from the reformed creed its passionate intensity of spirit. What was akin to his own nature he took, the rest he put aside with perfect unconcern. And Milton's first choice fell not upon a Biblical but upon a romantic theme—the deeds of Arthur, and there is little reason to believe that religious feeling dictated the final selection of *Paradise Lost*. Again if his subject was Christian, his models were certainly Pagan. However he may have been affected by Puritan theology, he suffered no imprisonment in the sombre dungeon of an aggravated and cheerless piety. A friend of Puritanism, we may call him, but a greater friend of beauty—" *Not with so much labour, as the*

---

[1] " John Milton is not only the highest, but the completest type of Puritanism " (Green, *Short History of the English People*), a statement only credible if we regard Milton as its sole representative.

[2] For example Milton never admitted the Puritan contention concerning the drama, and took pains to defend it. See his remarks on *Tragedy* prefixed to *Samson Agonistes*.

N

*fables have it, is Ceres said to have sought her daughter, Proserpine,
as I am wont day and night to seek for this idea of the beautiful
through all the forms and faces of things."*

On the whole Milton seems to be in his place in
the gap between Shakespeare and Dryden. Either he was
fortunate or there is another explanation. In any age or
country he would have attained to eminence. Talent needs
support, the good soil, the benign season, but genius sometimes arises which can root itself among rocks and draw
nourishment from any air. As a poet Milton was not easily
satisfied. The anxious care with which he prepared for his epic
undertaking was matched by equal care in his choice of subject.
The proof exists in a list of about one hundred themes, many
of them Scriptural, the rest from British history, written out
in his own hand about 1641. He desired, there is evidence, to
write for his countrymen,[1] but to write for them not a mere
story, rather to base his poem upon actual history. Three
considerations, we may assume, determined the final choice.
The Fall of Man was a subject of universal interest; it was, or
Milton believed it to be, an historical fact; and it offered a
larger field for the exercise of the speculative imagination, scope
for a vaster fabric of idealism than any other which suggested
itself, or indeed existed. Perhaps the very magnitude of the
scheme attracted him, the absence of limitations, the immense
abstractions, the scenes withdrawn from geographical space,
to include Heaven and Hell as well as Earth, and the middle
region of the abyss of stars,

" The stars terrific even to the gods."

That Milton rejected the dramatic form, first contemplated,
for the epic enhances our admiration for his judgment, that he
abandoned too the idea of a poem on Arthur. In the field of

---

[1] " *Native strains do I say ? Yea, one man cannot hope to accomplish all
things. It will be sufficient reward and honour for me, even if I remain for
ever inglorious among the other nations of the world, if only blond-haired Ouse
shall read me, and he who drinks of Alan Water, and the whirling Humber,
and the woods of Trent : above all, if my Thames shall sing my songs, and
Tamar mineral-stained, and the far-off wave-beaten Orkneys.*"—Moody's
Translation of *Epitaphium Damonis.*

romance the austerity of his nature might have become too apparent, nor can we believe that the human sympathies were strong in him. He was no realist, no student of the details of life. He chose and chose wisely a theme not far removed from the centre of his own thought and natural to his powers. It was doubtless a happiness, as Cowper said, that he fell upon such a subject, but a happiness it would not have been to a genius inferior to Milton's. Beside it most others appear easy— Virgil's, Ariosto's, Spenser's. Consider the difficulties and dangers. The *dramatis personæ*, God the Creator, God the Son, archangels and angels, Sin and Death, the first man, Adam, the first woman, Eve; *the background*, eternity; *the scene*, Heaven or Hell, elemental chaos or the new-formed earth; *the action*, battles and debates of beings wholly supernatural. How treat these things adequately, even tolerably? Things hard to conceive, harder still to describe, how sustain without instant contempt, how conduct without outrage this hardly imaginable, hardly approachable argument? " *The plan of ' Paradise Lost '* *has this inconvenience*," said Johnson—how eloquent is the word " *inconvenience* "—" *that it comprises neither human actions nor human manners. The man and woman who act and suffer are in a state which no other man and woman can ever know. The reader finds no transaction in which he can be engaged, beholds no condition in which he can by any effort of imagination place him- self : he has therefore little natural curiosity and sympathy*." On the very threshold of his undertaking Milton encountered serious problems, whether, for example, to adopt the Ptolemaic system of astronomy or the Copernican? The Ptolemaic regarded the earth as the fixed centre of the universe of stars and planets which revolved around it. The Copernican made our world one of a number of planets revolving round one great star, the sun. The latter system had the great advantage of truth and the approval of learned readers. But the former was still the popular belief. " The two systems of astronomy, from 1650 onwards," it has been said, " were still struggling with each other for the possession of even the most educated intellects in England," and though Milton was himself convinced of the truth of the discovery of Copernicus, it was not then generally accepted, and was much less convenient for his purposes.[1]

If there were difficulties in the proposed epic plan, however, there were for Milton also compensations. So comprehensive a scheme gave its author scope, magnificent if threatening—

> " Jehovah with His thunder, in the choir
> Of shouting angels, and the empyreal thrones "—

he passed them " unalarmed." *Paradise Lost* is an exposition of Milton's science, his religion, his philosophy, the epitome of his thought on almost every subject which can exercise the mind. " *Everything that is truly great and astonishing,*" said Addison, " *has its place in it. The whole system of the intellectual world, the chaos and the creation, heaven, earth, and hell, enter into the constitution of the poem.*" The literary suggestions and allusions alone, what great poems of the past, what legends and histories do they overlook? *Paradise Lost* is charged with references to the Bible, to the Greek mythology, to Homer, to Plato, to Euripides, to Virgil, to Dante, to Ariosto, to Spenser. Except the *Faerie Queene* there is no English poem with such wealth of literary and historic recollections. If it contained indeed no story of commanding interest, if the narrative were flat and insipid, these memories of the past, so dexterously interwoven into the narrative, would for many readers be a sufficient delight. It has been called the most artificial poem in the language. Doubtless it is the most artificial, it owes everything to books, it is the result not of the study of nature, nor a knowledge of human nature, it is the result of reading. But the fact increases rather than diminishes our wonder. With no other assistance than that of a library to project this stupendous world, to hang it in the heavens, to give us a sense of its reality can hardly rank below any other effort of the human imagination. If not believed with deliberation, at least the poet so presented his narrative as somehow to penetrate and colour the national

[1] In the end he compromised and so framed his plan that though to the imagination the action is conducted in a Ptolemaic universe, the exposition of the cosmic system in Book viii. is in accordance with the Copernican doctrine. Against the too inquiring reader the poet further protected himself by the rhetorical vagueness of his account.

mind, to make it as much a part of Christian tradition as the
Scripture history itself.

Paradise Lost opens with the statement of its subject and
scope.   " Hearken to the way," says De Quincey of this
opening passage, " in which a roll of dactyles is made to settle,
like the swell of the advancing tide, into the long thunder of
billows breaking for leagues against the shore,—

> " That to the height of this great argument
> I may assert eternal Providence."

Hear what a motion, what a tumult, is given by the dactylic
close to each of these introductory lines!   And how massily is
the whole locked up into the peace of heaven, as the aerial arch
of a viaduct is locked up into tranquil stability by its keystone,
through this deep spondaic close,

> " And justify the ways of God to man." [1]

The introduction over the epic action begins with the revolt
of Satan and his rebel angels, hurled by the Almighty Power
from the upper world of the unimaginable Heaven into the void
chaos, a terrific gulf, into which from the crystal battlements
of Heaven one might look down as into a confused night of wild
jarring atoms and homeless elements, the kingdom of shapeless
anarchy.   But beneath this, as figured by the poet, is a yet
profounder depth, an abyss of horror, into which the rebel host
is precipitated, a lower deep than chaos itself, a world of " *ever-
burning sulphur unconsumed*," a sea of fire.   Milton's horrors
are always physical.   Here the revolting angels find themselves,
and here, when they have partly recovered from their paralysing
defeat, they consult.   Satan, their leader, is still the first in
daring and resource—

> " Forthwith upright he rears from off the pool
> His mighty stature;   on each hand the flames
> Driv'n backward slope their pointing spires, and, roll'd
> In billows, leave i' the midst a horrid vale.
> Then with expanded wings he steers his flight
> Aloft, incumbent on the dusky air
> That felt unusual weight;   till on dry land
> He lights—if it were land that ever burn'd

[1] *Milton v. Southey and Landor*, Masson's ed., vol. xi. p. 456.

> With solid, as the lake with liquid fire. . . .
> Natheless he so endur'd, till on the beach
> Of that inflamèd sea he stood, and call'd
> His legions, angel forms, who lay entranc't
> Thick as autumnal leaves that strow the brooks
> In Vallombrosa." [1]

Here with high words this great spirit cheers the fainting courage of his followers, here his standard is erected which

> " Shone like a meteor streaming to the wind,
> With gems and golden lustre rich emblaz'd,
> Seraphic arms and trophies: all the while
> Sonorous metal blowing martial sounds:
> At which the universal host up-sent
> A shout that tore Hell's concave, and beyond
> Frighted the reign of Chaos and old Night.
> All in a moment through the gloom were seen
> Ten thousand banners rise into the air,
> With orient colours waving; with them rose
> A forest huge of spears; and thronging helms
> Appear'd, and serried shields in thick array
> Of depth immeasurable. Anon they move
> In perfect phalanx to the Dorian mood
> Of flutes and soft recorders." [2]

Here God's rebels build for themselves a kingdom of hell and Pandemonium, its high capital. In the second book the poet describes the debate of the leaders, the counsel given by his peers to Satan, and the plan which their great sultan himself proposes for their acceptance, whereby they may avenge themselves upon the King of Heaven. It is an attack upon the newly-created creature, man, for whom a world has been hung in the midst of the abyss through which they had been hurled— a creature and a world of which there had been word in Heaven before the revolt. For the arduous task of discovering in the deep infinite this new world Satan offers himself, and passing the dread guardians of Hell's gate, Sin and Death, plunges into " *the void profound of unessential night*." Journeying through these tremendous regions he reaches at length the verge of chaos, and discovers far off the towers and battlements of Heaven,

> " And, fast by, hanging in a golden chain,
> This pendent world, in bigness as a star
> Of smallest magnitude close by the moon."

---

[1] *Paradise Lost*, Bk. i., 221-229, 299-303.
[2] *Paradise Lost*, Bk. i., 537-551.

The third book opens with the famous invocation to light, " *offspring of Heaven first-born*," and the pathetic reference to the poet's blindness—

> " Thus with the year
> Seasons return; but not to me returns
> Day, or the sweet approach of ev'n or morn,
> Or sight of vernal bloom, or summer's rose,
> Or flocks, or herds, or human face divine." [1]

The scene then opens in the Heaven of Heavens, and God, the Father, discerning Satan's flight towards Earth, turns to his Son and foretells the Fall of Man. He has created Man a free agent, and Man is therefore responsible for his own undoing. But the Heavenly purpose remains a purpose of grace. The Son of God offers himself as a Redeemer, and a hymn of praise and adoration bursts forth from the choir of angels. Again the scene shifts, and Satan,

> " on the lower stair
> That scal'd by steps of gold to Heav'n-gate,"

arrests his flight to view the sublimest of all sublime spectacles, the universe of circling worlds—

> " Round he surveys (and well might, where he stood
> So high above the circling canopy
> Of night's extended shade) from eastern point
> Of Libra to the fleecy star that bears
> Andromeda far off Atlantic seas
> Beyond the horizon; then from pole to pole
> He views in breadth, and, without longer pause
> Down right into the World's first region throws
> His flight precipitant, and winds with ease
> Through the pure marble air his oblique way
> Amongst innumerable stars, that shone
> Stars distant, but nigh-hand seem'd other worlds.
> Or other worlds they seem'd, or happy isles,
> Like those Hesperian gardens fam'd of old,
> Fortunate fields, and groves, and flowery vales;
> Thrice happy isles! But who dwelt happy there
> He staid not to inquire: above them all
> The golden sun, in splendour likest Heaven,
> Allur'd his eye." [2]

There he lands, meets and converses with Uriel, regent of the sun—fit meeting-place for such divine ones—and at last towards " *the coast of Earth* " descends,

> " Nor staid till on Niphates' top he lights."

[1] *Paradise Lost*, Bk. iii., 40-44.
[2] *Paradise Lost*, Bk. iii. 555-573.

"*In reading 'Paradise Lost,'* " as Lowell said, "*one has a feeling of vastness.   You float under an illimitable sky, brimmed with sunshine or hung with constellations ; the abysses of space are about you ; you hear the cadenced surges of an unseen ocean ; thunders mutter round the horizon, and when the scene changes, it is with an elemental movement, like the shifting of mighty winds.*"

The fourth book contains Satan's amazing address to the Sun—

> " O thou that, with surpassing glory crown'd,
> Look'st from thy sole dominion like the god
> Of this new World—at whose sight all the stars
> Hide their diminisht heads—to thee I call,
> But with no friendly voice, and add thy name,
> O Sun, to tell thee how I hate thy beams." [1]

It contains, too, the splendours of the description of Eden, and of the new-created pair, the first parents of the human race in their happy state of innocence—

> " Adam the goodliest man of men since born
> His sons, the fairest of her daughters Eve."
> " For contemplation he and valour form'd,
> For softness she and sweet attractive grace;
> He for God only, she for God in him:
> His fair large front and eye sublime declar'd
> Absolute rule; and hyacinthine locks
> Round from his parted forelock manly hung
> Clust'ring, but not beneath his shoulders broad:
> She, as a veil, down to the slender waist
> Her unadornèd golden tresses wore
> Dishevell'd, but in wanton ringlets wav'd
> As the vine curls her tendrils, which impli'd
> Subjection, but requir'd with gentle sway,
> And by her yielded, by him best receiv'd
> Yielded with coy submission, modest pride,
> And sweet reluctant amorous delay—

" *a series of verses,*" said Landor, " *so harmonious that my ear is impatient of any other poetry for several days after I have read them.*" [2]   It concludes with the superb passage describing the angelic guardians of the newly created earth, warned by Uriel, drawing their cordon of protection around their charge.

---

[1] *Paradise Lost*, Bk. iv. 32-37.
[2] *Paradise Lost*, Bk. iv., beginning at line 297.   He adds, " I would rather have written these two lines " (the last quoted above) " than all the poetry that has been written since Milton's time in all the regions of the earth."

To select passages for quotation from these first four books, in which Milton put out his full strength as a poet, is hardly to do more than study a mountain from specimens of rock in a museum. And however legitimate to cite passages for praise, one can hardly hope to impress the indifferent or increase the admiration of readers who are in the secret. Is Milton widely appreciated? Admittedly one of the great epic poets of the world, does he not occupy the loneliest eminence, revered rather than read? Does he not resemble the colossal image of some god in a remote and rarely visited shrine? Had he been the author of no other poem than *Paradise Lost* one finds it difficult to believe that this poet would have stood where he now stands. For bring nothing to Milton and you take nothing from him. Bring to him some knowledge of classical poetry, some imaginative faculty, above all bring to him that rare gift, an ear not for the jingles but for the subtler harmonies of verse, and you share the transport of Landor—" *After I have been reading ' Paradise Lost ' I can take up no other poet with satisfaction. I seem to have left the music of Handel for the music of the streets, or at best for drums and fifes. . . . Averse as I am to everything relating to theology, and especially the view of it thrown open by this poem, I recur to it incessantly as the noblest specimen in the world of eloquence, harmony, and genius.*" It is to be feared, however, that those of us who are of Landor's mind belong to a minority, almost negligible even among readers of poetry themselves. For this art is barren of all forms of vulgar appeal. There are few simply human, there are no sentimental graces. Tenderness and romance, sweetness, pity, the child's heart, the social sympathies and affections—it deals in none of these. It is wrought in some incalculable fashion from materials overlooked by the other poets, a fabric which owes its strength and sublimity to exact relations, the science of spaces, the proportion of parts, to the formal laws which like those of mathematics govern the constitution of the world. It is in touch, though we fail to explain how or when, with some hidden principles of nature, a building whose foundations are laid close by the roots of being.

The early books of *Paradise Lost* present us with the whole

scheme, introduce us to the various scenes of the action and to
the *dramatis personae*.   Some critics find the remaining books
inferior.   They are, it may be admitted, inferior in general
interest, they are not inferior in metrical harmonies nor in
the quality of the greater passages.   Take some of Landor's
comments,[1] who blames as well as praises with judicial and
competent impartiality.   Of the passage in the sixth book,
beginning—

> " They ended parle, and both addrest for fight
> Unspeakable,"

he remarks, " *The battle of Satan and Michael is worth all the
battles in all other poets* "; of the description of Creation in the
seventh, " *The birds never looked so beautiful since they left
Paradise* "; of Adam's lament in the ninth (lines 1080-1090),
" *Certainly when we read these verses, the ear is closed against all
others for the day, or even longer* "; of the colloquy between Sin
and Death and the building of the bridge over Chaos to Earth,
in the tenth, " *From 293 to 316 what a series of verses!—a structure
more magnificent and wonderful than the terrific bridge itself, the
construction of which required the united work of the two great
vanquishers of all mankind.*"

Few critics have been bold enough to depreciate the poetic
art of Milton.   Here and there Landor has found a joint in his
harness, as when he says of the line

> " Burnt after them to the bottomless pit "—[2]

" *It is not a verse ; it is turned out of an Italian mould, but in a
state too fluid and incohesive to stand in English* " ; or of the line

> " To the garden of bliss, thy seat prepared "—[3]

" *This verse is too slippery, too Italian* "; or observes of two
consecutive lines in the second book (351, 352), " *two cadences
the same . . . this is unhappy.*"   But if Milton's be not absolute armour of proof, it approaches nearer magic invulnerability
than that worn by any poet since the world began.   To tilt

---

[1] *Imaginary Conversations*, xviii.   Southey and Landor
[2] Bk. vi. 866.   [3] Bk. viii. 299.

against it is the most dangerous critical pastime, and to be unhorsed the almost certain issue of the encounter. There have been good poets and good critics, not a few in England, but no such master of poetics.[1] That Landor has placed an accusing finger upon some metrical faults is proof not of Milton's ignorance or lapse of judgment, it is merely proof of his astonishing daring and dexterity. Forcing the measure he selected to yield all possible varieties of cadence and harmony, he hung a verse, as it were, now and again over the limits which metre imposes. He essayed at times a discord to heighten the value of the surrounding concords. It would seem indeed—the sensitive ear becomes aware of it—that in his later poems, *Paradise Regained* and *Samson Agonistes*, whether from weariness of harmonies already exhausted in *Paradise Lost*, or for purposes of experiment, Milton, like Shakespeare in his latest verse, became impatient with the restraints which metre implies and with which he had hitherto triumphantly complied. Few readers find the same music in his later as in his earlier blank verse. The cause is not a failure of power or a failure in sensitiveness. Departing with deliberation from a field already fully surveyed, in these poems Milton attempted new effects, tested the resources of his medium, and sacrificed the melodious arrangements he could produce at will for the sake of invention. He was sure of what he could do, he was not sure of what remained possible within the limits of the measure. A comparative study of the earlier and the later styles provides the best lesson in metric open to the student of our literature.

If Milton's pre-eminence as a poet is to be assailed, it must then be on other ground than that of poetics. To what censures is he open? Time has disposed of such general animadversion as that of Waller—" *The old blind poet hath published a tedious poem on the Fall of Man. If its length be not considered a merit, it hath no other.*" Let us pass to more particular objections. " *The great defect of ' Paradise Lost,' *" said Bagehot, " *is that after all it is founded on a political transaction.*" Goethe disliked the subject of the poem, " *its exterior was fair,*" he said, " *but*

[1] See an admirable passage in De Quincey's *Milton v. Southey and Landor.*

within it was rotten." Many even of Milton's admirers have
bemoaned its theology. The machinery, the demonology, the
cosmology, they say, once a part of the Christian creed are no
longer a part of it, the whole story has dipped, never to rise
again, below the horizon of belief. And with belief in the story
must go a great part of our interest. But how little it matters
to the value of the poem as a poem that the narrative is no
longer credible. We are not convinced of the truth of the
stories told by Homer or Virgil. We may wholly disbelieve,
as, let us say, when we read Ariosto and Spenser, and still find
the narrative fascinating and the poetry delightful. Nor is a
sense of reality, of verisimilitude required in epic as in dramatic
poetry. It is, one might almost say, expressly excluded. These
transactions, like those in *Beowulf* or the *Aeneid*, are not set
down to be believed, but to be admired; not to convince us,
but to give us the proper poetic pleasure. The defect, however
—there is no doubt of it—goes deeper. Parts of the poem—
the parts given over to the discussion of Predestination and
kindred matters—can provide no true pleasure and are artistically valueless. More than this. The modern reader cannot
rid himself of his Christian attachments, and is not merely
languid in his appreciation of the theology, he is even dis-
ressed by it. The Deity argues, and unhappily argues un-
convincingly; the charge against Satan is obscure, his actions
incredible in a great archangel, the crime for which he and his
followers are expelled from Heaven seems flimsy. And the
expulsion of our first parents from Eden appears equally hard.
So argues the modern age of rationalism and sentiment. Dis-
obedience in both cases is no doubt alleged, but there is no
wickedness discernible. They disobeyed commands, we are
told, but the commands exhibit no divine rationality. The
most disquieting thing of all is not that we find Satan more
interesting than Adam, but that we have a strong inclination
to prefer him to God. We feel with him as with Prometheus
against Jove. With the weaker, the defeated party one can
sympathise. Omnipotence, as Johnson said, neither commands
nor requires sympathy. Nor does Milton's God gain upon our

affections. It has been said, and said with perfect truth, he argues " *like a school divine.*"

The cardinal defect in *Paradise Lost* is hardly, however, Milton's, it arises, and almost inevitably, out of the epic form. That form, undoubtedly better suited for his general purposes than the dramatic, was yet inadequate because invented by a far different age with far different ideas. It was invented before spiritual religion, the art of an age that thought in pictures, of an age when gods were only a little higher than national heroes, immortal indeed, but human in intellect, human in passion. The epic demands as a condition of its existence, concreteness. God therefore, if God be introduced, can be no other than a resuscitated Zeus. War, if war is to be waged, must be war according to the approved epic *formulae,* war in the Homeric manner. Heaven and Hell, if the action lies in these regions, must be pictured, and when pictured remind us of the Elysian fields or of Olympus or of the Shades. These necessities lay within the chosen form. The machinery was epic, and in consequence we have such parallels to Homer as the athletic contests, the races, the chariot exercises with which the fallen angels endeavour to relieve the monotonous torture of Hell. We have the helmets and swords and spears, the fiery darts, the brazen chariots, and the engines invented by Satan with which " *the millions of fierce encountering angels* " fought. We have, as in Homer, the champions on both sides stepping out from the ranks, hurling derisive epithets at each other and clashing together in single combat. By a stupendous effort of imagination Milton realised this terrific, this planetary scene in which armies of immortal spirits engage in battle, in which the chariot of God himself flashes out from a gap in the crystal wall, " *Heaven ruining from Heaven* " to hurl the astounded rebel host in tenfold confusion to the yawning pit. He realised the desolation of chaos itself and the movements of Satan, poised on archangelic wings, amid the outposts of eternity. He made visible the scenes and actions he conjured into existence. But his very success is against him. Is not all this too real to be credible as a picture of the spiritual world?

It fails to convince because it was produced too late in human history, because we have outgrown the power of so considering these things. We cannot think of the eternal realities in these categories. Dismiss from the mind all modern prejudices, cease to regard the poem as having any relation to the religion of Christendom, view it as a poetic invention simply, waiving the impossible requirement that it shall represent the truths of a spiritual religion, and perhaps few reasons remain for denying to it an absolute and unparalleled success.

Bagehot quotes the Cambridge mathematician, who is reported to have said—" *After all ' Paradise Lost ' proves nothing*," and remarks, " *he was right, Milton proposed to prove something*." Nature proves nothing, nor does art. If indeed we ask from Milton a fulfilment of his proposal, the justification of God's dealings with men, we must admit that he has failed. But it is too much to ask: a poem is best justified by the attainment of poetic greatness. Milton failed in one of his aims—an impossible one—he succeeded in the other. The moral and didactic purpose which underlay his design is not negligible, though it be the fashion to believe that it matters nothing what a poet has said, but only how he has said it. Some critics have been understood to wish that poetry had no content, some have spoken with languid contempt of "*mere subject*." To Milton, at least, it would have appeared madness to strip poetry of its intellectual meaning, to regard it as no more than a decorative screen or a musical composition. Had this been his opinion we should not have possessed *Paradise Lost*. We owe it as much to a burning religious as to a poetic inspiration, to be obtained, in his own words, " *by devout prayer to that Eternal Spirit who can enrich with all utterance and knowledge, and sends out his seraphim with the hallowed fire of his altar to touch and purify the life of whom he pleases*." That Milton believed the Scriptures with inflexible conviction we cannot doubt, nor can one doubt that in *Paradise Lost* he believed himself to have set forth, in so far as human language was capable of representing such verities, the substantial truth, together with such poetic adornments as came natural to him as a poet and scholar. That we have outgrown his creed is natural; creeds, one knows, which are men's opinions on certain great problems, undergo change as do their other opinions. What has happened to Milton happened before him to Homer, to Virgil, and to Dante. In every work of art the perishable is blended with the imperishable, though we find the work at times so divine we forget for the moment that it is also human. When we observe the existence of the perishable in *Paradise Lost*, in certain aspects of its theology, we may also remind ourselves that it is not orthodox seventeenth-century theology. In his own day it was heretical. The fruit of Milton's private and prolonged searching of the Scriptures, the result of the exercise of his personal judgment upon the same body of material as that upon which the churches are founded, it is yet not coincident with the finding of the churches. The less negligible is the Miltonic creed therefore, the more welcome even, since it helps to make *Paradise Lost* the unique thing it is. For what one has suffered from this defect one has received compensation. Let us pass to a more serious charge. The poem, one often reads the complaint, lacks human interest. Milton appears to have taken small heed of ordinary humanity, of average men and women. A man on what Russell Lowell called " *such visiting terms with Heaven* " fell out of touch with the petty joys and sorrows of human life. He shared few interests with the millions of Earth's unremarkable, unheeded sons and daughters. Naturally his sympathies lay with the resolute and virtuous rather than with sinners or weak persons or humorous idlers, to whom Shakespeare was so friendly. And so he draws the line between right and wrong with a pen of iron, he separates the sheep and the goats. No sense of the sadness of human life, of the " *still sad music of humanity*," humanity wandering through trackless ways, endeavouring to make a home for itself in a strange incomprehensible world, suffering terrible things, clinging desperately to desperate hopes, like seamen afloat upon a raft in unknown seas, carrying on the struggle with the careless forces of nature—nothing of the compassion of Shakespeare for frail mortality touches him. There is certainly no condescension in Milton. " *His natural port*," as Johnson said, " *is gigantic loftiness*."

Whether we regard him as a publicist or a poet it is the same. His strength lay in his idealism, his immense confidence in ideas, his unceasing effort to apply general ideas to the conduct of life or to display great ideas in poetry. Consider for a moment the immense programme of reforms set forth in his prose pamphlets as a clue to his type of mind. There, as in the poems, the greatness of the ideas must compensate for any practical or intellectual errors. Living, as he did, a life consecrated to art and liberty, surrounded by the poets and philosophers of all the ages, leaders of the thought of the world, how difficult for such a character in such a situation to appreciate fully the difficulty of applying ideas to life, to gauge the stubborn resistance offered to thought by the unthinking, to realise the snail's pace at which society must be content to travel. Of the pitiful disabilities, the pathetic incapacities of human nature, most were beyond his ken. But more than this, the complexity of a world filled with individuals, the difficulty of adjustments in human communities, gave him little anxiety: the infinite diversities which clashed at every point, the idiosyncracies, the differences due to age, temperament, education, rank, surroundings, local prejudice. How hard a thing it is to found and maintain an ordered state, which must take account of the endless varieties of men! There appear to be some great minds which—a strange disability—cannot understand little minds, and Milton's was one of them. There have lived men so enamoured of great principles, of broad generalisations, of abstract propositions, that astonishment seized them when they met others unimpressed by their logical and mathematical methods. As well apply, one might say, abstract principles to a vast tropical forest as to the world of men, a forest riotously and inextricably complex, a restless, continuously moving and growing mass of vegetable and animal life, flitting bird and humming insect and travelling beast, endlessly employed amid all modes and forms of tree and leaf and flower and tangled undergrowth, world within world, circle investing circle, maze within maze, of

bewildering colours and energies and forms, before which analysis
is dumb.   In Shakespeare we have a knowledge of this complexity, we recognise that we are inhabitants of such a world.
Milton, who gives us no sense of it, abstracts and simplifies all
he touches by the omission of detail.   And his poetry, like his
prose, betrays the defects of its qualities.

In the sense in which Shakespeare or Dante provides human
interest Milton fails to provide it.   Comparing the *Divine Comedy*
with *Paradise Lost,* "*we are reminded,*" wrote Sir John Seeley, "*of
the difference between St. Paul's and Westminster Abbey.   Westminster Abbey is full of interest.   A line of kings and conquerors
is buried there; wherever we turn, the figures of great men,
sculptured in their most characteristic attitudes, confront us.
St. Paul's, on the contrary, is almost barren of such interest;
it is an empty building.   In the same way Dante's Hell and
Purgatory and Paradise are full of human beings.   In that
vast cathedral all the great men of the Middle Ages, all the
great personalities that make up mediæval history, lie in
glory, each one in his own place.   Beside the awful divine
realities are enshrined solemn and tender human memories; in the
bosom of the passionless eternity we see gathered the loves and
hatreds and the vicissitudes of time.   But of all such interest
Milton's poem is barren. . . .   Down this mighty Renaissance
temple as we walk we admire vast spaces, arches wide and graceful,
majestic aisles; but it has no monuments, no humanities; it is
an empty building.*"[1]   No unjust comparison this,[2] yet if
Milton's epic be like a mighty Renaissance temple, it has its
monuments, or at least, in the room of memorials, great pieces
of sculpture, the towering figures of Satan and Michael and
Gabriel, the figures also of Adam and Eve, classic statues like
the persons of the Greek drama, not human indeed as Chaucer's
or Shakespeare's characters are human, but like the beings
created by Michael Angelo on the walls of the Sistine Chapel or

[1] Seeley's *Lectures and Essays,* pp. 140-141.
[2] Dante's *Divina Commedia* is "*full of human beings,*" but is exposed to
Landor's criticism, that "*the characters are without any bond of union, any
field of action, any definite aim.*"   Scott thought its *plan unhappy; the
personal malignity and strange mode of revenge presumptuous and un-
interesting.*"

Q

in the chapel of the Medici, more than human, superb idealisations of humanity. Among them, it is true, fortunately or unfortunately Satan is pre-eminent, he is, said Dryden, "*the hero of ' Paradise Lost.'* "[1] From the first, since the poem opens with Satan's revolt, he engages our interest; upon him Milton, perhaps unconsciously, put forth all his poetic strength, and as Falstaff in *Henry IV.* exceeded his proper dimensions and usurped the position proper to the more heroic figures, so in *Paradise Lost* Satan grew to a natural sovereignty from which it was afterwards impossible to depose him. Milton's was, too, a revolutionary mind, charged with revolutionary theory in a revolutionary epoch. Can we be surprised that his mind took fire at the thought of the great arch-rebel, the antagonist of Omnipotence? How exactly, it has often been observed, the action of the poem resembles a republican movement against monarchy. The Sovereign announces to the peerage that his newly-begotten Son is to have rank above them. The great lords resist, their pride is wounded, their ancient privileges attacked. The political situation becomes strained, the peers withdraw from court, they collect their forces, they declare war upon their monarch. Who can doubt that unintentionally Milton's scheme reproduced the main features of the struggle which he himself witnessed in his own country? For a Christian poem the action has too much the character of a revolt against tyranny, the Deity is too monarchical, the Arch-fiend, to whom we are drawn by the very hopelessness of his cause, presents too magnificent a resolution, too noble a carriage. Did Milton expect us to restrain the thrill of sympathetic emotion when he describes him, rising to address his faithful followers?—

> " His form had yet not lost
> All her original brightness, nor appear'd
> Less than archangel ruined. . . .
> Thrice he essay'd, and thrice, in spite of scorn,
> Tears, such as angels weep, burst forth: at last
> Words interwove with sighs found out their way.
> ' O myriads of immortal spirits, O powers
> Matchless, but with the Almighty.' "[2]

[1] Compare Scott, " *The worst of all my undertakings is that my rogue always in despite of me turns out my hero.*"
[2] *Paradise Lost*, Bk. i., 591-593; 619-623.

The passages in which the great " Apostate Angel " is described
are always passages of splendour—

> " On th' other side,
> Incenst with indignation, Satan stood
> Unterrifi'd, and like a comet burned
> That fires the length of Ophiuchus huge
> In th' arctic sky, and from his horrid hair
> Shakes pestilence and war." [1]

> " Know ye not, then," said Satan, fill'd with scorn,
> " Know ye not me? ye knew me once no mate
> For you, there sitting where ye durst not soar;
> Not to know me argues yourselves unknown." [2]

From a theological point of view all this might, perhaps, be
accounted serious, but poetically the gain is immense. What
is lost to theology is gained by poetry. And although Satan
may attract the greatest interest—and Shelley's revolutionary
mind approved—Landor's contention is not without force—
*" there is neither truth nor wit in saying that Satan is the hero of
the piece, unless, as is usually the case in human life, he is the
greatest hero who gives the widest sway to the worst passions. It
is Adam who acts and suffers most, and on whom the consequences
have most influence. This constitutes him the main character ;
although Eve is the more interesting, Satan the more energetic, and
on whom the greater force of poetry is displayed."* [3]

Paradise Lost suffers, in the opinion of some, from a greater
defect than any yet enumerated. *" The event is unhappy."* Contrary to all the unwritten laws of romance, contrary to all the
practice of the epic poets, the hero is foiled, his enemy triumphs.
Yet here again the fault lies within the subject. And Milton,
conscious of the flaw, endeavours in the last book to mitigate
the sense of tragedy by common consent unsuited to epic.
The archangel Michael explains to Adam the plan for the
redemption of the world. Expelled from Paradise he is not left
in despair or for ever an exile from the divine mercy. Rarely,

---

[1] *Paradise Lost*, Bk. ii., 706-710.
[2] Bk. iv., 827-830.
[3] Landor notices too that the defect of *Paradise Lost*, that of exciting
the greatest interest in the feelings and exploits of a character other than
the principal agent, is shared with the *Iliad*.

only perhaps once, in the famous concluding passage, does the poet attempt or achieve pathos—

> " In either hand the hast'ning angel caught
> Our lingering parents, and to th' eastern gate
> Led them direct, and down the cliff as fast
> To the subjected plain; then disappear'd.
> They, looking back, all th' eastern side beheld
> Of Paradise, so late their happy seat,
> Wav'd over by that flaming brand, the gate
> With dreadful faces throng'd and fiery arms:
> Some natural tears they dropp'd, but wip'd them soon;
> The world was all before them, where to choose
> Their place of rest, and Providence their guide:
> They, hand in hand, with wand'ring steps and slow,
> Through Eden took their solitary way." [1]

Perhaps there is nothing more remarkable in a poem where all is remarkable than its air of every-day reality, the absence of diffidence, the absence of mystery, for strange indeed it seems to us, at no point in these transcendental regions does the author confess himself at a loss, never appears conscious that he should no longer personally conduct us. In this temple there is no Holy of Holies, no veiled sanctuary, its inmost shrine lies open to the gaze of the curious. Heaven is as easy to Milton as earth, his angels and archangels, celestial beings, are apprehended by the eye of sight, as the councils of eternity, the purposes of God are here intelligible to the simplest intellect. Thus Milton secures for his imaginative creation the credibility of a picture. There it stands, this building, complete, four-square, defiant; a wonder and an offence to the mystic. Its completeness and self-sufficiency torture him, as a philosopher might be tortured by the dogmatism of a vulgar disputant. But there is no help for it, Milton's manner is personal and peculiar to himself, it must be taken or left. With the accuracy of one who has seen and observed he describes the indescribable—

> " Betwixt these rocky pillars Gabriel sat,
> Chief of the angelic guards, awaiting night;
> About him exercised heroic games
> Th' unarmed youth of Heav'n, but nigh at hand
> Celestial armoury, shields, helms, and spears,
> Hung high, with diamond flaming and with gold." [1]

---

[1] *Paradise Lost*, Bk. xii., 637-649.   [2] Bk. iv., 549-554.

> —" to the ground
> With solemn adoration down they cast
> Their crowns inwove with amaranth and gold.
> Immortal amaranth . . . there grows
> And flowers aloft, shading the fount of life,
> And where the river of Bliss through midst of Heav'n
> Rolls o'er Elysian flowers her amber stream." [1]

Compare these passages with the spiritual reticence, the exquisite reserve of Milton's contemporary Vaughan, when he speaks of his friends who have gone over to the other world—

> " Dear, beauteous Death! the jewel of the just,
>   Shining nowhere but in the dark;
> What mysteries do lie beyond thy dust,
>   Could man outlook that mark! "

As in Homer Olympus has its definite geographical position, as Zeus and Apollo, Hera and Aphrodite are exalted men and women, so in Milton Heaven is a locality with definite limits, and its inhabitants a virtuous and noble race of superior human beings. So classical is the whole conception that to the Christian story is given the air of a Pagan legend. Where is one to look for an inward spiritual touch to distinguish *Paradise Lost* from the *Iliad*? Milton, again, is a classical artist, because his method is a straightforward method; he employs words with precision, without asking from them other than their customary suggestions. Perhaps alone among English writers he obeys the canon—"*In the truly great poets . . . there is a reason assignable, not only for every word, but for the position of every word.*" [2] Following closely in the steps of the ancients he adhered to firmly established principles and precedents. Though his subject differed his manner was the same. To the Greek writers, he said, " *I am indebted for all my proficiency in litera-ture.*" Trained in this school he avoided bizarre effects, effects which are calculated to startle or confuse the mind. He asked for no assistance from sensation which springs from a juxta-position of the familiar with the unfamiliar, which delights in the weird, the distorted, and the grotesque. In the Greek mythology every figure radiates beauty, every god and goddess, every nymph and naiad, every creature of the flood and field

---

[1] Bk. iii., 350-359.   [2] Coleridge, *Biographia Literaria*, chap. i.

seems, like Pygmalion's creation, to have lived first in marble and to partake of its serene perfection. That is the Hellenic secret, *Nothing but the beautiful*. The wonders wild created by the Eastern imagination, the monsters and genii, the Greek counted barbaric, barbaric too the grinning horrors and distorted deities, with elephant heads and a hundred mouths, the cruel-mouthed goddesses of Oriental religions. In such fancies, on the other hand, lurked for the Middle Ages a certain fascination, in the unlovely shapes that crowd the *Arabian Nights*, or in the hags and devils of popular superstition. There are signs of such a pleasure in the gargoyles and grotesque carvings of Gothic architecture, it appears in the forbidding shapes, the uncanny horrors of Dante's *Inferno*. This grimness is absent from Milton. Only in one passage, that in the second book where he describes the repulsive figures of Sin and Death, is the horrible anywhere suggested or depicted. For the rest *Paradise Lost* is a world in which the laws of beauty and of taste prevail—Apollo vanquishing the Python—over the presentation even of evil itself.

If we compare classical with romantic art, we notice, too, that with the former we seek finality rather than mystery, form rather than atmosphere. The romantic artists, on the contrary, delight in misty outline, in half-hidden details, in light and shade. Rain showers and clouds pass across their land-scapes, figures are dimly visible through the haze, here a shaft of sunlight streams through, there the shadows are deep to inky blackness. It is the contrast between the skies and scenery of the South, the Italian or Greek city with its high-built citadel, all its parts visible for miles in the pellucid air—a thing of beauty that loses nothing by its eternal radiance, its never-altering perfection—and the skies and scenery of the North, with its ever-changing soft and mystic tones—cloud and wind and weather incessantly at work, blotting out and revealing, now one part momentarily in shade and again in light, sug-gesting and concealing and altering a country which remains for ever interesting, because never seen twice under the same conditions.

A classic, it has been said, is an artist *"who possesses in a degree more or less eminent the qualities whose imitation, if it cannot do any good, cannot at least do any harm"* [1]—and judged by this canon also Milton is a classic. That is not, indeed, to say that great, even the greatest successes are unattainable in the romantic manner. It is to say only that you cannot predict them, they are not the qualities ascertained by the experience of the past to be fine qualities; they may be admirable, they have not been proved so. If you follow in the steps of the classical artists you may fail, but you do not court disaster. Theirs is an excellence conceded by generations of men, an excellence that has stood the test of centuries. A romantic may be admitted into the ranks of the classics, time may approve his methods, or for the sake of his genius condone them. *" A Romanticist,"* it has been argued, *" is simply a classic in the making."* He may or may not be. How far his spirit and manner are wholly human, how far he has not been governed by a passing fashion, a temporary mode of thought and feeling, must be left to the decision of the future, to the verdict of *" the incorruptible Areopagus of posterity."* Certain it is that in the unceasing expansion of the mind things once thought precious are precious no longer, old loyalties become impossible, old creeds wither, and only those thinkers and artists are secure of honour who by some divine instinct have probed or foreseen the requirements of the soul. One thing only we know, upon beauty alone time has no power. What once was beautiful, let us hold to it, remains beautiful for ever, and the safest of all rules of art is to be possessed by a vehement love of beauty and to pursue it, as did Milton, *" through all the forms and faces of things."* Genius, it is a commonplace, has often to wait for recognition, since, it has been acutely said, *" talent aims at a point which appears difficult to reach ; genius aims at a point which no one perceives."* [2] And so it happens that we often applaud talent and overlook genius. For in the first case we understand and appreciate the difficulties that have been over-

---

[1] M. Brunetière's *Essays*, translated by D. Nichol Smith.
[2] MacCarthy: " The Philosophy of Genius," *Proceedings of Dublin University Philosophical Society,* 1907.

come; in the second we but dimly perceive what time alone will make clear, and the mind only at a later stage of its development come completely to understand.

As Homer adorned his narrative with similes, so too Milton, and with a success certainly second to none. The Homeric simile served him for a double purpose—to decorate his verse in the classical manner and to introduce into the narrative, without impairing its unity, a wealth of illustration and suggestion really foreign to the subject, as, for example, when he compares Satan's shield to the moon—

> —" whose orb
> Through optic glass the Tuscan artist views
> At ev'ning from the top of Fesolè,
> Or in Valdarno, to descry new lands,
> Rivers, or mountains in her spotty globe." [1]

Never more splendid than when his learning is made to minister to his imagination, Milton's similes and historical comparisons seem to illustrate for us the saying of Longinus that *" the sublime is a certain excellence and perfection of language."* Here, one might almost say, we may make acquaintance with the whole art of poetry, here is a liberal education for those who seek it.

> " The birds their quire apply; airs, vernal airs,
> Breathing the smell of field and grove, attune
> The trembling leaves, while universal Pan,
> Knit with the Graces and the Hours in dance,
> Led on the eternal Spring.   Not that fair field
> Of Enna, where Proserpin gathering flow'rs,
> Herself a fairer flow'r, by gloomy Dis
> Was gather'd, which cost Ceres all that pain
> To seek her through the world; nor that sweet grove
> Of Daphne, by Orontes and th' inspir'd
> Castalian spring, might with this Paradise
> Of Eden strive." [2]

His use, too, of proper names instructs us.   Who has not felt the charm with which from his earliest years he could invest them?

> " Peor and Baalim
> Forsake their temples dim."

What historical perspectives, what endless vistas of unreturning time are thrown open to us in these lines—

---

[1] *Paradise Lost*, Bk. i., 287-291.   [2] Bk. iv. 264-275.

> —" what resounds
> In fable and romance of Uther's son,
> Begirt with British and Armoric knights;
> And all who since, baptis'd or infidel,
> Jousted in Aspramont, or Montalban,
> Damasco, or Marocco, or Trebisond,
> Or whom Biserta sent from Afric shore
> When Charlemain with all his peerage fell
> By Fontarabbia." [1]

Milton, said Coleridge, is "*not so much a picturesque as a musical poet.*" It is true that with all the density and lucidity, the clear cut definition of his style—a style which respects the value of words, which employs no unnecessary words, a style of magnificent economy—Milton is often content to suggest rather than describe, to lean upon the activity of his reader's imagination. Unlike Spenser, whose tapestries might be reproduced upon canvas, he paints in phrases invaluable to the mind, useless to the painter—

> " On th' other side Satan alarm'd
> Collecting all his might, dilated stood,
> Like Teneriffe or Atlas, unremov'd,
> His stature reach'd the sky, and on his crest
> Sat Horror plum'd."

It is true also that, as Lowell said, he is " *a harmonist rather than a melodist,*" and in proportion to our susceptibility to verse less highly charged with sentiment, to the purer and more formal music, will be our pleasure in Milton. Some, indeed, miss in him the lyrical cry, the gush of liquid melody, the Elizabethan wild-wood music, the trilling forest notes, the cadences that flutter through the songs of Shakespeare, like a bird through the summer leaves. They miss the *vox humana*, the mysterious, small, subtle, passionate cry of the violin, for which the solemn recitative, the " *sonorous metal blowing martial sounds* " will not entirely compensate. But the beautiful has many forms. Handel is great, but not greater than Bach. A careful student will learn from Milton how variety of cadence may be introduced into the single line by the inversion of stress—making, as it is called, a ripple on the larger wave of the period—which may occur in any foot—

> " Régions of sorrow, doleful shades—
> For one restraint, lórds of the world beside "—

[1] *Paradise Lost*, Bk. i., 579-587. See also Bk. xi. 385-411.

he will learn so to vary the measure, that in no period shall the same pause recur, he will learn to value the music of the paragraph—it is one of Milton's secrets—above that of the single line, he will learn so to connect the periods that the arch of each, like that of a wave, determined by its own weight and momentum, varied in respect of the stresses and pauses of which it is composed, shall mount and curve and fall, in ocean-like unending change, he will learn the art of selecting his words for the vowel or consonantal values required in the position they occupy, so that the rhythm, the vocal melody of one paragraph is succeeded by another of a wholly different character. He will come to know that the structure of this verse is comparable in its complexity to a sonata of Beethoven.

Poetry is the sum of two values, the intellectual and the musical, but somehow the effect is greater than their sum. The words of a poem belong to a double order, the order of thought and the order of sound; in so far as the requirements of the one order are sacrificed to those of the other the poet has failed. The task he undertakes is simpler or more difficult in proportion to the mass and complexity of his conceptions, the intricacy and variety of his measure. Milton's triumph consists in the undisturbed precision of his thought throughout, and despite the complex demands of the rhythm. Each word, like a stone in a cathedral arch, has its place and duty, each seems chosen as if for no purpose than to advance his meaning, to bear its portion of the weight of a vast structure, yet each, viewed from the other side, seems chosen only to play its part in the musical scheme. The pattern of the thought brooks no interference from that of the rhythm, nor that of the rhythm from the pattern of the thought. " *Qui perd ses mots, perd son air.*"

> " Anon out of the earth a fabric huge
> Rose like an exhalation, with the sound
> Of dulcet symphonies and voices sweet,
> Built like a temple, where pilasters round
> Were set, and Doric pillars overlaid
> With golden architrave; nor did there want
> Cornice or frieze, with bossy sculptures grav'n,
> The roof was fretted gold. Not Babylon,
> Nor great Alcairo such magnificence

Equall'd in all their glories, to enshrine
Belus or Serapis their gods, or seat
Their kings, when Egypt with Assyria strove
In wealth and luxury." [1]

It is related by Thomas Ellwood, Milton's young Quaker
friend, that, when returning to the poet the MS. of *Paradise Lost,*
he remarked, " *Thou hast said much here of Paradise Lost, but
what hast thou to say of Paradise Found ?* He made me no
answer, but sat some time in a muse, then broke off that discourse
and fell upon another subject." Some time later the poet handed
the MS. of *Paradise Regained* to Ellwood, with the remark,
" *This is owing to you.*" Few readers have contended that the
latter epic equals the earlier in interest. We are told by
Phillips that it " *was generally censured to be much inferior to the
other,*" but that the author himself " *could not hear with patience
any such thing when related to him.*" *Paradise Regained,* however, has had its defenders. Wordsworth thought it " *the most
perfect in execution of anything written by Milton,*" and Coleridge
asserted that " *in its kind it is the most perfect poem extant, though
its kind may be inferior in interest—being in its essence didactic.*"
What should one feel? Should we think of *Paradise Regained*
as " *the ebbing of a mighty tide,*" of the poet as weary, broken
with age, the riches of his mind already expended? Was Milton
here, as Landor said, " *caught sleeping after his exertions in
Paradise Lost* "? We shall, perhaps, be nearer the truth, if we
think of the poet as anxious to avoid competition with himself,
anxious to avoid the mere continuation of a work already
accomplished. In his latter epic he attempted something wholly
different from his undertaking in the earlier. One observes
that no great action is narrated, indeed nothing of any important kind can be said to take place. There are only two
persons, Christ and Satan, and the poem simply consists of a
conversation or debate between them, or as Pattison expressed
it, " *The speakers are no more than the abstract principles of
good and evil, two voices who hold a rhetorical disputation through
four books and two thousand lines.*" *Paradise Regained,* too, is
composed on severer lines than *Paradise Lost,* it is almost

[1] *Paradise Lost,* Bk. i., 710-722.

destitute of the decoration which the poet so lavishly expended upon his previous subject. Some of the finest poetry in the earlier epic appears in the similes, in which, it is clear, he took a particular pleasure, yet for the first three books of *Paradise Regained* Milton refrained, as Pattison notices, from indulgence in a single simile. The metre, again, is plainer, there is less of the sonorous splendour, the organ music. And we have nothing to compensate for the absence of such descriptions as those of Pandemonium and of Paradise. Yet after all it is only the question whether we have here " *an eagle in the nest or on the wing.*" Is it not probable that the author felt he had done enough for poetry, and perhaps too little for spiritual religion in his great poem, and desired to make good the omission? Is it not possible that though it represented his powers as a poet, he felt it barely satisfactory in itself as theology? The victory of God over evil in the persons of the revolting angels had been a physical rather than a moral victory, Satan, though defeated, had not been altogether unsuccessful, vanquished but not put to shame. In *Paradise Regained* Milton attempted to readjust the balance. He selects not the Crucifixion as his theme, but the Temptation. The Son of God is tempted as Adam was tempted, but the Tempter fails, a spiritual victory is won, and we are thus assured of the final triumph of good over evil in the great design of God.

Occasionally in *Paradise Regained* memories of the earlier epic are awakened, as in the description of the banquet in the second book—

> —" in order stood
> Tall stripling youths rich clad, of fairer hue
> Than Ganymed or Hylas; distant more
> Under the trees now tripp'd, now solemn stood,
> Nymphs of Diana's train, and Naiades
> With fruits and flowers from Amalthea's horn,
> And ladies of the Hesperides, that seem'd
> Fairer than feign'd of old, or fabled since
> Of faery damsels met in forest wide
> By knights of Logres, or of Lyones,
> Lancelot, or Pelleas, or Pellenore.[1]

but until we reach the fourth book this is almost the only passage in which the earlier Milton reappears. For most readers the

[1] *Paradise Regained*, Bk. ii. 351-361.

chief attraction of the poem is the lines where the poet, touched by his old passion, describes Rome and Athens, their architecture, arts, and literature in the undying and famous phrases: Rome,

> " With towers and temples proudly elevate
> On seven small hills, with palaces adorned;"

> " Athens, the eye of Greece, mother of arts
> And eloquence, native to famous wits."

The Satan of this poem is a far different figure from the magnificent apostate angel of the first epic, who thwarted the design of the Most High, and chose to rule in Hell rather than serve in Heaven, who claimed the empire of negation—" *Evil, be thou my Good.*" He now appears as " *an aged man in rural weeds,*" such as might seek stray fagots for his fire upon some winter's day. Yet no words spoken by the rebel Archangel in his pride are more thrilling than those which he now utters, when his disguise is penetrated by Christ, and he is known for what he is—

> " 'Tis true, I am that Spirit unfortunate."

Satan, now the subtle disputant, sets forth this world's glories, the work of men's hands, the Pagan victories in art, the triumphs of civilisation, the sky-searching philosophies against the simple virtues, the quiet obedience of the Christian life. The eternal antithesis emerges between the intellectual and the religious outlook. To the wisdom of this world—how often it has been said—Christianity seems to oppose but foolishness, to its wealth but poverty, to its culture but childish ignorance. In the debate between Christ and Satan Milton desires us to feel the majesty of the spiritual things. It is not indeed clear that he adopts the extreme Christian view that self-sacrifice and self-renunciation are of the essence of religion, that he would have placed in stern opposition the ideals of the Christian and the Pagan world. He may have thought it possible to add to the virtues found in the best men of pre-Christian times the virtues of the Christian saint. *Paradise Regained* makes no attempt to depress the intellectual while it exalts the moral and spiritual life. Whether compromise be possible, whether Christianity does not require that men shall resolutely turn their backs upon wealth and fame and learning and national pride, counting this world well lost for the sake of a better, belongs to another inquiry than ours. The modern age has taken, as one might say, the sting out of Christianity by accommodating the creed to its life rather than its life to the creed, and continues to call itself Christian. Perhaps Milton was himself partly conscious that he stood between incompatibles; he seems to approach as near hesitation as was possible to his unhesitating mind. Perhaps, again, he had more sympathy with the militant than the self-effacing qualities, as he was more of a soldier than a quietist. Into his study at least of the person and ideals of Christ in *Paradise Regained* he imparts something hardly to be found in the Gospels. As in many a Renaissance picture, the figure of Christ seems to be painted upon a classical background and touched with something of a philosopher's air and mien. Apart from its poetry, poetry in a deliberately subdued key, this poem is of interest as the first attempt, outside the Scripture narrative, to draw the portrait of the Founder of Christianity. Hardly the Gospel portrait, hardly Christ as preached in the evangelical churches, Milton's, as might have been expected, is none the less a majestic conception. What a contrast is presented between the hero of the first and of the second epic, the great militant figure of *Paradise Lost*, who, within sight of Eden, hurled his superb defiance at the noonday sun, and that of Christ, who rising superior to all temptations in complete self-mastery, retains the simplicity and humility of childhood, and when the trial is over, without shadow of self-gratulation or word of triumph, turns back to the life of every day—

> " He, unobserv'd,
> Home to his mother's house private returned."

There is no one with whom to compare this poet in our literature. Though a student of Chaucer and Shakespeare, he is far removed from their standpoint of cheerful acquiescence in a strangely assorted, multi-coloured patch-work world, where fools and

knaves jostle the good and great. Nor though he called himself
a disciple of Spenser did he share that dreaming poet's sweet
reflective mood, lost in the tangled woods of his own fairyland.
And if none preceded who were like him, none followed. Not
in Dryden or Pope, not in Burns or Shelley, not in Wordsworth
or Tennyson is heard again that clarion note of resolution and
certitude, of fortitude and faith. " *The large utterance of the
early gods* " died with him and cannot be revived. Though
without humour—the most repelling of defects—he retained
his hold upon generations to whom humour was the breath of
life; his intense religious fervour could not altogether discourage
the rationalists, nor his radicalism wholly estrange the Tories.
Addison devoted number after number of a society journal to an
appreciation of *Paradise Lost ;* Johnson, who hated Whig dogs,
growled a full confession of his greatness; Landor, averse to all
theology and particularly to Milton's, after a long and searching
criticism of his faults, remarks to Southey, " *Are we not somewhat like two little beggar boys, who forgetting that they are in
tatters, sit noticing a few stains and rents in their father's raiment?* "
Dryden, the Restoration playwright, places him above both
Homer and Virgil, Shelley ranks him third among the poets of
the world.

Yet the Romantics have triumphed, and other qualities than
his are the reigning qualities of art. Who now among the poets
puts himself to school with Milton? To-day we have with
us the ritual of the soul and its sorrows—" the dialogue of
the mind with itself has commenced "; we have the wistful
speculation, the vague desire, the frail wayward charm, the
delicate nuance, the dim half-tones, " an exquisite faintness,
une fadeur exquise." To the *poésie intime* they belong and you
prefer them, *le naïf*, the strange, the subtle; you prefer the
enchanted reverie.

You object that the beauty of *Paradise Lost* is outward, not
shy, modest, sheltered, elusive, pensive. There is no answer to
the objection. What you say, however, is true also of the
Parthenon.

CHAPTER XI

THE history of heroic poetry in the seventeenth and eighteenth
centuries, if we except Milton—a notable exception, indeed—is
a chronicle of failure. So that in speaking of it one may be
said to deal in the main with three classes of poems—those that
never lived, those now dead, and those more dead than alive.
Of these we may name as seventeenth-century examples, in
the first class Cowley's *Davideis*, in the second Davenant's
Gondibert, in the third Chamberlayne's *Pharonnida*. Cowley's,
like Waller's, which also once stood high, is a vanished reputation. At one time, however, his shorter poems were admired,
and a hundred years after his death Cowley still remained of
sufficient importance for Johnson to write of him at length and
with respect in one of the best, if not the best, of his " Lives."
But his fame was not derived from his epic. " Whatever is said
of Cowley," remarks Johnson, " is meant of his other works.
Of the *Davideis* no mention is made; it never appears in books,
nor emerges in conversation. By the *Spectator* it has been once
quoted; by Rymer it has once been praised; and by Dryden in
Mack Flecknoe, it has once been imitated; nor do I recollect
much other notice from its publication till now, in the whole
succession of English literature." The *Davideis, a sacred poem
of the Troubles of David*, is practically destitute of any kind of
interest. A very painstaking reader may undoubtedly discover
in it some good lines, and even a few tolerable passages, but,
unless he be very amiable, will probably feel himself insufficiently
rewarded for his previous toils. The thought that the *Davideis*
was left unfinished has never been the cause of pain. The
pedestrian portions of the narrative are without offence, but

when Cowley attempts sublimity his unfitness for an epic undertaking is startlingly apparent. Here, for example, is how he describes Satan's disappointment with Saul—

> " He trusted much in Saul, and rag'd and griev'd
> (The great deceiver!) to be himself deceived,
> Thrice did he knock his iron teeth, thrice howl,
> And into frowns his wrathful forehead roll:
> His eyes dart forth red flames, which scare the Night,
> And with worse fires the trembling ghosts affright;
> A troop of ghastly fiends compass him round,
> And greedily catch at his lips' feared sound.
> ' Are we such nothings then! ' said he, ' our will
> Crost by a shepherd's boy! and you yet still
> Play with your idle serpents here? dares none
> Attempt what becomes furies? Are ye grown
> Benumbed with fear, or virtue's spiritless cold,
> You who were once (I'm sure) so brave and bold?
> Oh! my ill-chang'd condition! oh, my fate!
> Did I lose Heaven for this? '
> With that with his long tail he lash'd his breast,
> And horribly spoke out in looks the rest."

When he recalls the destruction of Pharaoh and his Egyptians he presents us with this picture—

> " In his gilt chariots amaz'd fishes sat,
> And grew with corpse of wretched princes fat:
> The waves and rocks half eaten bodies stain;
> Nor was it since call'd the Red Sea in vain."

"*Cowley was not of God, and so he could not stand,*" said Rochester. But that he may not be judged by his worst—a test too severe for most poets, Shakespeare himself, perhaps—we may add a passage of greater dignity, near the beginning of the first book—

> " Beneath the mighty ocean's wealthy caves,
> Beneath the eternal fountain of all waves,
> Where their vast court the mother waters keep,
> And undisturb'd by moons in silence sleep;
> There is a place, deep, wondrous deep, below,
> Which genuine night and horror does o'erflow;
> No bound controls th' unwearied space but Hell,
> Endless as those dire pains that in it dwell,
> Here no dear glimpse of the Sun's lovely face
> Strikes through the solid darkness of the place;
> No dawning morn does her kind reds display;
> One slight weak beam would here be thought the day:
> No gentle stars with their fair gems of light
> Offend the tyrannous and unquestion'd Night." [1]

Both Davenant and Chamberlayne have stronger claims upon

---

[1] With the *Davideis* the curious may compare Prior's *Solomon*, in which the hero's thoughts not his acts are narrated by himself.

P

our attention than Cowley. Poetry which was once read excites greater interest and demands more respect than poetry which even its own age rejected. Or if that argument be disallowed, there remains another. These poets represent a very definite and curious type—the " *heroic poem*," as the term was understood by the seventeenth century, a type closely akin to the " *heroic romance* " and the " *heroic play*," which for a generation or two found an appreciative audience. It may be condemned, but it cannot be overlooked, unless we are willing to leave the seventeenth century, its ideals and aspirations, misunderstood. You may say Milton represents the century. He represents, undoubtedly, the spiritual side, the Puritan side. As its most perfect artist he represents too the sense of beauty, the golden legacy of the sixteenth century, in a measure unapproached by any other writer. But the later seventeenth century, emancipated from the Puritan strictness and constraint, bent upon pleasure, social in its aims, he does not represent. If we were to take Milton as the sole representative of his age, or Bunyan, how completely we should misconceive it!

The century which separates the England of Anne from the England of Elizabeth—though it may seem a strangely late date to assign—divides with distinctness modern from mediæval times. During the Civil War the deep change was somehow brought about, and one observes with interest how soon and how clearly the Augustans became conscious of it. Nowhere in the attitude of the latter age towards the former can we discern, as to us would seem proper, a sense of inferiority, everywhere is apparent rather a sense of high superiority. Hardly removed from it by more than a long lifetime, the men of Queen Anne's age thought of the Elizabethans as belonging to a remote and a barbaric past. A brief but sufficient exposition of their feelings appears in Addison's lines upon Spenser—

> " Old Spenser next, warmed with poetic rage,
> In ancient tales amused a barbarous age;
> An age that yet uncultivate and rude,
> Where'er the poet's fancy led, pursued,
> Through pathless fields and unfrequented floods.
> To dens of dragons and enchanted woods.
> But now the mystic tale, that pleased of yore,
> Can charm an understanding age no more."

Observe the phrases " Old Spenser," " a barbarous age,"
" uncultivate and rude " by contrast with " an understanding
age," the superior and altogether excellent age of Anne. Or
take this from *Evelyn's Diary* (1661), " *I saw ' Hamlet, Prince
of Denmark,' played, but now the old plays began to disgust this
refined age, since his Majesties being so long abroad.*" So swift
a change in the national mind and outlook upon life had
never before taken place, it has never taken place since. The
Elizabethan traditions were lost, the ideals forgotten, the manners
outgrown. The age of barbarism, it was assumed as beyond
debate, had given place to that of civility. Partly, no doubt,
the feeling arose out of the double victory of the Renaissance
and the Reformation. Literature and religion had together
thrown off the mediæval yoke. But we must add that at the
same time literature had ceased to be national, and become in a
high degree aristocratic. " *Poetry and criticism,*" wrote Pope
in 1716, " *being by no means the universal concern of the world,
but only the affair of idle men who write in their closets, and of
idle men who read there.*" To be unlettered, unable to read, was
no hindrance to the enjoyment of the works of Shakespeare
and his fellow dramatists. So little was our greatest writer
concerned with readers that he made no provision for the
publication of his plays. When the theatres were closed,
however, literature was altogether withdrawn from the people.
They had no other resources. The first daily newspaper was
not published until 1700, nor even at that date were readers
numerous. " The call for books," said Johnson, " was not in
Milton's age what it is at present. To read was not then a
general amusement; neither traders, nor often gentlemen,
thought themselves disgraced by ignorance. The women had
not then aspired to literature, nor was every house supplied
with a closet of knowledge. Those indeed who professed
learning were not less learned than at any other time; but of
that middle race of students who read for pleasure or accom-
plishment, and who buy the numerous products of modern
typography, the number was then comparatively small." [1]

[1] *Life of Milton.*

With the Restoration the theatres were indeed reopened, but neither the new drama nor the new poetry made any attempt to address the people. Both took their colour from the taste of the Court and fashionable society. Although the Civil War had ended in favour of the Puritans, the aristocratic party returned to place and power under the restored monarchy, bringing with it French preferences, and the reign of polite learning was established. Comedy apart, the taste of " the polite " was the " heroic drama," the " heroic romance," and the " heroic poem." To understand the last-named, a form of narrative peculiar to the seventeenth century, one must know something of the former two. The novel is an eighteenth-century invention, the romances which formed the favourite reading of fashionable society in the previous century, " *ponderous and unmerciful* " as Scott called them, were introduced from France during the Commonwealth period. The amorous Baron in the *Rape of the Lock*

> " every power ador'd
> But chiefly Love—to Love an altar built
> Of twelve vast French Romances, neatly gilt."

The earliest appears to have been de Gomberville's *Polexandre*,[1] which was followed by other translations, like the famous *Artamène ou le Grand Cyrus* [2] (1649-53) by Mlle. Scudéry, and by the works of English imitators, like Roger Boyle, Earl of Orrery (*Parthenissa*, 1654), or Sir George Mackenzie (*Aretina*, 1661). These *Romans de longue Haleine* were of mixed lineage. Their immediate forefathers were the pastoral romances, and though the marvels and enchantments of the earlier chivalric tales are gone, " *the love of honour and the honour of love* " remain to prove a relationship to these also, while the mingling of Moorish and classical personages recalls both Greek and Arabian fiction. But their chief recommendation to English society lay in their French manners, the elaborate code of sentiment and gallantry for which the Court of Louis XIV. was

---

[1] Unless we include *L'Astrée*, by Honore d'Urfé, part of which was translated in 1620.

[2] Upon which Dryden's heroic play, *Secret Love, or the Maiden Queen*, is founded.

famous. The long-suffering reader followed through many volumes a rambling story without coherent plot or interest of character, out of all relation to real life, but his education was not neglected. At every turn and on every page he was lectured upon the etiquette of heroic behaviour and instructed in the proper carriage of an amorous suit. He had too the satisfaction of moving only in the highest society. "Romances," said Congreve, "are generally composed of the constant loves and invincible courages of Heroes, Heroines, Kings and Queens, mortals of the first rank, and so forth; where lofty language, miraculous contingencies, and impossible performances elevate and surprise the reader into a giddy delight, which leaves him flat upon the ground whenever he leaves off."

The "heroic poems" of Davenant and Chamberlayne are of the same family as these romances, the poetical brethren of *Pandion and Amphigenia*,[1] in which the sentiment and reflections suitable to persons of "quality" overpower both plot and characterisation, in which a formidable thicket of commentary overarches and almost completely conceals a thin and trickling stream of narrative. They are close relations also of the "*heroic play*" of the same period, which, said Dryden, "*should be an imitation in little of an heroic poem*," "*drawing all things so far above the ordinary proportion of the stage, as that is beyond the common words and actions of human life*."[2] How may this species of drama, a species in which, to quote Dryden again, "we may justly claim precedence of Shakespeare and Fletcher," best be described? In its technical seventeenth-century sense the title has been the cause of some confusion. Directly derived from its being writ "*in that Verse*," as Rymer said, "*which with Cowley, Denham, and Waller I take to be most proper for Epic Poetry*," the "heroic play" is properly the rhymed play, of which, till he tired of it and changed his mind,[3] Dryden was so stout a champion. But all heroic plays were not rhymed. To describe it, therefore, one must note other

[1] By John Crowne, the author also of various " heroic plays."
[2] *Of Heroic Plays, an Essay.*
[3] See the Prologue to *Aurengzebe,* 1676.

features by which the species may be distinguished. Davenant's *Siege of Rhodes* has sometimes been claimed as the first of the kind, and with reason enough, but Davenant, not venturing in 1656 upon a direct breach of the law against dramatic performances, cast his drama into the form of a musical entertainment accompanied by dialogue, and called it "opera," a work or composition as distinguished from improvisation. If Davenant, however, the author of the first "heroic poem," be disallowed the authorship of the first "heroic play," the honour must go to the author of the first English "heroic romance," Roger Boyle. It was written, as was his prose story, in a new way, "*in the French manner, because I heard the king declare himself more in favour of their way of writing than ours.*" In effect the "heroic play" simply places upon the stage the romance of chivalry, a decayed and degenerate chivalry indeed, the child of a new generation, born and nurtured in France, modern in speech and manners, but with certain unmistakable marks of his blood and descent. A child of the French Renaissance, it need not surprise us that it preserved the unities and reduced the number of characters much below that usual in the Elizabethan drama. The mediæval material here meets the classical form. It chose, too, names historic and high-sounding, Greek or Moorish— *Mustapha, son of Solyman the Magnificent: Almanzor and Almahide ; or the Conquest of Granada : The Amazon Queen ; or the Amours of Thalestris to Alexander the Great.* It dealt almost exclusively with matter of love and honour, debated after the fashion of the mediæval courts of love, the aristocratic code of an exclusive society. "*Are these heroes ?*" inquires Boileau in his ridicule of the romances. "*Have they vowed never to speak of anything but love ? Is it love that constitutes heroic quality ?*"[1] Its preference was all for exalted characters, typical perhaps though in no sense real, tremendous in speech as they were superhuman in capacity. These majestic persons, "*kings and kaisars,*" stalk the stage like Tamburlaine, the extravagance of their whirling eloquence matched by a sentiment soaring above the human pitch. As in the romances the story is so

[1] *Les Héros de Roman.*

sheltered behind the amorous metaphysic, the love interest so predominates that what happens is matter only of secondary importance.

> " The play is at an end, but where's the plot?
> That circumstance the poet Bayes forgot." [1]

The directions for the composition of such a play, given by Tutor in *Reformation, a Comedy* (1673), succinctly set forth the requirements—

> *Tut.* Then, Sir, I take you some three or four or half-a-dozen Kings, but most commonly two or three serve my turn, not a farthing matter whether they lived within a hundred years of one another, not a farthing. Gentlemen, I have tryed it, and let the Play be what it will, the characters are still the same.
> *Pis.* Trust me, Sir, this is a secret of your art.
> *Tut.* As, Sir, you must always have two Ladies in Love with one man, or two men in love with one woman; if you make them the Father and Son, or two Brothers, or two Friends, 'twill do the better. There you know is opportunity for love and honour and fighting, and all that.
> *Ped.* Very well, Sir.
> *Tut.* Then, Sir, you must have a Hero that shall fight with all the world; yes, i'gad, and beat them too, and half the gods into the bargain, if occasion serves.
> *Ant.* This method must needs take.
> *Tut.* And does, Sir.[2]

Davenant has other claims to remembrance than his poetry. He was Shakespeare's godson. He succeeded Ben Jonson as Poet-Laureate. When condemned to death as a Royalist Milton's intervention is said to have saved his life. As for *Gondibert,* unlike the *Davideis,* it lived before it died. Not only was it praised by leading writers, like Hobbes, who declared that " *it would last as long as the ' Iliad ' or the ' Aeneid,' "* but it appears for a time to have ousted the French romances from ladies' favours. Cowley commended *Gondibert* for its freedom from romantic fiction, Waller too made handsome remarks in commendatory verses—

> " Now to thy matchless book
> Wherein those few that can with judgment look,
> May find old love in pure fresh language told,
> Like new stampt coin made out of angel-gold;
> Such truth in love as th' antique world did know,
> In such a style as courts may boast of now;

[1] Buckingham's *Rehearsal.*
[2] Quoted by Professor L. N. Chase in *The English Heroic Play : a critical description of the rhymed tragedy of the Restoration.* See also Scott's *Dryden,* Section 3.

> Which no bold tales of gods or monsters swell,
> But human passions, such as with us dwell;
> Man is thy theme, his vertue or his rage,
> Drawn to the life in each elaborate page;
> Mars nor Bellona are not named here,
> But such a Gondibert as both might fear;
> Venus had here, and Hebe been out-shin'd
> By thy bright Birtha, and thy Rhodalind."

Nor was Davenant himself slow to recommend his poem to a discerning public. To *Gondibert* is prefixed a long and, it must be allowed, a most interesting preface, in which are set forth the reasons for the author's choice of subject together with particulars of the plan and scope of the undertaking. Time, after his ironical fashion, has permitted the poem to perish, but continues to provide readers for the advertisement.

Davenant chose, he tells us, a Christian subject, as more likely to influence his own times; he chose the action from a past age, since great doings, he argues, are more credible if seen from a distance; and, because "*the most effectual schools of morality are courts and camps*," he took thence his exemplars, the heroes best fitted as patterns for imitation. His evilly-disposed characters were selected from those distempered by ambition or by love. "*The world is only ill-governed*," Davenant very wisely remarks, "*because the wicked take more pains to get authority than the virtuous*," and "*infinite Love*" is Lust, "*more dangerous in cities than the calenture in ships*." For his model—it is not easy to see with what good reason—he took the drama, "*proportioning five Books to five Acts, and Cantos to Scenes*," and preferred stanzas to continued couplets, as more pleasant to the ear, and less likely to "*run his reader out of breath*." The substance of his poem he designed to be *wit*, "*the soul's powder*." To the *heroic* he gave his strength as "*the most beautiful of poems*," and confesses that he took pains out of love of fame, reckoning it "*a high presumption to entertain a Nation (who are a Poet's standing Guest, and require Monarchicall respect) with hasty provisions*."

All this is excellent and not undiverting, but it offered a tempting target to the scornful—

> "Here is the mountain, but where is the mouse?"

Clearly Davenant sat down and considered before he laid siege to " *the chief city*," as Fontenelle called epic, in the broad empery of poetry.   Yet singularly enough, with all his thought, he omitted to borrow or construct a reasonable plot.   For six or seven thousand lines he spent himself unheroically upon sentiment and description, and in the middle of the third book a crisis in his political career extinguished the poem and came near to extinguishing the author's life.   " *Even in so worthy a designe*," he remarks in a postscript, " *I shall ask leave to desist when I am interrupted by so great an experiment as dying.*" Begun in France, where he had sought refuge from the Parliament, *Gondibert* was interrupted by the accident of the author's capture at sea by an English cruiser, and as a prisoner in Cowes Castle, expecting execution, he had no heart to proceed.   When released, Davenant was apparently no longer in the vein to finish his undertaking.

The story of *Gondibert* is nothing, common matter of love, in which the hero, Duke Gondibert, sways between the attractions of two rival stars, the ladies Rhodalind and Birtha.   The names, as in the romances, are far-fetched and mouth-filling—

> " Hurgonil, Astolpho, Borgia, Goltha, Tibalt,
>   Astragon, Hermogild, Ulfinor, Orgo, Thula."

One or two cantos, the least tiresome, deal with the wonders of the palace of the sage Astragon, a scientific and philosophical academy, in which, as in a modern university, were represented all manner of studies and laborious investigations of nature. Physics and chemistry, botany and zoology have here their museums, where " *olde busie men*," " *Nature's Registers*," study the objects supplied them by a " *throng of Intelligencers*," who search throughout the world in sea and earth and air for fish, fowl, and beast, minerals, roots, berries, simples, herbs, and flowers.   There are suitable observatories for astronomers, who " *seek the stars' remote societies*," for meteorologists—

> " He showes them now tow'rs of prodigious height,
>   Where Nature's friends, philosophers remain
> To censure meteors in their cause and flight,
>   And watch the wind's authority on rain."

Here too anatomy is studied, in " *The Cabinet of Death* "—

> " This dismall gall'ry, lofty, long, and wide,
>   Was hung with skelitons of ev'ry kinde;
> Humane, and all that learned humane pride
> Thinks made t'obey man's high immortal minde."

In the library, finely called " *The Monument of Vanish'd Minds*," are housed " *heaps of written thoughts, gold of the dead*," Egyptian and Chaldean rolls, the books of all the peoples of the past, Hebrew, Greek, and Roman, unwieldy volumes legal and theological and ethical, and to refresh the visitor after his long survey, " *the pleasant poets*," heralds of fame. No reader now attempts to enliven his leisure with *Gondibert*,[1] but one can see how it made an appeal to the philosophic Hobbes, and for the student of seventeenth-century criticism, as well as for the student of the " heroic " poem, it is important as a battle-ground of the wits and theorists. Though Cowley, Waller, and Hobbes had praised, Rymer, as Isaac Disraeli expresses it, " *opened his Aristotelian text-book* " and disapproved.[2] " A Club of wits," too, " *blending their brains together, plotted how to bespatter one of the Muses' choicest sons*," [3] in a series of satirical verses—

> " We thought it fit to let thee know it
> Thou art a damn'd insipid poet."

In the *Pharonnida* of William Chamberlayne, a work even less known to fame than *Gondibert*, the type to which both belong is best presented. It appears to have slipped into existence in 1659, eight years later than Davenant's poem, without attracting any attention, and probably in no single year since its birth has it numbered more than a dozen readers. Yet we have here a poem of curious and even abiding interest. *Pharonnida* is our first, and perhaps still our best novel in verse, a species of composition against which the Muse appears to have set her face, since no perfectly successful example can be cited. Why should it fail? Only, it would seem, because verse is inappropriate save in the conduct of elevated action, without due warrant where the key of feeling falls to the level of ordinary

---

[1] The latest appreciation of Davenant may be found in the *Retrospective Review*, vol. ii.
[2] See his *Quarrels of Authors*.
[3] From the title of a contemporary poem.

life.   In drama which admits only the critical situations and
critical moments verse is always legitimate, for it is then charged
with responsibility.   But verse, the aristocratic medium of
expression, revolts from servile occupations, refuses to perform,
or performs reluctantly, the workaday routine, the domestic
tasks of the novel.   It turns away from all menial service, it
is intolerant, haughty, exclusive, it abhors introductions,
explanations, details.   Nothing, therefore, would appear less
promising than such an attempt as Chamberlayne's to render
into verse a long and complicated story, with its many characters,
episodes, incidents, sentiments, and passions.   The mere linking
of part to part, the transitions from one matter to another, place
a heavy strain upon his medium.   The finest constructive art
was required of him.   Yet of such art he knew nothing.   A
nineteenth-century critic has spoken, indeed, of " *this beautifully
planned poem*," [1] but within the next few sentences remarks,
" The author lays the scene at one time in Greece, and at another
in Sicily; and with a strange and whimsical forgetfulness
describes the king's capital as being at one moment in the
Morea, and in the next, without the least warning, we find it
placed in the island; thus he transports us from one to the
other, with the most ludicrous gravity and unconcern.   The
confusion occasioned by this ubiquity of his *dramatis personae*
may be easily conceived.   Ariamnes is indifferently designated
by that name, and by the name of Aminander, and we learn
towards the conclusion of the poem, rather abruptly, and with
some surprise, for the first time, that the king of the Morea is
called Cleander."   As examples of " *beautiful planning* " these
are sufficiently astonishing, and though critics have been found
bold enough to praise *Pharonnida*—and its charm is undeniable
—the immense initial difficulty apart, the faults are so numerous
as to dishearten most readers.   Though epic in length, some
thirteen or fourteen thousand lines, it has no plot to speak of;
there reigns in it discursiveness beyond all reason.   Loose
rhymes afflict the ear, indifference to grammar the attention,[2]

---

[1] The *Retrospective Review*, vol. i.
[2] " *I could never get the blockhead to study his grammar*," said Swift of Pope.

doubtful meanings the intelligence. A conversational licence in abbreviations, an incredible carelessness in construction, which permits, for instance, characters we confidently believe dead to return not as ghosts but as living actors to the scene of the history, give to this poem a bad pre-eminence in artistic shortcomings. If Chamberlayne wrote only for his own pleasure and cared little for readers, there is of course nothing to censure or to pardon. In a sense no writer less deserves them. What saves him from utter and merited neglect is not this quality or that, it is simply that he is a poet, and so considerable a poet that one is willing to suffer many discomforts for the sake of his company. *Pharonnida* cannot be read like Chaucer for the story, like Pope for wit and epigram, or like Browning for intellectual speculation or dialectic subtlety. Rather, like Keats, it is exclusively for those who read poetry for poetry's sake. Its author provides no alternative, he is wholly and absorbingly occupied with the saying of "*heart-easing things.*" One moves slowly as through the flowery meadows of some misty pleasant land. Now and again the air clears, a prospect offers itself, we distinguish objects and persons, but presently the haze gathers, and without much sense of loss the grassy turf, the hedgerows, and the poet's quiet talk occupy and suffice us. His subject may be "heroic,"[1] but where in English narrative poetry are we to look for anything less like the heroic style than Chamberlayne's, which is "*nothing,*" as Professor Saintsbury says, "*if not starry and flowery.*"[2] There is no modern parallel save in Keats. Of nineteenth-century poems *Endymion* most resembles *Pharonnida*, which Keats indeed appears to have known and studied; it provides the same kind of pleasure in the same kind of verse.

In the "heroic" poems of this period the free run-on

---

[1] "I have made bold with the title of heroic, but have a late example that deters me from disputing upon what grounds I assumed it: if it suits not with the abilities of my pen, yet it is no unbecoming epithet for the eminence of those personated in my poem."—*Epistle to the Reader* prefixed to *Pharonnida*.

[2] See his invaluable *Caroline Poets* for Chamberlayne, Chalkhill, Kynaston, Marmion, and Bosworth. The third volume is long promised.

couplet makes for the ear a music never heard in the *staccato* rhymes of Pope.   They illustrate the "incorrect" as distinguished from the "correct" style recommended by Walsh and taught by Waller.   The rhyme frequently falls upon unimportant words, the pause comes as often (or oftener) within as at the end of the line, and a paragraph structure, as in blank verse, takes the place of successive emphasised couplets. The "incorrect" form of the couplet relieves monotony, offers opportunities of enrichment and variety of sound, and, in narrative poetry especially, may in the hands of an artist provide more musical pleasure.   But as in the case of Shakespeare's later blank verse, it may be so loosely built as to border upon, and, save for the rhyme, be barely distinguishable from prose.   Pope's, the "correct," form of versification undoubtedly best suited his purposes, and during the greater part of the eighteenth century no other seemed possible.   Yet this too had its dangers and defects.   So insistent is the tune that the verse seems perfect even when musically valueless.   It was easily learnt, and a hundred writers, who were without the rudiments of the art, fancied themselves poets.   It is not enough that the rhymes be true, the pauses kept, the accents regularly distributed; many thousands of correct and utterly inanimate lines were yearly produced in the eighteenth century.   Blank verse without merit creates suspicion even in the defective ear; there is nothing to veil its intrinsic poverty.   Rhyme—how little is it even among would-be poets understood—far more frequently conceals the absence of true melody than contributes to it, as Milton knew when he spoke of rhyme as "*no necessary adjunct*" to good verse, but a device often employed "*to set off wretched matter and lame metre.*"

Chamberlayne, like Davenant—knighted for his services to the Royalist cause at the siege of Gloucester—was so far qualified for heroic poetry that he knew something of camps and battles. A call to arms interrupted the composition of his poem.   "I must," he tells us at the close of the second book—

> "Let my pen rest awhile, and see the rust
> Scoured from my own sword"—

but if fortune favours he promises to return to his task—

> " If in
> This rising storm of blood, which doth begin
> To drop already, I'm not washed into
> The grave, my next safe quarter shall renew
> Acquaintance with Pharonnida.—Till then
> I leave the Muses to converse with men."

The reference is to the second battle of Newbury in 1644
Probably not long afterwards, since the war ended disastrously
for Charles in the following year, the poet exchanged the field
for the study, but the poem was not published until 1659, and
appears therefore to have been for long on the stocks.   The
story of *Pharonnida*, very similar to those told in prose in the
heroic romances, *Artamène* or *Parthenissa*, is too long to recall,
and extracts do it little justice, yet a quotation from a poem
which was praised by Campbell, and to which Southey was
" *indebted for many hours of delight*," needs no apology.[1]   Here
is a portion of the description of the palace in Pharonnida's
island—

> " Here did the beauties of those temples shine,
> Which Ephesus or sacred Palestine
> Once boasted in; the Persian might from this
> Take patterns for his famed Persepolis. . . .
> The sides, whose large balcones conveyed the eye
> T' the fields' wild prospects, were supported by
> A thousand pillars; where in mixture shone
> The Parian white and red Corinthian stone,
> Supporting frames, where in the like art stood
> Smooth ivory mixed with India's swarthy wood:
> All which, with gold, and purer azure brought
> From Persian artists, in mosaics wrought,
> The curious eye into meanders led,
> Until diverted by a sight that bred
> More real wonder.—The rich front wherein
> By antic sculpture, all that ere had been
> The various acts of their preceding kings,
> So figured was; no weighty metal brings
> Aught to enhance its worth, Art did compose
> Each emblem of such various gems—all chose
> Their several colours—under a sapphire sky
> Here cheerful emeralds, chaste smaragdi lie—
> A fresh green field, in which the armèd knights
> Were all clad in heart-cheering chrysolites,
> With rubies set, which to adorn them twist
> Embraces with the temperate amethyst;
> For parts unarmed—here the fresh onyx stood,
> And Sardia's stone appeared like new-drawn blood;

[1] The article in the *Retrospective Review* relates the story at some length.

> The Proteus-like achates here was made
> For swords' fair hilts, but for the glittering blade,
> Since all of rich and precious gems was thus
> Composed, was showed of flaming pyropus:
> And lest aught here that's excellent should want,
> The ladies' eyes were shining adamant."

The romantic manner, which endeavours to "*load every rift of the subject with ore*," which, careless of how time passes and adventure waits, lays colour by colour simply for the sake of their own beauty, is as admirably illustrated by Chamberlayne as the classical manner, where "*not a word is wasted, not a sentiment capriciously thrown in*," by Homer or by Milton. And in this very lingering nature of romance, this inclination to loiter by the way in pleasant places its weakness lies. Not so much a poetical as a narrative weakness, an inability to march is the characteristic of both verse and prose romances of this period. Chamberlayne succeeded bravely in bringing his story to a conclusion. Davenant and Chalkhill, after the author of *Pharonnida* the best poet among the "heroic" romancers, failed, as Boyle in his *Parthenissa* and Crowne in his *Pandion and Amphigenia* failed, to complete their undertakings. And since they are to be read for their embroidery, and the story and its characters are no more than fair excuses for the decorative pattern, though they are long poems, epic they are not. Yet in any history of epic one cannot overlook them, not only because they styled themselves "heroic," but because as a form of verse narrative they derive from the parent stem. Walton's preface to Chalkhill's *Thealma and Clearchus* describes it as "*a Pastoral History, in smooth and easy verse*," the second title of Kynaston's *Leoline and Sydanis* entitles it "*A Romance of the Amorous Adventures of Princes*." Place the two phrases together and they reveal the intentions of all the poets of this group. It would be difficult to say anything of Chamberlayne that is not true of Chalkhill except that as a poet he is perhaps superior in the same manner. *Thealma and Clearchus* was published by Izaak Walton in 1683, and ascribed by him to "*an acquaintant and friend*" of Spenser, and some critics [1] have

---

[1] *E.g.* Mr. Edmund Gosse (see his *From Shakespeare to Pope*, p. 209;) and the author of the article on " Thealma and Clearchus " in the *Retrospective Review*, vol. iv.

been bold enough to believe that since almost nothing is known of Chalkhill, Walton was himself the author. Compared with *Pharonnida* Chalkhill's poem is brief, three thousand lines. It concludes abruptly and a note is appended, " *And here the author died, and I hope the reader will be sorry.*" For the sake of a comparison with the passage quoted from Chamberlayne the following description of Thealma may serve—

> " She trick'd herself in all her best attire,
> As if she meant this day t'invite Desire
> To fall in love with her: her loose hair
> Hung on her shoulders, sporting with the air:
> Her brow a coronet of rose-buds crown'd,
> With loving woodbine's sweet embraces bound.
> Two globe-like pearls were pendant to her ears,
> And on her breast a costly gem she wears,
> An adamant, in fashion like a heart,
> Whereon Love sat a-plucking out a dart,
> With this same motto graven round about
> On a gold border: *Sooner in than out.*
> This gem Clearchus gave her, when, unknown,
> At tilt his valour won her for his own.
> Instead of bracelets on her wrists she wore
> A pair of golden shackles, chain'd before
> Unto a silver ring enamelled blue,
> Whereon in golden letters to the view
> This motto was presented: *Bound yet free.*
> And in a true-love's knot a T. and C."

This, with its mottoes and trinkets, is a very engaging but a very modern sentimentalism. The heroic spirit is gone, and by comparison with these romances even Crabbe in his realistic verse narratives makes a closer approach to epic interest. For at least with him we move again in a society that existed, and exchange the impossible princes and warriors we have never known, or can know, for fishermen and artisans, who have felt and suffered, whose experiences we can follow with understanding and sympathy. Such obscure and humble characters as appear in *The Borough* or *Tales of the Hall* dare not venture indeed to show themselves in epic camps or castles, but they live and have power upon us far beyond the phantasmal lords and ladies of pastoral fiction. Crabbe has virility without beauty, Chamberlayne and his group beauty without virility. Only when in a narrative poem virility and beauty are found together can any reasonable claim be advanced for it to consideration among the epics.

We now enter the most desolate region of English poetry,
a dreary " *No man's land*," forbidding desert, without sign of
human occupation or interest, a region reported to be barren
beyond hope, shunned even by the most hardy seekers for poetic
treasure, through which few, if any, living travellers have ever
forced their way—the epic poetry of Blackmore (1650-1729),
of Glover (1712-1785), and of Wilkie (1721-1772), in all con-
sisting of eighty-five books, and something between fifty and
a hundred thousand lines of verse. " Ce qui ne vaut pas la
peine d'être dit, on le chante." Of the redoubtable three Sir
Richard Blackmore, a city physician, who dealt " *at leisure
hours in epic song* " and wrote, said the critics, " *to the rumbling
of his coach's wheels*," is first in time as in the magnificence of
his industry, a giant author who successfully battles with
oblivion by the sheer bulk of his performances. Of no other
poet in the history of the world can it be claimed that he is the
author of four complete epics—*Prince Arthur, King Arthur,
Eliza, Alfred*. These massive achievements, not to speak of
such trifles as his *Creation, a Philosophical Poem*, in seven, his
Nature of Man in three, and his *Redemption, a Divine Poem*, in
six books, might well have staggered his contemporaries into
respect. Their contempt has served almost equally well to
preserve his memory. For if scorned by the critics, he was
at least not overlooked or neglected. Dryden, as Johnson said,
" *pursued him with great malignity*," Pope made " *the everlasting
Blackmore* " a constant butt, Dennis devoted a volume of over
two hundred pages to a condemnation of his first epic, *Prince
Arthur*. Though he had friends as well as enemies, Locke and
Molyneux, and Addison, who spoke of the *Creation* as " *one of
the most useful and noble productions in our English verse*,"
wherein " *the depths of philosophy* [are] *enlivened with all the
charms of poetry*," [1] Blackmore owes his fame, if we can call it
fame rather than notoriety, to scoffers rather than admirers.
Yet Johnson thought him worthy of a " Life," asserted justly,
and with his customary honesty, that he had " *been exposed to
worse treatment than he deserved*," found, like Addison, praise

---

[1] *Spectator*, No. 339.

for his *Creation*, defended his character as a man, and claimed for him " *the honours of magnanimity*." Dennis was right when he declared Blackmore " *neither admirable nor contemptible*." He is not admirable, for he never rises to distinction, nor is he contemptible, for he abounds in passages which reveal reflection, display poetic feeling, and if the end of poetry were, as he conceived it, " *to cultivate the mind with instructions of virtue*," might well be praised.

Blackmore is without poetry in the high sense, but he is not without powers of expression, and his achievements are certainly beyond the reach of the majority who have been taught to think them ridiculous. " *The ingenuous part of mankind*," he suggests with some point in one of his sensible prefaces, " *will not fall unmercifully on a writer of epic poetry, wherein only two men, I mean Homer and Virgil, have succeeded*."

With this sentence in our ears it is natural to ask ourselves why men like Blackmore should have attempted a task of such magnitude as the composition of an epic poem. We may ascribe the undertaking to an absurd self-conceit, or to sheer ignorance of its difficulty, or to both these failings. However explained, the state of contemporary criticism must share some part of the responsibility for their extraordinary efforts. To illustrate the critical attitude of the times towards poetry in general would take us far from the immediate subject, but the volume by Dennis, already mentioned, *Some Remarks on a book entitled Prince Arthur, an heroic poem*, and another by Pemberton, *Observations on Poetry, especially the Epic, occasioned by the late poem upon Leonidas*, which reviews Glover's epic, will instruct us in the current ideas which led, in Hayley's phrase, " *to the cultivation of epic writing*." Neither of these works appears to mention the need of any special talent or faculty, or of any unusual application to a study of the poetic art. Attention to the Aristotelian rules is indeed imperative, but the rules once mastered the rest of the undertaking would appear to be simple. Dennis lays down the usual Renaissance requirements—care for the integrity of the action, the manners of the characters, the propriety of the episodes. His complaints are that *Prince Arthur* is "*an empty fiction, without any manner of instruction*," that "*his machines are directly contrary to the doctrine of the Church of England*," that "*his incidents are not of a delightful nature*," that they "*are not surprising*," that "*the episodes are not pathetic*." He labours to prove that in particulars such as these Virgil's judgment was unerring, Blackmore's faulty. The qualities in which *Prince Arthur* fell short were apparently qualities in which a schoolmaster might have given the author instruction. The radical and essential defects, absence of imagination and insight, of poetic conception and expression, cause Dennis no concern. That Virgil was, that Blackmore was not a poet—the significance of this distinction appears not so much to have escaped as never to have occurred to his mind. Briefly he appears unconscious of the true nature of poetry, its genesis, its logic, its emotional attachments, its spiritual affinities.

With Pemberton in his appreciation of Glover it is the same. *Leonidas* is a great epic poem because in its action it exhibits "*the most shining example of military prowess and public spirit united in one person that the whole extent of history can furnish*," because the characters are well marked, the episodes well chosen. Pemberton devotes some space, it is true, to a consideration of the language and versification suited to heroic poetry, and finds his author "*attentive to the just measure of his verse*," and distinguished in the management of descriptions and similes, but seems powerless to discriminate between correct verse and inspired poetry. Had he designed a panegyric, he tells us, he "*might have desired the reader to compare this author with Milton in relation to the harmony of the numbers, with Virgil in point of character, and even with Homer himself in regard to sublimity of sentiment*." This is a strange deafness, the eighteenth-century deafness, from which Dr. Johnson suffered when he declared the diction of *Lycidas* "*harsh, the rhymes uncertain, and the numbers unpleasing*," when he wrote, "*By perusing the works of Dryden Pope discovered the most perfect fabric of English verse . . . to attempt any further improvement of versification will be dangerous. Art and diligence have now done their best, and what shall be added will be the effort of tedious toil and needless curiosity.*" [1]

Criticism like that of Dennis and Pemberton, preoccupied with mechanical and external matters of " plots " and " machines," " discoveries," " recognitions," " fables simple and implex," " unity," " characters," and "sentiments"—all the literary *patter* of the Renaissance—nowhere penetrates to the soul of the poem, nowhere asks about it the proper questions. Hearing around them no language but this, who can wonder that Blackmore and Glover were deceived, who can wonder that they mistook anatomic structure for animating spirit, that they conceived themselves epic poets when they had provided the necessary " *voyages, wars, councils, machines,*" and believed themselves to be creating life when they were carving a wooden block into its semblance? These writers were neither unintelligent nor unaccomplished. They were on the contrary able and talented. They were the luckless victims of misinformation, who followed faithfully enough the light, not the *vera lux* but the smoky lanterns of the ignorantly learned who prescribed the requirements. " *The flowers of the Ancients appear but withered when gathered by unskilful hands.*" [2]

To cite absurdities from Blackmore's epics were easy if it were not also tedious, but the general conduct of his narrative is insipid rather than ludicrous. Two specimens of his style, not at its worst, must suffice. The first is from *Prince Arthur*—[3]

> " To keep the birthday of the world, the Spring
> Does all her joys and frequent riches bring. . . .
> The air's so soft, such balmy odours fly,
> So sweet the fruits, so pure and mild the sky,
> The blissful states, too great to be exprest
> By all the pleasures of the wanton East,

[1] Less eminent sufferers from the malady were of course numerous, *e.g.* the Hon. Edward Howard, who spoke of " *The two elaborate poems of Blackmore and Milton, the which, for the dignity of them, may very well be looked upon as the two grand exemplars of poetry.*"

[2] Voltaire's *Essay on Epic Poetry*.

[3] " Begun, carried on, and completed," says the author in his Preface, " in less than two years' time, and by such catches and starts, and in such occasional uncertain hours as the business of my profession would afford me. And therefore, for the greatest part, that poem was written in coffee-houses, and in passing up and down the streets, because I had little leisure elsewhere to apply to it."

> By th' Arab's sweets, from Zephyr's tender wings
> Gently shook off, or what the merchant brings
> Of foreign luxury, with tedious toil,
> From Asia's coast, or soft Campania's soil."

The second, from *King Arthur*, describes that monarch—

> " His glorious belt he cross his shoulder flung,
> In which refulgent Caliburno hung.
> With his strong arm he grasp'd his spacious shield,
> Where a fierce Dragon guarded all the field.
> So bright it blazed, the metal when it came
> Red from the forge, did scarce more fiercely flame,
> Then his long spear he grip'd, which shone from far
> Bright, as if pointed with the Morning Star."

As he himself admitted he was an " interloper," not a member of any of the literary societies of his time, and the success of his first poem, *Prince Arthur*, with uncritical readers made him a target for the wits. "*Of his four epic poems,*" said Johnson, "*the first had such reputation and popularity as enraged the critics ; the second was at least known enough to be ridiculed ; the two last had neither friends nor enemies.*" Blackmore thus outlived the brief hour of his fame as a poet, but he was not without honours in his proper profession. As one of the king's physicians he received the honour of knighthood, and at Hampton Court was provided in his official apartment "*with stuff furniture, a large bed suitable, and bedding, and six back-chairs covered with the same stuff.*" Consolations such as these do not always await the unsuccessful adventurer into poetry. He dares to write bad verses and goes unpunished!

Unlike Blackmore, who surprised the world by a sudden entry into the lists for the poetic laurel when he was about forty years of age, Glover served an apprenticeship to the art, and gave promise of future distinction when he was but sixteen by a poem in praise of Sir Isaac Newton. A city merchant, it was not inappropriate that he should compose a poem upon *London, or the Progress of Commerce*—

> " Fair seat of wealth and freedom, thee my Muse
> Shall celebrate, O London: thee she hails
> Thou lov'd abode of Commerce "—

or write, with patriotic intention, the once celebrated ballad, praised by Fielding, *Admiral Hosier's Ghost*. That his attempt at the greater poetry in *Leonidas*, an epic in twelve books,[1] should have achieved immediate success and be six or seven times reprinted is, however, surprising, until we learn that it was supposed to give political support to the party opposed to Sir Robert Walpole, then in office. " *Nothing else was read or talked of at Leicester House,*" says Warton. " *Pray who is that Mr. Glover,*" wrote Swift to Pope, " *who writ the epic poem called ' Leonidas,' which is reprinting here and hath great vogue ?* " It is of some interest that Glover should have had the independence in Pope's lifetime to employ blank verse rather than the heroic couplet, a measure which he also adopted for his second epic *The Athenaid,* a continuation of the first, found among his papers and published after his death. Glover falls short of the singular eminence achieved by Blackmore in that he wrote only half the number of epics, but in some measure compensates for his deficiency. *The Athenaid* extends to thirty books, which " fell plumb," in Professor Dowden's phrase, " into the waters of oblivion." He entered, too, unterrified the dramatic field. *Boadicea* and *Medea*, the latter on the classical model, were both performed, though neither achieved any success. It is instructive that amid the general chorus of approval which greeted *Leonidas*—which, said Lord Lyttleton, " *will be handed down with respect to all posterity* "—some critics were concerned at the absence from the poem of the traditional mythological machinery. That it was poetry and good poetry none questioned. But a certain critical uneasiness was naturally felt at the reckless daring of an author who deliberately forbore to tread in the exact and sacred footprints of Homer and Virgil. Fortunately he had the example of Lucan, not indeed so safe, but at least a classical authority, and readers who had no suspicion that *Leonidas* was worthless as poetry, thus assured themselves that their author had not seriously imperilled his enduring fame.

A consideration of the satisfaction which appears to have been derived by their contemporaries from the verse of poets to modern ears destitute of musical delight, suggests the thought that we may now demand a more finished art, a richer and

---

[1] The first edition was in nine, and the poem was afterwards extended.

more subtle harmony than was required by our ancestors of a century or two ago. We would probably have little difficulty in believing it could we regard the progress of the poetic art as from the first continuous, if we could think of Chaucer as less skilled in verbal melody than Dryden, or Spenser than Pope; if we could forget Shakespeare and the Elizabethans, or Milton and the seventeenth-century lyrists. What appears incomprehensible is that the former lessons should have been so completely forgotten, the early and triumphant music overlooked or despised. We must believe the human ear to remain unchanged, and account for a satisfaction to us inexplicable by reference to influences outside the region of verbal sounds, which somehow create new tastes and new preferences. We must explain eighteenth-century fashions in poetry by directing our attention to civic and social conditions, to such matters as the state of learning, the intellectual *milieu*, or the number and interests of readers, rather than to the more technical aspects of literature. For it seems clear that the fortunes of poetry, as of the other arts, depend upon the national fortunes in ways impossible to foresee, and difficult to elucidate even when known. The history of art cannot be dissociated from the history of thought, from the history of the country to which it belongs.

To speak of the poetry of Glover as worthless may appear harsh and even insolent, when critics, like the poet Campbell, discuss his claims to attention, and find room in an anthology for twenty or thirty pages of quotation, but the judgment is quite compatible with such commendation as, for example, the following—" *in the general structure of the story, in the peopling of it with incidents and characters, and in the strain of feeling which he has diffused through the whole* [*of ' Leonidas '*], *he has displayed talents of no despicable order*." [1] One may go further and say that Glover's talents are even remarkable. But they are not poetic talents, they are not talents for expression which exalts and delights the mind. The smooth and easy conduct of narrative in verse implies no such talent. When exhibited, as

---

[1] *Retrospective Review*, vol. ii., to which, as to Campbell's selections, the inquiring reader may refer.

—to omit the greatest names—Sackville exhibits it, or Collins, or even Chamberlayne or Chalkhill, it is unmistakable—the sudden splendour like the flash of the sun's rays from a mirror. Glover, Blackmore at times, write with dignity, one might almost say, elevation, but the transporting and mysterious power which communicates often to thoughts or ideas not in themselves exciting, exciting quality—a music, or a poignancy like a sword thrust—of this power there is never at any time either the suggestion or the promise. "*I think nothing is of any value in books*," said Emerson, "*excepting the transcendental and extraordinary.*" We know his meaning, it was poetic quality only that he valued. Glover is admitted by scholars to have been a scholar, his abilities merit perfect respect, he is admirable as a citizen and as a patriot, he won a deserved popularity, but, with the increasing demand made by books and studies upon the brief years allotted to each of us, it would be folly to recommend readers to his pages. Since during the ascendancy of the heroic couplet he eschewed it, one might expect distinction in the measure he preferred, but, as Warton said, "*He has not availed himself of the great privilege of blank verse to run his verses into one another with different pauses,*" and "*appears,*" as the reviewer already quoted remarks, "*to have had an objection to the frequent use of the trochee;*" that is to say, he had learnt nothing from Milton. It will be sufficient here to illustrate his style by a single quotation from each of his epics. The first from *Leonidas* describes the song of the Priestess of the Muses before Thermopylae—

> " Of endless joys
> In bless'd Elysium was the song. Go meet
> Lycurgus, Solon, and Zaleucus sage,
> Let them salute the children of their laws.
> Meet Homer, Orpheus, and th' Ascræan bard,
> Who with a spirit, by ambrosial food
> Refin'd, and more exalted, shall contend
> Your splendid fate to warble through the bow'rs
> Of amaranth and myrtle ever young,
> Like your renown. Your ashes we will cull.
> In yonder fane deposited, your urns,
> Dear to the Muses, shall our lays inspire.
> Whatever off'rings genius, science, art,
> Can dedicate to virtue shall be yours,
> The gifts of all the Muses, to transmit

You on th' enliven'd canvas, marble, brass,
In wisdom's volume, in the poet's song,
In ev'ry tongue, through every age and clime,
You of this earth the brightest flow'rs, not cropt,
Transplanted only to immortal bloom
Of praise with men, of happiness with gods."

In the next, from *The Athenaid*, Themistocles foresees the renewed glories of Athens—

" Superb, her structures shall proclaim
No less a marvel than the matchless bird
The glory of Arabia, when, consum'd
In burning frankincense and myrrh, he shows
His presence new, and, op'ning to the Sun
Regenerated gloss of plumage, tow'rs,
Himself a species.   So shall Athens rise
Bright from her ashes, mistress sole of Greece.
From long Piraean walls her winged pow'r
Shall awe the Orient and Hesperian worlds."

We are told by Warton that when Thomson heard of Glover's epic, he exclaimed, " *He write an epic poem ! a Londoner, who has never seen a mountain !* " This singular qualification for the undertaking was at least possessed by William Wilkie, a Scottish contemporary, born in the parish of Dalmeny, afterwards minister of Ratho, and finally Professor of Natural Philosophy in the University of St. Andrews. As a parish minister he was, it seems, popular, though his habits were peculiar. It is recorded that he " *generally preached with his hat on his head*," " *often forgot to pronounce the blessing after public service*," and " *had been seen to dispense the sacraments without consecrating the elements*. His *Epigoniad*, an epic in nine books, was well received in Scotland, coldly south of the Border, and but for the remarkable intervention of the philosopher, David Hume, would probably have been forgotten within the author's lifetime. Admiration for Hume as metaphysician and historian must be exchanged for astonishment when one contemplates his unfortunate excursion into literary criticism. In a letter to the authors of the *Critical Review*, which had published an unfriendly article upon Wilkie, Hume claimed for the *Epigoniad* that it " *abounded in sublime beauties*," might be " *regarded as one of the ornaments of our language*," and referring to the tradition that Homer had taken the siege of Thebes for the subject of a poem, now lost, asserted that " *the whole turn of this new poem would almost lead us to imagine that the Scottish bard had found the lost manuscript of that father of poetry, and had made a faithful translation of it into English.*" Allow that Hume's patriotism inflamed his language, and we have but another example of that judgment according to the rules which so misled the eighteenth century. What adverse criticism did Wilkie himself anticipate? That he had "*chosen for his subject a piece of history which has no connection with our present affairs,*" or "*that the mythology will give offence to some readers.*" How remote are these from our present complaints! We allow that all the epic requirements are here in order—the combats, the games, the episodes, the similes. The reader will probably also allow that there are descriptions of merit, that the episode of Philoctetes, for example, in the seventh book, is a spirited one, he will allow that the poem taken as a whole is not unreadable—

> " Amid the fight, distinguish'd like the star
> Of Ev'ning, shone his silver arms afar."

> " Ah warriors! will ye fly, when close behind
> Dishonour follows swifter than the wind? "

> " His helmet fill'd with both his hands he rear'd
> In act to drink; when in the grove appear'd
> Th' Etolian prince. His armour's fiery blaze
> The dark recess illumin'd with its rays."

> " I climb'd a mountain's head,
> Where wide before me lay the ocean spread;
> And there no object met my wishing eyes
> But billows bounded by the setting skies,
> Yet still I gaz'd, till night's prevailing sway
> Extinguish'd, in the west, the ev'ning ray.
> Hopeless and sad, descending from my stand,
> I wander'd on the solitary strand,
> Through the thick gloom; and heard the sullen roar
> Of billows bursting on the desert shore."

There is no serious offence in these verses. As a poet Wilkie is perhaps more tolerable than either Blackmore or Glover, yet he is not sufficiently a poet. And if we have asked and answered in his disfavour the summary question, "Have we here a poet? " further criticism becomes unnecessary. There is no *via media* in this dangerous art between the good and the bad. "*Il y a de certaines choses dont la médiocrité est insuportable, la poésie, la musique, la peinture, la discours publique.*" We may agree or disagree with Hume in respect of such other matters as the design or the fable, we may, in the case of Glover, allow with Campbell that his characters are "*not so much poetical as historical recollections*," that his narrative "*wants impetuosity of progress*," or admit that *Leonidas* is of interest "*as the monument of an accomplished and amiable mind.*" We may apportion, or acquiesce in the apportionment of, praise or blame, but for us the matter is really at an end. The main issue in our day seems the only issue. Are we here on safe ground? Or are we in danger of neglecting the Greek canon, the canon of a people for whose judgments in poetry we cannot have too great a reverence, upon which Arnold so eloquently insisted? It is here set forth by him. "*All depends upon the subject ; choose a fitting action, penetrate yourself with the feeling of its situations ; this done, everything else will follow.*" May it be that in deciding against Blackmore and Glover, though the decision be just, it has been given on improper grounds, for irrelevant reasons? Is it possible that the first inquiry should have been, not "Are these men sufficient poets?" but, "Are the subjects chosen by them fitting subjects, were they penetrated with the feeling of the situations?" Behind Arnold's contention there lies surely a suppressed premiss. "All depends upon the subject," "all else will follow" only if the task be undertaken by a friend of the Muses. Arnold is here concerned with a tendency of modern, of romantic, criticism to overlook the whole, and admire, where they are admirable, the parts, to rest satisfied with fine lines and fine passages, to care most of all for the exhibition of the writer's personality, to care little, by comparison, for the design, "*the mere subject*," as Pater called it. The debate admits neither of a moment's hesitation nor doubt. We shall not, indeed, be called upon to reverse our judgments upon Glover or Wilkie, but that the Greeks, however misinterpreted by eighteenth-century critics, were right, the moderns wrong, seems indisputable. How brilliantly, to take an example, Browning exhibits his personality, how transporting are lines and passages in his works! But can we believe that we have here a poet who without loss neglected his design? Can we think that there is not here a waste of poetical power—the richest and most varied in its generation, perhaps in its century—pitiable and grievous? Shakespeare, it was said, wanted art; how much more did Browning want it! His longer poems will escape the fate of Blackmore, but they will escape it with difficulty. Not indeed for the same cause, lack of genius, but for a fault hardly compensated by genius — surplusage. Without personality, without the gift of expression, as the eighteenth-century epic failures prove, success in the greater poetry is impossible; it is almost, if not equally, impossible without design. Art without genius is barren, but genius without art is like a blind giant, a Polyphemus, stumbling over every obstacle, hurling with magnificent strength his ineffectual missiles.

CHAPTER XII

THE MOCK-HEROIC IN ENGLISH POETRY

VERSE, it is agreed, adds to the emotional force of expression. Words convey the poet's meaning, as they do that of the ordinary man, but through and by means of the rhythm something is added. That something is the intensity or enthusiasm which accompanies his thought, and without rhythm cannot be fully revealed or communicated. By verse, then, the key of speech is heightened, it is the natural utterance of passionate conviction or inspired vision. Thus with poetry seriousness is associated. We expect from it an exaltation the exaltation of language justified and compelled by the exaltation of idea and feeling. Or may we say that metre is symbolic of new conditions, that when we pass this gateway we know ourselves to have entered a new country, the home of ideals and beauty unveiled, that we expect new experiences? Seriousness then is implied in all the definitions—when Milton speaks of poetry as "*simple, sensuous, passionate,*" or Ruskin of its "*noble grounds for noble emotion,*" or Wordsworth defines it as "*the impassioned expression which is on the face of all science.*" But what then is to be said of verse when employed not to elevate but to lower the key of feeling, for purposes of derision rather than exaltation? The Muse of Satire is "*the least engaging of the nine,*" but is humorous verse even legitimate, is it not a contradiction in terms? Shelley, Peacock reports, "*often talked of the withering and perverting spirit of comedy,*" and when the language of a comedy was praised for the fineness of its expression, replied, "*It is true, but the finer it is the worse it is, with such perversion of sentiment.*" In satire, it may be argued, the emotion of indignation provides the necessary warrant, and the satirist may be justified in the use of verse on the ground that he is an idealist, angry and properly angry at the shortcomings he attacks. It is a possible, and doubtless, indeed, the just view of Swift that he was a fierce kind of philanthropist. But what of the use of verse when no warrant can be found for it either in the nature of the subject or in the feeling with which the writer wishes us to regard it? It may, perhaps, be justified as playful or ironical, designed to provide innocent entertainment or to emphasise—since metre attracts the attention—by means of an inappropriate medium, some absurd quality, which might otherwise be overlooked or even wrongly admired.

The poet fulfils his mission, let us say, when he makes men aware that there is an unrealised world of beauty lying around them, but also when he makes them aware that the world in which they have hitherto found satisfaction is neither admirable nor beautiful. He may deny as well as affirm. In some such fashion the defence of verse deliberately employed for derisive purposes may be attempted.[1] And the defence may be strengthened by reference to the existence and acceptance of humorous verse in the literature of all ages and countries. Humorous verse then, when its purpose is serious, as in *Hudibras*, is verse that denies, that exposes faults, deficiencies, disproportions, that turns aside from the praise of beauty, of grace, of order to note their absence or the presence of the ugly. It hales offenders before the bar of the ideal.

As comedy, at least in Athens, added point and humour to the treatment of subjects below the tragic dignity by a presentation which reproduced all the formality and elaboration of serious drama, was, in short, something of a parody, so from very early times epic elevation threw its comic shadow in

---

[1] The defence of verse which engages our sympathies *against* rather than *with* its subject might be summarised briefly as follows—(1) Indignation may make verses since satire involves an ideal, and would be pointless but for the existence of a standard from which the departure or decline is censured. (2) Verse gives epigrammatic point and force to expression, it feathers the arrow and drives it home. It is "*a stimulant of the attention*." (3) Since there is no thermometer of feeling, the precise temperature of emotion which warrants the use of verse cannot be determined: a low level has its rights. (4) Behind the *ironical* use of verse, as behind Plato's irony, there may reside the humour which is akin to pathos or paternal affection.

burlesque imitations. The trivial theme solemnly handled, the
hero selected for his ineptitude rather than his prowess—

> " Many arts he knew, and he knew them all badly," [1]

the mountain in labour to bring forth the mouse, are, in their
unexpectedness, sources of natural amusement. Probably that
Protean spirit, Humour, always opens its attack by its sudden-
ness, its surprise. When, so to say, mentally on guard to the
front, we are assailed on flank or rear. It lurks too in the
incongruous—the sublime manner, the worthless content—in
the disproportion when the great is made small, the small great.
Wherever, then, tragedy stalks, comedy may follow, aping its
magnificent gestures; wherever there is epic dignity, behind it
we may expect the mischievous imitation of the heroic gait.
Sacred as was Homer he had in Greece his burlesque copies, of
which the famous *Batracho-myo-Machia*, " The Battle of the
Frogs and Mice," once ascribed—perhaps to heighten the
absurdity—to the author of the *Iliad* himself, still survives.
A mouse, escaping from a weasel, pauses to drink from a pond,
where he is accosted by a frog of royal lineage, Physignathos,
" Puff-cheek ":

> " What art thou, stranger? what the line you boast?
> What chance hath cast thee panting on our coast? " [2]

Having disclosed his own illustrious descent and fame—

> " Known to the gods, the men, the birds that fly
> Through wild expanses of the midway sky,
> My name resounds: and if unknown to thee
> The soul of great Psycarpax lives in me,
> Of brave Troxartas' line—" [3]

the noble mouse accepts an invitation to King Frog's palace,
whither he is to be conveyed on his friend's back. The voyage
is begun, but a water-hydra suddenly rears its head, the alarmed
frog dives, and the mouse is drowned. News of his untoward
fate reaches his father and tribesmen, a council is called, and
war is declared upon the frogs.

> " Dreadful in arms the marching mice appear."

[1] The *Margites*, Murray's *Ancient Greek Literature*, p. 52.
[2] This and the following quotations are from the version by Thomas
Parnell.
[3] Psycarpax, *a plunderer of granaries*. Troxartas, *a bread-eater*.

The frogs heroically prepare to defend their kingdom, and devise stratagems.

> " Then dress'd for war, they take th' appointed height,
> Poise the long arms, and urge the promis'd fight."

At this point Jove calls a council of all the gods,

> " And asks what heavenly guardians take the list
> Or who the mice, or who the frogs assist? "

But Pallas is unwilling to take sides, the mice rob the lamps of her shrine of their oil, the frogs have kept her awake at night. She advises that the gods refrain from the war, and her words carry persuasion. Soon the battle is joined and great deeds of arms in single combat are done. Hypsiboas (The Far-Croaker) slays with a javelin Lychenor (The Licker); Artophagus (The Bread-Eater) strikes down Polyphonus (The Babler); Tyroglyphus (The Cheese-Scooper),

> " Prince of the mice that haunt the flowery vales,"

meets death at the hands of Lymnisius (The Lake-Dweller). Not javelins and spears alone the combatants employ, but one hero distinguishes himself as does Ajax in *Homer*.

> " A stone immense of size the warrior bore,
> A load for labouring earth, whose bulk to raise,
> Asks ten degenerate mice of modern days.
> Full on the leg arrives the crushing wound :
> The frog, supportless, writhes upon the ground."

So valiant are the mice that it seems as if the whole frog tribe will be exterminated, and Jove determines to interfere. First he casts a thunderbolt—

> " Then earth's inhabitants, the nibblers, shake,
> And frogs, the dwellers in the waters, shake."

But still the mice advance, and the King of Heaven at length sends forth a legion of crabs. Before this new and terrible enemy the mice give way—

> " O'er the wild waste with headlong flight they go,
> Or creep conceal'd in vaulted holes below. . . .
> And a whole war (so Jove ordain'd) begun,
> Was fought, and ceas'd in one revolving sun."

The Battle of the Frogs and Mice is a simple parody, designed to amuse by the application of the full machinery and apparatus of epic to a subject entirely without dignity. But clearly a wider application of the method—contrast between the trivial theme and the heroic style—was possible. It was obviously suited to the purposes of general satire. To the ironical humour of Italy it appealed with special force, and Italian literature of the sixteenth and seventeenth centuries is rich in types of serio-comic poetry. The most brilliant travesty of the epic style, employed with the double purpose of avenging a personal slight and satirising the poets of his own day, was Tassoni's *La Secchia Rapita*, " The Rape of the Bucket," founded upon an incident in the wars between Modena and Bologna. A bucket carried off by some Modenese soldiers was subsequently exhibited as a trophy in the cathedral of their city, where it is said still to hang, and became, in Symonds' phrase, " *The ' Helen ' of Tassoni's ' Iliad.'* " [1] Boileau's *Lutrin*, " The Lectern "—the most celebrated of French burlesque epics—has for its subject an ecclesiastical quarrel over a reading-desk—

> " Je chante les combats, et ce prélat terrible,
> Qui, par ses longs travaux et sa force invincible,
> Dans une illustre église exerçant son grand cœur,
> Fit placer à la fin un lutrin dans le chœur."

The classical *Battle of the Frogs and Mice* and the more famous stories which went by the name of Æsop had their mediæval counterpart in the *Roman de Renart*, a popular cycle of animal tales with the Fox, the Wolf, and the Lion as leading characters. Originating in the tenth century these edifying stories developed by the twelfth into something like a parody of the romantic epic. The attractiveness of the fable—according to Addison the earliest type of humour—appears in its currency both in the East and West, in the literature of the advanced and the folk-lore of the most primitive communities. The old *Reynard* faith, in the words of Carlyle, " rising like some river in the remote distance, gathered strength out of every valley, out of every country, as it rolled on. It is European in two senses; for as all Europe contributed to it, so all Europe has enjoyed it. Among the Germans, *Reinecke Fuchs* was long a house-book and universal Best-companion: it has been lectured on in universities, quoted in Imperial council-halls; it lay on the toilette of

[1] *The Renaissance in Italy*, vol. vii., p. 177.

R

princesses; and was thumbed to pieces on the bench of the
artisan; we hear of grave men ranking it only next to the
Bible." [1]

No English *Ysopet*, or narrative in which animals take
the place of men, can compare for humour and brilliance
with Chaucer's *Nonne Preestes Tale*, or " The Cock and the
Fox," derived from a French version by Marie de France, [2]
which may be classed either among the animal romances of the
Middle Ages or assigned a place among the mock-heroics.
Spenser, in his *Mother Hubbard's Tale*, followed Chaucer's lead
with the story of the Fox and the Ape, who determined to seek
their fortunes abroad, and turns it to satirical use, as, for
example, in the famous passage which reflects his personal
experiences as a courtier—

> " Full little knowest thou, that hast not tride,
> What hell it is in suing long to bide."

A claim might well be made for Chaucer as the first writer of
mock-heroic verse in English, a far better claim than for
Waller with his *Battle of the Summer Isles*, and better too than
for Dryden with his *Mac Flecknoe*, or Garth with his *Dispensary*,
a better claim, indeed, than for Philips' *Splendid Shilling* or
his *Cider*. But everything here depends upon definition. Is
Waller's poem to be classed among mock-heroics because it has
for its subject the attempt to capture two whales caught by the
falling tide in a pool among the rocks at Bermuda, and deals
with the incident in elaborate language?

> " Aid me, Bellona! while the dreadful fight
> Betwixt a nation and two whales I write:
> Seas stain'd with gore I sing, adventurous toil!
> And how these monsters did disarm an isle."

" *It is not easy to say*," as Johnson remarked, " *whether it is
intended to raise terrour or merriment. The beginning is too
splendid for jest, and the conclusion too light for seriousness.*"
Or again is Philips' *Splendid Shilling* [3] a mock-heroic, though it

---

[1] Carlyle's *Early German Literature*.
[2] See Skeat's *Chaucer*, vol. iii., p. 431.
[3] Imitated in Bramston's *Crooked Sixpence* and Miss Pennington's
Copper Farthing.

is in no sense a narrative, simply because it employs Miltonic diction upon unheroic matters in this style?—

> " With looks demure, and silent pace, a Dun,
> Horrible monster! hated by gods and men,
> To my aërial citadel ascends,
> With vocal heel thrice thundering at my gate,
> With hideous accent thrice he calls; I know
> The voice ill-boding, and the solemn sound.
> What should I do? or whither turn? Amaz'd,
> Confounded, to the dark recess I fly
> Of wood-hole; straight my bristling hairs erect
> Through sudden fear; a chilly sweat bedews
> My shuddering limbs, and (wonderful to tell!)
> My tongue forgets her faculty of speech;
> So horrible he seems! His faded brow,
> Entrench'd with many a frown, and conic beard,
> And spreading band, admir'd by modern saints,
> Disastrous acts forebode; in his right hand
> Long scrolls of paper solemnly he waves,
> With characters and figures dire inscrib'd,
> Grievous to mortal eyes (ye gods, avert
> Such plagues from righteous men!) "

Cider, a better poem than the *Splendid Shilling*, though an excellent and pleasing piece of work, is surely, though the claim is sometimes made for it, only mock-heroic in the sense that it applies humour and unusually dignified language, as does Virgil in his *Georgics*, to the affairs of the farmer and gardener.

> " The prudent will observe, what passions reign
> In various plants (for not to man alone,
> But all the wide creation, Nature gave
> Love and aversion): everlasting hate
> The Vine to Ivy bears, nor less abhors
> The Colewort's rankness; but with amorous twine
> Clasps the tall Elm."

Garth's *Dispensary*, a satire on men and doings now forgotten, which

> " Rose like a paper kite and charm'd the town,"

has a better right to the title, since a professional quarrel among the London physicians is at least treated in the epic fashion, and involves heroes, personal combats, battles, and councils. But though the verse is highly wrought and in places almost distinguished, the interest of the *Dispensary* has become anti-quarian beyond recovery. In his *Bathos, or the Art of Sinking in Poetry*, Swift discusses with examples " *the Magnifying and*

Diminishing Figures." Of the first, Blackmore's lines on a
" Bull-baiting " serve as an instance—

> " Up to the stars the sprawling mastiffs fly,
> And add new terrors to the frighted sky."

For the second he quotes the anonymous,

> " And thou, Dalhousy, the great god of war,
> Lieutenant-Colonel to the Earl of Mar."

In poetry intentionally humorous, if we omit the playful—
such verses as Cowper's *Retired Cat*, or Carey's *Sally in our
Alley*—what remains might be classified as (*a*) formal or direct
satire, like Byron's *English Bards and Scotch Reviewers*, or (*b*)
informal or indirect satire, of which the types are numerous.
Apart from drama or *fabliau* such as Jonson's *Poetaster* or
Chaucer's *Reeve's Tale*, it may be either, in Swift's phrase, of
the " Magnifying " or " Diminishing " type. In the former the
poet attempts to elevate a trifling subject to absurdity by the
adoption of a lofty tone or heroic manner, as does Pope in
the *Rape of the Lock ;* in the latter a dignified subject is reduced
to ridicule, as in Cotton's *Scarronides, or the First Book of Virgil
Travestie*. Pope's poem illustrates the true mock-heroic,
Cotton's the burlesque.[1] Chaucer's *Sir Thopas*, too, may be
classed with the burlesques, though the romances at which he
smiles are hardly travestied—a slight exaggeration of their
common features is sufficient. But there exist poems less easy
to classify, in which both methods are combined. In *Hudibras*
the Parliamentary Party is the object of the satire. Yet the
subject is not without dignity nor in itself trivial. " *Experience
had sufficiently shown*," in Johnson's words, " *that their swords
were not to be despised*." The victors at Marston Moor and
Worcester were in many respects above ridicule. How then
was their cause to be made ludicrous by heroic treatment?
Before applying it Butler burlesqued his persons and actions.
That is to say he first drew his caricatures and then provided
them with an epic frame. The satirist may or may not adopt

---

[1] In *parody*, a form of the burlesque, the notion of ridicule is not necessarily included. The form of a dignified work may be borrowed, as in
the *Battle of the Frogs and Mice*, not to make the original ridiculous, but
to amuse by the contrast between the subject and the form.

the epic machinery, but if he make use of it the subject must either be low, and unsuitable in itself for heroic treatment, or its inherent dignity must somehow first be obscured or obliterated.

Hudibras, beyond dispute the most brilliant as it was the most popular seventeenth-century satire, is often compared with *Don Quixote*, written fifty or sixty years earlier, to which it owed its general plan. But it would be difficult to name together two works which differ more widely in purpose and sentiment. The one is a work of humour, where humour approaches pathos, the other a work of wit which gives no quarter. The melancholy smile of Cervantes, his high Castilian air, belong to another world from Butler's angry sneer and unscrupulous vocabulary. The spirit of poetry shines through the romance, in the poem its presence is rarely felt. Whether Cervantes desired to provoke tears or laughter one hardly knows, so tender is the mood, so courtly the treatment of his victim. Merciless and inextinguishable hate reveals itself in every page of *Hudibras*. Cervantes employs the *arme blanche*, the gentleman's weapon, Butler never stays to make a choice, the stick or stone serves him, or the gamin's mud. The splendour of Cervantes' achievement is that he drew a portrait of strange human significance and universal meaning. Out of a satire upon the extravagances of chivalric romance there grew a far greater thing, a picture of the idealist at odds with the world, a picture which, like Dürer's "Knight and Death," remains for ever inexhaustible in its breadth of suggestion. Cervantes' melancholy knight, for all his disordered fancies and insane adventures, emerges a sad but infinitely engaging figure, undimmed by contempt, who rises in the scale of our affection as he falls in that of our judgment, a symbol of the great causes, the forlorn hopes which however unsuccessful engage human sympathy, for which the heroes and the martyrs have stood, the causes which ennoble history. The interest of *Don Quixote* goes far beyond its obvious and immediate meaning, that of *Hudibras* seems local, and, save for its coruscations of epigram, temporary. Yet Butler too had his vision, though an afflicting one. He made the tragic discovery that men may be betrayed

by their zeal for God and religion to follies and excesses no less
palpable than those of the vicious and ungodly, that the best
of causes have their ugly side. Hardly less tragic was the parallel
discovery that zeal for mundane truth and knowledge laid the
seeker open to the same risks, that the bigotry of religion is
matched by the bigotry of science. As a satirist he was entitled
to make the most of his discovery, for it was at a great price
that he had purchased his own liberty. He had eaten of the
fruit of the tree of knowledge, and its taste was bitter. In a
poem on *The Weakness and Misery of Man* he wrote—

> —" there is no good
> Kind Nature e'er on man bestow'd
> But he can easily divert
> To his own misery and hurt."

The blessings of Heaven are turned to curses, peace will
destroy a people with luxury and excess almost as swiftly as
war, wealth is a more deadly poison than poverty. Men per-
versely pursue the things that make for their destruction.
They will

> " Advance men in the church and state
> For being of the meanest rate."

They will

> " Grow positive and confident
> In things so far beyond th' extent
> Of human wit, they cannot know
> Whether they be at all or no."

Life itself is a cheat.

> " Our pains are real things, and all
> Our pleasures but fantastical . . .
> Our noblest piles and stateliest rooms
> Are but outhouses to our tombs.
> Cities, though e'er so great and brave
> But mere warehouses to the grave.
> Our bravery's but a vain disguise
> To hide us from the world's dull eyes." [1]

Isolate *Hudibras* among its author's works and you misunder-
stand him. He is written down in the histories of literature
as an enemy and satirist of Puritanism. But the roots of his
discontent lie deeper, it is of human nature he despairs. This
disillusioned and merciless archer directs his shafts equally upon

[1] *The Weakness and Misery of Man.*

the newly-founded Royal Society of Science,[1] upon the fashionable literary criticism,[2] upon plagiarism,[3] upon the gaming,
drunkenness, and licence prevalent in society,[4] upon marriage,[5]
upon French manners,[6] upon the Puritan scheme of thought
and life.

> " 'Tis a strange age we've lived in and a lewd
> As e'er the Sun in all his travels view'd . . .
> The good's received for bad, the bad for good;
> That slyly interchanges wrong and right
> Like white in fields of black, and black in white;
> As if the laws of nature had been made
> Of purpose only to be disobeyed;
> Or man had lost his mighty interest
> By having been distinguish'd from a beast;
> And had no other way than sin and vice
> To be restor'd again to Paradise."

The fame of *Hudibras* has obscured the true view of Butler—
the most independent mind of his generation. There is nothing,
for example, in seventeenth-century criticism to match the
clear-sightedness of his verses *Upon Critics*. He alone in that
age seems to have been conscious to what absurd lengths the
Humanist tyranny had gone:

> —" to handle
> The Muses worse than Ostrogoth and Vandal;
> Make them submit to verdict and report,
> And stand or fall to th' orders of a court."

Take these sentences—

> " That not an actor shall presume to squeak
> Unless he have a license for't in Greek;
> Nor Whittington henceforward sell his cat in
> Plain vulgar English, without mewing Latin:
> No pudding shall be suffered to be witty,
> Unless it be in order to raise pity;
> Nor Devil in the puppet-play b' allow'd
> To rear and spit fire, but to fright the crowd,
> Unless some god or demon chance t'have piques
> Against an ancient family of Greeks. . . .
> And only those held proper to deter,

[1] *A Satire on the Royal Society* and *The Elephant in the Moon.*
[2] *Upon Critics, who judge of modern plays precisely by the rules of the
ancients.*
[3] *Satire upon Plagiaries.*
[4] *Satire upon the Licentious Age of Charles II. Satire upon Gaming.
Satire upon Drunkenness.*
[5] *Satire upon Marriage.*
[6] *Satire upon our ridiculous imitation of the French.*

Who've had th' ill luck against their wills to err.
Whence only such as are of middling sizes,
Between morality and venial vices
Are qualify'd to be destroy'd by Fate
For other mortals to take warning at. . . .
Then are the reformations of the stage,
Like other reformations of the age,
On purpose to destroy all wit and sense
As th' other did all law and conscience. . . .
An English poet should be try'd b' his peers,
And not by pedants and philosophers. . . .
Besides the most intolerable wrong
To try their matters in a foreign tongue,
By foreign jurymen, like Sophocles,
Or tales falser than Euripides;
When not an English native dares appear
To be a witness for the prisoner."

Allow that this is doggerel—it has been called so—but allow
also that it is penetrating sense. How refreshing are these bold
and manly, these English tones amid the tiresome jargon of
false learning with which this age assails our ears! Doubtless
more elegant expression might have been found for the sentiments. It was not found, however, in Butler's century, nor in
the next were these sentiments, now commonplaces, uttered
either elegantly or inelegantly with the same emphasis, lucidity,
and conviction. Butler's patriotism has long been justified,
but to have held these views in his day argued originality of
mind as convincingly as did the authorship of *Hudibras*.

It is not known where Samuel Butler was educated, but he
appears to have resided for some time in the household of a
Presbyterian colonel of the Parliamentary army—Sir Samuel
Luke—and it is generally assumed that this Sir Samuel was
the original of Hudibras, and that while in his service, perhaps
as secretary, Butler learnt what he knew of Puritan manners,
habits, and religious life.

" 'Tis sung there is a valiant Mameluke
In foreign lands ycleped ——"

says the poem, and the hiatus is easily filled by " Sir Samuel
Luke." Hudibras—a name borrowed from *The Faerie Queene*—
represents the Presbyterians, Ralpho, his squire, the Independents, but the scope of the satire includes much more than
Puritan extravagances. Butler deals shrewd blows at legal,
philosophical, and scientific pedantry and the weaknesses of

human nature in general. In his commonplace book, to which
Johnson refers,[1] appear notes upon a multitude of matters to
which metrical form was given in *Hudibras*, a poem which
enshrines indeed the meditation of a lifetime. The first and
best part, published in 1662, describes the hero and his squire,
who sally forth to put down bear-baiting and other profane
practices of the vulgar, their adventures, defeat, and imprisonment in the stocks. The second (1663) describes their rescue
by a widow to whom Hudibras had paid his court, although

> —" for a lady, no ways errant
> To free a knight, we have no warrant
> In any authentical romance,
> Or classic author yet of France."

The lady requires of her lover that he shall administer a
flogging to himself. He consents, but afterwards proposes to
undergo his trial by proxy in the person of his squire, who
however rejects the proposal. Together they visit an astrologer,
from whom Hudibras makes inquiry concerning the probable
issue of his suit. In the third and last part (1678) he and
Ralpho visit the lady, who discloses her knowledge of his hypo-
crisies. Hudibras retreats to exchange his amorous proposals
for an action at law, but first writes to the widow, and with her
answer the work comes to an abrupt conclusion. The plan of
the poem is defective, one whole canto leaves the story at a
stand to ridicule the Rump Parliament, and the action often
waits upon wordy dialogues, which though witty grow tedious,
invention flags in the second part and altogether fails in the
third: the conclusion is lame and undiverting. The various
episodes of knightly adventure are however faithfully enough
reproduced in parody, the arms and accoutrements of the combatants, the challenges and defiances, the battle, the wounds,
the successes, and misadventures. The stocks stand for the
enchanted castle of romance—

> —" in all the fabric
> You shall not see one stone nor a brick,
> But all of wood, by powerful spell
> Of magic made impregnable."

[1] *Life of Butler.*

The influence of the gods is not wanting—

> " But Pallas came in shape of rust
> And 'twixt the spring and hammer thrust
> Her gorgon-shield."

The love suit of Hudibras gives abundant opportunity for the ridicule of the love metaphysic of the romances—

> " Madam, I do, as is my duty,
> Honour the shadow of your shoe-tie."

Romance itself, the whole idealistic structure, crumbles as we read—

> " Some writers make all ladies purloined,
> And knights pursuing like a whirlwind.
> Others make all their knights in fits
> Of jealousy to lose their wits."

> " Thought he, the ancient errant knights
> Won all their ladies hearts in fights,
> And cut whole giants into fritters
> To put them into amorous twitters. . . .
> So Spanish heroes with their lances,
> At once wound bulls and ladies' fancies;
> And he acquires the noblest spouse
> That widows greatest herds of cows."

Can we judge of a poet by the number of familiar sayings he has given to the language?　Adopt this test and Butler is raised to great eminence, not much below Pope and certainly above Shelley or Keats.　*Hudibras* is, however, a poem much more quoted than read, and many who use its phrases would be at a loss to indicate their source.　*" What should make a book valued when its subject is no more ?"* asks Johnson.　Since the story is neither attractive nor well conducted, the follies ridiculed no longer fashionable, the manners, men, and opinions of historical interest only, *Hudibras* lives not as a whole but in its parts—the wit and wisdom of its sententious phrases, the showers of epigram which give easy currency to shrewd observation and universal experience.

> " What makes all doctrines plain and clear?
> About two hundred pounds a year.
> And that which was proved true before
> Prove false again? two hundred more."

> " For loyalty is still the same,
> Whether it win or lose the game;
> True as the dial to the sun
> Although it be not shined upon."

" He knew what's what, and that's as high
As metaphysic wit can fly."

" He that complies against his will
Is of his own opinion still."

" He could distinguish, and divide
A hair 'twixt south and south-west side."

" He ne'er considered it, as loth
To look a gift-horse in the mouth."

" And force them, though it was in spite
Of Nature, and their stars, to write."

" The oyster-women locked their fish up,
And trudged away to cry No Bishop."

" And registered by fame eternal
In deathless pages of diurnal."

" For all a rhetorician's rules
Teach nothing but to name his tools."

" For rhyme the rudder is of verses
With which, like ships, they steer their courses."

" The world is naturally averse
To all the truth it sees or hears,
But swallows nonsense and a lie
With greediness and gluttony."

On almost every page they sparkle, these crystals of wit, while the unflagging play of fancy, the display of curious learning, the ingenuity of the rhymes provide the continual pleasure of surprise—

" Caesar himself could never say
He got two victories in a day,
As I have done, that can say, twice I,
In one day *Veni, vidi, vici.*"

Hudibras proves, if proof were needed, that there is, in Cowper's words, " *a sting in verse that prose neither has nor can have,*" [1] a fact more easily perceived in burlesque or satiric than in romantic poetry, since verse is in the former more nearly in competition with prose, occupied with the same order of

[1] Addison thought *Hudibras* " *would have made a much more agreeable figure in heroics.*" " *Why*, bless his head! " responds Cowden Clarke, " the whole and sole intention of the poem is *mock*-heroic, and the structure of the verse is burlesque." It may be added that Butler had compared the two metres by writing one of his poems, *The Elephant in the Moon*, *twice over*, once in each measure, an interesting and doubtless to the author a convincing experiment.

ideas, and addressed to the judgment rather than the imagination. Where one man appreciates the poetic value of—

> " She dwells with Beauty, Beauty that must die,
> And Joy, whose hand is ever at his lips
> Bidding adieu "—

a hundred understand—

> " Both parties joined to do their best
> To damn the public interest "—

or—

> " The trenchant blade, Toledo trusty
> For want of fighting was grown rusty,
> And ate into itself for lack
> Of some body to hew and hack."

Although in some cases, like that of Byron, serious poetry is welcomed with universal and unstinted applause, the pungent and malicious elements in satire attract more immediate attention and can count upon enthusiastic favour in at least one camp. *Hudibras* was well timed. The nation, or perhaps we should say the Court, welcomed rapturously the castigation of its enemies—

> " Such as do build their faith upon
> The holy text of pike and gun,
> Decide all controversies by
> Infallible artillery;
> And prove their doctrine orthodox
> By apostolic blows and knocks;
> Call fire and sword and desolation
> A godly thorough Reformation,
> As if Religion were intended
> For nothing else but to be mended.
> A sect whose chief devotion lies
> In odd perverse antipathies;
> In falling out with that or this,
> And finding something still amiss;
> More peevish cross and splenetic,
> Than dog distract or monkey sick.
> That with more care keep holy-day
> The wrong, than others the right way;
> Compound for sins they are inclined to,
> By damning those they have no mind to:
> Still so perverse and opposite,
> As if they worshipped God for spite." [1]

We have no reason to doubt the justice of the indictment. Butler was a man of acute intellect, he witnessed and bore

[1] For an account of the numerous imitations of *Hudibras* see the *Retrospective Review*, vol. iii., and for an article on his *Genuine and Spurious Remains*, vol. ii. of the same.

witness. But he stood so near the representatives of the Puritan cause as to lose perspective, he mingled personal with national issues, he failed to distinguish between the men and the principles they espoused. That the cause had its justification, that it was far from being wholly unworthy, that it made for political and religious liberty we must believe. Over against Butler stands the nobler figure of Milton. His sin is that he obscured the issues. If we have a quarrel with him, it is not with his hatred of cant, or contempt for the meaner instruments of the revolution. He is to be challenged on broader grounds. When it assists to preserve our intellectual sanity caricature is a legitimate weapon, but Butler dishonours not merely the instruments, he dishonours the motives and purposes of the Puritan cause itself. It is true that he is not so much a friend of the Royalists as a friend of moderation and good sense, yet there is in him no spiritual touch, no sympathy with the soul. He is of reason all compact. But somehow in the harvests of reason the wheat seems often to perish with the tares. With Butler, as with the more terrible Swift—and Butler resembles no other English satirist so closely—triumphant reason crashes through the ranks of hypocrisy and folly to a victory strangely desolating. Whether the author of a book the king carried in his pocket and all the courtiers quoted received any material reward for his contribution to the gaiety of Restoration circles seems doubtful. It was at least scanty and inadequate, and Butler, the tradition runs, feebly supported the character of a philosopher, and failed to conceal his disappointment. More than a generation after his death a monument to his memory was placed in the Abbey, a tardy tribute to celebrity which drew from Wesley's father the well-known lines—

> " See him when starved to death and turned to dust,
> Presented with a monumental bust;
> The poet's fate is here in emblem shown,
> He asked for bread, and he received—a stone."

Though both are serio-comic poems there are few points for fruitful comparison between *Hudibras* and the *Rape of the Lock.* The one is a burlesque of the chivalric romance, the other an imitation of the classical epic. In the former, a satire long meditated, the author is at work with deadly intention; in the second the purpose is rather playful than serious, and the occasion a chance one. Butler's poem had its source in a national, Pope's in a social quarrel. Nor can the subtle raillery and elegance of style which distinguish the *Rape of the Lock* fairly be weighed in any scale against the open and angry scorn, the vigorous colloquialism of *Hudibras*. Whatever may be said of Pope as a poet it will not be denied that in the *Rape of the Lock* he had a heaven-sent subject, admirably adapted for the display of his peculiar talents and congenial to the spirit of the times. A certain young Lord Petrie had snipped off a lock of a certain Miss Arabella Fermor's hair, the lady's family took umbrage, and a pretty social quarrel was in progress. Pope had chosen to begin poet at a time in which the poetic instinct was weak, but in which heroic poetry was none the less a favourite literary topic, and in this miniature epic—*heroi-comical* is his own word, as it was Boileau's—the epic of social life, of " *the tea cup times* " of Queen Anne, he achieved a double triumph. He satisfied himself since he touched, almost in his first effort, the type of perfection at which he aimed, perfection of form, convinced that his lines,

" Polished like marble, would like marble last ";

he satisfied " the town," since it was chiefly interested in life on its social side, by his matter—a tiff between lovers in the fashionable set. Because it is a work of art, not of magic, like the *Ode to a Nightingale*, we are sometimes asked to reject it, to reject Pope and all his works. But, inquires Hazlitt, " *shall we cut ourselves off from beauties like these with a theory ?* "

In so far as poetry is an approximation to complete or perfect expression Pope achieves it. He achieves it, of course, through choice of subject, and adequate handling of the subject, not through inherent poetic power, and this is his offence. Skilfully avoiding what lay beyond his intellectual range, exposing himself, as Johnson acutely said, " *to few hazards*," choosing his own ground, he may almost be said to defy criticism. That such virtue should lie in mere limitation of scope flutters romantic bosoms. Pope is often condemned not so much because he did not write poetry as because he never attempted it. Not a poet, if poetry be the language of the spirit, be what Shelley conceived it, or Keats, but certainly a poet if the title be allowed to a man of extreme intelligence employing verse with consummate dexterity upon social subjects. The ancient quarrel resolves itself, as do most quarrels, into a matter of definition. "*It seems not so much the perfection of sense,*" he wrote to his friend Walsh, "*to say things that have never been said before, as to express those best that have been said oftenest.*" And again, "*I found I could express them* [ideas] *more shortly this way* [in verse] *than in prose itself.*" When one is aware of his aims one recognises that Pope struck the centre of his target.

M. Brunetière in characterising the literature of France speaks of it as "*eminently social,*" and ascribes its faults and defects, for example its inferiority in lyrical poetry, to this cause — preoccupation with society and the interests of society. "The truth is that in obliging literature to fulfil, so to speak, *a social function,* in requiring the poet to conform his manner of thinking and feeling to the ordinary manner, in refusing him the right to put himself into his work, or merely to let himself appear in it, the living springs of lyricism had been dried up or shut off. French literature has thus paid by its too manifest inferiority in the forms which may be called *personal* for its superiority in the forms which are *common.*"[1] To the period most under the influence of France in our literature M. Brunetière's words apply with equal force. Pope is so arresting because he is so representative. He is the protagonist of a whole age, of a *weltanschauung,* of an attitude of mind and of a manner of writing. Shelley stands for himself, as does Coleridge, or Byron, or Browning, we speak of "*the school of Pope.*" He creates no intellectual ferment, he is never sensuous, rarely passionate, he himself confessed that he had culled all his thoughts from a careful course of reading, yet when Ruskin declares him "*the most perfect representative we*

---

[1] *Brunetière's Essays in French Literature,* a selection translated by D. Nichol Smith, p. 19.

have since Chaucer of the true English mind," it is difficult to resist the judgment. The very individuality, the personality, the poetic quality for which we praise his rivals are against them in this contention. They inhabit the imaginative uplands, he the plains of sense, but *" matched on his own grounds he neither has been nor can be,"* said Swinburne, whatever he has left us is *" as round and smooth as Giotto's O."*

That the quarrel from which it sprang should evaporate in laughter was the avowed aim of the *Rape of the Lock.* Successful as a poem, it appears, however, to have failed in its immediate purpose. *" The celebrated lady herself,"* wrote Pope, in a tone of vast surprise, *" is offended, and which is stranger, not at herself but me."* Modern readers are not at the same loss to account for Miss Arabella Fermor's annoyance. The tone of the dedication and indeed of many passages in the piece itself exhibited a taste that the author might well have recognised as doubtful. *" The Machinery, Madam,"* he explained with ironical politeness, *" is a term invented by the Critics, to signify that part which the Deities, Angels or Demons are made to act in a Poem : for the ancient Poets are in one respect like many Modern Ladies : let an action be never so trivial in itself, they always make it appear of the utmost importance. . . . As to the following Cantos, all the passages of them are as fabulous as the Vision at the beginning, or the Transformation at the end ; (except the loss of your Hair, which I always mention with reverence)."* No doubt Pope's general attitude to women belongs in part at least to his age, for is it not visible in the more genial Addison, who barely conceals his smile of superiority while he proposes to write in the *Spectator* for their amusement and edification ? *" The toilet is their great scene of business, and the right adjusting of their hair the principal employment of their lives."* [1] The mockery in the *Rape of the Lock* is unblushing—

---

[1] *The Spectator*, No. 10. It is pleasant to think that it was a contemporary of Pope and Addison (Steele) who paid to Lady Elizabeth Hastings the compliment that *" to love her is a liberal education"* (*The Tatler*, No. 49), but he was an Irishman.

> " With varying vanities, from ev'ry part,
> They shift the moving Toyshop of their heart
> Where wigs with wigs, with sword-knots sword-knots strive,
> Beaus banish beaus, and coaches coaches drive."

> " Not louder shrieks to pitying heav'n are cast
> When husbands or when lap-dogs breathe their last."

Genius, however, is easily pardoned. The brilliance of the execution induces tolerance for the hardly suppressed contempt here and elsewhere in Pope, and the critics—all men it must be confessed—agree with Hazlitt to regard the *Rape of the Lock* as " *the perfection of the mock-heroic.*" There is almost the same unanimity in ranking it as Pope's *chef-d'œuvre*. Not only does it abound in couplets exquisitely turned—

> " On her white breast a sparkling Cross she wore,
> Which Jews might kiss, and Infidels adore."

> " Fair tresses man's imperial race insnare,
> And beauty draws us with a single hair."

> " Beauties in vain their pretty eyes may roll;
> Charms strike the sight, but merit wins the soul."

> " The meeting points the sacred hair dissever
> From the fair head, for ever, and for ever! "—

the choice and management of the celestial machinery, the delicate verbal skill exhibited in the description of the toilet, the battle of the cards, the ethereal life and employments of the Sylphs and Sylphids, and the Cave of Spleen, the ingenuity, the sense of proportion, the airs of fashion and affectation, and the felicitous conclusion of the whole fairy fancy—poised as it were on a needle's point—which transforms the fatal lock to a shining constellation—

> " This Lock the Muse shall consecrate to fame
> And midst the stars inscribe Belinda's name,"—

extort admiration and disarm us of our principles. We laugh with the author at " *the little unguarded follies of the female sex.*"

Turn to the *Dunciad* after the *Rape of the Lock* and tedium succeeds pleasure. The form is still mock-heroic, but the rapier has become the bludgeon, and the vocabulary of the salon has been exchanged for the vocabulary of Billingsgate. Whatever interest the *Dunciad* possesses, and some have found it good reading, who will claim for it the interest of poetry? A

S

poem, like a picture or a piece of music, should explain itself without commentary, it should be independent of the historian's assistance. The *Dunciad* is loaded with notes, and what is worse, requires them. Pope, who in the eagerness of his malice stooped to all things, engaged Savage as an informer to provide him with details of Grub Street, and so crowds his canvas with strange faces and figures as to compete in dullness with the wretched starvelings he bespatters. To discover their weaknesses he employed all his own meanness, all his ingenuity to discredit them. His victims, the journalistic bores of their own times, are here, by a misdirected zeal, rescued from oblivion to weary succeeding generations. In his *Mac Flecknoe* Dryden had made an obscure poetaster,[1] who—

> " In prose and verse was owned without dispute
> Through all the realms of Nonsense absolute,"

abdicate the throne of dullness in favour of Shadwell, a whig writer, once Dryden's friend. 'Tis resolved, cries the aged prince—

> " for Nature pleads that he
> Should only rule who most resembles me.
> Shadwell alone my perfect image bears,
> Mature in dullness from his tender years;
> Shadwell alone of all my sons is he
> Who stands confirm'd in full stupidity.
> The rest to some slight meaning make pretence,
> But Shadwell never deviates into sense."

Following *Mac Flecknoe* Pope constructed his epic of the dunces, a work designed to extinguish in inextinguishable Homeric laughter his literary enemies and rivals together with the whole tribe of the starved Grub Street scribblers. The goddess of dullness, propitiated by Theobald [2] with a hecatomb of his own works, hails the author of " *works damned or to be damned* " as her worthy son, and exalts him amid the acclamations of his fellows to the throne of the dunces—

> " And the hoarse nation croak'd, ' God save King Log! ' "

---

[1] Richard Flecknoe (?-1678), a small but not a despicable poet, as Dryden suggests.

[2] Theobald, described by Professor Churton Collins as *The Porson of Shakesperian Criticism*, had angered Pope by the production of an edition of Shakespere superior to his own, which exposed some of his errors.

In the second book the king is proclaimed and the goddess institutes games, after the approved epic manner, to grace the occasion. These include races in pursuit of a phantom poet created by the goddess, a contest in vociferation, with its appropriate prizes—

> " Three cat-calls be the bribe
> Of him whose chatt'ring shames the monkey tribe;
> And his, this Drum, whose hoarse heroic bass
> Drowns the loud clarion of the braying Ass."

This competition ended, in which " Ass intones to Ass " so loudly that—

> " In Tot'nham fields, the brethren with amaze
> Prick all their ears up, and forget to graze,"

a contest in diving succeeds—

> —" where Fleet-ditch with disemboguing streams
> Rolls the large tribute of dead dogs to Thames,
> The king of dykes! than whom no sluice of mud
> With deeper sable blots the silver flood."

> " Here strip, my children!" (exclaims the goddess), "here at once leap in,
> Here prove who best can dash thro' thick and thin,
> And who the most in love of dirt excel,
> Or dark dexterity of groping well.
> Who flings most filth, and wide pollutes around
> The stream, be his the Weekly Journals bound;
> A pig of lead to him who dives the best,
> A peck of coals apiece shall glad the rest."

Among the rivals in this savoury exercise is Smedley, who relates on his return from the ooze—

> " how sinking to the chin
> Smit with his mien, the Mud-nymphs suck'd him in:
> How young Lutetia, softer than the down,
> Nigrina black, and Merdamante brown,
> Vied for his love in jetty bow'rs below,
> As Hylas fair was ravish'd long ago."

In the third book the hero, asleep in the temple of dullness, dreams of the future triumphs of stupidity, the decay of learning, the arts, and sciences, and the final conquest of all sense in a world given over to ignorance and inanity. Twelve or fourteen years later, at the suggestion of Warburton, Pope added a fourth book, and subsequently to wreak vengeance upon the most courageous of his rivals dethroned Theobald to instal Cibber in his room. " *The portentous cub never forgives*," said

Bentley, one of a number of distinguished men Pope in the blindness of rage or envy had placed in his pillory—

> " The mighty Scholiast, whose unweary'd pains
> Made Horace dull, and humbled Milton's strains." [1]

In its new form the *Dunciad* gained the final and most generally admired passage, which concludes—

> " Thy hand, great Anarch! lets the curtain fall,
> And universal Darkness buries All "—

a passage, it is said, the author could not read without betraying emotion, but in respect of the general plan Pope's second thought was unfortunate. No decay of power is visible in the *Dunciad*, rather it is the decay of character. Never able to control his malice, Pope disturbed a hive of enemies, their petty stings enraged him still further, and he grew more spiteful with the years. This satire, instead of ridding him of his foes, added to their number, fury, and pertinacity, and the delights of revenge brought him small compensation for the counter assaults it provoked. More than this, a life-long preoccupation with personal animosities injured his art, which suffered in judgment and breadth. " *The great fault of the ' Dunciad,'* " said Warton, " *is the excessive vehemence of the satire.*" No satire, however, fails from this cause. The victims of Pope's dislike are " monster-breeding," " blockheads," " coxcombs," " fools," " asses," " industrious bugs," " vaticides," " monkey-mimics," " blind puppies," " low-born," " cell-bred," " owls," " wolves," " zanies." But the violence of the abuse is a minor defect only. The only reason, but a good one, that it now finds no readers—for who but the student now reads the *Dunciad* ?—is to be sought elsewhere. It is steeped in interests purely local and temporary, it deals not in universals but in particulars, scores of particulars about Ozell and Ridpath, Eusden and Settle, Mears, Warner, Wilkins, Tutchin, Roper, Osborne, Welsted, Dunton, Arnall, Ralph, Concanen—is there

---

[1] Perhaps Bentley was not undeserving of the censure. " The world," as De Quincey said, " never before beheld such a scene of massacre as his *Paradise Lost* exhibited. . . . The carnage was like that after a pitched battle."

any need to extend the list of never-famous, now forgotten names? It may be argued and fairly argued that, its form apart, the subject-matter of a poem should, if translated into another language, retain a general and human interest. We need not inquire whether to a Frenchman or an Italian this chronicle of Grub Street can afford entertainment; it provides even for English readers little but instruction, with the help of the notes, in the life of the eighteenth-century literary slums. Pope wrote to suit the taste of his age; well, so did Shakespeare!

A complete survey of English mock-heroic poetry might be treated in a volume; a chapter could hardly do more than enumerate the names of authors who in some form attempted it, either for purposes of satire or pleasantry. The eighteenth century alone is strewn with *Scribleriads, Hilliads, Battiads, Fribleriads*. But the task of writing the history of tame genius, of the would-be Popes and Butlers, may well be postponed to that age foreseen by the goddess in the *Dunciad*, when—

> " This fav'rite Isle, long sever'd from her reign,
>   Dove-like she gathers to her wings again."

CHAPTER XIII

NARRATIVE POETRY IN THE NINETEENTH CENTURY—SCOTT, SOUTHEY, BYRON

UNLIKE its predecessor the nineteenth century in England made no attempt to comply with the requirements of formal epic. Possibly no attempt to comply with them will ever again be made. Have we not witnessed the triumph of what some call individualism and some caprice? In the century just closed romance was preferred; freer modes in art accompanied the freer modes of thought; it was discovered and preached that the only "laws of poetry" were those imposed by the nature of the subject chosen. What these were none knew, indeed, and few cared to inquire; the most competent judge—how could one doubt?—was the author himself. So far, however, from becoming an extinct species—though a serious rival, the novel, the "*comic epic poem in prose*," as defined by Fielding, had arisen—narrative poetry flourished in the nineteenth century as never before. But in what varied and bewildering forms! Recall the florid graces of Leigh Hunt's *Story of Rimini*, the mystic charm of *The Ancient Mariner*, the sensuous music of *The Eve of St. Agnes*, the Oriental embroideries of *Lalla Rookh*, the austere pathos of Wordsworth's *Michael*, the humours and amours of Byron's *Beppo* and *Parisina;* recall Shelley's *Revolt of Islam*, Landor's *Gebir*, Southey's *Thalaba*, Tennyson's *Enoch Arden* and *Idylls of the King*, Browning's *The Ring and the Book*, Morris's *Earthly Paradise*, Arnold's *Sohrab and Rustum*, Clough's *Bothie of Tober-Na-Vuolich*—to select a few names from the imposing series—and we perceive that no poet of any eminence forbore to essay the novel in verse, that the whole world was scoured for plot and pattern, all types and modes of narrative explored. Manifestly if narrative poetry were epic poetry, the nineteenth century was the great age of epic. But

278

as manifestly, however, make your definition as generous as you please, few if any of these stories in verse will fall within it. Is it possible to propose a clue by means of which this labyrinth may be traversed? Distinguish and divide we may, but frankly it is not possible. Type merges into type, classical forms melt into romantic to produce a confused panorama of scenes, characters, actions, where the distinctions that prevailed prevail no longer, where the old designations fail us. We have reached the ocean where all tributary streams and rivers are lost. At length, then, it seems we are about to reap the fruits of the folly censured by Croce, the folly of attempting to distinguish among works of art by a system of classification. Our main category has broken down; epic, if the word be any longer employed, is bereft of meaning. We have struggled to preserve it, but the attempt must at last, to all appearance, be abandoned. What then remains? Two courses seem open—either to close the survey by the declaration that the term is outworn and must be cast aside, that a category once useful is useful no longer, by the simple admission that epic poetry, even what proposes to be epic poetry, is no longer written; or confessing, as we have already had to confess, that we overstep the proper limits of the subject, so throw our net as to bring within consideration certain of the larger and more ambitious narratives, such as both represent the class to which they rightly belong, and at the same time by their structure, their breadth and scope, recall in some degree the features of the older poetry cast in the traditional epic form. We may attempt—and this is the course proposed—to test these modern narratives, as suggested in a previous chapter, by the quality of impressiveness, distinguishing greatness from that which is less great; we may say that for our purposes any narrative poetry, if it be sufficiently impressive, here claims consideration.

One is tempted, indeed, to stray from the immediate inquiry and to ask with Arnold [1] whether poetry, such narrative poetry, for example, as the nineteenth century produced, has not, after all, " *its boundaries and wholesome regulative laws,*" whether

[1] *Preface to First Edition of Poems* (1853).

success has in any large measure attended upon the departures
from the formal tradition; whether, too, the selection of subjects, where instead of action and the conduct of the action,
the presentation of " *a continued state of mental distress,*" occupies
and absorbs the poet, does not in the end lead to a period of
poetic exhaustion and depression. Arnold held that where
"*everything is endured, nothing done,*" where expression is
exalted above the situation which calls for expression, the
prospects of poetry are not bright, that the only remedy lies
in turning resolutely once more to the large and noble themes
and the presentation of such themes with the Greek regard for
simplicity and grandeur of design. Take what side you prefer
in such a debate, the infirmity of narrative poetry in the last
century—who can be unaware of it?—is the infirmity which
springs from the insistent, overwhelming presence of the artist
in his work. Whether we take Byron or Keats, Tennyson or
Browning, the reader never escapes the poet, who everywhere
thrusts himself in. But to be constantly reminded of the author
is to forget his theme. What, then, some one asks, do you
wish? I wish to be left uninterruptedly with the action, the
situations, the characters, that I may ponder them for the sake
of their own significance, their inherent interest and quality,
their immediate and native power. In *The Prisoner of Chillon,*
" *a continuous state of mental distress is prolonged, unrelieved by
incident, hope, or resistence,*" " *everything is to be endured, nothing
to be done.*" We are imprisoned with the prisoner's emotion.
When we recall *Isabella* it is to recall chiefly accessories and
lovely lines—

> " For them the Ceylon diver held his breath
> And went all naked to the hungry shark."

> " And thou art distant in mortality."

> " And she forgot the stars, the moon, and sun,
> And she forgot the blue above the trees,
> And she forgot the dells where waters run,
> And she forgot the chilly Autumn breeze."

We have here " *a poem which seems to exist for the sake of
single lines and passages.*" In *The Ring and the Book,* "*all
made out of an Old Bailey story,*" as Carlyle said, " *that might*

have been told in ten lines," we have a receptacle into which Browning hurled—the word is hardly too strong—anything of any kind that interested him. Over eighteen hundred lines are occupied with the remarks of Dominus Hyacinthus de Arch-angelis, over fifteen hundred with those of Juris Doctor Johannes-Baptista Bottinius. Individualism has certainly had its say! One inclines in such a case to agree with M. Brunetière that *" the English seem to write only to give themselves the exterior sensation of their individuality."* [1] One does not need to deny the merit, the pleasantness of nineteenth-century poetic narra-tives, to say this of them—their authors were their own heroes; they interested us greatly in themselves, less in the matters of which they wrote. But is it of Homer one thinks when the aged Priam stoops to clasp the knees of Achilles, the slayer of his sons, and kisses his hands, " terrible, man-slaying "? [2] Or of Virgil, even the romantic Virgil, when Aeneas in the shades addresses Dido, and the injured queen listens with averted eyes?

> " Nec magis incepto voltum sermone movetur,
> Quam si dura silex aut stet Marpesia eautes."

Or of Shakespeare when, after the murder of Duncan, Macbeth with the daggers still in his guilty hands, exclaims—

> " Methought I heard a voice cry, ' Sleep no more!
> Macbeth does murder sleep.' "

These things remind us that a situation may speak and speak convincingly for itself. Absorption such as Homer's in the matter in hand, the self-effacement of the artist that the work of art, like Donatello's " St. George," or Michael Angelo's " David," or a ballad like *Sir Patrick Spens*, may strike deep into the imagination of the spectator, remind us in some measure of the doings of Nature herself, *perdu* in her creations. When the theme, on the other hand, is merely the occasion for the display of the poet's or the painter's talent, is in itself nothing or no more than a point of departure, the artist must needs indeed refrain from too complete a knowledge of, too vital and dis-turbing a contact with, his subject.

---

[1] *Brunetière's Essays,* translated by D. Nichol Smith, p. 24.
[2] *Iliad,* Bk. xxiv., lines 478-479.

Among nineteenth-century narrative poets Scott alone stood close to his subjects, painted with some approach to real knowledge upon a background of actual history, was penetrated by the feeling of his situations, looked back, as one may imagine Homer to have looked back, upon an heroic age which had not long passed away, whose visible memorials remained. Upon Scott alone the past—and heroic poetry is the poetry of the past, as lyric is that of the present, and drama that of the past represented as present—upon Scott's imagination alone the past exerted a pressure as great, as thrilling as that of some keen personal experience. He only in the century to which he belonged desired passionately and sincerely to display an age and a society rather than himself, and in his eagerness to revive it surrendered, as it were, consciousness of his own personality. And with what result? That he approached nearer to success in epic than any modern poet. So near he came to it that had grudging Nature not withheld from him one gift, the gift of a sure and elevated style, he must have taken his place among the epic poets of the world. For even among what have been counted his disabilities we discern the necessary qualities. When Carlyle, the spiritual zealot, bewailed the lack in Scott of "*some kind of gospel tidings*," the absence of the prophetic mantle and message, he gave expression to a personal preference. But those who place Homer above, let us say, Shelley, have nothing to regret in Scott's freedom from the metaphysical and ethical fervours, in the fact that he stood so clear of the French Revolution, in the fact that he was an out-of-doors man, the descendant of hunters and reivers, who viewed the world simply as a fact rather than as a problem. For to this very freedom from the speculative, the abstract, we owe the frankness and animation, the vitality and buoyancy of his mind. The complaint of Carlyle proclaimed Scott's fitness for the epic undertaking. In a special degree, too, he answered to the call of a time which as no time before in the world's history cast wondering glances down the long vistas of the past, pondering the old bygone days and the deeds of men who had filled them. This new-born curiosity—a kind of wistful child's longing—meets one in Chatterton and the early Romantics, in Scott it is a passion full grown. Add the circumstance that in Scotland the heroic age—we may call it so—was hardly remote. It lay so near his own that with his own eyes he had seen its survivors, as he said, "*in arms*"—Alexander Stewart of Invernahyle, who had wielded the claymore under Mar in the Fifteen, and Charles Stewart in the Forty-five, who had crossed swords with Rob Roy, and had lurked in a cave near his own house when it was garrisoned by the English after Culloden; and his servant, "the grim-looking old Highlander," who had saved his master's life at Prestonpans. Consider, too, the nature of the material that lay around him in the Highlands and among the Border hills, not only the memorials of a feudal and fighting society in castles and watch towers, not only the countryside tales and traditions which survived on the lips of the dalesfolk, but these already wrought into song and ballad, and it is difficult not to think of Homer, who, we may believe, looked back upon a society not very dissimilar, as human history runs, to that of the old Border reivers and Highland tribes. One might easily, of course, emphasise the vast differences, but indulge the fancy, and how much of the Homeric narrative might have been drawn from clan and Border history. As Homer seems the last of the rhapsodists, so Scott "*the last and greatest of the Border minstrels.*" Each was a "*stitcher of lays,*" called upon not so much to produce original poetry as to add epic quality, unity, and dignity to the verses of his many predecessors. No one will deny to Scott Homer's aristocratic sentiment, his love of force of character, his delight in arms and armour, in local references. No one will deny to him the love of adventure which meets us in the *Iliad* and *Odyssey*, or contest that as in these poems, so in his, the story comes first, the doings, that the very things complained of in Scott, the eye for outward rather than inward things, "the plumed troop, the royal banner, the pride, pomp, and circumstance of glorious war," display kinship with the poet who

> "Drank delight of battle with his peers
> Far on the ringing plains of windy Troy."

Everything in Scott's birth and tastes, everything in the

circumstances of his youth seemed to point, as if with the finger of destiny, to the path he was to follow. Lineally descended from a famous Border chieftain, Auld Wat of Harden, the tales of these ballad heroes, Wat and Telfer of the fair Dodhead, were told him while yet in the nursery. Before he could read he knew by heart the ballad of *Hardyknute*, " *the first poem I ever learnt—the last I shall ever forget,*" and before he became a schoolboy he was in the habit of reading to his mother from Pope's *Homer*. Border lays ran, one may say, in his blood, and the day he first opened Percy's *Reliques* " *he forgot dinner,*" he tells us, " *notwithstanding the sharp appetite of thirteen.*" From childhood " *he fastened like a tiger upon every collection of old songs and romances.*" For natural beauty he developed an insatiable passion, " *more especially when combined with ancient ruins or remains of our forefathers' piety or splendour.*" " *Show me an old castle or a field of battle, and I was at home at once, filled it with its combatants in their proper costume, and over-whelmed my hearers by the enthusiasm of my description.*" His consciousness of existence awoke, he tells us, at Sandyknowe, overhung by Smailholme crags and the old ruined tower, the view from which " *takes in a wide expanse of the district, in which, as has been truly said, every field has its battle, and every rivulet its song.*" Wonder ruled his childish world, and he seemed, as it were, by intuition, to surprise the ancient secrets of the fields and hills. A coin or claymore or an old Border horn was enough to fire his fancy and paint a picture. During seven successive years he made raid after raid into Liddesdale, collecting the precious booty, " *the elements of a hundred historical romances* " which are preserved for us in *The Minstrelsy of the Scottish Border*. He thus, as Principal Shairp has so well described, came face to face with the feudal and historic past, in a district which was still redolent of the warlike traditions of the Border and of Scotland.[1]

Yet despite these concurrences of tastes with opportunities, of qualities with conditions, despite this close contact with the heroic past, despite the fact that, as Shairp said, there was

[1] *The Homeric Spirit in Walter Scott*, in Shairp's *Aspects of Poetry*.

between it and Scott's mind " a pre-established harmony," that if ever fortune favoured, if any man among modern poets seemed likely to succeed, Scott seemed likely to succeed, despite it all serious criticism discerns instantly that the poetry of Scott falls below epic level. One has no pleasure in emphasising it. Scott's well-wishers in his own day, such was the man's charm and the charm of his talents, were legion. He is still and must ever remain one of the best loved of English writers. His fluent and graphic pen has delighted millions of readers, he drew the eyes of all the world upon his country. So national is he that, as with Shakespeare, to speak in his dispraise suggests an attempt to dispraise his race. Yet, without a word spoken, that infallible critic, time, disposes of the most established reputations as of the most difficult critical problems. Before 1830 more than forty thousand copies of *The Lay of the Last Minstrel* had been sold in this country, *Marmion* was at least as successful, *The Lady of the Lake* even more so. Its success, the author wrote in 1830, " *was certainly so extraordinary as to induce me for the moment to conclude that I had at last fixed a nail in the proverbially inconstant wheel of Fortune.*" Popularity so immediate, however, is rarely prophetic of enduring fame. Great art usually makes its way slowly, often at first attracts the attention only of a few good readers. Nor must we expect for it in any single generation enthusiastic acceptance. The power to appreciate work of high artistic quality is only a little more common than the power to produce it. There are passages, indeed, in Scott of high artistic quality, passages so martial and ringing, so noble and affecting that the epics are recalled to us, there are descriptions which excite the fullest admiration. He can be but a languid lover of poetry to whom the famous battle-piece in *Marmion*, for example, is not altogether acceptable—

> " Amid the scene of tumult, high
> They saw Lord Marmion's falcon fly:
> And stainless Tunstall's banner white,
> And Edmund Howard's lion bright,
> Still bear them bravely in the fight:
>   Although against them come,
> Of gallant Gordons many a one,
> And many a stubborn Badenoch man,
> And many a rugged Border clan,

> With Huntly and with Home. . . .
> By this, though deep the evening fell,
> Still rose the battle's deadly swell,
> For still the Scots, around their king,
> Unbroken, fought in desperate ring.
> Where's now their victor vaward wing,
>   Where Huntly, and where Home?—
> O, for a blast of that dread horn,
> On Fontarabian echoes borne,
>   That to King Charles did come,
> When Rowland brave, and Olivier,
> And every paladin and peer,
>   On Roncesvalles died! . . .
> But yet though thick the shafts as snow,
> Though charging knights like whirlwinds go,
> Though bill-men ply the ghastly blow,
>   Unbroken was the ring;
> The stubborn spear-men still made good
> Their dark impenetrable wood,
> Each stepping where his comrade stood,
>   The instant that he fell."

Allow that Scott's " *light horseman sort of stanza*," as he himself
called it, is not in the " grand style," that it is never comparable
with the style either of Homer or of Virgil, still had he maintained the level to which in his best moments he could attain,
no matter how criticism had hesitated, he must have conquered
time.   But poetry—it is an essential—should be " *like Laconian
oratory*," all kernel, " *without rind*."   In some of his lyrics—one
thinks of *Rosabelle*, or *Where shall the lover rest*—Scott attains
perfection, a kind of faultless finality.   In general, however,
there is wanting in his poetry—in his narrative poetry for long
stretches it is wanting—a sense of form.   He lacked ear, or he
could never have written scores of passages, for instance, like—

> " Seem'd to the boy, some comrade gay
> Led him forth to the woods to play;
> On the drawbridge the warders stout
> Saw a terrier and lurcher passing out."

Scott cannot be trusted for a page to preserve, I do not say the
grand manner, even the distinguished manner, which the dignity
of his subject, or rather, let me say, which the nature of poetry
itself demands.   Turn to any poet who has captured beyond
question a place on the narrow ridge of fame, and his style, his
expression, whether his subject be epic or lyric, are found to
be arresting, impressive.   The character of the art is such that
there is but one path to success in it.   For what other purpose

do we read poetry than to experience the unqualified delight of a perfect rendering? We may overlook in poetry, in any art, lack of depth, of intellectuality; lack of form we cannot overlook, for form is the artist's *métier*. " *The Coryphaeus of balladists*," as Arnold called him, attempted to fashion for sustained narrative a style akin to that in which the history and traditions he loved had first been sung. He endeavoured to extend the range and heighten the tones of a rustic instrument. It was an interesting, a delightful and, let us add, a brilliant experiment. As a medium of narrative the qualities of Scott's style are undeniable. No man in his generation told a story in verse so well, perhaps no English poet since Chaucer had told one better. He retained something of the ballad charm in his longer poems, the charm of the unaffectedly simple. The homeliness, the natural speech of the ballad, by which it so often moves and delights us, as in *The Battle of Otterbourne*, for example, the lines in which Scott himself took his last and pathetic farewell of Douglasdale—

> " My wound is deep; I fain would sleep;
>   Take thou the vanguard of the three,
> And hide me by the braken bush,
>   That grows on yonder lily lea.
> O bury me by the braken bush,
>   Beneath the blooming brier,
> Let never living mortal ken
>   That e'er a kindly Scot lies here ";

or in *Jamie Telfer*—

> " It's I, Jamie Telfer o' the fair Dodhead,
>   And a harried man I think I be!
> There's naught left in the fair Dodhead,
>   But a greeting wife and bairnies three,"

this homeliness and natural speech, informed by the very spirit of its subject, so free from the intrusion of the subjective and personal, cannot be carried further. But this style had its limits, and they had been reached. Scott's instinct might have told him so. It might have told him that it was not possible to preserve the admirable qualities of the ballad, the simplicity of homeliness, and to add at the same time the qualities required in extended and elaborated narrative, narrative of substance, such qualities as weight, dignity, elevation. Perhaps, indeed, it did tell him, but he had not the patience to master a more suitable form. He had " a better knack," as he said, for his octosyllabics than for the other metres suggested to him, and preferred them, as a friend told him, because one takes pleasure in doing those things which one can do with the least fatigue. Scott's conception of poetry, moreover, is hardly ours. He himself preferred—and it is interesting to compare his preference with that of Byron for Pope—Johnson to any other poet, and confessed that " *he had more pleasure in reading ' London ' and ' The Vanity of Human Wishes ' than any other poetical composition he could mention.*" [1] He came—it is necessary to remember it—before Wordsworth had found acceptance or Coleridge, before poetry was thought of as the ally of philosophy or political ideals. He came before Keats and Tennyson, before it was thought of as the union between " a criticism of life " and the rare, the exquisite in rhythm and cadence. We who so think of it are scarcely in a position to do justice to Scott. From all other points of view than that of finish and perfection of style he is unassailable. He might, indeed, have been greater than he was, but of whom may this not be said? Though the tide of popular approbation has receded, by virtue none the less of creative and imaginative gifts comparable to those of Shakespeare himself he belongs to that select company who have profoundly impressed and shaped the thought of the world, who deserve from each succeeding generation that their memory be honoured with a festival, with incense and an ode.

How near Scott came to success in epic may perhaps best be judged if we compare him with Southey. "*Always a poet and never a good one,*" as Dryden said of himself, Southey, the most laborious and conscientious of writers, shared none of Scott's advantages, but did all that was possible to remedy the defects of nature. As a school-boy at Westminster he formed the " intention of exhibiting the most remarkable forms of mythology which have at any time obtained among mankind, by making each the ground-work of a narrative poem "—a remarkable ambition in

---

[1] Scott thought Joanna Baillie a better poet than either Wordsworth or Byron.

a youth—and with unflagging resolution carried to a conclusion a task hardly less tedious than prodigious. Nor, though he fell far short of Scott in popularity, did he lack admirers. Byron thought *Roderick the Last of the Goths*, " *the first poem of the time*." " *I have read ' Roderick ' over and over again*," wrote Hogg, " *and am the more and more convinced that it is the noblest epic poem of the age*." Coleridge spoke of " *the pastoral charm and wild streaming lights* " of *Thalaba*, Shelley imitated it in the opening verses of *Queen Mab*, and is clearly indebted to it in his *Alastor*. A later admirer, Cardinal Newman, declared it " *the most sublime of English poems*." " *I mean*," he added, " *morally sublime*." Scott himself, with a modesty so rarely found in poets, when he declined the poet-laureateship in Southey's favour, wrote, " *I am not such an ass as not to know that you are my better in poetry, though I have had, probably but for a time, the tide of popularity in my favour*." Yet open any volume of Southey at any page and you perceive that his was a moral rather than a poetic ardour. You respect the man more than the writer, you read for edification rather than for pleasure. " *Poetry, he held*," says his most sympathetic critic, Professor Dowden, " *ought rather to elevate than affect*." What is one to reply to such a doctrine? One must reply that it confuses the issues. Poetry has been very variously defined, and the definitions have not done much to elucidate its true nature. When we compare, however, the poems which continue to give satisfaction with those which have ceased to give it, those that are still read with those that are no longer read, when we compare the poems to which we return frequently and with enthusiasm with those which we take up seldom or reluctantly, we perceive that the secret of the successful work is simply its power to create interest. But what kind of interest? The interest proper to poetry, which is not that of science or philosophy or anything else. The interests of science or philosophy are not, indeed, excluded, but we do not ask for them. Nor are to-day's interests in science and philosophy to-morrow's. The successful poem does not draw its vitality from these, it is charged with an interest which belongs neither

T

to science nor philosophy. What is proper to itself is the interest of unique expression. The expression need not be faultless, though the nearer it approach to faultlessness the more impressive it must necessarily be. As there is probably no faultless organism throughout the whole realm of nature, so there are no faultless compositions, whether pictures, poems, or statues;[1] but an organism may be alive though faulty, and a work of art may be charged with expression, though, like the famous horse of Marcus Aurelius on the Capitol, it is in some measure defective in form. What we ask of a poem, therefore, is that it shall be so alive with expression that we can overlook blemishes. If the poem be a short one, comparatively few flat or insipid lines destroy its effect upon us; in a longer poem we may be so carried forward from the crest of one wave, as it were, to another, that the weaker passages escape our attention. If the number of unimpressive or commonplace expressions abound we become aware of it, and in proportion to their number the interest of the composition declines. Plutarch tells us that Zeuxis, when accused of painting slowly, replied, " *I admit that I do, but then I paint to last.*" It cannot be said that either Scott or Southey failed in industry, both were men who could toil terribly. Yet both wrote poetry at a pace which might well have excited the envy of Apollo himself. Scott prided himself upon his " *hurried frankness of composition.*" On one day Southey finished that formidable poem, *Madoc*, the next morning he rose early and wrote a hundred lines of another epic, *Thalaba!* While Virgil found eleven years of seclusion too short a time for the composition of a single poem of ten or eleven thousand lines, and proposed to give three more to its revision, about the same time sufficed Southey to produce two poems, *Madoc*[2] and *Roderick*, each almost as long as the *Æneid*, and two others, *Thalaba* and the *Curse of Kehama*, also of great length, together with many works in prose. How perilously near improvisation! What supreme poetic genius,

---

[1] " The only impeccable writers are those that never wrote."—Hazlitt's *Table Talk*.

[2] Southey himself thought this " The best English poem since *Paradise Lost*."

like Virgil's, found infinitely difficult these men found easy. So profound and deep-seated is the difference between one conception of poetry and another! It need not surprise us to meet the insipid and commonplace in Southey to a degree almost intolerable; in poems written with such haste nothing else is to be expected. For no genius has yet appeared in the poetical literature of any race or country so abundant, so fruitful of excellence, as to achieve greatness with ease and speed. Poetry is too high, too monumental an art. Excellence in it, *"as the Greek poet long ago said, dwells among rocks hardly accessible, and a man must almost wear his heart out before he can reach her."* [1]

As I have said, Scott came nearer success than Southey. One feels that he is more at home in the poetic world, one feels, too, that he is more disinterestedly a poet. Scott employs verse to serve poetic, Southey to serve ethical ends. Again, what we admire in the one we find wanting in the other. We admire in Scott the energy and animation, the spirited conduct of the action. It moves with a fluency and speed unrivalled in our narrative poetry. The most impatient reader can trust himself to Scott for the impetuosity of his style atones for its too fluent verbosity. The moral grandeur in which Southey outshines his contemporary somehow fails to communicate itself to his expression, his moral fervour to excite a corresponding fervour in his language. The fires of Apollo can be kindled from those of no other altar. But need we go further than the character of his subjects to account for Southey's inferiority in vigour and imaginative control? He stood at an infinite distance from all his themes, widely separated in race, religion, times, surroundings, from the men and events of which he wrote. He knew them only through the distorting medium of books. *Thalaba* is a tale of Arabia, *Kehama* of Hindostan, *Roderick* of Spain in the eighth century. Who can be at ease in all countries and times? The immediate sympathetic contact of Scott with the whole range of Scottish history and tradition, his lively familiarity with the country through which his heroes moved, the castles

[1] Arnold, *Essay on Milton.*

they attacked or defended, the scenes of the battles in which they fought, the knowledge, the confident sureness of touch in all particulars, as it were of an eye-witness, take hold of the imagination. Southey had no such resources, and the reader, moving among shadows, never feels that his foot is planted upon solid ground. Had one not been told one might have guessed that a poem like *Marmion* could hardly have come from the pen of a student writing in seclusion, that for such work was required a fusion of personal experience with poetic feeling. The soldier and the horseman in Scott contributed to it. "Many of the more energetic descriptions, and particularly that of the battle of Flodden, were struck out while he was in quarters with his cavalry." "In the intervals of drilling," Skene told Lockhart, "Scott used to delight in walking his powerful black steed up and down by himself upon the Portobello sands, within the beating of the surge; and now and then you would see him plunge in his spurs, and go off as if at the charge, with the spray dashing about him. As we rode back to Musselburgh, he often came and placed himself beside me, to repeat the verses that he had been composing during these pauses of our exercise."

De Quincey has a pleasant fancy about building a reputation "on the basis of *not* being read," and pictures the author who could point to a vast array of his works wherein no human eye had ever strayed. "*Such a Sabbath,*" he exclaims, "*from the impertinencies of critics!*" It is to be feared that an immunity of this kind has already been secured by Southey, that he has found his place finally among those authors who, like so many men who played a once conspicuous part in life, are for all succeeding time no more than names. Every age has its Southeys. What is fame for the statesman or the soldier is failure for the poet, whose success is to be measured not by the permanence of his name but of his verses. One might, indeed, desire for so elevated a spirit as his, so loyal to noble convictions, so heroic in life, a hold upon the future, an influence fixed and enduring. One might desire an increasing audience for a poet who pursued with passionate appreciation through Arabian and Indian mythology, through French and

Spanish history, through examples of perfect courage and lives
devoted to great causes the ideals of honour and valour, of
faith and fortitude most needed in the world.   But men take
ill to poetry which " *has designs upon them*," and when Southey
is most himself he is perhaps least attractive.   In *Roderick, the
Last of the Goths*, he found the subject best suited to his talents,
a pathetic tale of sorrow and hope and high endeavour, but
though one comes here most closely into contact with the real
mind and character of Southey, the magic and mystery, the
Oriental glamour and wizardry of *Kehama* and *Thalaba* excite
somehow a greater though now, indeed, a pallid interest.   Sham
sublimities, the modern man declares, painted devils, tales from
Eastern nurseries.   Demons and genii, spells and enchantments
—how languid the emotions these ancient terrors now excite.
Yet Southey displays both verbal skill and constructive imagination in his tales of marvel.   Here is a passage from the description of Padalon, the Inferno of Indian mythology—

> " Over these dens of punishment, the host
>   Of Padalon maintain eternal guard,
> Keeping upon the walls their vigilant ward.
>   At every angle stood
> A watch-tower, the decurion Demon's post,
> Where raised on high he view'd with sleepless eye
> His trust, that all was well.   And over these,
>   Such was the perfect discipline of Hell,
> Captains of fifties and of hundreds held
>   Authority, each in his loftier tower;
>   And chiefs of legions over them had power;
>   And thus all Hell with towers was girt around.
>   Aloft the brazen turrets shone
>   In the red light of Padalon;
>   And on the walls between,
> Dark moving, the infernal Guards were seen
> Gigantic Demons pacing to and fro."

In the midst was seen—

>   " Yemen's seat
>   Of Empire, in the midst of Padalon,
>   Where the eight causeys meet.
>   There on a rock of adamant it stood
>   Resplendent far and wide,
>   Itself of solid diamond edified,
>   And all around it roll'd the fiery flood. . . .
>   The Diamond city blazing on its height
>   With more than mid-sun splendour, by the light
>   Of its own fiery river!

Its towers and domes and pinnacles and spires,
Turrets and battlements that flash and quiver
Through the red restless atmosphere for ever;
    And hovering overhead,
The smoke and vapours of all Padalon,
Fit firmament for such a world, were spread,
With surge and swell and everlasting motion,
Heaving and opening like tumultuous ocean."

It may be safely assumed that in lyric there is nothing antagonistic to drama. The same poet may shine in both.
Between them there is a kinship, a blood-relationship one might
call it. For in drama, romantic drama certainly, it is not so
much the situation that counts, as the passion it arouses. Lear's
resentment, Macbeth's remorse, Othello's jealousy—these are
what make the play. The explosive force is in the personality,
a spark may fire it. For lesser men, placed in the same or similar
situations, men incapable of fierce emotions, who meet their
fates submissively, or who react mechanically upon circumstances, there is room in life, but little room in drama. Something akin to the poet's power of feeling belongs to all the heroes
of tragedy. Lyrical poetry, too, is ruled by passion, it is the
record of an emotional experience. The personal and passionate
experience of the lyrical poet may utter itself in a sonnet; there
is in the nature of things no reason why it should not be em-
bodied in a far different form, the dramatic. It may find an
utterance in the words of Richard II. or of Romeo. We have
been told, indeed, that Shakespeare was essentially a lyrical
poet, expressing himself in many moods through many of his
characters. A recent critic has claimed to prove from his
works that he " painted himself twenty times from youth to
age at full length." True or untrue, the remark points at least
to the sympathetic relationship between lyric and drama. In
both the interest is the interest of a climax, an intense moment,
a mental or moral crisis. Between lyric and epic there exists
no such relationship, for the epic, dealing with events rather
than emotions, avoids crisis and climax. There the situations
or circumstances, " *the real long-lived things* " out-last and overpower the momentary flashes, the sudden and violent storms of
feeling. The " nerve storms " have their place, but are seen

in perspective, as parts of the larger landscape of life. In Homer we take, as it were, a bird's-eye view of a great expanse in which the individual is but the individual, one man in a world of men. The anger of Achilles, Andromache's woe, the sufferings of Priam claim from us no more than a passing attention. " We must bury him who falls," says Homer, " steeling our hearts, when we have wept him for a day; for such as are left alive from hateful death must take thought of meat and drink, that yet more against our foes we may fight relentlessly ever."

In the epic then the lyrical cry is not heard, it is not heard from the poets of epic temper, like Milton or Scott. The subjective and passionate lyrists, like Shelley, on the other hand, avoid the large objective canvas of epic. They sympathise with feeling, with action they have little sympathy. And the epic hero, a man of deeds not of feelings, whose inner life is without hesitations, who reacts upon circumstances with the directness and simplicity of a child, cannot be made the mouthpiece of their poignant and soulful intensities. The individualism of the early nineteenth-century poets forbade success in the objective style. But among them was Byron. Substituting his own circumstances for the imagined circumstances of others, his own doings, his own sorrows, his own sentiments, for the doings and sorrows and sentiments of some historical group or society, though the true epic field was closed to him he broke new ground in a kind hitherto unattempted. The breach with tradition is, of course, complete. Nothing is to be gained by contrasting in this respect Byron's narratives with those of any other age or poet. He is his own hero, the creator of a type of poetry unknown before, which, but for the titanic force of character displayed in it, must have crumbled in the making. What astonishes one in Byron, what astonished Goethe, was the way in which he forced his personality upon the attention of the world. Is it too much to say, is it not literal truth, that he created a larger interest in himself, that he preserved it longer than any poet since the world began? His poems were like victories, his fame like that of a leader of

armies. The first two cantos of *Childe Harold*, those which
dealt generally with his travels in Spain and Greece, draw all
eyes to the noble author. He dealt in sentiments rather than
in thought, and in sentiments easily intelligible. The reflections
which he permitted himself were the obvious reflections—

> " By Heaven! it is a splendid sight to see
> (For one who hath no friend, no brother there)
> Their rival scarfs of mix'd embroidery,
> Their various arms that glitter in the air."

But these simple reflections were associated with descriptions
of men and countries themselves interesting. He was assisted
by his subject. The events of the Peninsular War were fresh
in the public mind, and the descriptions of places rendered
memorable by the events of that war, the references to the
battles fought in it, the dashing vigour of the verse, moving
rapidly from scene to scene, from topic to topic of contemporary
interest, naturally drew swift attention. When he pondered,
too, over the departed glories of Greece, though he added nothing
to the knowledge or appreciation of her great civilisation, his
verse gave to its readers the author's eyes, and their emotions
sprang to meet his own. Such descriptive poetry had never
before been written in England. As a guide to the ancient
glories of Spain, to the romantic history of the Moors, to the
slopes of Parnassus or the steep of Delphos, the new poet was
admirably equipped. His own love and knowledge of history
had vitalised his travel, it served him once again to enrich and
decorate his verse with famous names and episodes of the great
world's past. From Cadiz and Seville to Albuera and Barossa,
through Calpe's strait and past Calypso's isle, to Leucadia's
cape, past

> " the scenes of vanish'd war,
> Actium, Lepanto, fatal Trafalgar,"

he had journeyed, and in his references " *touched*," as Shelley
said, " *the chord to which a million hearts responded.*" Even
to-day when the freshness is gone, even to a critical generation,
sated with such travels and the obvious feelings they arouse,
there is possible a throb of answering pleasure.

Between the first two cantos of *Childe Harold*, not much more than a poetical journal of his early travel, and the third and fourth cantos which rise to a far higher level, Byron published his Oriental tales. In the interval, too, came the quarrel with his wife, the rupture with English society, and the final departure from his country. In these later cantos he passes from a description of Waterloo and the death-grapple of nations, to the Rhine and Switzerland, the rolling stream, the wild precipices, the forest's growth, the Gothic walls, the fertile country on its banks, still beautiful though empires fall, to the palaces of Nature, the Alps, pinnacled in clouds, which " *throne Eternity in icy halls*," and again to Venice, where " *a thousand years their cloudy wings expand* " around him, and Italy,

> " the garden of the world, the home
> Of all Art yields and Nature can decree,"

—Italy with its undying memories—Florence, the birthplace of Dante, the city which holds the dust of so many world-remembered men—

> " In Santa Croce's holy precincts lie
> Ashes which make it holier, dust which is
> Even in itself an immortality. . . .
>   Here repose
> Angelo's, Alfieri's bones, and his
> The starry Galileo, with his woes:
> Here Machiavelli's earth returned to whence it rose "—

and at last Rome, " *the city of the soul*," " *the Niobe of nations*," " *Childless and crownless in her voiceless woe*," the Rome of Virgil and Cicero, and Livy's " *pictured page*," of Sulla and Caesar, Titus and Trajan, the Rome of the Coliseum and the Pantheon and St. Peter's, where the mind expands to its true dimensions, finding in the genius of the spot a spell to evoke its own immensity and kindle the hope of immortality. Such is the colossal canvas upon which in this poem Byron chose to paint, to make the background of his reflections, his descriptions of nature, his portraits of the famous figures of every age. He pauses to recall the memory of " *the self-torturing sophist, wild Rousseau*," " *the apostle of affliction*," from whom came " *Those oracles which set the world in flame*," of Voltaire and Gibbon, who sapped

> " a solemn creed with solemn sneer,
> The lord of irony, that master spell,"

of Ariosto and Dante, Petrarch and Boccaccio, of Rienzi, "*last of Romans.*" He pauses before the statue of the dying Gaul, "*butchered to make a Roman holiday,*" before "*Laocoön's torture dignifying pain,*" before the radiant might and "*beautiful disdain*" of the Belvidere Apollo. He pauses to describe Lake Leman "*with its crystal face,*" "*the blue rushing of the arrowy Rhone,*" Clitumnus' happy lake and shore, turning in the end to the open sea in the famous apostrophe—

> " There is a pleasure in the pathless woods,
> There is a rapture in the lonely shore,
> There is society where none intrudes,
> By the deep sea and music in its roar."

It might well be supposed that a poem in this manner must necessarily dispense with even the semblance of unity, must from its nature fall apart into fragments. And yet this epic of the soul is not at all fairly represented in selected passages. Sustained energy—and its energy is unflagging—would not, indeed, suffice to bind the parts of such a poem into unity; and *Childe Harold*, for all its variety of interest, must have failed but for its revelation of the author's personality. It is fused into a whole by the passionate impress of that personality. There was nothing profound in Byron's creed, there was nothing novel in the sickness of soul from which he suffered save its intensity, to distinguish it from the same malady in other men, yet—

> " Thousands counted every groan
> And Europe made his woe her own."

The transience of all human things, the golden roofs and those that built them, the beautiful and brave, the lords of earth and sea, that thronged beneath them, all that had graced and ennobled life swept into the vast, never-glutted gulf of nothingness and oblivion; the ignorance of man, making his blind voyage across the uncharted waters, "*still striving for some false impossible shore*"—these and the like old and insistent reflections, presented again and yet again to the mind, and pressed home with new instances from every region of human experience, constitute the philosophy of *Childe Harold*. This age-worn indictment of human life drew its force from the

novelty and splendour of its setting. We are sometimes told
that the roots of Byron's disease were in his egoism, and in the
absence of any public or national cause to which he could
render a whole-hearted allegiance. But the roots lay deeper
still. While Shelley stayed his thoughts upon the ideal of a
regenerate human society, a world made beautiful by human
effort, Byron, with clearer gaze, foresaw the end of all societies,
civilised and uncivilised. What profit that one, or a dozen
generations, should labour and suffer that another might be
blest? Happiness, he saw, is no longer lived than sorrow, the
beautiful than the unbeautiful. He might have written the
words of a later poet—

> " Oh dreadful thought, if all our sires and we
>   Are but foundations of a race to be—
>   Stones which one thrusts in earth, and builds thereon
>   A white delight, a Parian Parthenon,
>   And thither, long thereafter, youth and maid
>   Seek with glad brows the alabaster shade,
>   And in processions' pomp together bent
>   Still interchange their sweet words innocent,—
>   Not caring that these mighty columns rest
>   Each on the ruin of a human breast,—
>   That to the shrine the victor's chariot rolls
>   Across the anguish of ten thousand souls! . . .
>   And yet these too shall pass and fade and flee,
>   And in their death shall be as vile as we,
>   Not much shall profit with their perfect powers
>   To have lived a so much sweeter life than ours,
>   When at the last, with all their bliss gone by,
>   Like us those glorious creatures come to die,
>   With far worse woe, far more rebellious strife
>   Those mighty spirits drink the dregs of life."

Byron, it appears, was not a philosopher. *"So bald er reflectirt,"*
said Goethe, *" ist er ein kind."* Perhaps, but what philosophic
reflections have disposed of his conclusions, what reasonings
have proved groundless his despair? He felt, as passionately
as ever man felt, the tragedy of the imprisoned soul. Who, with
a smile at his childish creed, has set it free? It is as literature,
as poetry, indeed, that we are here concerned with Byron, and
we may leave him to fight his own battle with the philosophers,
saying only this that they will find him a representative man.
Nowhere does he endeavour to escape the self-regarding attitude
of the soul. Carlyle, clad in Fichtean armour, breaks a lance

with him, comments sardonically on the poetic revelations of
a broken heart, and compares the poet to a rusty Meat-Jack,
eternally whining, growling, and screeching, " Once I was
hap-hap-happy, but now I'm meeserable! Clack-clack-clack,
gnarr-r-r, whuz-z. Once I was happy, but now I'm meeserable"
—and grimly adds, " My dear fellow, it isn't of the slightest
consequence ! " But Carlyle's despair is bleaker than Byron's.
Why is it of no consequence? Because, it seems, the day is
passing swiftly and " The night once come, our happiness, our
unhappiness—it is all abolished: vanished, clean gone; a thing
that has been: ' not of the slightest consequence ' whether we
were happy . . . as the fattest pig of Epicurus, or unhappy as
Job with potsherds, as musical Byron with Giaours and sensibilities of the heart; as the unmusical Meat-Jack with hard
labour and rust ! " Thus Carlyle, learned in German philosophy,
wise with the wisdom of Goethe, disposes of the childishness of
Byron, but with curious logic proceeds to advocate work—" our
work, behold it remains—for endless Times and Eternities,
remains ! " But does it? In what sense? As knit up into
the welfare of future generations? But they too must pass
into the night. And if it be " not of the slightest consequence "
whether the present inhabitants of earth are " as happy as the
fattest pig of Epicurus, or as unhappy as Job with potsherds,"
by what reasoning does one make the happiness or misery of the
future inhabitants of consequence? And Byron, who felt that
the welfare and happiness of society had no meaning save as the
welfare and happiness of the individuals who compose it,
remains unanswered. The whole of being, as far as we have
any knowledge of it, is parcelled out into individuals, and if
these fail in the satisfaction of their aspirations—and this is
Byron's cause of misery—how can the whole be satisfied, or
what remains of satisfaction in the world of being? He has,
too, this advantage over the philosophers, that where they
acquiesce he revolts against the acceptance of the futility of
life. The will to live, against which Buddha directed his
philosophy, and Schopenhauer, that occidental Buddhist, is
invincible in Byron. He recoils from the pessimistic con-

clusions which can find no remedy against the world's ills save
the extinction of the desire for existence itself. He passionately
desires individual life, he stands for immortality.

> " 'Tis life, whereof our nerves are scant
> 'Tis life, not death, for which we pant;
> More life and fuller that I want ";

and since he is thus the natural man, loving life and hating
death, he occupies a strong place with superior forces from
which the philosophers will find it difficult to dislodge him.

In *Childe Harold* Byron attempted the personal epic. The
fire and passion, the rebellious and tempestuous spirit abroad
in it carried the poem far on the pathway to complete success.
But Byron too, like Scott, fell, one might say, in the moment
of victory. Like Scott he had great gifts and great opportunity.
No poet since Shakespeare's day wrote English with more continuous ease, more consummate freedom, more fluent power or
richer variety. But how careless, how often undistinguished,
unharmonious, even ungrammatical. " On taking up a fairly
good version of *Childe Harold's Pilgrimage* in French or Italian
prose," said Swinburne, " a reader whose eyes and ears are not
hopelessly sealed against all distinction of good from bad in
rhythm or in style will infallibly be struck by the vast improvement which the text has undergone in the course of translation.
The blundering, floundering, lumbering, and stumbling stanzas,
transmuted into prose and transfigured into grammar, reveal
the real and latent force of rhetorical energy that is in them:
the gasping, ranting, wheezing, broken-winded verse has been
transformed into really effective and fluent oratory. . . . It
is impossible to express how much *Childe Harold* gains by being
done out of wretchedly bad metre into decently good prose: the
New Testament did not gain more by being translated out of
canine Greek into divine English."

Byron's first intention in *Childe Harold* was a poem in the
manner of Ariosto, mingling the grave with the vicious outlook,
and permitting himself within a few lines a transition from the
serious to the comic aspect. But the few attempts made in the
early cantos to introduce the jesting tone were not successful,

and soon abandoned. Nevertheless it was in comic epic that Byron finally and completely found himself. He made several discoveries—the first a discovery of the highest importance—that, as Moore said, " *It is far easier to rise with grace from the level of a strain generally familiar, into an occasional short burst of pathos or splendour, than to interrupt thus a prolonged tone of solemnity by any descent into the ludicrous.*" *Beppo* was a preliminary trial in a style brought to perfection in what must, when all deductions are made, be regarded as Byron's greatest achievement, *Don Juan*. Though Italy invented the burlesque romance, he owed most, perhaps, to his brilliant English predecessor, John Hookham Frere, who, in *The Monks and the Giants*, published in 1817, added a new kind of narrative to our poetical literature, a kind which to readers unacquainted with Italian, perfectly displays the ease and vivacity, the ironical humour and polished ridicule of Pulci and Berni.[1]

Though eclipsed by his great successor, Frere deserves remembrance. His work not only enters history, it should live as literature. No detached passage, more especially of a narrative poem, can display its full excellence, but the pleasant vein of *The Monks and the Giants* must at least be represented, however briefly. Here is the description of Sir Tristram, the darling of the romancers—

" Songs, music, languages and many a lay
 Asturian or Armoric, Irish, Basque,
His ready memory seized and bore away;
 And ever when the ladies chose to ask,
Sir Tristram was prepared to sing and play,
 Not like a minstrel earnest at his task,
But with a sportive, careless, easy style,
As if he seemed to mock himself the while.

His ready wit and rambling education,
 With the congenial influence of his stars,
Had taught him all the arts of conversation,
 All games of skill and stratagems of wars;
His birth, it seems, by Merlin's calculation,
 Was under Venus, Mercury and Mars . . .
Somewhat more learned than became a knight,
It was reported he could read and write."

[1] *The Narrative and Romantic Poems of the Italians. Quarterly Review,* April 1819. Whistlecraft (J. H. Frere), said Byron, speaking of *Beppo,* " *is my immediate model, but Berni is the father of that kind of writing; which, I think, suits our language, too, very well.*"

In this metre and style Byron wrote *Don Juan*, an epic in the modern manner, probably the only manner in which the taste of latter days would willingly accept it.

> " My poem's epic, and is meant to be
>   Divided in twelve books; each book containing,
> With love, and war, a heavy gale at sea,[1]
>   A list of ships, and captains, and kings reigning,
> New characters; the episodes are three:
>   A panoramic view of hell's in training,
> After the style of Virgil and of Homer,
> So that my name of Epic's no misnomer.
>
> All these things will be specified in time,
>   With strict regard to Aristotle's rules,
> The *Vade Mecum* of the true sublime,
>   Which makes so many poets, and some fools:
> Prose poets like blank-verse, I'm fond of rhyme,
>   Good workmen never quarrel with their tools;
> I've got new mythological machinery,
> And very handsome supernatural scenery."

As a poem *Don Juan* violates all the canons, is without middle-point or end, and could never have been brought to a satisfactory conclusion. To its hero, destitute of heroic qualities, Byron himself was perfectly indifferent, and was even prepared to guillotine him to bring about a finish.[2] Without form and void, the whole composition is a patchwork of irrelevancies. The author passes through half a dozen moods in half a dozen stanzas, tragedy and comedy are inextricably mingled. There is no apparent purpose, no design, no connection between the parts. It has been called the "*Odyssey of Immorality*," scandalised a large proportion of its readers, and so offended the taste of the Countess Guiccioli, Byron's mistress, that she implored him to discontinue it after the first few cantos. Yet it can never be dethroned from its place among the glories of

---

[1] " For your tempest, take Eurus, Zephyr, Auster, and Boreas, and cast them together in one verse: add to these, of rain, lightning and thunder (the loudest you can) *quantum sufficit*. Mix your clouds and billows well together till they foam, and thicken your description here and there with a quicksand. Brew your tempest well in your head, before you set it blowing. For a battle: pick a large quantity of images and descriptions from Homer's *Iliad*, with a spice or two of Virgil, and if there remain any overplus, you may lay them by for a skirmish. Season it well with similes, and it will make an excellent battle."—Swift, *Recipe for an Epic Poem.*

[2] " People are always advising me to write an epic. If you must have an epic there's *Don Juan* for you. . . . Poor Juan shall be guillotined in the French Revolution."—Byron's Letters.

our literature, fulfils, as Shelley said, "*in a certain degree what I have long preached, the task of producing something wholly new and relative to this age and yet strikingly beautiful,*" and its amazing poetic and humorous qualities apart, is above all a passionate and unsubduable charter of liberty. Whatever we deny, do not let us deny that *Don Juan* is a superb campaign in the sacred cause of human freedom. Like Blake, Byron was convinced that all law external to himself, all restrictions on liberty save those imposed by man's own nature, are torturing and intolerable. That as an individual he became the captive of his own appetites does not concern us. His significance lies in the fact that he declared for the inner as against the outer restraints—

> " I wish men to be free
> As much from mobs as kings,—*from you as me.*"

He dared to be himself, and when he drew the sword he flung away the scabbard. Those who require or desire an apology for *Don Juan* may be reminded that it is a comic and a satirical poem, and claims the licence of satire and comedy. Add to the names of Aristophanes and Juvenal, of Boccaccio and Chaucer and Swift, the name of Byron, and one apology will suffice. Society's ineradicable habit of assuming an air of virtue so imposes upon us that we take the mask for the person, and it is no uncommon thing for the critics of society to be charged with the vices they expose. " What are your motives," asked a friend of Byron, " for painting nothing but scenes of vice and folly? " " To remove," he replied, " the cloak which the manners and maxims of society throw over their secret sins, and show them to the world as they really are."

The first two cantos of *Don Juan* appeared in July 1819, but so savage was the outcry that the author threw aside the work for a time, and two years elapsed before the succeeding three cantos were published. The fifth canto, he replied to some one who asked whether it concluded the poem, " is so far from being the last of *Don Juan* that it is hardly the beginning. I meant to take him the tour of Europe, with a proper mixture of siege, battle, and adventure, and to make him finish, as

Anacharsis Cloots, in the French Revolution. To how many cantos this may extend, I know not, nor whether (even if I live) I shall complete it, but this was my notion. I meant to have made him a Cavalier Servente in Italy, and a cause for a divorce in England, and a sentimental 'Werther-faced man' in Germany, so as to show the different ridicules of the society in each of these countries. . . . But I had not quite fixed whether to make him end in hell or in an unhappy marriage; not knowing which would be the severest: the Spanish tradition says hell, but it is probably only an allegory of the other state."

Turn from the ethical to the poetical aspect of *Don Juan*, and he must be a very severe moralist who is not disarmed by its prodigious cleverness, a cleverness exhibited in the turn of its rhymes, like the famous—

> " But—Oh! ye lords of ladies intellectual
> Inform us truly, have they not hen-peck'd you all? "

or in punning sarcasm—

> " When Bishop Berkeley said ' there was no matter '
> And proved it—'twas no matter what he said ";

or in the witty juxtaposition of the serious and trivial—

> " They griev'd for those who perish'd with the cutter,
> And also for the biscuit casks and butter ";

or in unexpected snatches of literary criticism—

> " John Keats, who was killed off by one critique,
> Just as he really promised something great,
> If not intelligible, without Greek
> Contrived to talk about the Gods of late
> Much as they might have been supposed to speak.
> Poor fellow! His was an untoward fate;
> 'Tis strange the mind, that very fiery particle,
> Should let itself be snuff'd out by an article."

Yet wit, though a capital relish, could hardly itself support the reader through fifteen cantos. *Don Juan*, make what deductions please you in respect of the predominance of rhetoric over poetry—and our very scrupulous modern taste seems to disapprove of rhetorical verse—reveals pure poetical quality in an infinitely higher degree than any other humorous poetry in English literature. Poetical feeling as a rule blends ill with worldly wisdom, it is true, yet in the second canto we have the

U

exquisite pastoral of the loves of Juan and Haidee. Where are we to look for anything more delicately perfect than the stanzas descriptive of the island maid and her sublime unconscious innocence of entranced affection? Set here in the midst of this fierce, sardonic composition, it is like a smiling islet in an angry sea. The bitterness and scorn, the invective and ridicule roll back from it as the waves recoil from the white sands of the beach that seem to offer them no resistance, and its beauty shines the brighter from its surroundings. Or take the fine heroic episode of the death of the Pacha and his five sons in the eighth canto, and it will be difficult to deny the presence in *Don Juan*, as clearly as in any contemporary composition, of the chivalric temper. It is, as Goethe said, "*a work full of soul*," whatever its misanthropy and cynicism. In *Don Juan*, as one might expect, Byron often recurs to the sentiments he made familiar in *Childe Harold*—ambition, fame, the glory of the world, what are they but a fitful fury, a little whirling of the dust before it settles?

> " I've stood upon Achilles' tomb
> And heard Troy doubted; time will doubt of Rome."

> " I pass each day where Dante's bones are laid:
> A little cupola, more neat than solemn,
> Protects his dust, but reverence here is paid
> To the bard's tomb, and not the warrior's column:
> The time must come when both alike decayed,
> The chieftain's trophy, and the poet's volume,
> Will sink where lie the songs and wars of earth,
> Before Pelides' death and Homer's birth."

> " What is the end of Fame? 'tis but to fill
> A certain portion of uncertain paper:
> Some liken it to climbing up a hill,
> Whose summit, like all hills, is lost in vapour;
> For this men write, speak, preach, and heroes kill,
> And bards burn what they call their 'midnight taper;'
> To have when the original is dust
> A name, a wretched picture, and worse bust."

No poet perhaps, no English poet certainly, has found more eloquent speech for this philosophy to which men return when the things they have been taught or have believed fail them, but Byron's creed—

> " The dreary *Fuimus* of all things human,"

is relieved in *Don Juan* by the divine quality of action. He
kept his word, as he claimed—

> " You have now
> Had sketches of love, tempest, travel, war,—
> All very accurate, you must allow,
> And *epic*, if plain truth should prove no bar."

To the episodes of " love, tempest, travel, war," to the solid
core of invigorating, health-giving circumstances, absent from
Childe Harold, Don Juan owes its easy superiority, its spring
and buoyancy, its air of largeness. We are out of doors, under
the bright sunlight or the stars, afloat on the current of life.
Here too, for the first time, as Swinburne said, his style " is
beyond all praise or blame, a style at once swift and supple,
light and strong, various and radiant." One rises from it with
some understanding of his European fame.

Byron's star has been for a generation or more if not in eclipse,
certainly overcast. He has been in the descendent rather than
the ascendant during the latter half of the nineteenth century.
While Tennyson filled the horizon of readers and while Wordsworth was slowly climbing to his station among the greater
luminaries, Byron receded from his former pride of place. But
in England only; on the continent of Europe his star has never
paled its fire. " *He led the genius of Britain,*" said Mazzini, " *on
a pilgrimage throughout all Europe.*" After Shakespeare he seems
to all countries not English the greatest poet of his race. It is
and will remain impossible for us to accept this verdict, and
difficult for the foreigner to understand our rejection of it. He
will ascribe our judgment to our insular morality, to our Puritanism. He perceives Byron's breadth and freedom, his bold
design, his dazzling eloquence, he will not perceive the absence
of the delicate tints, the subtle graces, the haunting cadences,
the exquisite and refined phrasing which we associate with the
masters of our language; he will not perceive his " *feeble and
faulty sense of metre.*" Among us Byron speaks to the many,
to an audience not fastidious in the aesthetic and technical
values. To the connoisseur in the art of poetry, then, he proves
disappointing. Yet it is of the highest moment that a reputa-

tion should rest upon a broad popular basis. If it does so, and passes the critical test even with difficulty, it takes an altogether different rank from those reputations which pass the critical test with much to spare, but make no wide or general appeal. Though Byron did not belong to the highest type of creative minds, though his imagination was limited by his experience, though his expression is often rhetorical rather than just or exquisite, after these and all other necessary deductions have been made, the undeniable splendour and attraction of the man and his poetry remain. If you argue that he belongs to the negative, the iconoclastic movement, that we miss in him the spiritual, the reconstructive touch, I answer that he is none the less dæmonic. He is not easily to be numbered with the saints, but it is not the saints only who are magnificent. Byron is magnificent also—

> " Beholding whom, men think how fairer far
> Than all the steadfast stars, the wandering star."

CHAPTER XIV

NARRATIVE POETRY IN THE NINETEENTH CENTURY—
TENNYSON, MORRIS, ARNOLD

" *I almost feel hopeless about Alfred now—I mean about his doing what he was born to do,*" wrote Fitzgerald, after the publication of *The Princess*, a view assuredly remote from the popular one, which found Tennyson everywhere and at all times flawless and consummate. Anything more whole-hearted than his acceptance by his own generation need never be looked for. A plant of slower growth than Scott's or Byron's, his fame appeared to root itself more firmly, and so increased with the years as to place him high above all rivals. During his lifetime—so immense was the attraction—Poe's reiterated declaration that of poets he was " *the greatest that ever lived* " seemed a pardonable exaggeration. A cloud of glory encircled him, a veritable halo rested upon his head. For long, therefore, criticism of Tennyson —and what a prodigious volume of it poured through journals and reviews—was praise of Tennyson. Hardly at all in public utterances, here and there only in private letters or conversations, one met with a certain dubiety or hesitation. Fitzgerald alone among Tennyson's friends made no effort to conceal his disappointment. He had looked for a work of epic proportions and epic grandeur, something to match the great things in poetry, and looked in vain. Then came *The Idylls of the King*, in which, it was abundantly proclaimed, Tennyson had passed the final test, and Fitzgerald's last hopes expired. Something had gone wrong, " *the cursed inactivity of the nineteenth century had spoiled him* " or he " *had not the wherewithal to work on.*"

The judgments of contemporaries are sometimes curious, rarely trustworthy, but of the verdicts upon Tennyson Fitzgerald's more nearly represents, perhaps, the opinions of to-day. Yet that these will prevail there remains room for doubt. Not the verdicts of a poet's own generation only, those of the generation succeeding his own are also open to suspicion. To judge of a work of art we must stand well away from it, as clear of the retreating wave of reaction as of the advancing wave of enthusiasm. Few of us probably now believe that Tennyson is best represented by *The Idylls of the King*, or if he is best represented by them, that his station in English poetry is with Spenser or Milton, perhaps not even with Byron or Keats. *Childe Harold*, for example, may be read when Tennyson's Arthur and Guinevere are forgotten. The question how far Tennyson succeeded in his longer poems is still among his admirers an open question, and as an open question intelligent curiosity may be employed upon it. May not, we may ask, the depreciation of Tennyson, which has undoubtedly set in, have already gone too far? Is perfect success ever attained, and in the *Idylls* has he not achieved all that was possible? Or again, are we sure that the Arthurian story, rejected by Milton, was as suitable for epic treatment as it was alluring? These and questions like these, more easily, indeed, asked than answered, suggest themselves, but they are secondary to the question how far in the treatment of this theme Tennyson succeeded in capturing the human interest of the familiar story, in heightening the large and lovely elements, in fashioning to new shapes of tragic sadness or immortal beauty the wonderful figures of the ancient legend.

Let us note the character of the legend and his manner of handling it. How will it strike the reader who knows the romances, who takes pleasure in the version of that supreme editor, Malory? It will strike him that the marvels have become of less, the symbolism of more account, that while new interpretations have been offered of it, the story as a story has faded. This is no less than a great change. The Arthurian story, whatever its origin, took up a transfigured matter not its own, fables the most beautiful, the fables which belong to the childhood of the race, the floating marvellous tales with which all primitive peoples explain to themselves the everlasting miracle of the world.   It drew to itself all the wonders, the terror and delight of simple societies in simple times.   It embraced the whole region of miracle, nothing of the mysterious or amazing lay beyond it, of dream-built forms and fancies.   Mediæval Christianity did not make these things, they were its fortunate heritage from the immemorial and pagan past.   But by some excellent touch of genius it impressed upon them its spiritual seal, the stamp of chivalric and religious ideals, or at least suffered them to keep their place in the legends unaltered.   Thus the plain wonders, invented to delight the imagination, the happy isles, the healing wells, the enchanted armour and moving towers and dreamy woods, the dragons and ogres and sorcerers, became signs and symbols of the invisible, instructive matter for the soul.   The Celtic Arthur became a Christian knight, and his war against heathen enemies a holy war.   At no time, we may believe, were readers drawn to the romances of chivalry otherwise than out of naked delight in marvel and adventure.   Yet from the first the parable, if one cared for parable, lay within, a source of mystic power. Spenser preserved it in the *Faery Queene*, and Tennyson, who believed that there was "*no grander subject in the world than King Arthur*," when he chose to make his poem an allegory, "*shadowing sense at war with soul*," neither violated nor out-ran the tradition.   To compass it, however, to avoid arbitrary and absurd symbolism, purely forced and fanciful meanings, cost him much anxious concern.   And to his needs he sacrificed the old delightful fictions, the magic and marvels of the enchanted land of faery.

The price paid for the allegory was thus a heavy one, and Tennyson appears at a serious disadvantage beside Spenser, who knew that, as Bacon said, without a touch of strangeness there is no excellent beauty, with whom the allegory was secondary to the miracle.   The expulsion of the pagan elements—necessary perhaps in the interests of the Christian interpretation—abates the curiosity with which one followed the old and true romance, which is nothing if it be not a house of adventure, a banquet of surprise.   Tennyson cannot hold his own with Malory, for how disastrous is the change of balance when the centre of interest shifts from the story to the meaning of the story, from the oldest and most natural kind of pleasure in the noble and strange and moving to the pleasure of quite another kind—the sophisticated, the pleasure in ideas and sentiments and philosophical reflections. At best, then, Tennyson's *Idylls* are not epical but metaphysical poetry, the poetry of contemplation remote from the type which glories in martial prowess and rings with adventure, which exalts deeds of bodily strength and feats of endurance and daring, as in the ancient epics, remote, too, from that in which the knights " gallop for ever on their enchanted coursers, within enchanted armour, invincible, invulnerable, under a sky always blue, and through an unceasing spring, ever onwards to new adventures." [1]

Tennyson never plunges into battle like a warrior, for not the acts of men but their ideas and feelings occupy him. Lancelot's knightly achievements yield him little satisfaction, for he is distressed by his morals. And how significant it is that with the most famous and wonderful of all the legends, the story of Tristram and Iseult, he could do nothing. Paralysed by Victorian sentiment, this, the passionate rose of the mediæval romance, the most elemental and moving, the most lovely and pathetic of all tales of love, falls from his hands, the peerless story which lives by the beauty of inextinguishable affection. His mind misgave him for it was lawless. In the interests of the poem as a whole, Tennyson did right, no doubt, to abandon the legend in its mediæval form. Manifestly among the *Idylls* nothing could have been more incongruous, but manifestly also the romance of passion has thus been sacrificed, no less than the romance of marvel. And this sacrifice, too, is for the sake of the symbolism, the inner meaning, the " dark conceit."

Allegory is at all times in poetry a dangerous ally. Emphasise it and you rob the narrative of its human and living charm, you imperil its reality, your characters cease to be fellow creatures, and become unsubstantial puppets summoned from the shades to lesson us. Neglect it, and there is little justification for the

[1] Vernon Lee: *Euphorion*, p. 323.

use of so clumsy a contrivance. Success even, the most shining, what has it to show? It may well be doubted whether in the *Idylls* the philosophy materially assists the poetry or the poetry the philosophy. No one will deny the legitimacy of Tennyson's method, but one may question its efficacy. More especially may one question it when, as the reader soon perceives, the inward sense, by which certain critics lay such store, is fitful and uncertain, too obvious for pleasure in some of the tales, wholly absent from others, so that one is painfully unaware when and where it should be looked for. In the end not as allegory but as poetry the poem must be judged. "*By Arthur I always meant the soul, and by the Round Table the passions and capacities of a man.*" [1] It is well, perhaps, to know it, but is our appreciation of the poetry heightened by the knowledge, our delight in it more rare? In this world so purely idealistic a sense of vacancy oppresses us. Like the combatants in the last of Arthur's battles, when

" Friends and foes were shadows in the mist,"

it is as if we too

" beheld the faces of old ghosts
Look in upon the battle."

All that eloquence could do to give these phantoms breath, the filed phrase, the delicate cadence, are there, but we desire a blunter, bolder speech to match the heroic spirit. Of sweetness and sadness these poems are full, but who associates sweetness and sadness with great adventures, with voyages and sieges and all the matter of epic? And if epic pretensions are set aside and we agree to take it for what it is, a modern and philosophical poem, one is impelled to ask whether Tennyson was justified in selecting a mediæval legend to enforce modern sentiment. Taste lies beyond argument, and in some sort it may be a matter of taste. Yet when Arthur, for example, lectures Guinevere, as Meredith said, " like a curate," who does not feel that something like violence has been done to the simplicity and beauty of the old legend, that to think of such a story in such a way is

[1] Conversation of Tennyson with Mrs. Ritchie.

unnatural and afflicting? As well might one attempt to relate the terrible old legends in the Volsunga Saga, or the mythic tales upon which the Greek drama was founded, to modern morality. One has difficulty, too, in believing that we have here the inspired words of a final philosophy of human emotion and human conduct, that these ideals, though the ideals of the poet's own age and society, English society in the nineteenth century, clearly outline the divine idea, and have nothing to fear from the march of mind.

If Tennyson's *Idylls of the King*, then, are to be praised, it must be for qualities which none can deny him, in which he stood above all his contemporaries and high among poets of all times, qualities more fortunately and favourably presented, the future will incline to believe, in many of his other works—the skill in words, the sense for form and colour, the lucidity and equality of style everywhere preserved by him. He understood in its breadth and height the meaning of the word art, he knew that no art required more unremitting, more anxious, more strenuous labour than poetry which is " *the queen of arts*," and devoted to it the allegiance of a lifetime. Tennyson's greatness as a poet is, of course, not at all here in question. If he was not strong enough to support epic—

" The sacred, old, traditionary verse,"

in other fields his was no common success, for, make what reservations you will, he possessed the one gift of account in poetry, *fervor quidam exquisite inveniendi et exquisite dicendi quod inveneris*.

" I thought," said Tennyson, when the news of Byron's death reached England in 1824, " I thought everything was over and finished for every one—that nothing else mattered. I remember I walked out alone and carved ' Byron is dead ' into the sandstone." To the next generation Tennyson himself seemed, in like fashion, to fill the whole horizon, to leave no room for successors. " *We all had the feeling*," relates Canon Dixon of Morris and his friends at Oxford, thirty years later, " *that after Tennyson no further development was possible,*

that we were at the end of all things in poetry." There is
nothing unnatural, or even unusual, in such feeling, yet one is
surprised to think of it as shared by William Morris. Superficial
resemblances in their art may, one sees, be traced, but who
could fail to recognise that their aims and motives as poets were
radically dissimilar? Of necessity Morris came under the prevailing Tennysonian influence, which none, indeed, escaped,
echoes of Tennyson's verse are heard in his early poems, yet the
blended romanticism and realism of *Sir Peter Harpdon's End*
or *The Haystack in the Floods*, the strange modern quality of
such lines as those in *King Arthur's Tomb*, in which Guinevere
clings passionately to earth while she looks for heaven—

> " If even I go hell, I cannot choose
>   But love you, Christ, yea, though I cannot keep
> From loving Lancelot; O Christ, must I lose
>   My own heart's love? "—

show Morris already far from Tennyson, beginning not where
his predecessor ended, but remote with the remoteness of that
originality and independence of mind, which, judge him to have
been a great or a middling artist, are visible in every act of his
life, every poem from his pen, or pattern from his hand.

In all essentials Tennyson was a modern poet, and his preferences were for classical models. In Morris the mediæval revival
culminated, the movement which, springing out of the reaction
against the classicism of the Augustans, renewed the life of the
artistic spirit in England in the late eighteenth century. Till
his advent Chatterton's passionate devotion to mediævalism
remained unmatched. No other, not even Keats, had so loved
the outer and inner life of the Middle Age, its body and its soul,
had fingered so lovingly the fringes of its raiment, the old black
letter or the yellow parchment, had walked with the same
emotion within the dim splendours of a Gothic minster, under
the columns and carvings, " *the cross aisles and the arches
fair.*" Chatterton, indeed, had lived too soon and died too
early to realise the Middle Age save in its outward pageantry of
colour, its banners and coats-of-arms, its helms and lances; for
Morris the vision extended beyond the archæology, though that

too, of course, was fuller and more exact, a man's knowledge beside that of a child. " I am fairly steeped in mediævalism generally," he said. Like Chatterton, he desired to lure beauty back again into everyday life, the beauty which, in his age and ours, with its drab and dusty commercialism, none seem to miss, and for which few seem even greatly to care, but with Morris, and this is his signal distinction, definite aims based upon a reasoned scheme added a novel force and inspiration to his labours as an artist, so that we are to-day his debtors not for poetry only, which others have given us, but for a deeper consciousness of our practical necessities and counsel how we may supply them. One hardly knows whether to admire most his success in poetry or in his mission. An engaging simplicity marked his character and career. Believing that he knew the needs of his age, as " poet, artist, manufacturer, socialist," he took so direct a path that the aims he pursued in the art of words are hardly to be distinguished from those he followed in the weaving of his tapestries, his doctrines as a man from his doctrines as a painter.

In narrative poetry, it may be said at once, for all are agreed, no writer since Chaucer excelled William Morris in literary quality, in mastery of pure English, in the art of retaining the attention of his readers. Our literature is less rich in narrative than in almost any other poetic form, elegiac, satiric, didactic, lyrical, dramatic, and Morris, peculiarly fitted to excel in it, knew his gift, and followed its bidding with unwavering allegiance. I know no poem in the language which equals *Jason* in length, which in ease of movement can rival it, in spring and assured quality of quiet rhythm. Through all episodes and incidents, all conditions of wind and weather, his *Argo* keeps the seas with buoyant grace. Compare it with *Pharonnida*, for example, the heroic romance of the seventeenth century, and how astonishing the advance in sheer craftsmanship! Every forbidding fault of construction, all trace of florid and tiresome verbiage has vanished. Morris, in some miraculous fashion, has solved the problem, so often declared insoluble, of writing a poem in many books from which tedium is altogether expelled, in which, if never greatly moved, we are at least never fatigued, which we may open at any page to find pleasure, and can hardly close anywhere without regret. Undoubtedly there is here displayed a talent which, if not the highest in poetry, is at least rare to the degree that never in our literature has it been more amazingly exhibited. The surprising, nay the magical, thing consists in the triumph wrought not by deft diversity of tone or variety of manner, but simply by the succession of exquisite, cool, clear pictures in verse, whose liquid murmur is as little wearying as the tune of a woodland brook. The manner of *Jason*, indeed, is not epic, the antithesis of epic rather, however heroic the theme. The heroes are there, the antique gods and goddesses, the classic names and associations, but all else altered, transformed, so that one is reminded of Landor's lines on Shakespeare, who—

> " called up
> The obedient classics from their marble seat,
> And led them through dim glen and sheeny glade,
> And over precipices, over seas
> Unknown by mariner, to palaces
> High-arch'd, to festival, to dance, to joust,
> And gave them golden spear and visor barred,
> And steeds that Pheidias had turned pale to see."

It is not that we have mediæval trappings or pageantry, some subtle metamorphosis of the spirit has taken place, subduing the old legends to a key of feeling utterly unclassical, which produces a sense of bewilderment, as of a man who takes up again a favourite book of his childhood, and is puzzled by its new and unfamiliar print and pictures. In *Jason* the old fabric is dissolved, and though beautiful in a new way the story was designed not to make us in love with heroism but to lull us to acquiescence in our own dull lives, sad though it be with the sense which pervades all the writings of Morris, that " *beauty passes like a dream.*" Nor is it so much the persons or their acts which hold us as the direct simplicity and suggestiveness of the style whereby each episode and scene is made, as in a fairy tale, to serve the moment by arresting rather than furthering the swift action of the mind. Take two scenes, the first describing the departure of Jason and his crew on their great adventure, the second the return of Jason and Medea to the ship with "*the sea-born wonder of all lands,*" the fleece of gold—

> " But silent sat the heroes by the oar,
> Hearkening the sounds borne from the lessening shore;
> The lowing of the doomed and flower-crowned beasts,
> The plaintive singing of the ancient priests,
> Mingled with blare of trumpets, and the sound
> Of all the many folk that stood around
> The altar and the temple of the sea.
> So sat they pondering much and silently,
> Till all the landward noises died away,
> And midmost now of the green sunny bay,
> They heard no sound but washing of the seas
> And piping of the following western breeze,
> And heavy measured beating of the oars:
> So left the Argo the Thessalian shores."

> " Then swiftly did they leave the dreadful place,
> Turning no look behind, and reached the street,
> That with familiar look and kind did greet
> Those wanderers mazed with marvels and with fear.
> And so unchallenged, did they draw anear
> The long white quays, and at the street's end now
> Beheld the ship's masts standing row by row
> Stark black against the stars: then cautiously
> Peered Jason forth, ere they took heart to try
> The open star-lit space; but nought he saw
> Except the night wind twitching the loose straw
> From half-unloaded keels, and nought he heard
> But the strange twittering of a caged green bird
> Within an Indian ship, and from the hill
> A distant baying: yea, all was so still,
> Somewhat they doubted, natheless forth they passed,
> And Argo's painted sides they reached at last."

The style of Morris, moving always at the same level, never low, never exalted, a level sward, like a smooth meadow daisied o'er, a style which in its own way touches absolute perfection, challenges all other styles. So never-failing, so adequate it seems, supporting without effort poetic undertakings the most lofty, that to better it, we believe at times, would be impossible, the final touch has been given to language, the last improvements made. And astonishment increases when we recall the ease with which it was written. "*Well, if this be poetry,*" Morris is reported to have said, when praised for some of his early verses, "*it is very easy to write.*" There is, too, the story, hardly less significant, even were it untrue, that he wrote in one day seven hundred lines.[1] We possess at least, *The Earthly Paradise* in forty-two thousand lines, *Sigurd* in ten thousand, *Jason* in about the same number. There the volumes lie; not the product of an otherwise idle, but of an otherwise full and active life. How amazing such dexterity would have appeared to some of our poets, how amazing, for example, to Wordsworth or Gray, who were accustomed to brood over their verses with inexhaustible patience, with incredible anxiety.

Is poetry, then, easy to write? May we say, in Johnson's words of Pope, that Morris discovered " *the most perfect fabric of English verse*," compact of all the virtues. We suffer, of course, from an illusion if we think it. Some instinct should tell us that this style appears so satisfying because it declines the higher tasks, that only when his thoughts are not greatly engaged is such facility at the command of any man, that when he takes hold of life it abandons him, and his difficulties begin. Some instinct should tell us that this admirable ease and fluency do not march with intellectual depth, with the attempt to render the clash of motives and conflict of wills, the invisible and crucial crises of the soul. As the poetry of pageant, whose figures are without flesh and blood, as tapestry—and the author intended it for no more—a dim far-off reflection of the spectacle of moving life, adding nothing of comment or interpretation, though there are here no gains for the mind, though in it we taste the " *last honey of decay*," it captures by its pictorial charm. To tell a story such as children, and we are all children, love to hear, of *Argo* afloat upon the ridgy seas, of landscapes seen through the summer haze, of marble wharves and palaces, of strange and new-seen lands, of streams and grassy slopes and gardens in the wooded vales, of shell-strewn beaches and flowery shores, places

> " not made for earthly bliss
> Or eyes of dying men,"

—no style has sweeter chords. In *The Earthly Paradise*, as in *Jason*, it does all that is required of it, hardly if at all is one

---

[1] " The verse flowed off his pen. Seven hundred lines were once composed in a single day."—Mackail's *Life of Morris*, vol. i., p. 186.

conscious of inadequacy, of any shortcoming. Only when we remember that as Arnold said, " *the noble and profound application of ideas to life is the most essential part of poetic greatness,*" do we perceive what is lacking. Perhaps never in literature has an author more exquisitely veiled the absence of power, declined the more hazardous themes with such consistent and consummate skill. No writer certainly of his century knew his own limitations better or covered them more brilliantly. " *That talk of inspiration is sheer nonsense,*" said he, " *I may tell you that flat ; there is no such thing, it is a mere matter of craftsmanship.*" One can believe it of Morris, with him it was a mere matter of craftsmanship, of admirable craftsmanship. He spoke of what he knew and understood.[1] But there are passages in Shakespeare, as there are in many lesser men, of which one declines to believe it. One can believe it of Morris, for there is in him nothing dæmonic, there are no sudden elevations to be accounted for, no divine moments when he " *utters somewhat above a mortal mouth,*" no revealing flashes as from the god who, as it were, " *contrives a voice for himself through a mortal instrument.*"

> " Est deus in nobis, agitante calescimus illo;
> Sedibus aethereis spiritus ille venit."

If we desire then to walk " *with Epicurus on the right hand and Epictetus on the left,*" or if we desire the imperial accent in poetry, the accent of

> " You do me wrong to take me out o' the grave,
> Thou art a soul in bliss "—

or of

> " 'Tis true, I am that Spirit unfortunate "—

---

[1] The evidence of the poets is, of course, altogether against Morris, from Pindar to Goethe. Take two witnesses. " I appeal to the greatest poets of the present day," said Shelley, " whether it is not an error to assert that the finest passages of poetry are produced by labour and study. The toil and the delay recommended by critics can be justly interpreted to mean no more than a careful observation of the inspired moments, and an artificial connection of the spaces between their suggestions by the intertexture of conventional expressions." " I compose only when under an inspiration," said Leopardi, " . . . without inspiration it were easier to draw water from a stone than a single verse from my brain."

we must seek it elsewhere than in *Jason* or *The Earthly Paradise*.[1] Is it to be heard in *Sigurd the Volsung?*   In this poem, which Morris regarded as his crowning achievement,[2] he attempted something different, something in a style and upon a theme of which *The Lovers of Gudrun* is an anticipation.   Here, we have been told, he deserted the romantic for the true epic manner, in *Sigurd* we have " *the most Homeric poem which has been written since Homer.*" [3]   One may perhaps be excused some hesitation in accepting this verdict, in believing that, with all his brilliance, the author of *Jason* should find it easy to accumulate successes, to exchange at will romance for epic, and display so decisive a superiority in the grand style.   The phrase " the most Homeric poem since Homer " suggests an eminence in heroic poetry not merely unquestionable but outstanding, an excellence akin to Homer's, of exceeding and divine splendour. Let us take a specimen.

" But that night, when the feast was over, to Gudrun Sigurd came,
   And she noted the ring on his finger, and she knew it was nowise the same
   As the ring he was wont to carry; so she bade him tell thereof:
   Then he turned unto her kindly, and his words were words of love;
   Nor his life nor his death he heeded, but told her last night's tale:
   Yea, he drew forth the sword for his slaying, and whetted the edges of bale;
   For he took that Gold of Andvari, that Curse of the uttermost land,
   And he spake as a king that loveth, and set it on her hand;
   But her heart was exceeding joyous, as he kissed her sweet and soft,
   And bade her bear it for ever, that she might remember him oft
   When his hand from the world was departed and he sat in Odin's home."

---

[1] I do not know that the final impression created by the poetry of Morris is anywhere better described than in his own words upon Swinburne's *Tristram of Lyonesse*, when he glances at his own work: " As to the poem, I have made two or three attempts to read it, but have failed, not being in the mood I suppose: nothing would lay hold of me at all.   This is doubtless my own fault, since it certainly did seem very fine.   But to confess and be hanged, you know I never could really sympathise with Swinburne's work; it always seemed to me to be founded on literature, not on nature . . . in these days the issue between art, that is the god-like part of man, and mere bestiality, is so momentous, and the surroundings of life are so stern and unplayful, that nothing can take hold of people, or should do so, but that which is rooted deepest in reality and is quite at first hand; there is no room for anything which is not forced out of a man of deep feeling, because of its innate strength and vision.

" In all this I may be quite wrong and the lack may be in myself: I only state my opinion, I don't defend it; still less do I my own poetry."— Mackail's *Life of Morris*, vol. ii., p. 74.

[2] " This is the Great Story of the North," Morris wrote, " which should be to all our race what the Tale of Troy was to the Greeks."—*Ibid.* vol. i., p. 330.

[3] *Ibid.* vol. i., p. 332.

Can we recommend this to readers unacquainted with the Greek as Homeric? The truth is the passage has neither distinction of phrase nor rhythm. There are better, there are many striking passages in *Sigurd*, inspiring and noble, which one reads with delight and admiration, but there are no Homeric passages. *Sigurd* is not a poem of action, it is a resonant chant, rising and falling like the long ocean swell, it is—and in Swinburne's *Tristram of Lyonesse* we have a parallel—a piece of music woven about a great story, which rises at times into lyrical splendour. But to compare it as narrative, as a record of things attempted and done, with Homer or with Scott, these descriptions so slow, cloudy, and indefined with the bright clear pictures, the swift movement of the *Iliad* or the *Odyssey*, can only make for confusion. Any one who has a sense for poetry does not need to be told that Morris was here overweighted, that he undertook a task as much beyond his strength as it was outside his natural province, that to have given of this terrific old-world story a final and worthy, that is a sublime version, would have taxed the resources of a poet far greater than he, that his style, exquisitely adapted, perfectly equal to such narrative as one reads with pleasure in *The Earthly Paradise*, a delicate and charming style, contained few elements of real greatness, the spiritual virtue, the burning sincerity, the moral depth which we associate with lofty eminence, without which grandeur is unattainable. In the style of *Sigurd*, moreover, there is a great defect, a defect which in the close grapple with Time must prove fatal to any poem—its wordiness. " *It is not*," as Lowell said, " *the great Xerxes army of words, but the compact Greek ten thousand that marches safely down to posterity.*" The quality to which above all others the classic style owes its superiority is its economy, its hatred of the superfluous. In style there should be, as Schopenhauer said, a certain trace of kinship with the *epigraphic* or *monumental.* What delights one in Homer as in Milton is that every word counts. And the reader who wishes in nineteenth-century poetry to catch, though it be from far, an echo of Homer, must turn not to *Sigurd*, but to the work of another poet, to Arnold's *Sohrab and Rustum.*

Whole-heartedly an adherent of the classical tradition, Arnold—
one can hardly dispute it—lacks freedom. Both in his prose
and verse there is something academic, and the academic note
is not welcome in poetry. Yet since Landor's *Gebir* what
statelier narrative has been written, what more impersonal
and impressive?

In *Sohrab and Rustum* some readers feel indeed that, so far
from being wholly absorbed in his subject, the author has his
eye too constantly upon his model, the ancient model of which
he was from first to last a consistent worshipper, and that he is
in consequence not spontaneous enough, not natural enough.
Arnold felt, and felt rightly, however, that in our literature
generally, in these days particularly, unpruned luxuriance,
verbosity, laxity in rhythm and language, a too careless freedom
were the common and prevailing faults. English writers he
thought self-indulgent, capricious, and as a result unequal, often
spirited and inspiring, as often jejune and insipid or rhetorical
and hollow. He aimed and aimed consciously at a pure and
concise, a severe and disciplined style, which even when uninspired remained at least dignified and sufficient. Is such a
style unreservedly to be preferred? Place, for the sake of comparison, a passage from Morris side by side with one from
Arnold, and a conflict of ideals, of styles emerges, the conflict
between the style of ease and affluence and the style of economy
and restraint. The first passage describes the death of Brynhild
in the third book of *Sigurd*, the second is taken from the conclusion of *Sohrab and Rustum*—

" Then she raised herself on her elbow, but again her eyelids sank,
　And the wound from the sword-edge whispered, as her heart from the
　　　iron shrank,
　And she moaned: ' O lives of man-folk, for unrest all overlong
　By the Father were ye fashioned; and what hope amendeth wrong?
　Now at last, O my belovèd, all is gone; none else is near,
　Through the ages of all ages, never sundered, shall we wear.'
　Scarce more than a sigh was the word, as back on the bed she fell,
　Nor was there need in the chamber of the passing of Brynhild to tell;
　And no more their lamentation might the maidens hold aback,
　But the sound of their bitter mourning was as if red-handed wrack
　Ran wild in the Burg of the Niblungs, and the fire was master of all."

　　　" So, on the bloody sand, Sohrab lay dead,
　　　And the great Rustum drew his horseman's cloak

> Down o'er his face, and sate by his dead son,
> As those black granite pillars, once high-rear'd
> By Jamshid in Persepolis, to bear
> His house, now, mid their broken flights of steps,
> Lie prone, enormous, down the mountain side—
> So on the sand lay Rustum by his son.
> And night came down over the solemn waste,
> And the two gazing hosts, and that sole pair,
> And darken'd all; and a cold fog, with night,
> Crept from the Oxus. Soon a hum arose,
> As of a great assembly loos'd, and fires
> Began to twinkle through the fog; for now
> Both armies mov'd to camp, and took their meal:
> The Persians took it on the open sands
> Southward; the Tartars by the river marge:
> And Rustum and his son were left alone."

Preference for one or other of these styles will be, doubtless, a matter of temperament. If one asks, however, which outgoes the other in moving quality, which makes the deeper and more lasting impression, to which are we most likely to return, there seems little room for doubt. How are we to reconcile ourselves to the rhythm of such lines as—

" Now at last, O my belovèd, all is gone; none else is near "—

and its immediate successor, or to such vague phrases as *for unrest all overlong* or *shall we wear*, so evidently due to the necessity of rhyme? The future will deal more kindly with the severe and restrained style, which displays a continuous respect for the exact meaning of words, than with the fluent and easy style, which employs them to fill a gap, or to eke out a line without much regard for their precise significance. Schopenhauer was surely right, there should be in style a touch of the epigraphic, the monumental. What is to last must be written upon stone, must have the quality of sculpture. In *Sohrab and Rustum* Arnold illustrates his own principles—the need of a careful choice of subject, the need to subordinate the interest of expression to the interest of the action and characters, the need of attention to form, the need of a style of few and decisive words, neither capricious nor ornamental, but at once noble and disciplined, like an athlete in training, whose movements are marked by a continual and sinewy firmness, and are beautiful only because they are perfectly adapted to his undertakings.

The long poem has not flourished in our literature since Milton. In closing a survey of the kind attempted in this volume, a survey of our greater narrative poetry for a thousand years, one has to confess the result in some measure disappointing—the strength of English literature is not so conspicuous here as in other fields. Putting *Beowulf* aside, putting aside also *Paradise Lost*, no intelligent critic will claim for this country any signal success in formal epic. Since the word " epic," however, admits of various interpretations, we have passed in review the chief of our more ambitious narrative poems, to which the highest honours might in a moment of enthusiasm be assigned. Disregarding the convention altogether, judging these works simply as poems, how seldom has it been possible to praise unreservedly, how often when the severest tests were applied have they been seen to come short of the grandeur, even of the excellence which the high aims and pretensions of such poetry lead us to expect. How many outright and irredeemable failures there are, like Wilkie's and Glover's, how many very partial successes, like Scott's or Byron's, how many of the spirited attempts remain, like the *Hyperion* of Keats, mere fragments. The same causes cannot be assigned for all these failures. The reason of Blackmore's failure was not the reason of Tennyson's, the failure of Scott differs from that of Morris, and Cowley's from both. What, then, are the true causes? Many, one might say, indeed, most failures in poetry arise from an insufficient appreciation of its difficulty. Poetry appears to some easy to write. The truth is, there is no success in the world so ardently pursued, so frequently missed. So high and rare is the gift for it that an hour's inspiration, a few lines like Landor's—

" I strove with none, for none was worth my strife "—

a few stanzas, like Shelley's *Ode to the West Wind*, confer immortality upon their author. And when we come to the greater poetry, for which a happy hour, a momentary inspiration will not suffice, the chances of success, even for a man of extraordinary poetic talent, are terribly reduced. What is required of a poet is that he shall have at command not merely unflagging invention, but a sure sense for style which never forsakes him. No people has possessed a richer national genius for poetry than the English. Their ill success in the longer narrative, the objective as distinguished from the subjective type of poetry, cannot, therefore, be traced to any fundamental disability. But in the greater poetry, natural genius is not enough. Our poetry, as Arnold never wearied of insisting, failed through neglect of form, or through indifference to qualities of style which may be absent even where genius is present. That he was right the poetry reviewed in this book abundantly proves. In no writer since Milton can we feel that the sense for style is continually evident, " *the certain excellence and perfection of language* " of which Longinus speaks; he is " *our one first-rate master in the grand style.*" For the most part also our poets rarely foresaw the end from the beginning, rarely so planned their works as to subordinate the parts to the whole and to bring them to a natural and fit conclusion. They embarked on their voyages without charts, sometimes, one might fancy, without thought of any port of destination. What an eloquent example is Spenser. His *Faerie Queene*, though longer than the *Iliad* and the *Odyssey* combined—a royal barque, indeed—never reached harbour. But in a long poem, if its success is to be measured by its pretensions, not only is form necessary, a sustained nobility is necessary. " *Beware*," said Goethe, " *of attempting a large work. . . . What exertion and expenditure of mental force are required to arrange and round off a great whole ; and then what powers, and what a tranquil, undisturbed situation in life, to express it with the proper fluency.*" A lyric may be supported during its brief flight by the spirit and fervour of its initial impulse. In the long poem the author must frequently conduct us through stretches of level country, along the lower slopes of Parnassus, where the pressure of inspiration is barely felt. Through such stretches, along these lower levels, if he be master of an assured style he will continue to give us pleasure, though pleasure of a quieter kind. But many of our poets who attempted epic or the longer narrative, though the true nature of poetry was not hidden from

them, though, like Browning in *The Ring and the Book*, they
wrote at times with genius, were incapable, through some
deficiency of ear or musical invention, of producing, except
in their happiest moments, verse that was more than correct,
that had in it any arresting or satisfying quality. They were
wrecked on the shallows of commonplace, on the shoals of the
superfluous, or on the rocks of rhetorical magniloquence. Our
longer narratives are poems great in passages rather than great
poems, splendid elevations are followed by melancholy and
forbidding depressions. The English poets, following each his
own vein, display marked originality, an originality so pronounced as to amount in the eyes of our foreign critics to
eccentricity. They give full scope to their individual tastes,
often to their displeasing idiosyncracies, unrestrained by any
regard for tradition, or any inquiry into the principles of their
art. They write to please themselves, " *to give themselves
the exterior sensation of their individuality*," rather than to
please others, or to create objective and visible shapes of
beauty. The metaphysical bent, too, the subjective tendency
of the English nature, wars against success in narrative,
in the objective style. Characteristic of the English nature
in general, this metaphysical bent discovers itself more
and more as we approach our own times, it has become a
feature of modern thought. More and more the world seems
impelled towards the theoretic, the interior, the mental region,
so that for the artist to escape from it, to create bright, clear
pictures, like those of the visible and real world, pictures such as
Homer gives us, or *Beowulf*, seems for the present beyond hope.
If Hegel is to be believed, we have even less to expect from the
future. For if ours be a reflective age, coming ages will be even
more reflective. Our ways of thought infect the artist, " *the
whole spiritual culture of the age is of such a kind that he himself
stands within this reflective world and its conditions.*" Art is,
and will remain, " *on the side of its higher destiny*," concludes
Hegel, " *a thing of the past.*" [1] Let us trust that the philosopher

[1] *The Introduction to Hegel's Philosophy of Fine Art*, translated by
Bernard Bosanquet, p. 55.

was deceived in this matter. Even philosophers have been known to err, and prophecy is dangerous work. But when Professor Bradley accounts for the ill success of the longer poems of Wordsworth's age by the same tendency, the bent of that age towards the intellectual and analytical mood, its keen interest in ideas, in abstract questions, his argument seems conclusive.[1] Nothing, as he shows, can be more unfriendly towards the production of the more ambitious narrative poetry —which to interest us must make its ideas visible, must give them objective shape and value—than this preoccupation with abstract and critical modes of thought. The poets of that age exhibited this inward tendency, this speculative habit of mind. Fascinated by such ideas as lay at the roots of the French Revolution, they concerned themselves with the future and schemes for the reconstruction of society, whereas the poets of earlier epochs, undistracted by the clash of conflicting theories, were free to ponder and to shape anew in clear sculptured forms, in vivid scene and action, the ideas already familiar and fixed in the national imagination. Criticism may thus, partially at least, account for the defects in our longer narrative poems.

There are readers, however, who are far from deploring these defects, who, as we saw,[2] have no liking for the long poem, or believe it under the friendliest conditions impossible. " You say that one half is very good," said Byron, in reply to some criticism of *Don Juan*, " you are wrong; for if it were, it would be the finest poem in existence. Where is the poetry of which one half is good? . . . No—no; no poetry is generally good—only by fits and starts—and you are lucky to get a sparkle here and there." If not wholly good, however, there exist poems, like those of Virgil and Milton, so admirable, of such noble quality throughout, that the true lovers of poetry would sacrifice much to retain them, even in every word and line. If we are to have no more such poetry, if the long poem is doomed, we can only say with Professor Bradley

[1] *The Long Poem in Wordsworth's Age, Oxford Lectures on Poetry.*
[2] Chap. ix., p. 176

that "*something of inestimable worth will perish.*" And we may, perhaps, take some comfort to ourselves by recalling the history of poetry, and how often that history shows her powers of revival and renewal; when

> " she herself hath burnt, and spicy nest,
> The lovely bird with youthful pens and comb,
> Doth soar from out her cradle and her tomb."

APPENDIX

For the following translations I am indebted to my friend Mr. RITCHIE GIRVAN, *Lecturer on English Language in the University of Glasgow.*

" EXODUS," 154-168

Pharaoh's Approach

Hopeless in mind they stood
After they saw from out the south advancing
Pharaoh's army, bearing on high their spears
Close ranked like forest trees, the troops agleam,
The banners reared aloft, a nation's force
Treading the boundary ways—embattled close
They came, with spears arrayed, and glancing shields,
And blare of trumpets.   Over the corpses screamed
The birds of battle lusting for the fray,
Their wings all dewed, and he who claims the slain,
The raven, hastened to that place, and wolves
Their hideous call of the night-time cried aloud
In hope of carrion, brutish and ruthless beasts,
Which savagely followed with the foe and boded
The host's destruction—such as at mid of night
Watch howling round the outposts where men dwell.

" GENESIS," 1982-1995

The Battle of the Kings

Fierce for the fray the hosts drew nigh, with lances
Loud ringing, while around the spear shafts screamed
The raven, swart bird of battle, on his wings
The dew still wet, and in his breast high hope
Of feasting on the slain.   In mighty columns
Hastened the heroes forward, high of heart,
Helmed for the onset, till the companies closed

330

From south and north together. Stern game of war
Was there, exchange of murderous dart, the din
Of battle joined, and war's loud note. Their swords
Ring hilted, trenchant, from their scabbards loosed
The heroes, and he who never yet had drunk,
Insatiate, his fill of war, each noble there
Hard by his hand might find barter of battle.

"ANDREAS," 369-377

A Storm at Sea

There was the sea
Troubled and roused, the swordfish in its play
Glided across the ocean, the grey mew
Circled intent on prey, the day's bright lamp
Darkened, and waxed the winds, and the waves crashed,
And ocean's streams were moved, the cables shrieked,
And lashed the deep the while there rose upon them
A terrible sea which smote them with the violence
Of its unnumbered waters. Then the thanes
In mind were all a-tremble . . .

"FINNSBURG"

" [These gables] are never burning? "
Then spake the king young in warfare: " This is no dawn
from the east, no dragon flies here, nor are the gables of this
hall afire, but [our foes] bear forward [their arms]. The birds [1]
sing, the grey corselet [2] rattles, the war-spear rings, shield
responds to shaft. Now shines out this moon, wandering [3]
amid clouds; now shall arise deeds of sorrow which shall bring
to end this affliction of our nation. But rouse ye, my warriors,
grasp your bucklers,[4] set your minds to prowess, haste to the
front of battle, be resolute of heart."
Then arose many a thane gold-decked, and girt his sword upon
him. To the door went the noble warriors, Sigeferth and Eawa,
and drew their swords, and at the other door Ordlaf and Guthlaf
drew theirs, and Hengist himself followed behind.
Then further Garulf urged Guthere [5] that he should not bear
in harness to the hall door for the first assault a life so noble,
since the stern warrior was intent to spoil it. But he, the brave

hero, loud over all challenged who held the door. " Sigeferth is my name," said he. " I am a prince of the Secgans, an exile of wide renown. Many evils have I come through, many stern battles, and still here for thee is appointed whichsoever of the twain thyself wilt seek at my hands."

Then at the rampart was the din of mortal conflict. In the hands of the brave must needs burst in sunder the bossy shield, the guard of the limbs [6]—the floor resounded—until in the warfare, first of all mortals,[7] Garulf went down, Guthlaf's son, and around him many a goodly man. Over the corpses of the slain [8] wandered the raven, swart, dark-hued; the flash of swords shone like as all Finnsburg were aflame. Never have I heard in the warring of men of sixty warriors better acquitting themselves in nobler fashion, nor [9] yielding better requital for sweet mead than his young retainers paid to Hnaef.

Five days they fought [10] in such fashion that no one of them, of the retainers, fell, but they held the door. Then a wounded hero turned him away, declared that his corselet was shattered, useless his mail-shirt, and his helmet pierced besides. The keeper of the folk questioned him then how the warriors survived their wounds, or which of the two young men . . .

Cetera desunt.

[1] Perhaps " birds of battle," but possibly " birds of morn " roused in untimely fashion.

[2] Some render " wolf." It may be so. I follow what seems the greater probability.

[3] *waðol* may be a noun in apposition with *mona*, meaning " full moon." I tend to that belief, but have translated in the more usual fashion, since the matter is all uncertain.

[4] The text is doubtful. Some emend *linda*, some *handa*—" Grasp your shields," or " Stir your hands;" but in any case the idea is that of setting hand to shield.

[5] Garulf might also be the object. I take him as subject because his name stands first.

[6] *ban-helm* has been emended but needlessly. It is in apposition to *bord* and means also " shield."

[7] Some translate *eorð-buendra* as " dwellers of the land, natives, Frisians," but I see no reason for it.

[8] This passage is doubtful, and the text corrupt. No really satisfactory emendation has been proposed.

[9] The text is corrupt in this place. Some read *swanas* for the recorded reading *swa noc*, rendering it " swains," but this seems to me improbable. I have omitted the words.

[10] Probably two half lines are lost after " fought," but the sense does not suffer.

I have left unmentioned other emendations and interpretations adopted.

INDEX

Addison, 8, 196, 223, 226, 241, 267, 272
Admiral Hosier's Ghost, 245
Æneid, 1, 15, 99, 204, 231, 290
Æschylus, 13
Æsthetic as Science of Expression, 25
Agincourt, Ballad of, 181
Agincourt, Battle of, 181
Ainslie, Douglas, 25
Alastor, 289
Albion's England, 174, 176
Albo, 104
Alexander, 4
Alexander, 113, 114, 116, 140
Alfred, King, 97
Alfred, 241
Almanzor and Almahide, 230
Alonzo of Ercilla, 9
Amazon Queen, 230
Anacrisis, 4
Ancient Danish Ballads (Prior's), 30
Ancient Greek Historians (Bury's), 125
Ancient Mariner, 278
Andreas, 92, 96, 332
Angelo, Michael, 209, 281
Anne, Queen, 226, 270
Antimachus, 126
Anyte, 19
Apollonius Rhodius, 152
Apology for Actors, 174
Appreciations (Pater's), 174
Arabian Nights, 110, 214
Araucana, 9
Archesilaus Prytanoeus, 171
Aretina, 228
Argonautica, 75, 120
Ariosto, 6, 17, 101, 103, 146, 148, 151, 152, 161, 162, 166, 182, 195, 196, 204, 301
Aristophanes, 304
Aristotle, 1, 3, 4, 10, 21, 23, 59, 110, 116, 123, 146, 149
Arnold, M., 45, 78, 176, 251, 278-280, 287, 291, 320, 322-324, 326
Artamène, 228, 238
Arthur, King, 108-114, 132-135, 164, 194

Athenaid, 11, 246, 249
Augustine, 163
Augustus, 166
Aurengzebe, 229

Bach, 217
Bacon, Francis, 149, 311
Bacon, Roger, 1
Bagehot, 176, 203, 206
Baillie, Joanna, 288
Bale, John, 173
Barbour, 29, 138-143
Barons' Wars, 183, 184
Bathos, or the Art of Sinking in Poetry, 259
Batracho-myo-Machia, 255, 256
Battle of Otterbourne, 287
Battle of the Frogs and Mice, 255-257
Battle of the Summer Isles, 258
Baxter, 193
Bede, 92
Beethoven, 218
Beginnings of Poetry, 33, 34, 35
Benoît de Sainte-More, 115
Bentley, 276
Beowulf, 13, 15, 17, 21, 24, 26-28, 39, 47-77, 80, 84, 86, 89, 90, 92, 95, 98-100 104, 106, 110, 111, 127, 136, 166, 204, 325, 327
Beppo, 278
Berni, 302
Beves of Hamtoun, 111
Biographia Literaria, 176, 213
Blackburn, Prof., 92
Blackmore, 11, 150, 241-245, 248, 250, 260, 325
Blair, 5, 30
Blake, 193, 304
Boadicea, 246
Boccaccio, 117, 120, 304
Bodel, Jean, 105
Bodley, 171
Boiardo, 117
Boileau, 8, 230, 257, 270
Bolton, 172
Book of Old English Ballads, 33
Bosanquet, Prof., 327
Bossu, Le, 2

333

THE TEMPLE PRESS, PRINTERS, LETCHWORTH